ISBN 978-1-332-82266-9
PIBN 10044645

1 MONTH OF
FREE
READING

at

www.ForgottenBooks.com

By purchasing this book you are eligible for one month membership to ForgottenBooks.com, giving you unlimited access to our entire collection of over 700,000 titles via our web site and mobile apps.

To claim your free month visit:

www.forgottenbooks.com/free44645

English
Français
Deutsche
Italiano
Español
Português

www.forgottenbooks.com

Mythology Photography **Fiction**
Fishing Christianity **Art** Cooking
Essays Buddhism Freemasonry
Medicine **Biology** Music **Ancient
Egypt** Evolution Carpentry Physics
Dance Geology **Mathematics** Fitness
Shakespeare **Folklore** Yoga Marketing
Confidence Immortality Biographies
Poetry **Psychology** Witchcraft
Electronics Chemistry History **Law**
Accounting **Philosophy** Anthropology
Alchemy Drama Quantum Mechanics
Atheism Sexual Health **Ancient History**
Entrepreneurship Languages Sport
Paleontology Needlework Islam
Metaphysics Investment Archaeology
Parenting Statistics Criminology
Motivational

Wisconsin War History Commission: W⁵

Michigan War History Commission:

32nd Division Historical Detail:

Dedication

In my official reports and comments and in general orders quoted in the following pages I have in a way indicated my most inward thoughts as to the quality of the personnel of the 32nd Division and as to the value of their achievements in the great battles of the World War. Since the deeds recorded in this history resulted from the combined efforts of every member of the Division, may not all those of us who are still living dedicate this brief and unboasting record of events to OUR HERO DEAD.

Major General, U. S. Army.

Introduction

O many a student of the history of our civil war has come the belief that Abraham Lincoln was born into this world Divinely destined to preserve the Union. To many a student who ponders over the history of the Red Arrow Division in the World War may come the belief that the union of Michigan and Wisconsin in that now famous command was an inspiration.

Certain it is that no happier combination of state soldiery was to be found overseas; certain it is that even when its battle casualties had rendered necessary heavy replacements, hailing from a dozen other commonwealths, Michigan and Wisconsin ever predominated— ever gave the tone to the entire array.

Almost forgotten in 1917, that combination had been strong and significant nearly three generations ago. Badger and Wolverine, the grandfathers of many a soldier of the 32nd Division fought side by side in the civil war. Well remembered now, one of the four infantry regiments of the Red Arrow Division was led for a time by the son of the leader of one of the five infantry regiments of the Iron Brigade, Wolverines both, they were both comrades in battle with the men of Wisconsin.

As was said in an address at the first reunion:

"Over sixty years ago the soldier comradeship of Michigan and Wisconsin had its birth. Sixty-one years ago it was at its old-time highest point, when Detroit and Milwaukee cemented their friendship, when the finest military organizations in the West, the Detroit and the Milwaukee Light Guard, uniformed almost exactly alike, in the dark blue, swallow-tailed coats turned up with buff, the towering bearskin shakos and broad white cross belts, paraded alternately in the two cities, visited each other at intervals, exchanged caps, souvenirs and stirring sentiment at every banquet. Each had been captained and drilled by veteran soldiers, West Point had done its share; each had been assigned as the first company of the first regiment of its commonwealth, and, possibly foreseeing how soon it might be put to the test, each had vowed its knightly fealty to the Union of States, and asked only that when the time should be ripe, Badger and Wolverine, they might go into action together.

"Two years later the summons came. Two years later, in May, '61' the first captains of those foremost companies appeared on President Lincoln's first list of some thirty brigadier generals of volunteers. The first regiments marched away to the Potomac with the very first draft under the call for 75,000, and the First Michigan, in front of Washington, under Mc-Dowell, the First Wisconsin near Harper's Ferry, under Patterson, had their baptism of fire in July; reorganized for the war in August; furnished one or two more generals apiece and a score of field officers between them, but they were separated.

"In the Army of the Potomac, however, there was from the first to the last of the great civil war just one brigade of infantry made up exclusively of western troops. In the fierce battle summer of '62 it won the title of The Iron Brigade. Its prized insignia has five branches, yet its membership in August, '62' had but four regiments, the Second, Sixth, Seventh Wisconsin and the Nineteenth Indiana. But so reduced were they in numbers by the casualties of Gainesville, Groveton, Second Bull Run and Antietam that a fresh regiment was sent to join them —the Twenty-fourth Michigan. 'Big as the whole brigade,' said the Badgers, when, under gallant old Morrow, it came striding into camp, and big as the whole brigade's were the fearful casualties of the Twenty-fourth in their first pitched

8

battle — Gettysburg. Here on this cross are inscribed the names of that martial quintette, unchanged so long as that bloody war should last. Here again Michigan had stood in soldierly rivalry with Wisconsin, and when the final muster out was ordered here again Michigan and Wisconsin struck hands and prayed that should ever in the future the honor of the nation be imperiled Michigan and Wisconsin should again stand shoulder to shoulder in the same brigade, and further cement, with their blood if need be, the compact of the old Guardsmen of '59 and '60·

"And so it came—so it was ordered by the powers at Washington, as though ordained of the God of Battles himself, Michigan and Wisconsin were destined in the most destructive, stupendous war the world has ever known, out of a combination of 48 states and heaven only knows how many possibilities, to be linked, not as had been their fathers, in a single brigade of some 5,000 men, but in a huge division, built upon modern lines to a strength of 27,000, almost every man of whom at the outset hailed from those sister states of the now Middle West."

Born of such a union, it was to be expected that the fruit would be of surpassing merit. Proud as were our people of their Guardsmen thus called into the national service, confident as we were that our sons would do their uttermost to uphold the honor of the Flag and the standards of their respective states, even we, who thought we best knew them, could not have predicted the triumphant award that awaited them.

Among our citizens before the call there had long been a large element opposed to any expenditure for military purposes, any semblance of military service, any symptom of that which they termed militarism, but which was in fact a patriotic endeavor to prepare at least a certain few of our young men for the national defense should ever the national honor or safety be threatened. Even the press for many a year, and in too many an instance, threw its influence against the annual encampment for training purposes. It came, therefore, as a surprise to very many honest souls that, while they had been slumbering in fancied security, some scattered thousands of their more observing, not to say more patriotic, fellow citizens had been diligently schooling themselves for service in war. It gradually dawned upon many eloquent and influential men and persuasive women,—not because of anything, but in spite of everything, they had said and done,—Michigan and Wisconsin, under competent instruction, had been earnestly striving to perfect their few Guardsmen as soldiers. It eventually aroused in the minds of the really conscientious citizens of this class a realization of the error of their original ways, and an earnest desire on part of some of their best and worthiest to atone for the past neglect or active opposition, by even more earnest interest and support. Still, they were not quite prepared to hear of the young men who flocked to the ranks of the 32nd Division that they should so early in their career be declared foremost in training and discipline; but when, later still, they listened to the citations and reports as to what the Red Arrow had done in Alsace, and in the Marne and Aisne and Oise offensives, and finally in the Argonne, the scales fell from their eyes, and, joining with the kith and kin, the friends and neighbors of their soldiers overseas, there went up a chorus of pride and rejoicing such as these sister states had never heard before.

And now it seems they are seeking something beyond the brief official reports and the individual missives, strictly censored, of the sons, husbands or brothers in the ranks. It was for them, the mass of our people—the plain people of whom Lincoln said "the Lord must deeply love them since he made so many," that the 32nd decided to prepare its history—a story one and all could read and understand. It was to aid in placing before the people the narrative of the service and sacrifices of all their sons that the War History Commission was established, and our people will little know the difficulties which beset that same Commission.

First to be published comes this modest recital of the campaigns of the 32nd Division, soon to be followed by the official report, accompanied by excellent maps, of that able soldier who so skillfully trained and then so admirably led our chosen through the terrific campaigns which proved the climax of the World War. As the pages of both these military narratives were studied by the members of the Wisconsin Commission (for not until five months later were their associates of Michigan designated and sent to take part), the utter suppression of individual exploit, the sinking of battalion or battery claims for recognition in favor of a simple recital of the deeds of the Division as a whole, became the subject of no little discussion. The people who were behind that Division and whose money paid for the preparation of its history were eager for something more. The personal element, the soldier story of comrades' daring or heroic deaths had been given no place in these pages. These were things their fathers and mothers, wives, sisters and sweethearts would long and expect to see, and with one accord the chairman of the Commission was instructed to endeavor to draw them out. With this in view he wrote to a score of prominent officers, begging that the lid might be lifted—that the seal to their soldierly silence might be broken, but it was in vain—the 32nd would not talk or write of its manifold deeds. "They could fight like all hell," said one of their number, "if need be, but they somehow couldn't be got to brag about it." And so at last the work had to go to press without what one of their foremost staff officers termed the touch of human interest, and so it is launched upon its untrumpeted way to perhaps ten thousand firesides in the two states.

This at least the 32nd will say: It was a united household, a military family that knew neither envy nor malice in respect to other commands. It had brotherly regard for all, but sought favor of none. It "minded its own business," said one of its best, and if it had internal differences it kept them there: No one else need know them. Moreover, said he, it was a happy family. It was a highly favored and fortunate division in spite of certain disappointments in its early days. It was a loyal division, devoted to its chief and proud of its brigade and regimental commanders, proud of its Staff, and well it might be! Had any division a chief-of-staff to match with theirs ever alert, driving, vigilant, yet ever kind and courteous? Was any division better fed, clothed and supplied? and would the 32nd swap their Badger quartermaster for any other in the business? Was there better organization of the medical, surgical and sanitary service in any other division? and would the 32nd admit anywhere the superior of their chief surgeon? Was there anywhere more cordial, helpful, pull-together spirit than between the brigade leaders, and between those leaders and the Division head? and by the time they launched out on the climax of the whole campaign, the Argonne offensive, would they have exchanged division or brigade commanders with any in the American Expeditionary Forces or elsewhere? Sorrows they had, as what soldiers have not? They grieved, Badger and Wolverine alike, over the loss early in the campaign of the brigade and regimental leaders from their respective states, but in silence and subordination accepted their successors—total strangers as a rule, yet how soon they gained the confidence of their men, how soon that confidence ripened into respect and admiration, how strong eventually became the regard in which they were held!

Other sorrows they had, as what soldiers have not when called upon to take leading part in such destructive warfare? Fourteen thousand, in round number, were the casualties, and their roll of honor embraces many and many a beloved name, and yet what division won higher honors? Fighting earlier and longer the First and Second regulars had lost more men, and had probably gained more kilometers—captured more "objectives," yet at the final round-up, when it came to the final ceremonies of the campaign, to what division was assigned a prominence equal to that of the 32nd, holding, as has been said, "the very center of the stage" beyond the Rhine, with the castled fortress of Ehrenbreitstein, Germany's boast and pride, at their back, the stars and stripes flung to the breeze from the lofty battlements that for generations had been garrisoned by Prussia. Verily, in the story of the 32nd as told by its chosen scribes, there is so little made of all this that it well may be that the Division admiring

12

INTRODUCTION

Frenchmen named "Les Terribles" thought but casually of their own exploits.

Not so with us, however, we others who so often with sleepless eyes and straining hearts watched prayerfully for tidings of their progress, mourning over their dead and dying, yet glorying in their deeds. First of all our army to cross the frontier into Germany, second to none in the tremendous task of breaking the German hold in the Argonne, and finally, honored and acclaimed throughout the forces overseas as one of the five "shock" divisions, we of the home folk can find no words in which to tell the pride we feel in these, the brother Guardsmen of these sister states.

For the Wisconsin War History Commission.

CHARLES KING,
Chairman.

13

MAJOR GENERAL WILLIAM LASSITER,
Commanding General, 32nd Division, during March to the Rhine and Army of Occupation.

MAJOR-GENERAL JAMES PARKER.
First Commanding General, 32nd Division.

1. CAPTAIN DANIEL D. THOMSON, Inf.; Aide to General Haan, Training Period; Occupation of Sector in Alsace; Aisne-Marne Offensive; Oise-Aisne Offensive; Meuse-Argonne Offensive; March to the Rhine.

2. CAPTAIN LEROY PEARSON, Inf.; Aide to General Haan and Assistant C-3, Training Period; Occupation of Sector in Alsace; Aisne-Marne Offensive; Oise-Aisne Offensive; Aide to General Haan, Army of Occupation.

3. CAPTAIN DOUGLAS C. CRAWFORD, A. D. C.; March to the Rhine and Army of Occupation.

Contents

		Page
DEDICATION		5
INTRODUCTION		7
ORGANIZATION OF THE THIRTY-SECOND DIVISION		25
HIGH LIGHTS IN THE HISTORY OF THE DIVISION		26

THE HISTORY:

CHAPTER I.	Birth of the Thirty-Second Division	27
CHAPTER II.	The Thirty-Second Division in France	33
CHAPTER III.	First on German Soil	41
CHAPTER IV.	Into the Big Battle	49
CHAPTER V.	The Baptism of Fire	57
CHAPTER VI.	"Les Terribles" Report to General Mangin	69
CHAPTER VII.	The Capture of Juvigny	77
CHAPTER VIII.	The Red Arrows Join the First American Army	87
CHAPTER IX.	Breaking the Kriemhilde Stellung	97
CHAPTER X.	Our Last Fight and the Armistice	113

GRAPH OF CASUALTIES OF THE 32ND DIVISION		125
CHAPTER XI.	The March to the Rhine	127
	March Table of March to the Rhine	140
HISTORICAL CHART		141
CHAPTER XII.	Die Wacht am Rhein	143
CHAPTER XIII.	Leaders of Thirty-Second Division	147
CHAPTER XIV.	Cited in Orders	155
CHAPTER XV.	Reading the General's Mail	193
CHAPTER XVI.	The 32nd Division Veteran Association	213

ROLL OF HONOR		217
CASUALTY REPORT CONSOLIDATED		296
OFFICERS AND MEN AWARDED THE DISTINGUISHED SERVICE CROSS		297
OFFICERS AWARDED THE DISTINGUISHED SERVICE MEDAL		302
OFFICERS AWARDED THE LEGION OF HONOR		302
OFFICERS AND MEN AWARDED THE CROIX DE GUERRE		303
OFFICERS AND MEN AWARDED BELGIAN DECORATIONS		308
OFFICERS AND MEN CITED IN GENERAL ORDERS 32ND DIVISION		309
ABBREVIATIONS AND UNCOMMON WORDS USED IN THE HISTORY		313

1. COLONEL J. G. PILLOW, General Staff, Assistant Chief of Staff, G-3; Aisne-Marne Offensive; Oise-Aisne Offensive; Meuse-Argonne Offensive; March to the Rhine; Army of Occupation.
2. LIEUTENANT COLONEL PAUL B. CLEMENS, General Staff, Assistant Chief of Staff, G-2; Training Period; Occupation of Sector in Alsace; Aisne-Marne Offensive; Oise-Aisne Offensive; Meuse-Argonne Offensive; March to the Rhine; Army of Occupation.
3. COLONEL ROBERT M. BECK, General Staff, Chief of Staff; Aisne-Marne Offensive; Oise-Aisne Offensive; Meuse-Argonne Offensive; March to the Rhine; Army of Occupation.
4. MAJOR ROBERT CONNOR, Acting Assistant Chief of Staff, G-1; Meuse-Argonne Offensive; March to the Rhine; Army of Occupation.
5. LIEUTENANT COLONEL JOHN H. HOWARD, General Staff, as Major, Infantry, Division Adjutant; as Lieutenant Colonel General Staff, Assistant Chief of Staff, G-1; Training Period; Occupation of Sector in Alsace; Aisne-Marne Offensive; Oise-Aisne Offensive; Army of Occupation.

Organization of the Thirty-Second Division

Division Headquarters. Commanding General, Aides and Staff.

Headquarters Troop and Detachment.
63rd Brigade Headquarters.
    125th Infantry Regiment.
    126th Infantry Regiment.
    120th Machine Gun Battalion.
64th Infantry Brigade Headquarters.
    127th Infantry Regiment.
    128th Infantry Regiment.
    121st Machine Gun Battalion.
119th Machine Gun Battalion.
107th Engineer Regiment.
107th Field Signal Battalion.
32nd Military Police Company.

57th Field Artillery Brigade.
    119th Field Artillery Regiment.
    120th Field Artillery Regiment.
    121st Field Artillery Regiment.
    147th Field Artillery Regiment (Attached).
    107th Trench Mortar Battery.
    107th Mobile Ordnance Repair Shop.
107th Train Headquarters.
    107th Supply Train.
    107th Sanitary Train.
    107th Ammunition Train.
    107th Engineer Train.
    107th Motor Supply Truck Unit.

158th Field Artillery Brigade (Attached).
    322nd Field Artillery.
    323rd Field Artillery.
    324th Field Artillery.
    308th Trench Mortar Battery.
    308th Ammunition Train.

High Lights in the History of the Thirty-Second Division

Six months under fire—from May to November, 1918, with but 10 days in a rest area.

Fought on five fronts in three major offensives—the Aisne-Marne, Oise-Aisne and Meuse-Argonne.

Losses—14,000 casualties from all causes.

Met and vanquished 23 German Divisions from which 2,153 prisoners were taken.

Gained 38 kilometers in four attacks and repulsed every enemy counter attack.

In action east of the Meuse when the Armistice was signed.

Marched 300 kilometers to the Rhine as fiout line element of the Third U. S. Army and occupied for four months the center sector in the Coblenz bridge-head, holding 63 towns and 400 square kilometers of territory.

First American troops to set foot on German soil—in Alsace in May, 1918; captured Fismes in the Marne offensive after an advance of 19 kilometers in seven days; fought in the Oise-Aisne offensive as the only American unit in General Mangin's famous Tenth French Army, breaking the German line which protected the Chemin des Dames; twice in the line in the Meuse-Argonne offensive, fighting continuously for 20 days, penetrating the Kriemhilde Stellung, crossing the Meuse and starting drive to flank Metz.

Over 800 officers and men decorated by American, French and Belgian governments. The colors of all four Infantry Regiments, three Artillery Regiments, and three Machine Gun Battalions wear the Croix de Guerre of the Republic of France while every flag and standard in the Division has four American battle bands.

Composed of Wisconsin and Michigan National Guardsmen; insignia a Red Arrow, signifying that the Division shot through every line the enemy put before it; given the name of "Les Terribles" by the French; commanded in all its actions by Major General Wm. G. Haan and in the Army of Occupation by Major General Wm. Lassiter.

Arrived in France in February, 1918, being the sixth Division to join the A. E. F. Left Germany, Homeward Bound, in April, 1919. Arrived in the United States and demobilized in May.

CHAPTER I.

Birth of the Thirty-Second Division.

THE 32nd Division was organized under War Department orders of July 18th, 1917, from National Guard troops from Wisconsin and Michigan. Details of this organization are given in G. O. No. 101, War Department, 1917.

Wisconsin furnished approximately 15,000 and Michigan 8,000 troops of all arms. Later 4,000 National Army troops from Wisconsin and Michigan were transferred to the Division shortly before it left for France.

When war was declared on Germany, April 6th, 1917, there were two National Guard infantry regiments, one from each of these states, in the Federal Service; the 33rd Michigan, which had never been mustered out since its services on the Border, and the 3rd Wisconsin which had been called out for guard duty on war plants. In July the remainder of the state troops were mobilized at the state camps, and early in August the movement of the troops to the Division's training camp at Camp MacArthur, Texas, commenced.

The units thus assembled at Camp MacArthur included all the troops from Michigan and Wisconsin which had been on the Border in 1916. Six of the nine infantry regiments and most of the cavalry, artillery, engineers, and auxiliary troops had this Border experience. There were, however, in the new Wisconsin regiments, a large number of recruits who enlisted after the Declaration of War.

On August 4th, 1917, Battery F, 121st Field Artillery regiment, was the first unit of the new division to arrive at Camp MacArthur. From that time until late in September troops continued to pour in as rapidly as railroad facilities could be provided to transport them from the north.

Training commenced immediately upon the arrival of the first units at Camp MacArthur, and proceeded under the direction of the Division Commander and the National Guard brigade commanders.

Under instructions from the War Department, the Division was reorganized in accordance with the "Tables of Organization, 1917," on September 22, 1917. Generally speaking, the 63rd Infantry Brigade was formed of Michigan infantry and the 64th Infantry Brigade was organized entirely from Wisconsin infantry.

The 31st, 32nd and 33rd Michigan regiments, and, later on, the National Army recruits from Camp Custer and Camp Grant, went to form the 125th and 126th Regiments of Infantry and the 120th Machine Gun Battalion.

The 1st, 2nd and 3rd Wisconsin Infantry Regiments formed the bulk of the troops of the 127th and 128th Infantry Regiments and the 121st Machine Gun Battalion of the 64th Infantry Brigade. These two regiments were brought up to war strength by transferring enough troops to them from the 4th, 5th, and 6th Wisconsin Infantry regiments. These latter three regiments were in the 2nd Wisconsin Brigade, which was designated to function as the 57th Depot Brigade. From this brigade the various new units of the new Division were organized in accordance with the "Tables of Organization, 1917." The 57th Field Artillery Brigade included the Wisconsin and Michigan field artillery and cavalry and men from the 57th Depot Brigade. The 107th Engineer Regiment was organized from the Wisconsin and Michigan Engineer Battalion and men transferred from the 57th Depot Brigade. Whole companies were transferred from the Depot Brigade to make up the 107th Trains and Military Police and the 119th Machine Gun Battalion. The 107th Sanitary Train included the Wisconsin and Michigan Field Hospital and Ambulance Companies. The National Guard organizations which lost their identities to form these new units of the 32nd Division follow:

1st, 2nd, 3rd, 4th, 5th and 6th Wisconsin Infantry Regiments.

31st, 32nd and 33rd Michigan Infantry Regiments.

1st Wisconsin and 1st Michigan Field Artillery.

1st Wisconsin and 1st Michigan Cavalry.

1st Battalion Wisconsin Engineers and 1st Battalion Michigan Engineers.

1st Michigan Field Signal Battalion, and 1st Wisconsin Field Signal Battalion.

Wisconsin Ambulance Companies Nos. 1 and 2.

Wisconsin Field Hospitals Nos. 1 and 2.

Michigan Ambulance Company No. 2.

Michigan Field Hospital No. 1.

Major General James Parker, U. S. A., assumed command of the Division on August 26th, 1917, in accordance with War Department orders. On September 18th, 1917, he left for France on special duty with his Chief of Staff, Lieut. Col. E. H. DeArmond. They did not return until early in December, 1917, and General Parker was almost immediately transferred to the 85th Division at Camp Custer, Michigan.

GENERAL HAAN ASSUMES COMMAND.

Upon General Parker's departure for France, Brigadier General Wm. G. Haan, U. S. A., succeeded to the command of the Division, being senior brigadier general by virtue of his Regular Army commission.

The reorganization of the Division was effected a few days after he became the Division Commander. Brigadier General Louis C. Covell, formerly the brigadier general commanding the Michigan National Guard troops, was assigned to the command of the 63rd Infantry Brigade, and Brigadier General Charles R. Boardman, the senior Wisconsin brigadier general, who commanded the 1st Wisconsin Brigade, was assigned to the command of the 64th Infantry Brigade. Brigadier General R. A. Richards of the 2nd Wisconsin Brigade, who commanded the 57th Depot Brigade until his troops were all disposed of, was ordered to Camp Wadsworth, Spartanburg, South Carolina.

The 125th Infantry, Colonel John B. Boucher commanding, included all of the 33rd Michigan Infantry with the exception of one company, and five companies of the 31st Michigan Infantry.

The 126th Infantry, Colonel Joseph P. Westnedge commanding, was formed from the entire 32nd Michigan Infantry and five companies of the 31st Michigan Infantry.

The 120th Machine Gun Battalion was formed from surplus companies of the Michigan Infantry Brigade and Major David E. Cleary, formerly in command of the 3rd Battalion, 31st Michigan Infantry, was assigned to the command.

The 127th Infantry was organized with Colonel Wilbur N. Lee, formerly of the 2nd Wisconsin Infantry, in command.

Colonel John Turner, formerly in command of the 3rd Wisconsin Infantry, was assigned to the command of the 128th Infantry.

Major Frank H. Fowler, formerly in command of the 1st Battalion, 3rd Wisconsin Infantry, was assigned to the command of the 121st Machine Gun Battalion.

Major Percy C. Atkinson, formerly battalion commander of the 6th Wisconsin Infantry, was assigned to the command of the 119th Machine Gun Battalion.

Major William Mitchell Lewis, of the 1st Wisconsin Signal Battalion, was assigned to the command of the 107th Field Signal Battalion.

Colonel P. S. Bond, U. S. A., was assigned to the command of the 107th Engineers.

Colonel Robert B. McCoy, formerly in command of the 4th Wisconsin Infantry, was assigned to the command of the 107th Trains and Military Police.

Brigadier General Wm. G. Haan, while acting as Division Commander, was also in command of the 57th Field Artillery Brigade.

The 119th Field Artillery, composed largely of Michigan artillery and cavalry troops, was commanded by Major Chester B. McCormick, later promoted to the rank of Colonel.

The 120th Field Artillery was made up almost entirely from troops of the 1st Wisconsin Cavalry, and the commanding officer of the latter organization, Colonel Carl Penner, continued in command.

The 1st Wisconsin Field Artillery regiment became the 121st Field Artillery, the heavy artillery regiment of the 57th Field Artillery Brigade. The Commanding Officer of the Wisconsin Artillery, Colonel Philip C. Westfahl, became Commander of the new regiment.

The organization of the Division Staff was completed in September, 1917. Upon the departure of Lieut. Col. DeArmond for France, Major Geo. M. Russell, F. A. N. A., who reported at Camp MacArthur on September 14th as Division Inspector, became acting Chief of Staff. Major John H. Howard, Inf. N. A., reported on War Department orders as Division Adjutant. Lieut. Col. Hjalmer Erickson, Q. M. C. N. A., the Division Quartermaster, was the first member of the staff to report, arriving at Camp MacArthur on August 22, 1917. Lieut. Col. P. L. Boyer, M. C. N. A., the Division Surgeon, arrived a few days later. Lieut. Col. Gilbert E. Seaman, M. C. Wis. N. G., reported at the same time as Division Sanitary Inspector. The Judge Advocate was Major Samuel D. Pepper, J. A. Mich. N. G. Major Herbert L. Evans, S. C. N. A., was the Division Signal Officer, and Major J. P. Smith, F. A. N. A., the Division Ordnance Officer. Later Major John G. Salsman, Wis. N. G., reported as Assistant Division Adjutant. Major Chas. R. Williams, Q. M. C. Wis. N. G., reported for duty as Assistant Division Quartermaster. Major Mathew Hansen, Q. M. C. Mich. N. G., who was one of the first officers to arrive at Camp MacArthur, and who, as Constructing Quartermaster, was largely responsible for the speed with which the camp was completed, also became Assistant Division Quartermaster upon the completion of his duties as Constructing Quartermaster.

To the various staff departments were assigned for temporary duty a number of officers who assisted in the administrative work connected with the organization and training of the Division. In addition, there was a camp staff, which labored throughout the organization and training period to complete the equipment of the Division.

In the reorganization of the Division it was the policy to preserve original company organizations, but some consolidation was necessary to bring the companies up from the formerly prescribed strength of 150 men to the new tables of organization strength of 250 men. It was also necessary to change the commands of a number of line officers, but this was all accomplished with a minimum of friction, and the new organization started its training period with excellent spirit. A number of officers became surplus in the Division because of the reorganization, and were assigned special duties in the various regiments and separate organizations and in the divisional schools.

Early in September, 1917, a large number of the Reserve Corps Officers from Camp Roots reported to the Division for further instruction, and they were distributed among the various units. A number of these Reserve Corps Officers later accepted National Guard commissions and were recommended by organization commanders for permanent assignment to duty. Others took advantage of an opportunity to be transferred to organizations from their several home states in other camps, and those remaining who were surplus in the Division just before it left for France were assigned to Camp Dodge, Iowa.

FIGHT FOR EQUIPMENT.

The various National Guard units which were sent south for the new Division arrived fairly well equipped for campaign service similar to that on the Border in 1916, but with very little of the equipment prescribed for overseas. The necessity of securing, at the earliest possible moment, the equipment necessary for duty abroad was immediately apparent to the Division Commander and his Staff, and their energies from the first were bent upon so equipping the Division.

Upon the completion of the reorganization, training, of course, took precedence, but there never was a let-up in the efforts to secure the equipment for service as a combat unit in France. In this work the Camp Quartermaster, Major Edward H. Andreas, co-operated with the Division Commander and the Division Quartermaster to an important extent, and to him a measure of the credit is due for what was achieved in the next three months in getting the Division ready to sail.

TRAINING PROGRAM STARTED.

At the time the reorganization of the Division was completed troops were training in accordance with War Department instructions contained in a pamphlet entitled "Infantry Training," prescribing a course of sixteen weeks' training for all elements of the Division. The first four weeks' program was completed shortly after the reorganization had been effected, and when the second four weeks' period was taken up the Division was organized on a permanent basis and the schedules throughout the various units were uniform. An infantry school of arms was established, and various officers and non-commissioned officers were assigned for training in infantry specialties. Upon the completion of their course they became instructors, and returned to their organizations to instruct companies, platoons and squads in the use of new infantry weapons. This school was commanded first by Colonel Marshall Cousins, of the 6th Wisconsin Infantry, and later by Colonel Peter Piasecki, formerly of the 5th Wisconsin Infantry. To this school Captain Allen L. Briggs, A. D. C. to General Parker, devoted all his time. Captain Briggs was in Europe when the World War broke out in 1914, and had had an opportunity to observe the methods used in the various military schools in France. Later five French officers and four British officers, with several French and English non-commissioned officers, arrived as instructors, and during the latter part of the training period gave valuable assistance in preparing the Division for the part it was to play in the Great War.

30

A trench system was constructed just outside the camp, and in this system trench warfare was practiced. Infantry and artillery target ranges were prepared early in the training period, and a thorough course of instruction in service firing was given to every man in the Division. From these two features of the training program excellent results were obtained.

The War Department training program prescribed that certain hours of the week be devoted to athletics, and advantage was taken of this opportunity to organize a divisional football team, which was an important factor in creating a divisional *esprit de corps*. The team played elevens representing other military camps, and finished its schedule without being defeated by a soldier organization.

TROOPS DRILLED, RAIN OR SHINE.

The training was greatly expedited by the excellent weather which prevailed at Camp MacArthur. The policy of the Division was to carry out the program, rain or shine, and this policy was rigidly adhered to, especially in the schedule of trench maneuvers. However, there was very little rain, and interruptions of the program were rare.

All elements of the Division trained with equal energy, and all ranks soon realized that the 32nd would "get into the war" at a much earlier date than many had at first realized. This was a point which the Division Commander frequently emphasized in his daily conferences with the field officers. It was quickly evident to everyone that there was no time to waste, and the Division accordingly wasted none. In spite of handicaps due to lack of equipment, the Artillery Brigade developed as steadily as the infantry, the machine gun battalions rapidly gained knowledge of their weapons, the signal battalion, the engineers and the sanitary troops found practical work to do to supplement the required drills, and the trains, truck companies and trench mortar battery, without the "tools of their trade" with which to practice, took up infantry training, and organized schools to learn what they could about their specialties. Indeed at several division reviews the trains were commended by the Division Commander for the fine showing which they made, marching as infantry, and became rivals of the best "doughboy" battalions for smartness on parade.

Rigid discipline was required in everything that the Division did. Even games—the exercises prescribed as part of the training—were played at attention. Laundry work was done by schedule, during hours set apart for that purpose; and facetious "doughboys" used to say that they took their shower baths "by the numbers." But if the stern military rule to which they were subjected irked the men they did not show it; early in the game they demonstrated a willingness to implicitly obey orders, and after the Division had been in training two months it became apparent to everyone that the 32nd was to be a thoroughly disciplined organization. Both officers and men had cause, later, to be thankful for the careful attention given to this important feature of the training during the formative period.

SCHOOLS FOR EVERYBODY.

The men worked hard, and the officers worked even harder. With the organization of the School of Arms, many junior officers and non-commissioned officers were ordered there for courses in specialties, leaving harassed Captains, First Sergeants and company clerks to handle the administration of the companies. At drill a company commander was fortunate to have even one Lieutenant to help him handle a company of 250 men, and the First Sergeant likewise was forced to "carry on" with his best non-com assistants away at school during drill hours. Each evening there was an officers' school which all commissioned grades were required to attend, and frequently the non-commissioned officers were called together for special instruction "after hours." A school for Brigade, Regimental and Battalion commanders, with General Haan himself as director and instructor, was held daily.

The Division was fortunate in possessing a wealth of excellent officer material in the ranks of the enlisted men of the National Guard, and, when opportunity finally offered, certain enlisted men, who had shown exceptional ability in training activities, were examined, and later, on recommendation of the Division Commander, they were commissioned as Second Lieutenants and assigned to fill vacancies in the lower commissioned grades. A number of older Second Lieutenants also were promoted. Some of the best officers developed in the great campaign of the Division in 1918 were men promoted from the ranks during the training period at Waco, and all fully justified the confidence which General Haan expressed in these young officers at the time their commissions were announced.

While camp life at Waco was strenuous, and the duties of all ranks most exacting, it wasn't entirely a case of all work and no play. The people of Waco proved themselves to be highly hospitable, and born and bred Southerners, who admitted that they had reached the age of maturity without knowing that "damned Yankee" wasn't all one word, went out of their way to entertain these stalwart soldiers from the North. Many fine friendships were formed, and when the Division left for overseas Waco people took the parting as they would for their own sons. In fact the local papers always referred to the 32nd as "Waco's Own," and followed closely and enthusiastically the gallant career of their friends from Michigan and Wisconsin. And in 1919 when the Division returned from abroad it is a record that many of the men went back to Waco and "lived happily ever afterwards."

DIVISION ORDERED OVERSEAS.

During the latter part of November and early in December the Division was visited and carefully examined by War Department artillery and infantry inspectors, and was judged ready for overseas service. Their reports to Washington indicated that the 32nd was more advanced in its training at that time than any other division then in the U. S. Its equipment was very nearly complete, and the spirit which had developed no doubt also influenced the inspectors. Accordingly notice was shortly forthcoming from Washington that the Division would be sent to France at the earliest practicable date.

In those days information regarding troop movements was carefuly guarded, but before Christmas it was generally known throughout the camp that the 32nd was on the "sailing list." Many officers and men, of course, desired furloughs to say good-bye to the folks at home; but the journey north was a long one, and there was considerable uncertainty as to just when the movement would begin, so leaves were impracticable, and relatives who took the hint that there might shortly be "something doing" came to Waco for the final farewells.

Following the receipt of orders from Washington for the transfer of the 32nd to the Port of Embarkation at Hoboken, N. J., the first troops left Waco on January 2d. From that time on the movement was steady, until the camp was cleared by the first of March of all but a few casuals. Division Headquarters left Waco January 14th. The infantry was moved first, arriving at Camp Merritt before Division Headquarters sailed. The artillery movement did not get under way until February.

CHAPTER II.

The Thirty-Second Division in France.

ON January 24th, 1918, the advance party of the 32nd Division arrived at Brest, France. Division Headquarters sailed on January 31st and were at sea when the Tuscania, on an earlier convoy, was sunk by a German submarine. The Tuscania carried a detachment of 32nd Trains, and the Division suffered its first war casualties when 13 men lost their lives as a result of the attack. The Tuscania was one of the few American troop ships to meet with disaster, and her sinking caused a sensation in the United States. The papers, of course, carried the news that there were certain 32nd Division troops aboard, and relatives of all the men of the Division who might have been on the seas at the time had several anxious days until the identity of those on board was established.

Aside from the misfortune of the Tuscania, the transport of the Division abroad was accomplished without accident and quite expeditiously for the facilities available

PRAUTHOY (Hte Marne) - Entrée Nord

PRAUTHOY, HAUTE MARNE, FRANCE,
A little town about 20 kilometers south of Langres, where Division Headquarters was opened on February 24th, 1918.

at the time. Some of the troops landed in England, and nearly every port in France received its quota. Division Headquarters landed in Liverpool the middle of February, went to the rest camp at Winchester for a few days, crossed the channel to Havre, and after another brief wait went by train to Prauthoy, Haute Marne, France, (a little town about 20 kilometers south of Langres), where the first "P. C." abroad was opened on February 24th, 1918. The area in the vicinity of Prauthoy had been designated by General Pershing as the training ground for the 32nd.

The Division was the sixth to join the American Expeditionary Force, and was, in accordance with General Headquarters plans made before it was known exactly which would be the sixth division to arrive, designated as a replacement organization for the First Army Corps.

MADE A REPLACEMENT DIVISION.

The news that the 32nd was to be a replacement organization came as a blow, indeed. It took the heart out of everybody. The 125th, 126th and 127th Infantry regiments were assigned as temporary labor troops immediately after their arrival, and went to work on important projects in the Service of Supply, so that only scattered detachments and casuals reached the 10th Training Area during the first month the Division was in France. The Artillery Brigade went to the artillery training area at Camp Coetquidan, and the 107th Engineers were assigned to engineering work in the Service of Supply. The 128th Infantry, however, reached the 10th Area in March, and bore the brunt of the replacement blow, just as it was destined to bear the brunt of other blows later on. For about four weeks the Division

"All the privates and captains of the 128th Infantry were transferred to the 1st Division as replacements."
RAYAUMIEX, FRANCE, MARCH 21st, 1918.

functioned as a replacement organization, and during that time all the privates and captains of the 128th who were present for duty were transferred to the First Division as replacements.

It was a sad day in the towns occupied by the 128th when the time came for the men to be separated from their comrades, for the captains to leave the commands which they had so painstakingly trained. The officers and their men were not even to go together, the captains being assigned to one brigade of the First Division and the privates to another. There was, however, some consolation for those who were going away. The First Division had completed its training and was in the trenches, and the replacements had the assurance, at least, of seeing some speedy action. Many non-commissioned officers asked to be reduced to the ranks so that they could accompany their "buddies," but the "non-coms" were needed to train men who would come to take the place of the 128th "bucks" and their requests, of course, could not be granted.

FLOWER OF 32ND GOES TO 1ST.

The parting was pathetic, from the point of view of all concerned, but once under way the replacements started out with the 32nd Division spirit expressing itself in the "rarin' to go" attitude which always was evident on the eve of anything big. Officers who accompanied the replacements to their destination said the First Division officers who received them certainly were grateful. The First Division had received replacements before, but never such men as these. And subsequent reports which came in when the two divisions later found themselves side by side at the front indicated that the 128th replacements with the First fought as valiantly and as skillfully as their comrades who remained with the 32nd.

General Haan felt the blow as keenly as anyone else—perhaps more keenly—but when the replacement order went into effect he called a conference of officers and told them that replacement units were necessary; that we had trained one set of men to fight and could train another; that if it was our lot to do our part in the war by training men to fight instead of fighting ourselves, then it was up to us to put our whole heart and soul into the effort. The officers left the conference and went back to their skeleton units, and training soon was under way with the same energy, and, outwardly at least, the same enthusiasm.

But while General Haan gave his officers no reason to believe that there was any way out of it, he nevertheless set to work to present certain facts and figures to the General Headquarters, with the result that shortly there were no further requisitions for replacements; and then, by undertaking some diplomatic work where it would do the most good, the Division Commander finally got the 125th and 127th relieved from labor duty in the Service of Supply, and the three regiments were sent, early in April, to the 10th Training Area, where they had all arrived by April 10th.

A considerable number of troops were, however, detached from the infantry regiments and held on duty in the Service of Supply, so that during this period approximately 7,000 men were transferred from the Division. The Division was short 2,000 men upon its arrival in France, so that at the end of the replacement period it was approximately 9,000 men short, practically all from the infantry. The companies of infantry in the Division consequently had been reduced to somewhat less than 100 men each, after reassignments equalizing the various rifle companies.

"PINCH HITTING" IN THE SERVICE OF SUPPLY.

While the labor duty required of the 125th, 126th and 127th infantry regiments was unfortunate in that it took the edge off the fine state of discipline these troops had reached, the work they accomplished in the Service of Supply was of great importance in the American Expeditionary Force. According to a statement recently made by Colonel Charles J. Symonds, in command of the depots at Gievres, the 32nd Division arrived in France at a crucial moment, at a time when the completion of depots, etc., was absolutely imperative in order to supply the increasing flow of troops which was expected. Owing to the high state of discipline in the regiments detailed for labor duty, and to the fact that in their ranks many men were found with civilian training in just this kind of work, the 32nd Division was able, in a comparatively short time, to complete the construction work so urgently required, and to tide the Service of Supply over a critical period in its career.

The replacement spectre removed, and the Division being together again, with the exception of those who had gone from the 128th, the artillery, and the engineers who were still on important construction work, the overseas training prescribed by General Headquarters went forward with all the zeal that hard-working officers and willing enlisted men could put into it. The 128th was patched up by assigning to the regiment a number of captains who had been on special duty throughout the Division, and transferring men from the 125th and 126th, so that all four regiments were of about the same strength, approximately 150 men per company. In this training period considerable attention was paid to specialties; there were a number of exercises in open warfare problems, and selected officers and men were sent to the American Expeditionary Force schools at Gondrecourt and Langres to come back with the latest wrinkles on how to make war. The 42nd Division sent back a number of officers who had had some experience in the trenches, and they gave our eager men many pointers on how to apply the principles they were being taught. The practically new subject of Liaison was carefully studied, especially in the higher echelons, and the first practical demonstrations of its workings were conducted. From the first a solid foundation was laid for the divisional liaison which later came to be known as the most nearly perfect in any division in the American Expeditionary Force.

PREPARING FOR THE TRENCHES.

The weather in April, when the bulk of the 32nd Division's overseas training was done, was wretched; but the men were out, rain or shine, day in and day out, Sundays included, drilling, working out problems, conducting demonstrations with live grenades, shooting on the rifle ranges, perfecting themselves in the use of the gas mask, and, in general, finding out all there was to find out about war; and their hearts were in their work.

When the officers from the 42nd came down to help out, they were busy all day on the schedules which had been arranged for them, but at night they conducted volunteer scouting and patrolling classes, and after a hard day's work there always were more applicants for permission to go on these practice raids than there were places in the parties planned. The progress made by the Division was highly satisfactory, and when the fine days of early May came everybody felt that the time was at hand when we would get near enough to the enemy to put some of our knowledge to a very practical use.

THE THIRTY-SECOND DIVISION IN FRANCE

FIRST IMPRESSIONS OF FRANCE.

The Division's "first impressions" of France and the French people were acquired in the Tenth training area, where the troops occupied about thirty small towns and villages, the largest of which was· Champlitte, where the headquarters of the 63rd Infantry Brigade was located. The Division arrived in France at what is probably the worst season of the year—February and March. At Prauthoy, where Division Headquarters was established, it snowed twice, and the first two months were cold and damp. The infantrymen, who, when they first landed, were scattered in detachments from a company up to a battalion, had to do manual labor on construction enterprises in weather that was totally miserable. After they came to the Tenth Area the work was different, but the weather was not. Until the first of May there were but few pleasant days, and in cold, raw, wet weather doughboys drilled, rain or shine, day in and day out, and wondered who the merry jester was who first called the country "sunny France."

A part of the training consisted in the construction of trenches. In the rocky soil of·this part of France trench digging was more of a mining than an agricultural operation. A weary soldier one afternoon stopped for breath while wielding a pick and confided to his "buddy" as follows:

"I know what this war is about. The French are trying to make the Germans take this country and dig holes in it."

The environment was not conducive to the creation of a deep love for France— for the country, not the nation, that is. Few of the men could talk the language, and those who had learned their French from books found that the peasants of this district "didn't understand their own language." But in spite of exasperations, difficulties, and above all the depressing weather, some mighty fine friendships between American soldiers and French civilians sprang up. The French matrons "mothered" the doughboys who were billeted in their homes or barns, the French kiddies just naturally joined the O. D. Army and had new daddies and big brothers by the score, and generous and happy their new relations were, too. The French girls— they weren't exactly like the girls we left behind us, but girls are girls the world over—readily learned to "compree" the most expressive of the doughboy slang, and quickly taught their big American friends certain French phrases. How well the young folks got along is indicated by the number of requests for leave to visit the Tenth Area that were submitted a year later, when the Division was engaged in oconpying Germany and the men were getting the first overseas furloughs.

The Americans, in their early association with the French, found many of the French ways of doing things open for criticism, but they also quickly found that the French war spirit was something constantly to admire. As they became better acquainted in this peasant country, the admiration of the Americans grew, and gradually formed one of their lasting impressions of France—lasting even through the period of profiteering which ensued when the American Expeditionary Force grew from a few to many thousands.

THE "Y" MADE GOOD HERE.

Y. M. C. A. huts in every town occupied by American troops quickly supplemonted the social centers that the men·themselves arranged. The "Y" in France never attained the proportions of the institution in the United States, and during the period of active operations later in the year it did not function exactly as anticipated, and sometimes described, by its admirers; but in the Tenth Area the "Y" did

37

everything that was expected of it. The huts were places where the men could write letters, buy limited, but generally sufficient, quantities of candy and cigarettes, read not-too-old magazines, and meet one another in the evening. The huts also provided the military with a place to hold lectures and classes, and in them on Sundays the chaplains conducted services, the bands gave concerts, and movies now and then entertained the men. Whatever may be said of the "Y" in the field—and plenty of things have been said—there is no doubt but what it made good in the Tenth Training Area.

1. LIEUTENANT COLONEL CHARLES S. CAFFERY, General Staff, Assistant Chief of Staff, G-2; Training Period; Occupation of Sector in Alsace.
2. LIEUTENANT COLONEL ALLAN L. BRIGGS, General Staff, Assistant Chief of Staff, G-3; Training Period; Occupation of Sector in Alsace.
3. COLONEL GEORGE M. RUSSELL, General Staff, Division Inspector.
4. BRIGADIER GENERAL E. H. DEARMOND, as Lieutenant Colonel, General Staff; First Chief of Staff of the Division; Training Period.
5. COLONEL HJALMER ERICKSON, Infantry; Division Quartermaster, Training Period.
6. MAJOR MATHEW HANSEN, Q. M. C.; Assistant Division Quartermaster.
7. MAJOR EDWARD D. ARNOLD, A. G. D.; Personnel and Division Adjutant.

39

CHAPTER III.

First on German Soil.

THE German offensive of March 21st, 1918, was undoubtedly one of the reasons why the "powers above" listened to General Haan's plea for an interruption of the plan to make the 32nd a replacement division. The success of the enemy offensive made it imperative that all the available American troops in France be utilized for combat duty, and after the scattered 32nd had been assembled in the 10th Training Area in April an inspection of our troops was made by the Training and Operations Section of the General Staff, General Headquarters. Their reports resulted in a decision to designate the 32nd for combat duty, and a program of training for four weeks was prescribed to prepare the Division for its front line debut.

This training program had not been completed when, early in May, there were indications that the Division would soon get its long expected chance. During the month of April some replacements were received from the 41st Division and the rifle companies were brought up to a strength of about 160 men. Early in May equipment arrived to fill shortages and certain garrison equipment was turned in, rolling kitchens replaced, field ranges and water carts arrived, packs were reduced by the salvaging of extra clothing. Yes, it looked like the front, at last!

About the middle of May orders were received directing the Division to proceed to the region of Belfort in Alsace and report to the Commanding General of the 40th French Corps for further orders. Then for a few days there was hustle and bustle. Entraining points were designated for each of the rather scattered battalions, and orders regarding the movement were carefully issued by each echelon. The destination was known at Division Headquarters of course, but few others shared the secret, and the battalions packed up, marched to their trains and again made the acquaintance of "Hommes 40" without knowing where they were going, but happy in the knowledge that they were on their way.

ON OUR WAY TO GERMANY.

It was a pleasant trip, all things considered, through a beautiful country, and we finally arrived in picturesque Alsace. On German soil, too!—though the Alsatians carefully corrected us when we made that statement, and pointed out that it was Alsatian soil, not German, though maps issued prior to 1914, showed the towns we were going to were within the former borders of the German Empire. "The first American troops to set foot on German soil." Pretty good stuff to write the folks as soon as the censors would allow it—if they ever would! But it was too good a story for the censors to hold back for long; and a few days later, when the 32nd had been identified by the enemy, there was no reason for keeping the secret from the

"The First American Troops to Set Foot on German Soil." The striped pole near the center of the picture is a marker of the 1914 boundary between France and Germany.
SENTHEIM, ALSACE.

42

people in the United States, and it was announced from Washington that the Wisconsin and Michigan National Guardsmen were holding the line in Haute Alsace.

On May 18th, 1918, the first troops of the 32nd Division, consisting of four battalions, were assigned to front line duty in Haute Alsace, relieving elements of the 9th and 10th French Divisions. It was intended that each of the infantry battalions should remain in the front line twelve days for instruction and other battalions were to be trained in the reserve areas during these periods. The plan contemplated a thirty-five-day course of instruction. However, the success of the German Offensive begun on March 21st caused a speeding up of the training, and on June 15th, eight battalions of the 32nd Division were placed in the front line and the other four battalions in support, the Division thus taking over a front of 27 kilometers, from Aspach le Bas to the Swiss border.

In the middle of June the 57th Field Artillery Brigade joined the Division in Alsace, and a few days later was firing in support of the infantry. The 107th Engineers joined the Division about the same time, so that on June 15, 1918, the Division was practically complete, except for a shortage of about 2,000 enlisted men, mostly from the infantry.

Upon the recommendation of the Commander-in-Chief, American Expeditionary Force, the French authorities undertook to complete the training of the 32nd Division at the earliest practicable date, with a view of placing it on the active battle line on the Western Front. The Division Commander and his Staff up to June 15th had not functioned in command of the Divisional troops in the sector. At this time, however, after a careful investigation by the 7th French Army Commander, he decided that the American Division Commander and his Staff should be placed in tactical control and in command of the troops of the 32nd Division, and also in command of the troops of the 9th French Division, who were occupying a part of the same sector. Accordingly the Division Commander and his Staff assumed tactical command of the sector from Aspach le Bas to the Rhine-Rhone Canal with all the troops therein, both American and French, the latter forming the major portion of the 2nd line and reserve. The training was continued, with the assistance of many French officers and non-commissioned officers as instructors, until July 15th, when orders were received to withdraw the 32nd Division from the sector and prepare it for transportation to the active front.

FIRST TO SET FOOT ON GERMAN SOIL.

The Division went into the Alsace sector in high spirits, the troops being the first Americans to set foot on German soil. They proved to be keen students of trench warfare, and their training progressed rapidly. During their occupancy of the sector there were no operations of a pretentious nature, but few offensive raids being attempted by either side, and none of these was on a large scale. There was plenty of action, however, as patrols were meeting in "No Man's Land" almost nightly, and after the sector came under the command of the Americans successful efforts were made to obtain and retain complete control of "No Man's Land."

Among companies which distinguished themselves, either in offensive or defensive operations in Alsace, were the following:

Companies D, E and I, of the 125th Infantry.
Companies C, D, M and K, of the 126th Infantry.
Companies B, D, H, L and M, of the 127th Infantry.
Companies B, C, D, G, I and L, of the 128th Infantry.

Company A, of the 107th Engineers.
Companies A, C and D, of the 121st Machine Gun Battalion.
Companies A, B, C and D, of the 120th Machine Gun Battalion.
Companies A and B, of the 119th Machine Gun Battalion.

All these organizations had casualties as a result of the affairs in which they participated.

Eight enemy prisoners were captured and eight Americans were taken by the enemy.

OUR LOSSES IN ALSACE.

In the. Alsace sector our losses were: Killed, 1 officer and 39 men; severely wounded, 3 officers and 79 men; slightly wounded, 9 officers and 211 men; died of wounds, 1 officer and 15 men. Total losses from all causes: 368.

The losses inflicted on the enemy were fully equal to our own, according to reports of our raiding parties, and of prisoners captured.

In the Alsace sector 3 German Divisions, the 30th Bavarian Reserve Division, the 44th Landwehr, and the 25th Landwehr, were in the trenches opposite the 32nd Division.

In their skirmishes with the enemy in Alsace the infantry acquired a fine degree of confidence. If ever there was any question as to whether the German, with his four years of experience, his many years of training and his reputation for military knowledge, was a better soldier than the young American volunteer, our first experiences with the enemy at close hand settled the argument. Our men knew the German had nothing that we feared. In short order we learned most of the tricks it had taken him four years to perfect and had figured out a few on our own account, to the great delight of the French non-com instructors who were assigned to look after us. These French non-coms were perhaps rather dubious about our doughboys at first, and counseled more moderation than we had a mind to use in our negotiations with the foe. Haute Alsace was a "quiet sector," and neither the exhausted French nor the busy Germans had a desire to make it anything else. Accordingly the French, while they were with us, stifled a lot of budding initiative; but as they gradually were withdrawn, to let the Americans run things in their own way, the sector livened up appreciably. After our 57th Artillery Brigade came there was an increase in activity both in front and behind the observation posts, as the most advanced positions were termed, and the Germans more or less readily accepted the Yankee challenge. Soon shells were falling on both sides of the line, where no shells had fallen for months, and the front line trenches were no longer a place to spend a quiet evening.

The 32nd Division found Alsace a super-quiet sector, and they left it anything but that.

WE "PARLEY BOCHE."

In Alsace the Americans were thrown into contact with a class of "French" people different from those they met in the Tenth Training Area. The Alsatians did not, as a rule, impress the soldiers in olive drab as being so wholly keen for "La Patrie" as the peasants of Haute Marne. In Haute Marne the people were "Frenchmen." In Haute Alsace they were "Alsatians."

With them the Americans got along quite comfortably. The average doughboy could talk a little French by this time, and the Alsatians could all speak German, which gave them a medium of understanding with the Wisconsin and Michigan

"After our 57th Artillery Brigade came there was an increase in activity both in front and behind the Observation Posts as the most advanced positions were termed."

FRONT LINE TRENCH IN ALSACE.

troops that the peasants of the Tenth Area did not have. Many of our men could speak German, and accordingly one of the difficulties of being a stranger in a strange land was made less acute.

. The friendships formed between soldiers and civilians in Alsace were neither as numerous nor as lasting as those made in the Tenth Area, but in Alsace our officers and men had their first opportunity of meeting the French fighting men at the front. The admiration of the two armies was mutual. As Americans and French became better acquainted a spirit of true fellowship grew steadily, and today many officers of the 32nd Division count among their best friends officers of the Ninth French Division with whom the 32nd was associated in Alsace.

TWO HOLIDAYS IN ALSACE.

Two great holidays were celebrated during the Division's tour of duty in Alsace— the Fourth of July, the birthday of the United States of America, and the Fourteenth of July, the natal day of the French Republic. The Fourth was the occasion for ceremonies in all Alsatian towns which contained Americans, and which were a sufficient distance from the front line to prevent Fritz from taking a hand in the fireworks. French soldiers and Alsatian civilians assisted the Americans in observing the day—there were parades, speeches and felicitations. On July 14th the Americans returned the compliment, helping the French to observe the holiday, which they will always remember as being celebrated on the eve of the turning point of the war.

"Soon shells were falling on both sides of the line where no shells had fallen for months and the front line trenches were no longer a place to spend a quiet evening."

THE ABOVE IS NEAR HECKEN, ALSACE.

46

1. LIEUTENANT COLONEL GLEN GARLOCK, Infantry. Lieutenant Colonel, 128th Infantry, Training Period; Occupation of Sector in Alsace; Aisne-Marne Offensive; Division Inspector, Oise-Aisne Offensive; Meuse-Argonne Offensive; March to the Rhine; Army of Occupation.
2. LIEUTENANT COLONEL FRANK H. FOWLER, Infantry, as Major commanded 121st Machine Gun Battalion, as Lieutenant Colonel, Division Machine Gun Officer, Training Period; Occupation of Alsace Sector; Aisne-Marne Offensive; Oise-Aisne Offensive; Meuse-Argonne Offensive; March to the Rhine; Army of Occupation.
3. LIEUTENANT COLONEL S. D. PEPPER, J. A. D., Division Judge Advocate, Training Period; Occupation of Sector in Alsace; Aisne-Marne Offensive; Oise-Aisne Offensive; Meuse-Argonne Offensive.
4. LIEUTENANT COLONEL CHARLES R. WILLIAMS, Q. M. C., Division Quartermaster, Training Period; Occupation of Sector in Alsace; Aisne-Marne Offensive; Oise-Aisne Offensive; Meuse-Argonne Offensive; March to the Rhine.
5. COLONEL HAROLD C. FISKE, Engineers, Division Engineer; Training Period; Occupation of Sector in Alsace; Aisne-Marne Offensive; Oise-Aisne Offensive; Meuse-Argonne Offensive; March to the Rhine; Army of Occupation.
6. COLONEL GILBERT E. SEAMAN, Medical Department, as Lieutenant Colonel, Division Surgeon.
7. MAJOR WILLIAM A. WOODLIEF, A.G.D., Division Adjutant, Training Period; Occupation of Sector in Alsace; Aisne-Marne Offensive; Oise-Aisne Offensive; Meuse-Argonne Offensive; March to the Rhine; Army of Occupation.
8. MAJOR AMOS ASHLEY, F. A., Division Ordnance Officer; Aisne-Marne Offensive; Oise-Aisne Offensive; Meuse-Argonne Offensive; Army of Occupation.
9. LIEUTENANT COLONEL JOHN SCOTT, S. C.; Division Signal Officer; Oise-Aisne Offensive; Meuse-Argonne Offensive; March to the Rhine; Army of Occupation.

47

CHAPTER IV.

Into the Big Battle.

ARLY in July General Pershing came to Alsace to inspect the Division. He visited every unit, and made a very thorough examination of everything and everybody. During the visit of the Commander-in-Chief, General Haan told the head of the American Expeditionary Force that the 32nd had been thoroughly rehearsed in the various drills prescribed in the training pamphlets, and that in their exercises our men were easily kept in hand; that they were getting a trifle weary of training, and were anxious to get into a real fight.

"Fed up on it," General Pershing commented, smilingly.

General Haan expressed the opinion that his men would give a good account of themselves, and hoped that he would soon get orders to go to an active front.

"Early in July General Pershing came to Alsace to inspect the Division."
NEAR SENTHEIM, ALSACE.

"During the visit of the Commander-in-Chief, General Haan told the head of the American Expeditionary Force that the 32nd had been thoroughly rehearsed in the various drills prescribed in the training pamphlets."

A maneuver showing infantry advancing to 1st Objective. See picture on page 104, showing troops advancing on machine gun nests in actual battle. How similar to the above when only at drill!

NEAR ST. GERMAIN, ALSACE.

General Pershing, with a bit of a twinkle in his eye, and a pleased expression on his face, developing into an appreciative smile, replied:

"I like the snap in your Division, and unless I am mistaken you will be on your way to a more active front in the very near future. Tell your men I like their spirit."

After General Pershing's inspection there were whispered rumors of an impending movement of the Division. With accumulating signs that the rumor was based upon something more substantial than the usual trench gossip, came speculations as to the probable destination of the outfit. Most guesses were that the journey would be up to the "big front." The doughboys out in the trenches received the papers daily and were familiar with the situation created by Marshall Foch's counter-offensive of July 18th. They knew that Americans had been in the thick of it, and that the U. S. troops had distinguished themselves. They knew that there were only a few divisions in the American Expeditionary Force that had been over longer than the 32nd, and the thoughtful officers and men figured that it was about our turn.

Others thought that the Division would be withdrawn for a rest, refitting and some more training. Those who had good imaginations thought the Division might go to Italy—we were closer to the Italian border than any other troops on the line. A few "strategists" who had recently returned from the schools at Langres and Gondrecourt, and had seen signs of other American troops in the vicinity of Alsace, thought perhaps there might be a contraction of the front with the idea of an offensive in Haute Alsace.

INTO *THE BIG BATTLE*

The "strategists" were the first to be disillusioned. A few days after the mess sergeants' details brought back from the railhead the first rumors of a move an order came out directing the withdrawing of all troops from the trenches to entraining points. On July 19th the first elements of the Division crowded the well-known "Hommes 40" and rattled away. It soon became apparent that the imaginative doughboys who had guessed we were going to Italy were all wrong, for the troop trains headed north. There were still three guesses left—was it to be a training area, Chateau-Thierry, or the British front?

BID GOOD-BYE TO ALSACE.

The doughboys didn't care much. They were, as General Pershing had suggested, "fed up" on Alsace and quiet sectors. If they were going to a training area they knew it was to prepare for something big, and if they were on their way to something big they felt that they were ready. Officers and men who had been away to the American Expeditionary Force schools and who had talked to soldiers from other divisions who had had a taste of the real thing, were especially keen for the initial try-out.

Real summer weather prevailed during the troop movement. It was "sunny France" at last, and the men enjoyed the trip northward through the beautiful country. It soon became apparent that the journey was not to a training area, as the trains passed through the section in which the American forces were preparing for action. We were headed straight for Paris, and those who had guessed that we

General Pershing, Major General Haan, and Colonel Laucagne of the 9th French Division in conference.
GENERAL PERSHING'S INSPECTION OF 32ND DIVISION, ALSACE.

51

"The 32nd Division had been thoroughly rehearsed in the various drills prescribed in the training pamphlets."

ARTILLERYMEN OF 57TH FIELD ARTILLERY BRIGADE
AT GAS DEFENSE DRILL IN ALSACE.

were bound for Chateau-Thierry indulged in "I told you so." Some of the trains were fortunate enough to pass through Paris in the daytime, and as the toy French engines jerked the toy French box-cars through the outskirts of the French capital the people in the street stopped and waved at us. They crowded the windows of the buildings and shouted "Vive L'Americain!" and the doughboys yelled back in good American fashion.

To those who had passed through Paris on their way into France some months before the change in the attitude of the people was very noticeable. In March the crowds in the streets looked up as the American troop trains passed, and some of them waved; but there was nothing spontaneous or particularly enthusiastic about it. But lately the Americans at Chateau-Thierry and on the Marne had saved Paris, and the bulletins in the papers the day the 32nd Division passed through Paris indicated that these same Americans were about to save France. And so the French folks waved—all of them—and "vive-d" for "les Americains."

The troop trains passed Paris and continued on their way. Those who had guessed in favor of Chateau-Thiery began to weaken. We seemed to be headed for the British front. Many rather hoped so. The doughboys "liked the French fine," and had a sincere admiration of their ability to make war, but they "sure were hard to talk to." Yes, going up with the British wouldn't be so bad. They were good fighters, too; we would learn some new tricks from them, no doubt, and then we would "slam into the Germans" and win our niche in the Hall of Fame.

INTO *THE BIG BATTLE*

NEAR THE "BIG FRONT" AT LAST.

But it wasn't to be the British front after all. The same day that we passed through Paris the trains pulled up at a station in the vicinity of the forest of Compiègne where the German drive had been stopped a short time before. The troops detrained and were billeted in a number of small towns in the neighborhood of Pont St. Maxence with Division Headquarters at Bethisy St. Martin.

Still, our destination wasn't exactly apparent. Maybe the General and his staff knew where we were going to get our baptism of fire, but nobody else did, or cared particularly. All rather hoped it would be around Chateau-Thierry. That was known as an American sector, and if we got in there it would be something to write the folks back home when we got out. We wouldn't have to tell them that it was a quiet sector.

The Division spent a few days in the small towns west of the forest of Compiègne, during which the entire Division was assembled there. The First Division had recently been in that neighborhood—we met some of the 32nd Division men who had been transferred to the First in our replacement days. They had been in the thick of it, and we listened to their tales with interest. Back from the front came news that the 42nd Division was smashing the German lines for daily gains. All the news indicated that the Allies were gaining and we were impatient to be off.

We had not long to wait. By July 24th the whole Division was in the vicinity of Pont St. Maxence southwest of Soissons. We were under the orders of the 10th French Army, which was operating around Soissons, and were in the Army Reserve. On July 26th orders were received to proceed by trucks to the region of Chateau-Thierry and report to the 38th French Corps of the Sixth French Army.

The Troops embussed at once and rode through a country recently swept by a tremendous battle. Whenever a road block developed and the truck train stopped the men jumped off and went souvenir hunting. There were plenty of evidences of the German retreat and evidences also of what had caused them to fall back—the French *poilu*. Belts of machine gun bullets, helmets and German equipment were scattered over the fields. But the search for souvenirs had its disadvantages. The Germans who had been left behind hadn't been buried very deeply, and certain salvaging expeditions met with rather grewsome surprises now and then. The men picked up a lot of souvenirs and carried them until they left the trucks—and maybe for an hour afterwards. Then most of them decided that a pack which was some pounds heavier than the man who wrote Field Service Regulations had figured on was enough baggage—and besides, where they were going there would be souvenirs in plenty.

AT CHATEAU-THIERRY.

Debussing at Chateau-Thierry just after nightfall, the troops marched to billets in the town and in small villages in the vicinity. Up ahead the war was going on, all right. The sky throbbed with red flashes from the big guns; their constant cough and rumble told us plainly that this wasn't Alsace. There was some speculation as to when we would be up there, but the immediate concern was in regard to billets. Some of them were quite a distance from the debussing point and the hike put thoughts of future danger and glory out of our heads. That night, for the first time since coming to France, many of the men billeted without a roof over their heads—some took to the fields in pup-tents, while others took their chances in wrecked buildings and hoped it wouldn't rain.

The next day the 32nd Division got its first real look at Chateau-Thierry and the towns in the tip of the famous Marne salient. The sight-seeing was of brief duration, however, for late in the afternoon orders were received directing that the troops march at nightfall, to arrive in the immediate rear of the divisions up ahead who were at grips with the Germans. The rolling kitchens and field trains had marched from the Pont St. Maxence region and had not yet arrived, so that the meals on the 27th were from the reserve rations and the vegetable gardens in the vicinity.

Just before dark, July 27th, the doughboy regiments lined up on the Paris-Metz road and started forward. The 32nd Division was going into battle at last! How different from the scene a good many had visualized! There were no bands, no flags, no pomp, not even a riffle of any excitement. If the men had any feeling in the matter they didn't express it. Their immediate concern was the difficulty of marching with their blouses on, on that hot night. But the order said what uniform should be worn and how it should be worn, and the 32nd was a well disciplined division; the men wore their blouses, but they compromised by tucking their olive drab shirts into their packs.

As the Division struggled along the hot and dusty road, frequently halted by blocks up ahead, the rumbling of the big guns became louder; their coughing deeper. The red blotches in the sky were continuous. There was sure-enough fighting not far away, but nobody worried especially about that. "What in hell was the matter with that regiment up in front? Couldn't they hike, or what? Let's go!"

Just as day was breaking, the Division reached its destination and bivouacked in the Foret de Fere, near le Charmel and right in the rear of the 3rd and 28th U. S. divisions, which were in the line. Division Headquarters came up to Jaulgonne—the 63rd and 64th Brigade P. C.'s were established at le Charmel.

PREPARING FOR THE BATTLE.

The next day regimental and battalion commanders went up to reconnoiter and make their plans for relieving the 3rd Division. The troops remained concealed in the Foret de Fere, and worried a great deal more about the fact that the rolling kitchens were still some distance behind, than they did at the imminence of their participation in a major offensive and one of the decisive battles of the great war.

The junior officers were a little thoughtful, wondering when the relief would be made, and what the plan of action would be. But their minds, too, were on the "chow" wagons, more or less, and they hoped the mess sergeants would catch up before the big show started. There was no change in the situation on July 28th. The Division and Brigade P. C.'s remained as on the day before. The regimental and battalion commanders had reconnoitered the front, and were ready for the order which would send their outfits up to strike a blow for Democracy.

After midnight of the 28th, the 38th French Corps ordered the relief of the 3rd Division by one brigade of the 32nd, the relief to take place the night of July 29th-30th. Orders for the relief at once were issued. The command of the sector was to pass to the Commanding General of the 32nd at 11 A. M., July 30th, and arrangements were made to move the Division P. C. to le Charmel Chateau, near the village of le Charmel, on the morning of July 30th.

NO THOUGHT OF POSSIBLE FAILURE.

In the Foret de Fere the men waited through the day for the word to move out. They didn't know exactly what they were expected to do, but they knew they were going to do it. Nine months later, when the war was over and the men were crossing the ocean on their way home, General Haan made a speech at a banquet of officers of the Division in which he said that the possibility of failure never entered his head at the time his Division was preparing to go into action on the Ourcq and while the 32nd was driving at the Germans in the long smash to the Vesle. That is exactly the way every officer and man in the Division felt at the time. A major offensive was a new one on them; but they had trained for it, and they knew in theory what they should do—attack, dig in, hold and prepare to attack again. They thought a little about some concrete things that might actually happen, but the possibility of failure was not one of the visions they entertained.

At nightfall the 64th Brigade started filtering forward to make the relief, while the 63rd Brigade remained bivouacked in the Foret de Fere. From this time on the battle raged, and for the next eight days hammer blows were rained upon the enemy whenever he was found. In the savage fighting that ensued the German line was forced steadily back, over difficult ground, including the strongly fortified position on the Ourcq river, for a distance of 19 kilometers to the Vesle river, where, as a brilliant climax to the brilliant American attacks, the 64th Infantry Brigade captured by storm the important town of Fismes, and the 63rd Brigade took the important German railhead on the Vesle in the left of our sector.

"As a brilliant climax to the brilliant American attacks, the 64th Infantry Brigade captured by storm the important town of FISMES."

A STREET IN FISMES.

55

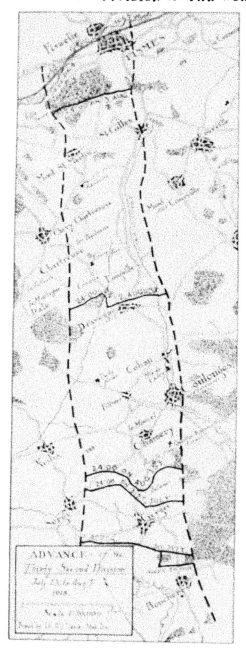

CHAPTER V.

The Baptism of Fire.

THE memory of that relief which started as the mantle of darkness fell on the war-racked slopes of the Ourcq on July 29th and which was completed in the misty midsummer morning of July 30th, is indelibly impressed upon the minds of the men of the 127th Infantry who stumbled forward through the Stygian night to take their places in the front line. They were guided into place by details from the tired 3rd Division and by their own reconnoitering parties which had been over the ground in the daytime, but the night was so utterly black that the long relieving column had to grope its way blindly along, harassed by false gas alarms and all the exasperating delays to which a movement of this kind is always subjected. The big gun flashes as the troops passed through the American battery positions gave the sweating soldiers glimpses of a smashed and dusty road, the center of which they were forced to avoid in favor of the necessary ambulance and supply traffic. Although the distance covered was far less than the long hike a few nights before when they moved up from reserve to support, the effort was more trying to both nerves and muscles, but Colonel Langdon's regiment and Colonel McCoy's 128th, which followed in close support, finally made their way through the blind night, and when the damp darkness started to dissolve in the early morning hours, they had taken the places of the fatigued regulars from the Third and were in position on the line of the Ourcq in the vicinity of Roncheres. Fortunately, the necessary noise made by floundering through the inky night had not apprised the enemy of anything unusual, and the movement was completed without undue hindrance from the German artillery.

Dawn found the front elements of the 127th facing the Bois des Grimpettes, a strong German position in a clump of woods, which had held up the 3rd Division after the famous conquerors of the Marne had fought their way from Chateau-Thierry, having been in continuous action since the German offensive started on July 15th. On our left were Pennsylvania National Guardsmen of the 28th Division, who had been through some bloody fighting, and on our right were grizzled *poilu* veterans of the 4th French Division who had been tenaciously hanging to the German retreat since the enemy had started falling back from the Marne.

IMMEDIATE ATTACK PLANNED.

The 127th was fighting the foe before command of the sector passed to the Commanding General of the 32nd Division. The transfer of authority from the staff of the 3rd to the 32nd took place at 11 A. M., and General Haan, after getting reports that the relief had been completed and that the dispositions which he had ordered had been verified, immediately held a conference with the Commanding General of the 3rd Division Artillery, which had been left in the sector to support the 32nd, the 57th Field Artillery Brigade having not yet come up. The 28th Division had reported during the morning that the Pennsylvanians would be unable to advance in their sector until the menace of the Grimpettes woods was removed from their flank, and General Haan accordingly planned to take the German position at once. Liaison was established with the 28th, and the support of the 28th Division artillery was secured for the projected assault on Grimpettes. The plan contemplated the advance of the 28th Division as soon as the 32nd had taken the woods.

In accordance with this plan, at 2:30 P. M., just three and one-half hours after the Division had taken over its first active sector, troops of the 127th Infantry went over the top and followed a rolling barrage into the Bois des Grimpettes. There had been a brief but intensive artillery preparation on the German position before the attack was launched, and some snappy work by runners and officers was necessary to get the troops in position to go over at the proper time. For some of the assault platoons zero hour was the moment they got their orders, but in spite of the close work necessary the Division's first major attack was entirely successful and was made exactly according to the schedule arranged. The 127th dashed across the clearing which the enemy woods commanded, pushed through the tangle of wire and fallen trees, and cleared the Germans out, until their advance was halted by machine gun fire from another clump of woods on their right flank.

On this flank, from positions in the Bois des Cierges, the enemy continued during the day to pour a deadly fire, and successfully hindered the 127th in its efforts to enlarge its gain. However, as darkness fell, the Americans made their way to the edge of the Cierges woods, and established themselves in position there with the idea of clearing the place out in the morning. During the night, the Germans discovered the menace and delivered a counter attack, about midnight, with a force from the Bois de Meuniere. Determined not to be dislodged from their position of vantage, the 127th met the attack and a sanguinary bayonet melee raged for hours in the dark tangle of the woods. The attacking force finally was routed, and retired, leaving many dead.

Unable to loosen the American grip on the woods by a direct attack, the enemy, during the rest of the night, tried to make the position untenable by making it the target of a heavy concentration of artillery fire. The survivors of the German attack were able to give the enemy artillery very exact information as to the American position, and toward morning our troops were slightly withdrawn so as to avoid the mounting losses from shell fire. We continued to command the Bois des Cierges, however, and the front line was relieved from the galling fire it had suffered from that direction on the late afternoon before.

MICHIGAN TROOPS GO IN.

During the night of July 30th-31st, the 63rd Brigade moved up from support for its baptism of fire, relieving the 28th Division, which had made a slight advance following the fall of Grimpettes. The Michigan soldiers duplicated the feat of their Wisconsin comrades on the night before, by making a successful relief in the face of trying circumstances, and on the morning of July 31st, were in a position for their share of the glory about to be won by Les Terribles. On that morning, the two brigades of the 32nd, in line side by side, the 63rd on the left and the 64th on the right, occupied the entire front of the 38th French Corps, which previously had been held by two Divisions. The line extended across the sector through the Bois des

"The 63rd Brigade moved up from support for its baptism of fire."
THE ABOVE SCENE IS NEAR COURMONT, FRANCE.
See exploding shell just to the right of the tree on extreme left of the picture.

Grimpettes, one-half kilometer south of the village of Cierges, to Ferme Caranda on the left, where the 63rd Brigade connected up with the Rainbow troops.

In front of the 32nd loomed Hill 212 above the village of Cierges, a hornet's nest of German machine guns. It was apparent to the Corps Commander that these two spots were the menace of his front, and, in compliance with his request that an attempt be made to capture them, an attack was prepared in which both brigades were to participate.

Directly in front of us was the long, open slope of the Ourcq Valley, reaching to the small woods leading up to the woods of Les Jomblettes on Hill 212, a spur of Hill 230. This objective constituted one of the strongest German positions on the line of the Ourcq, and the success of the contemplated operation meant the breaking of the Kaiser's last formidable line of resistance south of the Vesle.

Les Jomblettes at this time was holding up not only the 32nd Division, but machine gun nests there and in the Bois Pelger, further back, flanked the open ground in front of the 42nd Division and absolutely prevented any advance by the Rainbows.

The assault planned was on much the same order as the initial attack of the day before. After a brief artillery preparation, the troops advanced under the protection of a barrage. On the left the 63rd Brigade made its "big league" debut in a workmanlike manner, promptly reaching its objective, Hill 212. The Michiganders dove into Les Jomblettes and mopped it up, and then cleaned out the Bois Pelger, allowing the 42nd Division to advance. It was hot work, and some wicked fighting took place before the enemy was forced to retire his line to the Bois de la Planchette, where the Americans could see another tough job in store for them.

While the Michigan boys were roughing it with the foe on the left, the 127th was struggling for further advantage on the right. The Wisconsin troops pushed their attack through the village of Cierges and passed beyond, only to be held up by a withering hail of machine gun bullets from Bellevue Farm, which had been organized into a very strong center of resistance and which the artillery had failed to smother. Officers leading the attack saw the impossibility of taking the position by a frontal assault, and so broke off the attack until the night of July 31st, when the right flank of the 64th Brigade succeeded in filtering through as far as Hill 230.

Unfortunately, however, the Fourth French Division had also been held up in the afternoon attack, and in consequence the Americans who reached Hill 230 were wide open on their right flank to machine gun fire from in front of the French in the vicinity of Reddy Farm and on their left rear to fire from the vicinity of Bellevue Farm. When it became apparent that the whole front could not be straightened out and brought up to the advanced position, the troops in the fire-swept salient were withdrawn from Hill 230 and took shelter on the reverse slope between the village of Cierges and Bellevue Farm.

GERMAN LINE DENTED.

The day's attack had been launched with the hope of breaking the German line of the Ourcq. Owing to the courageous German resistance and a cunningly arranged machine gun defense, the line had not been broken, but it had been badly battered

"The Michiganders dove into Les Jomblettes and mopped it up."
BOIS JOMBLETTES, NEAR CIERGES.

"The troops • • • took shelter on the reverse slope between the village of Cierges and Bellevue Farm."
CIERGES, WITH HILL 230 AND BELLEVUE FARM IN BACKGROUND.

61

and actually pierced in some spots. It appeared that the German hold on the line had been shaken, and, with victory in sight, the Division Commander decided to attack along the entire front on the morning of August 1. The Bois de la Planchette was the objective of the 63rd Brigade, and Hill 230 the goal of the Wisconsin outfit. The 64th Brigade had the added mission of turning the strong position at Bellevue Farm which had stopped the attack of the day before.

During the night, the Brigade and Regimental commanders disposed their troops according to orders, based upon the problem before them, and by dawn were ready for what was regarded as the 32nd Division's most critical test. The day would prove whether or not the Americans could continue to deliver the punch with which they had entered the offensive, whether they had the power of sustained effort, or whether they had "shot their bolt" in the brief but bitter struggle of the past few days.

The attack started with much promise of success, but reports from every section of the front indicated that the Germans opposed to us were not of the fleeing kind. They resisted desperately, and dozens of groups died at their posts rather than "kamerad" before the American waves which surged forward. The German Command was under no misapprehension as to the importance of the position, and had put in fresh troops to attempt to hold the Ourcq against further American attacks. These troops were amply provided with machine guns, strongly supported by artillery, and they put up a game fight.

KEY TO OURCQ CAPTURED.

But Les Terribles were not to be denied. Although new to the vicious kind of warfare in which they found themselves, they rushed the enemy defenses with irresistible determination, captured the Bois de la Planchette and Hill 230, maneuvered the foe out of Bellevue Farm, and finally completely overwhelmed the strong position which was the day's objective and the key to the entire enemy line to the north of the Ourcq.

The capture of Bellevue Farm and Hill 230 was a triumph of tactics as well as bravery. It was accomplished by a converging movement of the two regiments of the 64th Brigade, the 127th Infantry on the left attacking from Cierges in a northerly direction to the left of Bellevue Farm, and the 128th Infantry on the right going out of the Division sector into the French front through the western edge of the Bois de Meuniere and attacking Hill 230 and the woods to the right of the hill, at the same time turning Bellevue Farm on the right. Early in the afternoon, the forward elements of the 128th were in Bellevue Farm, and about the same time, the leading platoons of the 127th passed the position on the left and continued up the road nearly to Reddy Farm. After dark, the 128th, still operating on the edge of the Division sector, got troops into the Bois de Meuniere on the right of Hill 230, where they were joined by liaison troops of the Fourth French Division. The two flanks of the Brigade thus enveloped Hill 230 and completely dominated it.

The possession of Hill 230 and the high ground extending across the sector to the left had been especially valuable to the Germans, and they held tenaciously to the position. When it fell, they could do nothing but retreat. They seem to have promptly sensed their danger and hastened their withdrawal while the Americans were making sure of victory. From information secured during the night, it was apparent that the enemy was pushing his retirement with great rapidity to escape a further blow.

The 42nd Division, which fought grimly during the day on the left of the 63rd Brigade, succeeded in breaking the German resistance which had been holding up the

"The 57th Field Artillery Brigade was finally all in position."

A CAMOUFLAGED GUN, 57TH FIELD ARTILLERY BRIGADE.

Rainbow advance. By the night of August 1st, the 42nd Division line was well forward, and on the right of the 32nd, the Fourth French Division, under cover of the darkness, came up on a line with the Wisconsin men who held Hill 230.

The situation was now such that the commander of the 6th French Army deemed it probable a consolidated advance could break through, and such an advance was accordingly ordered to begin on the morning of August 2nd. In the meantime, the batteries of the 57th Field Artillery Brigade, which had been coming into the line since the night of July 30th-31st, was finally all in position and set to fire the barrage which was to protect the infantry in their final push.

There were early indications, on the morning of August 2nd, when the new drive started, that the Germans were abandoning their positions without the stubborn resistance which had made them worthy foes for the past three days. On the 32nd Division front, the forward movement progressed rapidly, and early in the day our troops had passed Reddy Farm and advanced to a line a little south of Chamery, which was the day's objective. "Sacrifice" machine gun crews had interrupted the progress to a certain extent, but none of the organized resistance of previous experience had been encountered, so it was decided to press on beyond the objective. The pursuit was continued energetically to a line north of the village of Dravegny, which the 32nd Division reached by nightfall, after advancing a distance of approximately 6 kilometers.

The extent of the American victory was now apparent, and the allied command planned to drive on to the Vesle. Accordingly, on August 3rd, the pursuit was resumed, and our troops continued to steadily gain ground, although meeting with increased resistance, especially from the left flank, where the 42nd Division, on account of the many patches of bothersome woods from which the sacrifice machine guns operated, was unable to advance as rapidly as the 32nd.

GERMANS STAND ON VESLE.

By the end of the day, the Division's front line had advanced 7 kilometers, to the hills overlooking the valley of the Vesle, about 1 kilometer south of the Vesle on the left and two kilometers south of Fismes on the right flank. Here considerable resistance was encountered from the German rear guard organization, which was making a stand to protect the withdrawal over the river. After ascertaining that the enemy intended to make a stand, the advanced forces were thinned out and withdrawn, to prevent heavy casualties from the continuous stream of machine gun and artillery fire from the well organized German positions on the heights north of the Vesle.

About midnight on August 3rd, the Corps Commander ordered the 32nd Division to push forward to the Vesle and provide the means of crossing. Immediately dispositions were ordered with the idea of overcoming the German rear guard and establishing the American forces in command of the river crossings.

When the pursuit of the Germans started on August 2nd, the Division front was held by elements of all four infantry regiments, the 126th on the left being in liaison with the 42nd Division, with the 125th, 127th and 128th, in the order named from left to right, the 128th being in liaison with the Fourth French Division on the right. When the advance was started on August 2nd, the 125th and 126th moved

"The Division's front line had advanced 7 kilometers to the hills overlooking the Vesle."
MONT ST. MARTIN.
Note German shell exploding—center of picture.

"The enemy • • • by means of very active trench mortar fire, was able to hold the town."
"Captured—10 trench Mortars."

A GERMAN "MINNIE."

out side by side, with the 128th, taking the lead in the right sub-sector, followed by the 127th. On August 3rd, the 63rd Brigade also echeloned in depth, the 125th taking the lead with the 126th in support. The 128th continued in the lead on the right. In two days the leading regiments advanced the Division's front line a distance of 13 kilometers for the greatest gains ever recorded by the 32nd.

With another attack in prospect, the 128th was relieved at St. Gilles on the night of August 3rd, and on the afternoon of August 4th, Colonel Langdon's regiment moved out of St. Gilles toward Fismes, while the 63rd Brigade attacked the railroad yards on their front. The enemy, however, had no intention of yielding without a bitter battle, and by means of very heavy artillery and machine gun fire was able successfully to hold the town and railroad yards during the early hours of the afternoon.

"In the eastern part of the town German and American patrols clashed in fights for possession of sheltering walls."

FISMES.

THE BAPTISM OF FIRE

"LES TERRIBLES" TAKE FISMES.

In its attack on Fismes, the 127th Infantry was badly cut up, and late in the day Colonel Langdon organized a provisional battalion out of what was left of his regiment and sent this force forward to storm the town. His shattered companies made a desperate assault and finally succeeded, about nightfall, in passing through the town and establishing a position on the south bank of the river. On the left, the 63rd Brigade took the railroad yards and succeeded in getting a few small patrols across the river during the night, but was unable to maintain them there, and they were withdrawn.

On August 5th, the troops of the 127th, who were in Fismes, gave their attention to mopping up the west half of the town. Attempts also were made to cross the river, but without success. On the night of August 5th, the Third Battalion of the 128th Infantry, which was the only strong battalion left in the 64th Brigade, was ordered into Fismes to reinforce the 127th, and on the morning of August 6th, all four companies of the reinforcing battalion entered Fismes, relieving the 127th.

There were still German snipers in the town, and the 128th continued to mop up the place. In the eastern part of the town German and American patrols clashed in fights for possession of sheltering walls and buildings, and it was not until nightfall that the Americans could claim anything like control of the city.

By this time, it had become apparent that an organized attack would have to be made if the Allies were to secure bridge-heads across the Vesle, and the 28th Division was ordered up to relieve the 32nd and prepare for the effort. On the night of August 6th-7th, the Pennsylvanians came up from the rear, where they had been following in support of the 32nd since their relief from the line over a week before by the 63rd Brigade. The Keystone soldiers took over Fismes from the battered battalion of the 128th on the morning of August 7th, and relieved the 63rd Brigade in the left sub-sector during the night before. The relief in the town was made in the presence of enemy patrols, and, though the Americans continued to hold the city, Fismes was a No-Man's Land and fair game for both sides for several weeks thereafter.

CHAPTER VI.

"Les Terribles" Report to General Mangin.

THE last tired doughboys sifted out of the front line positions during the forenoon of August 7th, and dragged their weary feet back to the shattered, filthy towns which a few days before they had rushed through in the heat of their first big battle. They found some shelter, such as it was; they found their rolling kitchens with plentiful hot food, and they found more or less rest, punctuated, however, by airplane bombs and heavy shells at frequent intervals. In twenty-four hours they felt a lot better, and began to take an interest in hearing what they had accomplished. Each small unit knew, of course, that it had gained its objectives, that it had fought well; but had the Division as a whole demonstrated that it was the shock outfit we all believed it to be?

"They found their rolling kitchens with plentiful hot food."
NEAR MONT ST. MARTIN.

69

It had. Up at Dravegny, a town about in the center of the territory the Division had just wrested from the enemy, the 128th Infantry had a battalion headquarters. On the day after the relief a runner, coming from regimental headquarters, brought the news that all was well.

"General Haan was just out to see Col. McCoy," he told the company runners gathered around battalion headquarters. "The Old Boy was all smiles. I guess he's satisfied."

He was; and soon the story of the General's smile was going the rounds of every mess line. Little by little the men during the next few days heard the story of what their Division had done. They learned that in seven days of fighting—which means shooting, marching, rushing, digging, sweating, bleeding, enduring hunger, thirst, exhaustion, cooties and all manner of the manifold hardships of war—they had gained 19 kilometers; captured eighteen villages or fortified farms, captured four pieces of heavy artillery, five pieces of light artillery, ten trench mortars, and 28 machine guns, many of which they turned on the foe, besides hundreds of rifles and artillery and machine gun ordnance which they did not use. They learned that the ammunition and war material which they had captured was being collected and hauled to the rear by the trainload. They found it was the Fourth Prussian Guards who had first tried to stop their rush on the Ourcq and whom they had so terribly punished and completely vanquished. They learned that the 200th and 216th German divisions had then been thrown in against them in an attempt to stay their rush for the Vesle, and they knew where all that were left of those two divisions were now. They were north of the Vesle, and thanking their stars that they were fleet enough of foot to outdistance those mad soldiers from across the seas whom the French were calling "Les Terribles."

EARN NICKNAME OF "LES TERRIBLES."

For it was in this battle that the 32nd Division got its name. When the fight first started General de Mondesir, commanding the 38th French Corps, under whose orders the 32nd was serving, came up to see how the Americans were conducting the battle. He looked over the plans at the Division P. C., and asked questions concerning the methods by which expected results were to be achieved; then he shook hands with everybody and expressed himself as "tres content," which means, of course, that he thought it would work.

Not satisfied with visiting Division Headquarters, the French Corps Commander, in order to inform himself further, went to the front, found a good observation point, and with his own eyes saw our soldiers as they climbed the heights to the north of the Ourcq containing the strong position included in Bellevue Farm, Hill 230, the Jomblettes Woods and the heights in the left of our sector. He saw them clearing the enemy out of those powerful positions with a regularity and determination which contented even a fiery Frenchman, and when he later learned that our troops had that day taken all the strong positions to the north of the Ourcq and were solidly entrenched there and holding them, he said, "Oui, Oui, *Les soldats terrible,* tres bien, tres bien!"

And the name stuck. General Mangin heard of it and referred to the 32nd Division as "Les Terribles" when he asked for the Division to join his famous 10th French Army of shock troops north of Soissons, and he later made it official when he incorporated it in his citation for their terrific punch at Juvigny.

70

Owing to the sanguinary character of the fighting in the Aisne-Marne offensive, the number of prisoners taken was less than might otherwise have been the case. The Prussian Guards shot it out with us on the Ourcq, and when they broke it was because there weren't enough left of them to stop the American rush. The two divisions that succeeded them did not die as gallantly, but they retired skillfully, and there was little "kamerading." As a result, but one German officer was captured, and only ninety-six men passed through the Division cage.

Our burial squads interred more German dead than the 32nd Division's total of killed and missing.

Our own casualties were heavy, numerically, but light in comparison with the results achieved and the losses known to have been inflicted on the enemy. Our casualties were: Killed and died of wounds, 777; severely wounded, 1153; slightly wounded, 2009; missing 12; captured, 2 officers and 6 men. Total losses from all causes, 4187. This total does not include the reduction of fighting strength suffered by every regiment through the evacuation of men who were taken ill on the field of battle and who could not keep up with their hard marching outfits. Only the stoutest hearts and strongest constitutions reached the Vesle on the heels of the foe, and pitiful indeed were some of the handfuls which company commanders mustered as their units when they took their men out of line on August 7th.

32ND STOOD TEST.

This operation tested the ability of the Division in almost every phase of warfare. The men demonstrated that they could outfight the German in hand to hand encounters; that they could take his positions by assault; that they could outmaneuver the enemy when maneuver tactics were desirable; and that they would go without food and sleep when it became necessary to leave their supplies behind and relentlessly pursue a retreating foe. During the operation, they learned to use the auxiliary infantry arms, and special weapons that were not called into use in the early fighting were utilized to great advantage when the enemy resistance south of the Vesle was broken.

The operation was fought almost entirely under the 38th French Corps, the 3rd U. S. Corps, commanded by Major General Bullard, taking over the sector on the morning of August 5th after the 32nd Division had occupied the south bank of the Vesle.

For a few days after the relief the division rested in the small towns between the Ourcq and the Vesle to which the troops had been withdrawn. Up ahead the 77th and 28th Divisions were trying to cross the Vesle and finding it impossible. It appeared that a period of stabilization on the Vesle front would follow, and orders were received for the 32nd to resume training. A redisposition of forces was required which took the men from the towns where they were billeted and sent them to bivouac in the shelter of woods not far from the front, always within range of the German artillery, and constantly exposed at night to the airplane bombers. However, the men remained well concealed; their positions were apparently not discovered by the enemy, and the casualties during the time that the Division served as a reserve for General Bullard's Corps were slight.

The training program provided for instruction in the use of infantry specialties, and maneuver problems, including a division terrain exercise. A few replacements were received to fill the gaping ranks, but the new men were only partially trained, and, of course, had never been under fire. They brought the strength of the rifle companies up to about 110 men and two officers each. In less than twenty days after they joined the Division these new men were thrown into one of the fiercest bits of action of the whole war. But so thorough was their limited instruction and so quickly did they assimilate the aggressive spirit of the Division, that they conducted themselves like veterans when the test came, and contributed greatly to the prestige which the Division gained in its famous Juvigny campaign.

ORDERED TO REPORT TO MANGIN.

The training had proceeded less than two weeks when orders were received to move the Division again to the vicinity of Soissons and report to the Commanding General of the Tenth French Army, the great Mangin.

The order came rather suddenly, and provided that the movement be made by trucks for the foot troops and by marching for the artillery and mounted elements. The 57th Field Artillery had remained in action when the 32nd was withdrawn, and was supporting the 28th and 77th Divisions.

On August 23rd the artillery brigade was withdrawn from the Vesle and the infantry embussed for the new sector. The Division moved to the vicinity of Perrefonds, and after a few days in the Army reserve was sent across the Aisne to a position in the rear of the 127th French Infantry Division, with instructions to prepare to relieve that division at an early date. The 32nd had no sooner reported itself in the new reserve position than the order for the relief came.

The sector north of Soissons seemed, as we marched toward the front on the night of August 26th-27th, every bit as active as did the Chateau-Thierry sector when we marched in there just a month before. Up ahead were the same rumbling guns, coughing their barrages at the foe. In the summer sky was the same feverish red glare, throbbing throughout the night, as our batteries and theirs poured back and forth their deadly hates.

"JUST BEFORE THE BATTLE."

But this time we knew what we were going into. While the men were training back of the Vesle they had hoped that their next move would be out of the war zone, for a week or two anyway, away from the shells and the airplanes and the cooties. The hope survived in the breasts of some even during the 'bus trip to the new sector, but when they debussed they knew this was no rest area. Well, fair enough, the doughboy ruled; anything was better than those damned woods in which they had been camping since their last fight. This coming action looked like it might be a whole lot like the last. The country appeared to be much the same. It wasn't raining anyway, but there sure was a sight of dust. "C'est la guerre!" If it wasn't one thing it was another.

We wondered whether Heinie would stick as he did on the Ourcq or run as he did afterwards. Some of the doughboys would just as soon he didn't stick; those Prussian Guards were sure hard to lick. Others hoped he would.

"Might as well wipe him up all in one place," they figured. "Besides when we're chasing Heinie we're running away from our chow." The memory of those eatless days during the Aisne-Marne pursuit survived longer than the horror of the bloody fights which ensued when the chase was temporarily halted.

As they marched into their second battle the men voiced some ideas that they had not expressed as they went into their first fight. They were veterans now, and they had the assurance of veterans. They knew their companies were down to 50 per

"The French had pushed the Germans out of the trenches through which the road we were using drove toward the front. Well, if they could make the Boche move, so could we."

NOUVRON, FRANCE.

73

cent. of the authorized strength, but they also knew that what there were of them were as good as full companies before Chateau-Thierry. And again the possibility of failure was never thought of. The French had pushed the Germans out of the trenches through which the road we were using drove toward the front. Well, if they could make the enemy move, so could we. The doughboys hoped the front line wasn't too far ahead of the support position. These approach marches were a nuisance. Who wouldn't rather fight than hike?

The relief order provided that the 32nd should occupy the position then held by the 127th French Division on the night of August 27th-28th. It was decided to put the 63rd Brigade in the line and the 64th in support, and orders were issued accordingly. As soon as darkness furnished a cover the troops started moving up and again the battle was on.

It was a different fight from the Aisne-Marne operation. It was a fight all the time—every minute. There was no respite while we were catching up to the enemy. We were caught up to him from the instant we got into the front line zone until we pulled out of it—five days of hell on earth. The 63rd Brigade went over the top at the very minute General Haan took command of the sector and the 64th Brigade was stabbing machine gun nests five days later when the Moroccans came up to take the job off our hands.

1. MARSHAL PETAIN.
2. GENERAL MANGIN, Commanding 10th French Army.
3. MARSHAL FOCH, Commander of all Allied Forces.
4. MAJOR ARMAND GOEZ, French Army, Liaison Officer with the 32nd Division during all operations.
5. LIEUTENANT COLONEL STANILAUS LOBEZ, French Army, Chief of French Corps of Instructors with the 32nd
     Division during Training Period in France; Occupation of Sector in Alsace, Aisne-Marne Offensive and
     Oise-Aisne Offensive.

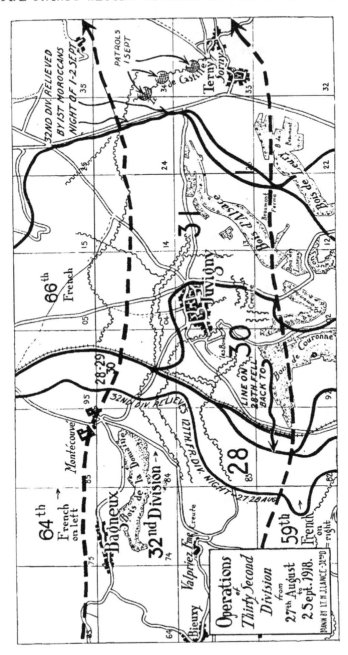

Operations
of
Thirty Second
Division
from
27th August
to
2 Sept. 1918.

DRAWN BY LT. M.J.LANCE·31ST·D

CHAPTER VII.

The Capture of Juvigny.

THE 63rd Brigade veterans made the relief of the 127th French Division with neatness and dispatch, and without any of the confusion which characterized the relief on the Ourcq a month before. The Americans were guided into their positions by the retiring French, and slipped into the trenches in perfect order. By 2 A. M. the relief had been accomplished, and reports to that effect were made to the two French divisions on either side of us. As soon as he learned that the Americans were in position, the Commanding General of the French division on the right notified the Commanding General of the 32nd that he had planned an attack to take place at 7 A. M. for the purpose of correcting a dangerous salient in his front line. As the immediate objective was about opposite the point of liaison between the two divisions, the Americans were asked to participate in the attack.

In spite of the fact that the hour set for the operation--7 A. M.-- was the precise hour at which command of the sector passed to General Haan, the 32nd Commander sent word to the French that we would assist in the attack. General Covell, then commanding the 63rd Brigade, was informed of the French request and of General Haan's assent to it, and the Brigade Commander in turn instructed Colonel Westnedge, in command of the front line, to get in touch with the French and assist in the operation. This was promptly done, and, regardless of the fact that no preliminary reconnaissance of the front by the relieving troops had been practical, a plan of action was agreed upon, objectives fixed, and at the appointed hour the Michigan troops went over the top for the first clash of what was to be a continuous struggle for five bloody days.

The Americans readily gained their objective—the railroad track west of the village of Juvigny, the village which was destined to be one of the high spots in the career of Les Terribles. The 63rd Brigade turned in over one hundred prisoners as a result of their push, and the captured Germans all testified as to their complete surprise at the presence of Americans in the sector. Their surprise was a testimonial to the careful manner in which the approach to the sector had been accomplished and the relief made.

During the day, the 63rd Brigade found that it is often a lot easier to gain ground than it is to hold it. The advance in the morning had been made with comparatively light casualties, but the position captured was on high open ground on the slope of a hill facing the enemy. There was little cover to be had except in shell holes, and our men were subjected to artillery and machine gun fire from enemy positions that had our front lines under excellent observation. Under this galling fire, the casualties were heavy; but there was nothing to do but stand it, as the position could not be abandoned without endangering the French.

77

"There was little cover to be had."

EAST OF VALPRIEZ FARM NEAR JUVIGNY, FRANCE.

78

THE CAPTURE OF JUVIGNY

Shortly after noon, the Germans decided to attempt a counter attack for the purpose of dislodging the Americans. Preceded by an artillery and machine gun barrage, they struck at the point of contact between the French and Americans. The 59th French Division on our right was forced to fall back several hundred meters, and the right of our line was bent back to maintain liaison. Our machine gunners, however, held their ground and poured an effective fire into the attacking Germans, and our artillery also got into action quickly. After their first recoil, the French also delivered a telling fire, and the counter attack was broken up without having accomplished its object. After that, the Germans resumed their harassing artillery and machine gun fire on the troops in the vicinity of the railroad tracks, but they thinned out, took what shelter they could find, and weathered the storm as best they could.

WHOLE ARMY ATTACKS.

General Mangin ordered a general attack by the entire 10th French Army to take place at 5:25 A. M. on the morning of August 29th, with the pretentious object of a complete break through the German line. For this operation, the Division was disposed in the same manner as when it entered the sector, namely with the 63rd Brigade in the front line and the 64th Brigade in support. The two regiments of the 63rd were side by side, with the 126th on the right and the 125th on the left, each in liaison with a French division. Two companies of tanks and a troop of Moroccan cavalry were attached to the Division to be used as necessary. The 57th Field Artillery Brigade came into the sector and the artillery command was taken over on the night of August 28th-29th by Brigadier General G. Leroy Irwin, who had under him several units of French artillery in addition to his own 32nd Division guns.

A tremendous artillery preparation had been ordered during the night, and was carried out; but the enemy organization of machine gun defense was so effective that the artillery failed to put the numerous nests out of commission, and the barrage which rolled ahead of the attacking infantry did not keep the German gunners from operating so as to cover the entire front. The numerous caves in this region lent themselves admirably to the German plan of defense, the machine gunners remaining safely far underground during the artillery preparation and until the barrage passed, when they suddenly appeared and poured their fire into the advancing doughboys. It also appears that the enemy had been expecting a general offensive, and was well prepared for it with artillery.

At any rate, there was a very heavy machine gun fire across our entire front from both flanks, and a counter barrage of great intensity was laid down just as our troops jumped off. In consequence, little progress was made. On the left, the 125th made a slight advance and captured a few prisoners. On the right isolated groups which could find cover crossed the jump-off line and penetrated the woods to a considerable depth, but it was never possible to get enough troops forward to bring the whole line up to the position reached by the most advanced patrols. The net result of the day's fighting was that no ultimate advance was made, and the positions maintained after the attack were practically the same as on the night before, except for a few minor advantages which the Americans had gained.

This was true on the front of the entire Army. Everywhere General Mangin's storm troops had been stopped, none of the divisions on either our right or left having anything to show for their powerful thrust. Our casualties from artillery and machine gun fire were heavy, as were those of the French. The Germans, too,

For protection, from machine gun and artillery fire, these men from the 121st Machine Gun Battalion, took to a shell hole near Juvigny at meal time to snatch a few minutes' rest. (August 29th, second day of the drive on Juvigny.) A U. S. Signal Corps photographer snapped this picture, a moment later a machine gun bullet pierced his hand. "Troops in the vicinity of the railroad tracks * * * weathered the storm as best they could."

"Two companies of tanks were attached to the Division."
NEAR JUVIGNY, FRANCE.

it developed later, suffered mightily during the day, and their defenses were far more badly shaken than was apparent at the time.

During the forenoon the Division Commander made a personal reconnaissance of the positions held by his troops, and found that the men were suffering severely. Accordingly, instructions were issued to thin out the front line and hold the forward positions, which were under intense fire, merely as an observation line. The position of our troops was not of the best, and early in the afternoon, the Commander of the 63rd Brigade asked for authority to move his brigade forward and attack the woods to the southwest of Juvigny with a view of capturing that town and getting a more favorable position. Arrangements were made for the attack, which was to be delivered at 5:30 P. M., but at 4:30 a telephone message from the Corps Commander directed that no attack be made, and gave the information that another general attack was to be made the next day.

In preparation for this attack, the 63rd Brigade, which had suffered heavily in the fierce fighting of the two days it was in line, was relieved on the night of August 29th-30th by the 64th Brigade, the relieving brigade being disposed with the two regiments side by side, the 127th on the right and the 128th on the left, each with two battalions in the front line and one in support.

ASSAULT ON JUVIGNY ORDERED.

The contemplated general attack, however, was not ordered, and information received from the Corps Commander indicated that no infantry attack was intended for the 30th. This situation left the 32nd Division front line still exposed on the hill to the west of Juvigny, with the troops suffering heavily. While corrective measures were being considered, word was received from the 59th Division on our right that its right flank had advanced in close liaison with the division on the right of the 59th, which had found a weak spot in the German line and had broken through. By closely following the progress of this operation, it became evident that the movement was destined to meet with considerable success, and preparations were immediately made to participate in the shove. Shortly after noon, the Corps Commander informed the 32nd that the Germans on our right were giving ground, and instructed us to advance our right flank in liaison with the 59th Division. This gave us our looked-for opportunity to attack Juvigny, and the plans which had been considered were immediately put into effect.

While progress was being made by troops on our right, such was not the case on our left, where the 66th French Division was held up by heavy fire from machine gun nests located on the plateau directly in front of it. Accordingly, it seemed probable to the Division Commander that the blow at Juvigny would have to be a turning movement, with the right of the Division swinging on Juvigny while the left kept liaison with the 66th French. This was exactly what happened. When the attack was launched, the left flank, together with the division on our left, was held up by heavy fire coming from the northeast. The right flank, however, moved forward, and while it encountered determined opposition in going through the woods, it succeeded in making its way through the ravine to a position to the south of Juvigny with the extreme right partially enveloping the town to the east. One battalion of the 128th Infantry in the left sub-sector moved forward west of Juvigny

"TToops entered the town and mopped up, encountering some wicked fighting."
JUVIGNY, FRANCE.

and finally reached a position north of the town, and in this way the two forces practically surrounded the village.

The enemy was taken by surprise by the direction of the attack, but recovered and delivered a counter attack on our left flank from a point to the north of Juvigny. This attack was repulsed by the 128th, which had been reinforced on its left by a battalion of the 125th. This battalion had been moved in to keep liaison with the 66th French Division, which had been unable to move forward. The left of the 128th, which tried vainly to push forward, suffered intensely from fire coming from in front of the French, and had lost so many men that reinforcements were necessary.

With Juvigny virtually surrounded, troops from the supporting battalion of the 127th entered the town from the southwest and mopped up, encountering some wicked fighting. Over one hundred and fifty prisoners, three of them being officers, were captured in the town and a large number were killed. The day's operation netted 189 prisoners.

WHOLE GARRISON WIPED OUT.

The attack cost the Division severely in casualties, especially in the 128th. The troops on the right, which gained the ground and captured Juvigny, suffered comparatively light casualties, owing to the fact that the enemy's attention was given principally to the troops on the left. The swinging movement of the right flank took the enemy by surprise and blanketed his machine guns, located to the north and northwest of the village. Juvigny was in our hands for some hours before any enemy shells fell in the town, probably due to the fact that the German command did not know that the village had been lost. It is thought that none of the garrison escaped through the surrounding cordon, the troops holding the village being all either captured or killed.

Instructions had been given to the Commanding General of the 64th Brigade to place his troops on the road running north and south just east of Juvigny, and after gaining that ridge to organize the position for defense against possible counter attacks, and at the same time prepare for a further advance. The troops of the reserve brigade were hurriedly disposed so as to insure the safety of our flanks in case of a heavy attack by the enemy. Telephonic communications with the new front were quickly established, so that the artillery might be instantly informed of indications of enemy activity.

As a result of the action which culminated in the brilliant capture of Juvigny, the front line of the 32nd Division on the morning of August 31st was considerably in advance of that of the divisions on our right and left. The division on the left had made no advance whatever, and was about a kilometer to the rear, while the division on the right, which had fought sturdily all day, was about half a kilometer to the rear.

General Mangin ordered his second general attack to take place at four o'clock in the afternoon on August 31st. He ordered an artillery preparation of four hours to precede the infantry attack and smash up the enemy defenses which had been so badly battered for three straight days of almost continuous artillery fire. The entire 57th Field Artillery and the artillery of the First Moroccan Division, which was supporting the 32nd, was assigned to General Haan for this attack. A plan to make a novel use of this abundance of artillery was discussed by the Division Commander and the Artillery Commander, with the result that it was decided to place a triple

"Telephonic communications with the new front were quickly established."

NEAR JUVIGNY, FRANCE.

rolling barrage in front of the advancing infantry. It had been learned from previous experience in this sector that the German machine gunners were able to remain safely concealed during the artillery preparation, and that they did not come out of their caves until after the barrage had passed over them, when they had plenty of time to attack the advancing infantry unless the doughboys were following the barrage very closely. To overcome this, a double barrage had been tried by some of the French divisions, the second barrage often catching the machine gunners. But not all of them apparently had left their shelters in time to be caught by the second barrage, so the Americans planned to improve the scheme and use a third barrage. There were also other factors, namely the peculiar alignment of the Division front, which commended the triple barrage for the occasion. Owing to the inability of the Division on our left to advance on the 30th, the right half of the Division was considerably in advance of the left. It was planned to place a standing barrage in front of the advance half of the Division while a rolling barrage was to start in front of the left and bring it up on a line abreast of the right. Then the entire barrage was to move forward across the whole front.

THE TRIPLE BARRAGE.

The triple barrage was to cover a depth of about 1½ kilometers, in order to flank machine gun nests which might be too far to the west to be covered by the single barrage and which might succeed in preventing our troops from moving forward. The 128th Infantry, in the left of the sector, was required to move forward, the troops adjusting themselves at the same time to the barrage. A time schedule was carefully arranged, and the delicate operation was carried out with great skill and exactly as intended. When the rolling barrage arrived on a line with the most advanced portion of the front, the troops in the right half of the sector moved forward and successfully carried the German trenches.

Progress across the whole front continued until the Division reached the Terny-Sorny-Bethancourt road. On the extreme right of the sector, however, in ravines and sheltered places, machine gun nests succeeded in holding up the advance of the French division on our right and some of the elements of the right of the 32nd. The general advance stopped at the Terny-Sorny road, and infiltration was resorted to for the purpose of stalking machine gun nests and reducing strong points that were harassing the right flank. It was not possible, however, in the short remaining period of daylight to clear out all of these obstacles. The ground was therefore organized to guard against counter-attacks, and a reorganization of the attacking troops was undertaken to prepare for a continuation of the advance on the following day.

Our casualties for the day, while considerable in number, were small when compared with the magnitude of the operation, the result accomplished and the stubborn resistance of the enemy. The total number of prisoners captured from 4 o'clock in the afternoon until 10 o'clock at night was 550. From them were obtained many amusing stories concerning the effect of the triple barrage. Some of them thought the Yanks had a machine gun which sprayed seventy-five shells. Their officers characterized the American artillery fire as "crazy," and frankly admitted that they did not know what was happening during the terrifying afternoon. The morale of the Germans was evidently badly shattered by the tremendous pounding to which they had been subjected, and the prisoners all expressed complete satisfaction with the fact that they were behind, instead of in front of, the American artillery.

On the morning of September 1st, further attempts were made to improve the positions of our advanced elements, and a number of troublesome machine gun nests were cleaned up. An effort was made to assist the 59th French Division to come up to the road on our right, and the Division was engaged in this operation when the order came for our relief by the First Moroccan Division. This sterling division, which included some of the crack French Colonial troops, the Foreign Legion and other famous units, had followed closely in support of the 32nd, and upon accomplishing the relief on the night of September 1st-2nd, took up the task where the Americans had left off, and on September 2nd continued the advance to Terny-Sorny.

CHAPTER VIII.

The Red Arrows Join the First American Army.

AFTER our relief in the front line the Division remained for a couple of days in support of the advancing French Army. The 63rd Brigade at one time nearly got back into the fight. There seemed to be a chance to split the German line by putting another brigade in to assist the Moroccans, who were striking some mighty blows in the salient which the 32nd Division had formed, and the Corps Commander ordered a brigade of the 32nd alerted for the purpose. But the opportunity for its use did not develop, and on the night of September 5th orders were suddenly received to the effect that the 32nd was to be transferred to the First American Army. The next day the Division started moving back across the Aisne to its former billeting area near Pierrefonds.

There is no record that after the battle of Juvigny General Haan came out to Col. McCoy's P. C. and smiled, but there is a record that after the brilliant

IN THE GREAT CAVE AT TARTIERS WHERE GENERAL MANGIN VISITED THE 32ND DIVISION.

maneuver which drove the Germans from the Juvigny plateau, General Mangin came to the 32nd Division P. C. in the great cave at Tartiers and smiled. And when he smiles he looks as happy as he looks fierce when he does not smile. He told General Haan how pleased he was with "Les Terribles," and the way he later gave out decorations to the Division demonstrated that he meant what he said. General Mangin wanted to decorate the Division then and there, but learned that it must "go through channels," and through channels it went, arriving over six months later, when the war was over and General Mangin and "Les Terribles" were again neighbors keeping "Die Wacht Am Rhein." He decorated the colors of all four infantry regiments and all three machine gun battalions with the army order of the Croix de Guerre, and cited some 500 officers and men for gallantry in action while under his command. Later he issued an order decorating the colors of the artillery regiments which participated in the fight.

Upon its withdrawal from the Oise-Aisne offensive the Division required considerable replacements. For five days the battle raged with terrific intensity, both sides fighting with grim determination and striking blow for blow. In spite of the sanguinary nature of the operation and the constant exposure of our troops to every weapon with which the enemy was supplied—and he had them all—our casualties were not unusually heavy.

Our losses were: Killed and died of wounds, 485; severely wounded, 599; slightly wounded, 1251; missing, 14; captured, 5 men. Total losses from all causes, 2504.

Five German divisions were used up in an attempt to hold the position which the 32nd stormed—the 7th, the 7th Reserve, the 223rd, the 238th, and the 237th. From these divisions 937 prisoners were captured, 9 of them being officers.

The material captured included 2 pieces of heavy artillery, 2 of light artillery, 16 trench mortars, 112 machine guns, 700 rifles and great quantities of ammunition and material.

A few of the required replacements arrived while the Division was in the vicinity of Pierrefonds, waiting for orders. It was generally known that we were to join the new American army then in the process of formation. Rumor had it that there was to be an all American debut shortly in the Toul sector, and thither we expected to be sent, for a rest and refitting, we hoped, before another drive.

MOVE TO REST AREA.

The move wasn't to the Toul sector, but to a rest area in the vicinity of Joinville, north of Chaumont. Division Headquarters opened there on September 10th, the troops moving from Pierrefonds by train. There everyone prepared for a well-earned rest.

Well earned it was! The 32nd had in less than six weeks engaged in two major offensives, and had won victories which contributed decisively to the upper hand the Allies were now maintaining all along the front. In the Aisne-Marne Offensive, the 32nd, by forcing the Germans back from the Ourcq to the Vesle, had finished what Marshal Foch had planned for this phase of the action when his offensive of July 18th was launched on the Marne. The Germans were too solidly established north of the Vesle to be ousted by a frontal attack, except at great loss, so a flanking movement north of Soissons was inaugurated and it was in this movement that the 32nd participated at Juvigny.

There, in an operation against an enemy disposed in great depth, supported by adequate artillery, and entrenched in highly organized positions, in a country which lent itself naturally to defense, the Division had again broken through the German's key position, penetrated his line to a depth of 6 kilometers and started an enemy withdrawal, thus paving the way for a forward movement by the whole 10th French Army, which outflanked the positions on the Vesle and allowed the Americans and French there to push forward to the Aisne.

Yes, the doughboys and their officers figured, they had a rest coming, and for a few days they enjoyed it, in a peaceful, lovely section of agricultural France in which American troops had never before been billeted. Then came replacements, and, of course, a training program. About 5,000 new men arrived, including some officers. Many of the replacements had had but little training, and intensive instruction was necessary, as the First American Army had struck its initial blow with great success at St. Mihiel, and the word had been received that the Division might at any time be called upon again to go into action. Special attention was paid to gas defense drill, target practice and exercises in attack formations for small units.

ORDERED TO THE ARGONNE.

We were just getting acclimated to the Joinville area, and learning to like it immensely, for a change, when the Division was ordered forward as a reserve unit. We were still short three officers and about fifty men per rifle company, but the new men had caught the spirit of "Les Terribles," as all of our replacements readily did, and reports from regimental commanders, while indicating that the new-comers were not sufficiently trained, spoke highly of their morale and their eagerness to profit by the knowledge of the veterans.

"The Infantry followed in trucks on September 22nd."
NEAR SOUILLY, FRANCE.

"The artillery went forward to the vicinity of Verdun."

The 57th Field Artillery brigade, which had again remained in line north of Soissons when the infantry was withdrawn, supported the Moroccans until the whole Division was transferred to the American Army. The artillerymen won the unqualified praise of the French big gun chiefs with whom they were associated, and before they pulled out were assured of the Moroccan commander's appreciation of their services. They arrived in the Joinville area some time after the infantry, and the order sending the 32nd up as a First Army reserve provided that the artillery movement should begin at once, the marching to be entirely at night. The artillery and all animal drawn transportation of the Division started at once. The infantry followed in trucks on September 22nd.

We did not see the artillery until about three weeks later, when we were in the thick of the Argonne battle. The artillery went forward to the vicinity of Verdun, and immediately was assigned a mission in support of the 79th Division, which was to jump off in the Argonne-Meuse Offensive, launched on September 26th.

The infantry followed the trail of the artillery to the vicinity of Verdun, where the Division was assigned to the Fifth Army Corps as reserve. When the battle started on September 26th, orders were received to march forward and prepare to occupy as a garrison the original front of the Fifth Corps, which had that morning gone over the top and attacked the enemy in the Argonne.

We had listened to the great barrage which opened the Meuse-Argonne offensive on the night of September 25th-26th, and our doughboys, who had heard some sizeable barrages up Chateau-Thierry and Soissons way, sensed at once that this was something new in the way of a battle. There was something American about it. We knew we were going to be in it pretty quick, and all ranks were glad they were going to fight as part of an American Army. Not that they didn't like to fight

90

with the French—the *poilu* was a bully front line pal—but the doughboy likes a change, and besides we were Americans, and this was an American punch. "Let's go!"

MISERABLE WEATHER SETS IN.

About the time we were ordered up in immediate support of the three divisions of the Corps which had jumped off that morning, the miserable weather, which was one of the most disagreeable features of the long drawn out Argonne battle, set in. The Division marched during the night of September 25th-26th and the afternoon of September 26th, some of the latter part of the way under a little shell fire, to a position in the Foret de Hesse, about 4 kilometers south of what for four years had been No Man's Land.

Foreseeing that the Division might at any moment get instructions to relieve one of the divisions in the front line, the brigade commanders were directed to reconnoiter the front for the best means of crossing No Man's Land, and our engineers and some of our infantry were put to work on the roads. Liaison was immediately established by means of mounted agents with each of the divisions in front of us, and the staff kept a close watch on developments, so that we might be informed of the situation on any front the 32nd might be required to take over.

In the wet, cold Foret de Hesse the troops waited for whatever might be in store for them. Back from the front came reports that success had crowned the attack, that every division in the corps had made big gains and that losses had been small. Then the reports indicated that the going was becoming harder. Then the gains practically ceased. Late in the afternoon on September 28th a report came back that

"What for four years had been No Man's Land."

NEAR AVOCOURT, FRANCE.

"There was only one road across No Man's Land and that was by the way of Avocourt."
THIS WAS AVOCOURT, FRANCE.

the 37th Division, directly ahead of us, had been counter-attacked and had lost some ground. The Corps alerted the 32nd Division and actually had one brigade started for the front, when it was discovered that the report was erroneous. So the 63rd Brigade, which drew the assignment, had its thrill of again going into action postponed for twenty-four hours.

INTO BATTLE ONCE MORE.

Just as darkness was setting in on the cold and rainy night of September 29th, the order was received to go forward and relieve the 37th Division. This order had been anticipated, and full reconnaissance had been made as to the best routes for marching. There was only one road across No Man's Land, and that was by way of Avocourt. This was only nominally a road. It was impracticable, for any but the lightest vehicles. Moreover, when General Haan, with a part of his Division Staff, rode forward that night with the order in his pocket for the relief of the 37th Division, he found that this road, so-called, was blocked for more than 5 kilometers by a double line of vehicles, all standing perfectly still. We were so near the front line that no lights of any kind were allowed. It was, furthermore, a very dark night—no moon—with heavy clouds and a continuous fall of rain which had been going on for several days. On the sides of the so-called road, through No Man's Land, there was much barbed wire, and it was difficult to get through even in the day time, but the order required that we go through that night.

Fortunate indeed it was that General Haan and his Brigade Commanders had carefully reconnoitered this ground; otherwise it would have been impossible to get through at all at night. General Haan, in person, had reconnoitered the trail further on through the woods to the Headquarters of the 37th Division the day before, and was familiar with this trail. He himself, therefore, led his own staff to their new headquarters, using now and then an electric flash lantern to make sure that his staff officers, all of whom were mounted, would not lose their horses in the deep shell holes that were on all sides. He reached the Headquarters of the Commanding General of the 37th Division about midnight, and reported to that officer the disposition of the 32nd Division, which was making its way forward as best it could, one brigade marching on each side of the so-called road, across No Man's Land, in single file. The troops marched all night, arriving in the Bois de Montfaucon at early dawn, with the heads of the columns.

This approach march, made by the 32nd Division, is considered by General Haan one of the greatest pieces of work that the Division did in all of its battles in France. Each man was carrying on his back a load weighing approximately 78 pounds, and during this dark and rainy night, floundering all the distance through the mud, falling frequently over broken barbed wire and broken down brush and trees, many of the men marched more than 18 kilometers, which means about 11 miles. But these men were hardened to their work, and the Division Commander felt sure that although the task he was giving them was about the limit of human endurance, yet they would respond to his command, and they did. Not only this, but after arriving in these shot-to-pieces woods, and after resting from two to three hours and snatching a bite of breakfast, the 63rd Brigade was moved forward under cover of mist and fog to relieve most of the elements of the 37th Division during the day-time of September 30th.

93

"On the sides of the so-called road through No Man's Land there was much barbed wire."
NEAR AVOCOURT, FRANCE.

94

"It was at this same headquarters, while the report was being prepared by the Division Commander and his Staff, that a direct hit was registered on this little building."

DIVISION P. C. IN BOIS DE MONTFAUCON, FRANCE.

General Haan established his Headquarters in a half sunken building erected by the Germans for headquarters, and found that this place was more or less comfortable, although facing in the wrong direction. It was shell proof from the south, but we were now receiving the shells from the north.

It was in this same "shack" that General Haan, three weeks later, when our troops were withdrawn after their terrific work, again sat down to write the account of the employment of his troops in the great battle. It was at this same headquarters, while the report was being prepared by the Division Commander and his Staff, that a direct hit was registered on this little building by the long range German guns. During this period the troops billeted in shell holes and any places that could be found through these woods, and were bombed nightly from airplanes.

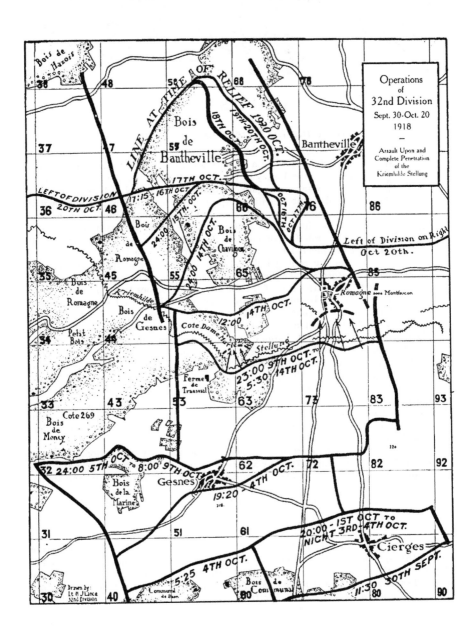

Operations
of
32nd Division
Sept. 30-Oct. 20
1918
—
Assault Upon and
Complete Penetration
of the
Kriemhilde Stellung

CHAPTER IX.

Breaking the Kriemhilde Stellung.

IT WAS in front of a village called Cierges that Les Terribles had faced, in the Valley of the Ourcq, their first considerable problem of the war; and again, on that misty last day of September, they found themselves lining up in battle array before another town of that same name and size and general appearance. The 63rd Brigade had barely gotten into the sector by dawn, and no part of the relief, except the establishment of a few headquarters, had been effected before broad daylight. But a heavy fog hung low over the rolling hills between the Meuse and the Argonne, and, hid from enemy aviators and artillery observers by this welcome veil, the Michiganders proceeded, during the rest of the day, to take over positions from the weary and disheveled Ohioans. By nightfall, all elements of the 37th Division had been relieved or located, and as soon as darkness fell, the troops in the front line were changed, and the 32nd Division was again toe-to-toe with the Germans.

The morning of October 1st, found the 63rd Brigade holding the entire front line, that had been occupied by the 37th Division, a front of about 4 kilometers, extending east and west and about one-half kilometer from the village of Cierges. It was immediately apparent that this Cierges, like the bloody obstacle of two months before, was a thorn in the side of the front line. Our troops were in the open, exposed to the observation of the enemy, and the Germans were very active in taking advantage of their knowledge of the position of our troops. Artillery fire rained down upon them, and from Cierges, and other points of vantage where nests were located, came a constant swarm of machine gun bullets.

The front line commanders quickly sensed the necessity for action. The information from the retiring 37th Division was to the effect that the Germans were not holding their front very heavily, so it was decided to exploit the ground immediately before us by means of combat patrols, cleaning out, if possible, the bothersome German garrisons, and permitting our front line to advance to a better position.

FIRST ATTACK SUCCESSFUL.

This plan was promptly and successfully carried out. Our front elements were pushed through the village of Cierges and to a point about one-half kilometer north of the town, the advance being accomplished without a great deal of fighting. There were a few rather rough tussles between American and German patrols, but the net result of the day's work was that the front was permanently shoved forward for a gain of about one kilometer. The position obtained was a better one than that taken over from the 37th, but was such that any further forward movement in the limits of our sector was easily observed. Directly in front of our new line was a section of terrain completely dominated by the strong position of the enemy south of Romagne and on the heights to the west of that place. Although the Germans knew exactly where the American advanced positions had been established, and were therefore able to considerably harass them with artillery, there was shelter from machine gun bullets and a good field of fire for defense.

On October 2nd, the Corps Commander began preparations for a new attack, and the 32nd Division, being in place, was not called upon for any action. However, as a part of the plan for the next blow, two new Divisions were sent in to relieve outfits which had jumped off in the attack on September 26th. This necessitated a slight change in frontage, and on October 3rd, an order was received for the 32nd to relieve the 91st Division, on our left, and we, in turn, to be relieved of a part of our front on the right by the 3rd Division, which had come in the night before to take the place of the 79th.

The 64th Brigade was ordered up to make the relief of the 91st Division, and the 63rd Brigade gave up part of its sector to the 3rd Division. This arrangement left our two brigades in line side by side, with the 64th on the left and the 63rd on the right. The relief was accomplished during the night of October 3rd-4th, and in the morning our troops found themselves in a position with all the disadvantages of the front they held on the morning they took over the line in front of Cierges.

CAPTURE OF GESNES.

This time the town of Gesnes, which had changed hands several times in previous fighting, was the sore spot. Combat patrols were at once sent out to test the German strength, and found that the enemy had taken advantage of the lull of the past few days to get better organized for defense. The patrols found the enemy too strongly disposed to be ousted by infantry action alone, and so artillery support was secured and the line promptly advanced to a position running from northeast to southwest, just south of the village of Gesnes. The town was taken by a mopping-up party, but was not garrisoned, as the Germans laid down a heavy artillery fire on the place, right on the heels of its departing defenders, and made the town too hot to handle. So it remained a part of No Man's Land and a fair field for patrol combats. Gesnes had been a sort of rest resort back of the German front line in the Argonne, with pleasant army cottages, a Casino with a band-stand and beer-garden and various kindred places of amusement, calculated to make Heinie continue to love his Fatherland. It was reported that one reason the American patrols liked to reconnoiter 'round the town and why the Germans also liked to come around that way on their trips out in front, was that the beer-garden stock had not been entirely destroyed by the avalanche of artillery, which, first one side and then the other, had loosened on the place.

When the 64th Brigade completed its relief of the 91st Division, the famous 1st Division was found on our left, the American Expeditionary Force veterans having come in as the right division of another Corps at the same time the 91st was withdrawn. Both divisions at once sought to establish the proper liaison, but the point of contact was the hot spot of the entire line and continued to be during the next few days, with the result that the troops charged with maintaining the connection had some terrific fighting and suffered serious losses.

The operation of October 4th, which had wrested Gesnes from the enemy, had put the 64th Brigade practically in front of the Bois de la Morine, which bristled

PANORAMA FROM HILL 255, 1 KILOMETER N. W. OF GESNES.

HILL 288 FROM SLOPE OF HILL 255, 1 KILOMETER N. W. OF GESNES.

99

with well placed machine gun nests. These nests were adequately protected from the searching fire of our artillery, and all efforts to reduce their effectiveness failed. After the first artillery preparation, the 64th Brigade tried to take the woods in an attack covered only by the fire of infantry weapons. While some progress was made, the German positions proved to be too thoroughly organized for an operation of this nature to be entirely successful, and, accordingly, a further and more destructive artillery preparation was ordered to be followed by an infantry assault, assisted by a barrage.

TANKS AID DOUGHBOYS.

This attack was made on the morning of October 5th, the troops driving in a northeasterly direction towards the southeastern edge of the Morine woods. For this operation, the 64th Brigade was echeloned in depth, the 127th Infantry having three battalions in line, closely supported by the 128th Infantry, which followed the attack with one battalion behind the other. On the right of the Division sector the 63rd Brigade also attacked, with the 126th in the front line and the 125th supporting. Gas and flame troops and tanks were assigned to the attacking units, and were used to assist the doughboys.

The operation was successful. The Bois de la Morine was overwhelmed and its pestiferous machine gun nests cleaned up. The direction of the attack was then changed to the north, with the idea of reducing the Bois de Chene Sec. Considerable determined resistance was met with in these woods, and hand-to-hand fighting developed when our men followed the barrage into the thick undergrowth and found that the enemy had not yet had enough. The Bois de Chene Sec was finally mopped up and remained securely in our hands, but further advance became impossible because of the strong position on Hill 255 and Hill 269.

During the attack on October 5th, the 127th Infantry was relieved in the front line by the 128th, and on the night of October 5th-6th, the 126th Infantry was relieved by the 125th in the sub-sector of the 63rd Brigade. Both of the retiring regiments had suffered heavily in their struggle to advance, and the supporting troops were pushed in to give the Division the punch to carry on the attack in case a further forward movement seemed advisable.

However, no general attack was ordered, and during the next two days the 64th Brigade strove valiantly to reduce, by local attacks, the strong points which had halted the advance. Efforts were especially directed at obstinate German detachments directly in front of the point of liaison between the 32nd and the 1st Divisions, and finally, through the efforts of brave combat groups on both sides of the corps dividing line, the worst of the obstacles were removed.

In the meantime, the 125th Infantry gave its attention to small patches of woods on its immediate front, which were unusually heavily garrisoned with cunningly arranged machine gun nests, so well protected as to be invulnerable to artillery fire. After considerable effort, these nests were finally cleaned up.

The sector of the 32nd Division was at this time nearly six kilometers wide, and the Corps Commander decided on another change, placing between the 1st and the 32nd Divisions, one brigade of the 91st Division which had been held in the Corps reserve since its relief in the line. The Brigade took over from the 32nd Division about 2 kilometers of front and we in turn took over from the 3rd Division, on our right, about one kilometer. This change in the sector necessitated a rather complicated relief, and it was decided to again place one brigade in the line, with a front of about 5 kilometers, with the other in support. The 63rd Brigade was given the

PANORAMA FROM HILL 269, LOOKING TOWARD HILL 255 AND TRONSEL FARM.

PANORAMA FROM HILL 269, LOOKING TOWARD HILL 255 AND TRONSEL FARM, ABOUT
1 KILOMETER N. W. OF GESNES.

101

front line, and the 64th withdrawn to a support position. This movement was executed on the night of October 7th-8th. On the morning of October 8th, the new front was on a line about two kilometers north of the village of Gesnes.

BLOODY APPROACH COMPLETED.

Les Terribles had now completed their bloody approach to the Kriemhilde Stellung, and were directly in front of what was known as the strongest position on the whole Hindenburg line in the Argonne-Meuse sector. The struggle to reach the ramparts of the bristling natural fortress which our men now faced had been over a dangerous terrain, and every outpost to the Kriemhilde line had been desperately defended by an enemy fully aware of the deadly peril he would be in should the Americans continue their success. Forced, finally, into the position he had cleverly chosen for his final stand, the German Commander issued orders to his troops to hold the line at all costs, and reinforced his points of vantage with all the men available.

On our side, preparations were at once made to attack before the foe had longer in which to set himself for the expected shock. The Division Commander's idea was to capture the strong points by maneuver, and a special maneuver map was prepared under his direction, showing graphically the movements to be executed by the various units when the attack was launched. This map was distributed down to company commanders. The general plan was to penetrate the wire and works at some point south of Romagne and then to roll up the remainder of the position by a movement to the left, taking the heights from the rear.

October 8th was devoted to disposing of the troops for the attack. On the morning of October 9, the assault was delivered. Our troops closely followed the barrage right up to the wire, and on the right, the 126th Infantry, supported by tanks, succeeded in breaking through and reached the southern outskirts of Romagne. On the left, one battalion of the 125th Infantry fought its way to the top of Hill 258. Along the rest of the front, the attack was stopped by organized positions about 1 kilometer south of Romagne.

The next day, October 10th, the fighting was continued, and after repeated efforts, the 125th Infantry captured one of the outlying defenses of La Cote Dame Marie and held it in spite of the efforts of the enemy to loosen our grip. La Cote Dame Marie was the name given to a frowning hill which now lay immediately in the path of the 32nd and seemed to effectually bar further progress. It was flanked by similar crests, and the approaches were regarded as extremely difficult. Indeed, the Germans thought they were invincible. It was one of these smaller crests which the 125th took on October 10th and to which they clung with so much tenacity.

KRIEMHILDE STELLUNG REACHED.

The same day, the right of the line was advanced by the 126th Infantry, which reached the Tranchee de la Mamelle, an important bulwark in the Kriemhilde Stellung. In this deep and well fortified trench, the 126th met the enemy in a hand-to-hand conflict and succeeded in occupying a part of the system. In the center of the line, the enemy held firm and succeeded in turning back every effort the Americans made to storm the approaches to the trench.

On the following day, the different front line groups devoted themselves to consolidating the advanced positions they had won and organizing for a further attack. Various local operations were undertaken to improve the position of certain exposed troops, and some fierce fighting resulted from the clashing of our combat patrols

"Over 500 prisoners were taken, * * * most of them surrendering in the Tranchee de la Mamelle."

and those of the enemy, now alert and vigilant and with his back to the wall. There were some especially sanguinary struggles in the vicinity of La Cote Dame Marie, where our men were trying to gain control of the approaches; but the net result of the day's work was that no substantial gain was recorded.

In the fighting of October 10th-11th over 500 prisoners were taken; most of them surrendered to the 126th Infantry in the Tranchee de la Mamelle. The smash had brought the 32nd Division up to the wire of the Kriemhilde Stellung with both flanks almost astride of the German line.

When it became apparent that the Kriemhilde line was almost within our grasp, a further push was decided upon, with the hope of driving through at points where the 32nd Division had already partly penetrated. In preparation for this movement, the brigade of the 91st Division, which had been in action between the 1st and 32nd, was relieved on the night of October 11th-12th by the 127th Infantry, and the 126th Infantry, which had suffered heavily in the bloody battling in the Tranchee de la Mamelle, was relieved by the 128th Infantry. This put three regiments of the 32nd Division in line. At the same time, the 42nd Division relieved the 1st on our left, the 1st having sustained heavy casualties in battering its way up to the Kriemhilde line.

The re-arrangement of the forces was not completed in time to plan any organized offensive action for October 12th, and the day was largely devoted to the straightening out of troops. Developments in the general situation then caused the Corps to again change the sector limits, and the 42nd Division was ordered to take over the part of the 32nd Division front held by the 127th Infantry. The 127th was moved over to the right, to take over a part of the line held by the 125th, which was too low in effectives to hold the front assigned to it. This necessitated again

103

"When the barrage lifted, the Americans flung themselves at the German positions."
NEAR ROMAGNE, FRANCE.

placing the 126th in line to take over the rest of the 125th sector, so that on the morning of October 13th, our front line from right to left was as follows: two battalions of the 128th Infantry, one battalion of the 126th Infantry, one battalion of the 127th Infantry with the 125th Infantry in support. The Commanding General of the 64th Brigade was placed in command of the front line, both of his regiments being in contact with the enemy.

GERMAN LINE CRUMPLED.

On October 13th, the Corps Commander directed a renewal of the attack, and in accordance with his instructions orders were issued for an assault to be delivered at 5:30 A. M. on October 14. While the realignment of infantry forces had been taking place on October 12th and 13th, our artillery had been delivering a heavy fire on the enemy defenses, and when the attack started, on the morning of October 14th, a barrage was laid down on the enemy trench system along the entire front and held there for five minutes, while our troops moved forward as close to the wire as possible. When the barrage lifted, the Americans flung themselves at the German positions and sought to tear through the tangle of wire and trench wreckage before the German infantry could get into action.

The battalion of the 126th, in the center of our front, had the best luck, springing forward from its position on Hill 258, surging through the wire and closely following the barrage as it advanced to the first objective of the attack. On the right, the 128th Infantry, by some vigorous and heady work, succeeded in getting through the trenches south of Romagne, and by skillful maneuvering virtually surrounded

"Their officers said they quit as soon as they discovered they were surrounded."
BOIS DE MONTFAUCON, FRANCE.

"Mopping up parties were sent into the village."
ROMAGNE.

the town and established a line on the northern outskirts. The 128th had been forced to avoid the town in its rush ahead, and, accordingly, mopping-up parties were sent into the village from the 125th Infantry, which had been following in support, ready to take advantage of just such a situation. The 125th had its hands full, but the Germans at length gave up the fight and some 200 prisoners were taken. Captured officers said they quit as soon as they discovered they were surrounded. In the meantime, the 128th was stretching its left flank north of Romagne, and the 126th was reaching out with its right, liaison finally being established and the position consolidated.

While the 126th and 128th were thus breaking through the Kriemhilde Stellung, the 127th on the left was flinging itself in vain against the impregnable defenses of the hills which flank La Cote Dame Marie. Colonel Langdon's men found that the artillery preparation had not cut up the wire to any appreciable extent, and the first wave which dashed over the top as the barrage lifted found itself caught in the impassable tangle. Into this wire strong enemy groups poured a withering machine gun fire, and effectually halted all efforts of the 127th to advance.

But, while La Cote Dame Marie was successfully resisting every effort at a frontal conquest, her doom was being sealed by the valiant battalion of the 126th, which had been the first to break the line in the morning. This battalion drove straight forward, concealed and protected from view of the Cote, and passed the hill on the right. Its objective was north of La Cote Dame Marie, and this objective the battalion reached, there establishing the position which it had extended to the right to meet the 128th.

COTE DAME MARIE FALLS.

The support battalion of the 126th, which followed in the wake of the troops who had forged ahead from Hill 258, sent a mopping-up party from Company M under command of Captain Strom to make a turning movement to the left and attack the defenders on Dame Marie from the flank. This mopping-up party, by an effective use of rifle grenades, put to rout the group which had been holding the German left flank on the hill, and allowed the whole 126th line in the center of the Division sector to move forward to the objective north of Dame Marie.

In the meantime, the 127th had despaired of taking the position frontally or of obtaining a footing from which a further attack might be launched. Accordingly, a maneuver around the German right flank was decided upon and immediately undertaken. It was as successful as Captain Strom's attack on the other German flank. Mopped up on one side and outflanked on the other, there was nothing left for the defenders of the German stronghold to do but give it up. This they did, and when darkness came, and the 127th decided upon an audacious march across the top of Dame Marie, expecting to meet and battle to the death with whatever of the enemy remained, they found the wicked machine gun nests deserted by all but the dead.

By morning of October 15th, the 127th had moved its line over Dame Marie, establishing liaison on the right with the 126th and on the left with the flanking detachment which had gone forward the day before. This detachment had already gotten in touch with the 42nd Division, which had come up to the new line reached by the 32nd. This completed the establishment of the new front and the complete penetration of the Kriemhilde Stellung. The line extended from a point about one-half kilometer north of Romagne to 300 meters north of La Cote Dame Marie.

"This completed • • • the penetration of the Kriemhilde Stellung."
THE ABOVE IS A PORTION OF THE KRIEMHILDE STELLUNG,
THE STRONG GERMAN POSITION.

There was a bulge in the center of the line caused by the activity of the 126th in exploiting the front after its objective had been reached, the center being about a kilometer in advance of the two flanks. The exploitation was made necessary, and its success possible, by reason of the fact that this part of the sector was covered by woods, whereas both the right and left flanks were exposed to fire across an open country in front of them.

Although the great attack had been crowned with success and the objectives gained, there were still advantageous positions on our front which it was advisable to take, and fighting was resumed on the morning of October 15th and continued during that day and the 16th and 17th. Special artillery fire was employed on obstinate points, machine gun concentrations were utilized to assist small infantry attacks, and the doughboys relied upon their own weapons in cases where artillery and machine guns were not available. Our line was pushed steadily forward until it extended across the sector about two kilometers north of the village of Romagne. In all this fighting, through a tangled wilderness of shattered woods, over small bare hills, across fire-swept gulleys where machine gun bullets ripped and where deadly gas hung low, up difficult slopes, always struggling for the mastering of a terrain that presented a new problem the moment the one immediately in hand had been solved, there had been constant action, varying from the clash of large units using everything from heavy artillery to hand grenades, to those ferocious hand-to-hand conflicts between our combat patrols and the enemy outposts left in sacrifice positions in machine gun nests as the foe retired.

"Fighting through a tangled wilderness of shattered woods."
ENGINEERS REPAIRING ROADS IN ARGONNE.

NEW LINE CONSOLIDATED.

But the line sought was finally won and consolidated. The position, north of Romagne, which the Americans occupied on October 17th, was an excellent one from which to launch a systematic offensive, and an order for another general operation was consequently awaited. Pending the expected attack order, attention was devoted to the exploitation and penetration of the Bois de Bantheville, a considerable stretch of woods in front of our sector. This exploitation was carried on vigorously during the next few days. On October 17th, the work was started by directing a heavy machine gun fire at sensitive points in the woods. The section north of the road running southwest from Bantheville, crossing our sector, was sprayed by fire from all the machine guns that could be brought to bear upon this part of the woods. Our observers from points on Hill 286 and the slopes of Hill 288 were able accurately to direct artillery fire on any evidence of enemy activity, while for twelve straight hours the woods were harassed by the combined fire of six machine gun companies, augmented by captured German Maxims, minenwerfers and 77 mm. field pieces.

At the end of the period of preparation strong exploitation patrols were sent forward into the woods with instructions to report back at a definite hour. These patrols returned to our lines at noon on October 18th with the word that they had advanced to the northwestern edge of the woods, about a kilometer and a half to the front, and had discovered only small groups of the enemy.

Accordingly, it was decided to push forward and occupy the woods in force, and on the night of October 18th-19th this operation took place. Infantry posts and machine gun positions were established on the northern edge of the woods. In the left sub-sector, the movement was promptly completed, very few Germans being encountered. In the right sub-sector, on account of the long echelonment necessary, the task of mopping up the woods proceeded at a slower rate. When morning came on the 19th, patrols were still pushing forward on the right, when they drew fire from enemy positions on Hill 274 and Hill 275. The front line established, bulged considerably in the center and put the Division in a salient, this however, being well protected by the Bantheville woods, in which the men found adequate concealment.

Late in the afternoon of October 19th, came the long expected relief order, the 89th Division being designated to take over the sector. That night the relief was accomplished without incident, the 89th electing to hold a line through the center of the woods instead of taking over the further outposts on the northern edge of the woods.

1. LIEUTENANT COLONEL W. E. MARBLE, Ordnance Department, Division Ordnance Officer; March to the Rhine; Army of Occupation.
2. LIEUTENANT COLONEL J. A. HOWELL, J. A. D., Division Judge Advocate, Army of Occupation.
3. LIEUTENANT COLONEL GUY M. WILSON, Infantry, as Major, commanded the 2nd Battalion, 125th Infantry, Training Period; Occupation of Sector in Alsace; Aisne-Marne Offensive; Oise-Aisne Offensive; Meuse-Argonne Offensive; Commanded the 126th Infantry, March to the Rhine; as Lieutenant Colonel, Division Inspector.
4. LIEUTENANT COLONEL WILLIAM MITCHELL LEWIS, Signal Corps, as Major commanded the 107th Field Signal Battalion, Training Period; Occupation of Sector in Alsace; Aisne-Marne Offensive; Oise-Aisne Offensive; Meuse-Argonne Offensive, as Lieutenant Colonel, Division Signal Officer; Army of Occupation.
5. COLONEL L. H. CALLAN, as Lieutenant Colonel commanded the 107th Engineers, TTaining Period; Occupation of Sector in Alsace; Aisne-Marne Offensive; Oise-Aisne Offensive; Meuse-Argonne Offensive; March to the Rhine; as Colonel, Division Engineer, Army of Occupation.
6. LIEUTENANT COLONEL JAMES R. SCOTT, Medical Department; as Major, Division Sanitary Officer; as Lieutenant Colonel, Division Surgeon.
7. MAJOR FRED A. RODGERS, J. A. D., Division Judge Advocate; Meuse-Argonne Offensive; March to the Rhine; Army of Occupation.
8. MAJOR A. W. FLUEGEL, M. T. O., Division Motor Transport Officer; Training Period; Occupation of Sector in Alsace; Aisne-Marne Offensive; Oise-Aisne Offensive; Meuse-Argonne Offensive; March to the Rhine; Army of Occupation.
9. MAJOR J. E. BARZYNSKI, Q. M. C., Division Quartermaster; March to the Rhine; Army of Occupation.

111

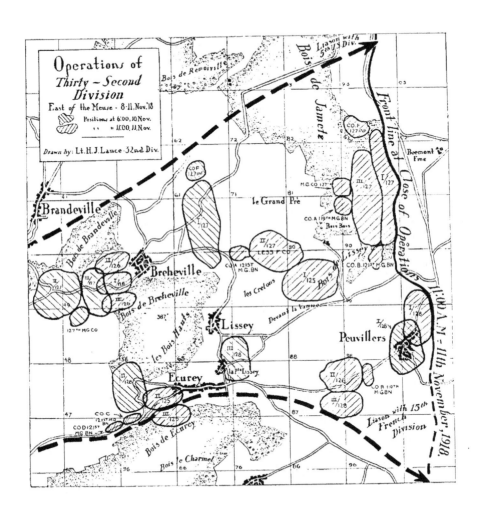

CHAPTER X.

Our Last Fight and the Armistice.

URING the night of October 19th-20th, our troops not actually on the line succeeded in getting back to the corps reserve position, which was where the German front line troops had been located when the offensive of September 26th opened. Our outposts, however, were not relieved until about daylight, and it was noon before the last of the 32nd Division left the forward area and staggered away from the scene of their three-weeks' nightmare. During this period it had rained almost continuously; the nights were always raw and cold, the men were nearly always in the open, and there was scarcely an hour of the day or night in which they were not under fire. They had gone over the top in attack after attack, sometimes gaining their objectives in the first rush, sometimes being forced to re-form their shattered ranks and try again, but always in the end sending back the message, "Objective gained." They had dug themselves in after taking position after position in the formidable Kriemhilde Stellung, and they had easily repulsed the few counter-attacks that the harassed Germans had had the heart to launch. They had followed each formal attack by exploiting the new front gained, and had spent the days between their big pushes in reducing machine gun nests and improving their position so as to be ready for the next shove.

They had finished three weeks of constant fighting. They had broken through a whole series of lines like the position on the Ourcq where three months before they had received their baptism of fire. They had been through three smashes like the battle of Juvigny. There had been no pursuit like the chase in the Second Battle of the Marne, but there had been dozens of those small but vicious fights with machine guns for every one that took place in the Aisne-Marne Offensive.

The Division had encountered everything that troops in modern battle might be called upon to face. The struggle was over the most difficult terrain that any soldiers in the great war were ever asked to conquer. There were commanding hills on which the enemy could make his stand, deep open ravines which he could sweep with machine guns and fill with gas, patches of weeds tangled with wire which were difficult to penetrate even when not garrisoned by the deadly Maxims of the Kaiser's machine gunners. There were open spaces on which the enemy had perfect observation, and which could be crossed only at the cost of a heavy toll of lives. East of the Meuse the enemy had batteries, which kept our rear areas under observation, and frequently shot up troops forming for attacks who thought themselves concealed and who were out of view from the front.

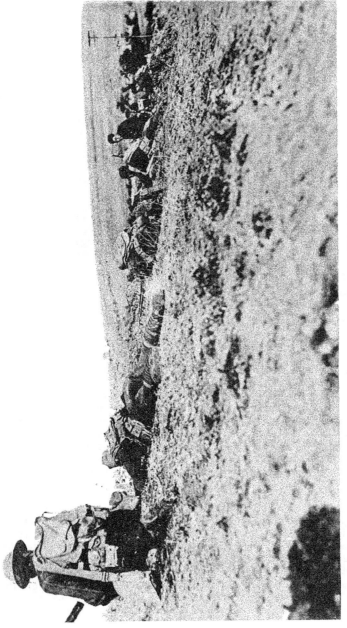

"But always in the end sending back the message 'Objective Gained'."

NEAR ROMAGNE, FRANCE.

114

"There were commanding hills on which the enemy could make his stand."

OPPOSED BY KAISER'S SHOCK TROOPS.

The enemy realized the importance of holding the line at this point. His positions were organized with every means that four years of experience in trench warfare had suggested. The troops which opposed the 32nd were shock units of the first order, and their instructions, as captured prisoners invariably stated, were to hold the line at all costs. The enemy was well supplied with machine guns and artillery. He was fully familiar with every detail of the country in which the fighting took place. He was hampered by no problems of supply, for he was being forced back upon an abundance of every required material, and had an ample system of strategic wagon roads and narrow-gauge railways. All the advantages of combat were with him; yet he was completely beaten in every clash with the 32nd Division; the famous Hindenburg line of the Meuse was wholly broken, and not only was the Kriemhilde Stellung over-run, but the Freya Stellung, the German third line position, was penetrated in its outpost zone by the capture of the Bantheville woods during the last few days in which the Division was in line. This was a daring operation, performed largely by our patrols, after the enemy had been shot out of the woods by a terrific machine gun barrage. Combat groups then exploited the woods, seized vantage points, and effectually prevented the enemy from re-occupying the territory.

It is significant that our losses in the Meuse-Argonne Offensive were not greatly in excess of the casualties in the Aisne-Marne. Although in the line nearly three times as long, and engaged in heavy fighting all the time, contesting every inch of the ground won, the Division had 1179 killed, and dead of wounds; 1006 severely wounded; 3321 slightly wounded. Total losses from all causes, 6046.

115

In the approach and penetration of the Kriemhilde line the 32nd Division met and vanquished 11 German divisions, including the 5th Prussian Guards, the 3rd Prussian Guards, and the 28th Division, known as the "Kaiser's Own." The others were: the 37th Division, the 52nd Division, the 115th Division, the 39th Division, the 123rd Division, the 236th Division, the 41st Division, and the 13th Division.

During our long tour of duty in the front line, the 79th, 3rd, and 5th U. S. Divisions occupied the sector on our right, and the 91st, 1st and 42nd U. S. Divisions the sector on our left.

The haul of prisoners made in the Argonne was the heaviest in any sector, 28 officers and 1067 men being captured. The material captured included 2 pieces of heavy artillery, 6 pieces of light artillery, 51 trench mortars, 50 machine guns, and 800 rifles.

GAINED 8½ KILOMETERS.

The total depth of advance in this offensive was 8½ kilometers. In the whole period of twenty days of continuous fighting the weather was miserable. It rained almost constantly, and the fields over which the fighting took place were knee-deep in mud. In spite of all the heart-breaking difficulties it was called upon to encounter, the high spirit of the Division, which had been forged in the flames of two previous major offensives, constantly manifested itself, and it was the grim determination of the veteran framework of the 32nd that carried the newly trained replacements to the magnificent victory which the Division achieved.

"All the advantages of combat were with him, yet he was completely beaten in every clash with the 32nd Division."

GERMAN PRISONERS.

"The material captured included * * * 50 machine guns."
GERMAN HEAVY (MOUNTED) MACHINE GUN AND AUTOMATIC RIFLE OR LIGHT
MACHINE GUN.

In a hammock of chicken wire suspended over a shell-hole, this 32nd Division doughboy makes himself comfortable on an Argonne battlefield. (Oct. 18, 1918.)
"The men came out of this battle more completely exhausted than had yet been their experience."
IN THE ARGONNE, FRANCE.

117

The men came out of this battle more completely exhausted than had yet been their experience. The battle had lasted longer, and the conditions of weather and the terrific fighting told very much on the physical strength and endurance of the men. Their equipment was badly depleted, their clothing was largely worn out, but their spirit was still with them—a spirit that it seemed nothing could break.

These men needed only rest and refitting to make them ready for another great battle. It was not practical to remove them far from the front. They had to go immediately into reserve of the 3rd Corps, where there was shelter in the Mont-faucon Woods, immediately surrounding General Haan's Headquarters. The remark that they were "sheltered" needs some explanation. There was no shelter in the proper sense of the word. There were dug-outs which a survey indicated would accommodate 2400 men, but the Division still had some 18,000. Moreover, these dug-outs, many of them, were filled with water, and those which were not were unhealthy, and every single one of them contained that pesky beast which had come to be known as the "cootie"; all of our men, including the officers, had become well acquainted with this little pest, and were now in the very center of the area in which the insect thrived most plentifully. For twenty days, the Division had been fighting in the rain and mud; but just as the men were assembled by regiments in various places in these woods, there was a gleam of sunshine in the afternoon. General Haan visited the various regiments, called together as many as he could get, and spoke to them something about as follows:

"You men are to be congratulated upon the splendid success you have again achieved, in that you have taken every objective against which you were sent, and indeed, you have gone beyond. You are the first division that succeeded in getting through the great Kriemhilde Stellung. You have just been through perhaps the greatest battle that has ever been fought in the world, and you were in the very center of that, and every one of you is glad of it. You are now located in a so-called 'rest area,' which, without doubt, is from every viewpoint the rottenest and worst in all of France, and you ought to be glad of that, because see what stories you can tell to your friends when you get home, without the least exaggeration."

"ALL THE COMFORTS OF HOME."

In this general line, General Haan encouraged his men everywhere to return to their smiles and good humor. He told them that he would send for the bands next day; that they should have concerts and all the comforts that could be had in such a home. The sun kept on shining, and the men kept on smiling, and it was a revelation to see how these men pulled themselves together; how they got rid of those little animals, "the cooties"; how the supply departments strained every nerve to get them new clothing, new blankets; how the engineers constructed those famous "palace baths," where the "cooties" and the old clothing were gotten rid of all at the same time, and where new clothing and blankets were issued. For five days the weather was fine, neither too cold nor yet too warm, and at the end of a short period of three days, training was again started, training by schedule—everything was done by schedule. General Haan insisted on schedule for everything, and what a difference it was in the training! How the men understood what was going on! How easy it was to correct the few errors that were still noticeable here and there, and how mobile this force had become! The orders were carried out as by habit, and when the Division a few days later was called again to move out, the Commander had but to

118

"You have just been through perhaps the greatest battle that has ever been fought in the world."

"It was a revelation to see how these men pulled themselves together; how they got rid of those little animals 'the cooties'."

IN THE ARGONNE, FRANCE.

say a few words, the Staff formulated the order, and hardly had the order gotten off the mimeograph when the Division was in motion.

Shortly after coming out of the line five hundred men were permitted to go on leave, and it was planned to send an equal number when the first fortunates returned. But when they got back the Division was again preparing to go into battle, and it was months before any more leaves were granted. Except in a few individual cases— a very few—these were the only 32nd Division officers or men to be granted leaves from the time the Division arrived in France until a year after our landing.

TRANSFERRED TO THIRD CORPS.

The Division remained in reserve of the 5th Corps until November 1st, when it was transferred to the 3rd Corps, on the eve of the renewal of the Meuse-Argonne Offensive. When the 89th, 90th and 5th Divisions jumped off in the big attack of November 1st and started their successful drive up the left bank of the Meuse, the 32nd followed in their wake, in close support and ready to go to the relief of any one of them. Our troops marched forward again through the country they had fought over, and finally bivouacked in the Bantheville woods, while the Corps front line was being pushed to the river bank and the left flank of the First Army was edging toward Sedan.

The 57th Field Artillery, which had supported the 79th in the opening of the Meuse-Argonne Offensive on September 26th remained in the sector when the 3rd Division relieved the 79th, until the 3rd Division's artillery could get into position,

120

several artillery brigades in the meantime supporting the 32nd. On October 7th the 57th Brigade again reverted to the 32nd and supported their comrades of "Les Terribles" until the 89th took over the front. In spite of its long tour of duty and its heavy losses in horses, the 57th Brigade was held in line to support the 89th, and fired in the barrage which opened the November 1st attack. But when the First Army surged forward in victory, the 57th was without the motive power to follow, and was withdrawn for refitting. To supply the 32nd with artillery, the 158th Brigade, which had been assigned to the Division when the 32nd first came up to the Argonne, but which had never fired for us, reported and accompanied us as we marched up in support of the divisions on the Meuse.

On November 4th the 5th Division, which was fighting on the right flank of the 3rd Corps front, forced a crossing of the river at Dun-sur-Meuse, and, in a brilliant attack, formed a bridge-head there. Up to that time the Corps axis of march had been northward. Now it turned to the northeast on the right flank, in an endeavor to connect with the French and American divisions, which had been driving up the right bank of the river, but considerably in the rear of the Third Corps front. The 5th Division, however, was too widely distributed on its front to make the contact required on its right flank, and the divisions east of the Meuse were slow in coming up. So on the night of November 5th the Corps ordered the 32nd to send a regiment to report to the Commanding General of the 5th Division for use in support of the right flank. The 128th was designated for this duty and crossed the Meuse on the night of November 5th. On November 6th the 128th took up a position on the right flank of the 5th, but the contact, which was being sought for in the front line, was not made, and on the 7th the 128th was put into line on the right of the 5th Division. The regiment attacked on the 7th and 8th, capturing the town of Brandeville and finally connecting with the 17th French Colonial Division.

On November 9th orders were received for the remainder of the Division to cross the Meuse and go into line in the sector the 128th was holding, between the 5th U. S. Division and the 17th French Colonials. The 32nd crossed on the pontoon bridge during the night of the 9th, the 128th Infantry reverting to the command of General Haan and going into line on the right of the new Division sector, with the 127th on the left.

The information of the enemy contained in the Corps order which sent the 32nd Division again into the fight, was to the effect that the Germans were retreating, and the Division accordingly went into battle in pursuit formation. The 64th Brigade furnished the advance guard, while the 63rd Brigade, with most of the artillery and the divisional troops, made up the main body.

MEUSE CROSSED IN DARKNESS.

The crossing of the Meuse was made under cover of the darkness and was not interrupted by the enemy. It was an all night operation and was not completed until dawn, when the leading battalion of the 127th reached the front line, occupied by the 128th, and relieved a battalion of that regiment which then moved into the right sub-sector where the 128th had been concentrated. The two regiments, side by side, verified their liaison, and prepared to attack at 6 A. M. November 10th.

In accordance with the instructions contained in the Corps order for the attack, the advance guard moved forward in two columns, one in each sub-sector. There was not a continuous front line, the space intervening between the routes of march of the two columns being covered by patrols. There was no artillery support available

"The 32nd crossed on the pontoon bridge."
DUN-SUR-MEUSE, FRANCE.

122

except the one battalion which had been assigned to the advance guard, the remaining artillery being engaged in a struggle to move forward from the river and get into position.

A heavy fog hid the advance. The leading elements of the First Battalion of the 128th, which was at the head of the column, made rapid progress. The troops had been in the sector long enough to have some knowledge of the terrain, and wasted no time in getting off. They encountered enemy troops almost at once, but fought their way through the Bois Pommepre and part way up a hill called the Cote de Mont. A combat liaison group on the right, which was there for the purpose of maintaining contact with the French Colonials, advanced even farther.

At about this time the fog lifted and the 128th discovered that instead of pursuing a fleeing foe they had fought their way right into the middle of a strong German position which the enemy apparently had no intention of abandoning. The fog had prevented the Germans from effectively defending their works, and the only clashes of the early morning had occurred when our advancing doughboys happened on groups of the enemy.

LIKE BALAKLAVA.

As the mist cleared the advance guard found itself in a position similar to that of the famous "Gallant Six Hundred" in the charge of Balaklava. "Cannon to right of them, cannon to left of them"—and behind and in front of them, too,—"volleyed and thundered"; only in this case the cannon were mainly machine guns located in nests, which the 128th had passed by in the thick morning. The German artillery, hearing the sudden rattle of machine guns, opened up with a barrage where the front line ought to have been, and the Americans seeing the shells bursting in their rear thought their own artillery was falling short. It was a situation which would have been fatal to less seasoned troops. It was immediately apparent that liaison had been lost on both the left and right, and that neither the 127th on the left nor the French Colonials on the right had been able to advance as rapidly as the 128th.

Our men were almost completely surrounded, unable to go ahead against an opposition that was showing increasing strength, subjected to a galling flanking fire by machine guns where they were, and confronted with the alternative of filtering back through a barrage that they feared was thickened by both their own and the enemy artillery. But in a pinch they proved themselves veterans, and in good order made their way back to a position on a line with the units on the right and left.

In the meantime the 127th in the left sub-sector had moved forward cautiously, encountering considerable machine gun resistance, which increased as the troops advanced. As they approached the River Thinte minenwerfers made further gains impossible and they organized to hold the line, having gained 3 kilometers during the day.

ENEMY NOT RETREATING.

By nightfall it was apparent that the information that the enemy was retreating was erroneous, and arrangements were immediately made to adopt different tactics. The artillery, which had been coming into position all day, was informed of the conditions which the 128th had encountered and the positions which were holding up the 127th. Fire was ordered on points of apparent enemy strength and plans were made for a formal attack to dislodge the enemy. Reports coming back from divisions on our right and left indicated that they had likewise been able to make but little progress and that they also had found that the enemy was not retreating. The

Division Commander made a personal reconnaissance of the front line to verify reports of the situation, and, after conferring with the commanders of the front line troops, a plan of action for the next day was decided upon. The Corps issued Instruction to continue the operation on November 11th, and preparations for an attack to occur at 7 A. M. November 11th were perfected early in the evening of November 10th. Orders were issued to the artillery to keep up a heavy fire during the night which was to increase in volume early in the morning and gather into a barrage to precede the scheduled advance of the infantry.

Out in front the troops were tired and cold and wet and miserable. For five days the 128th had been fighting and marching from one point in the sector to another as the regiment's punch appeared to be needed. During the day the gallant command's casualties had been heavy and the morale had not been improved by the unfortunate foray in the fog. The 127th had spent a night in a long hike over horrible roads to get into position, and a day in a struggle against a wicked machine gun resistance. Most of the night of the 10th-11th was spent in getting units into position to go over the top in another drive. But when day-break came they were ready, all set to deliver one of the blows for which Les Terribles were becoming more and more famous.

Finally the last relief was verified, the last reports that all was in readiness had been sent back to regimental and brigade headquarters. Overhead the preparatory fire of our artillery was shrieking toward the German lines, and the enemy, conscious, no doubt, of the impending attack, was raining shells on where he thought our assault troops might be forming, and on the back areas where the support troops were concentrated, ready to follow up the shove. At 6:30 officers in command of the take-off line were issuing their last instructions; fifteen minutes later they were looking at their wrist watches, not with the tense excitement which characterized the approach of zero hour on the Vesle, not with the savage elation with which they waited for their turn in the tremendous smashes at the foe at Juvigny, not with the grim determination with which they entered each succeeding struggle in the Argonne, but with the calm deliberation of veterans who had a day's work ahead of them, a day's work the like of which they had done before and which they knew just how to do, a disagreeable, dangerous day's work; but, well—it was all in a day's work—c'est la Guerre!

"FINIS LA GUERRE!"

Five minutes to seven! The men started to stir around, getting a toe-hold for the take-off, shaking their equipment into place, gripping their guns. Seven o'clock and some of them were off, over the top. Others had been stopped just in the nick of time, and after the advancing skirmish lines of those who had gotten away went panting runners from headquarters with the magic words:

"FINIS LA GUERRE!"

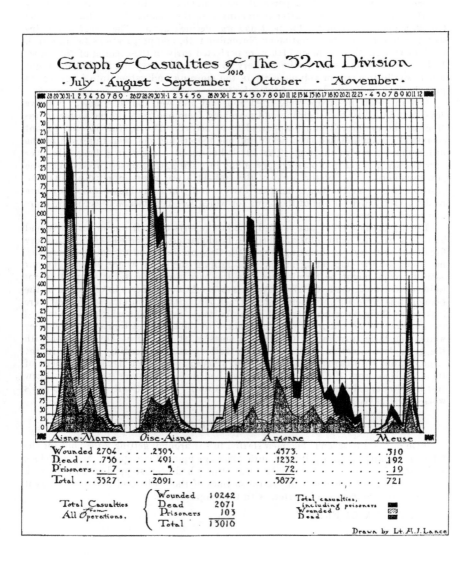

Graph of Casualties of The 32nd Division
1918
· July · August · September · October · November ·

Aisne-Marne   Oise-Aisne   Argonne   Meuse

Wounded 2704 . . . . . 2393 . . . . 4573 510
Dead . . . . 756 . . . . . 491 . . . . 1232 192
Prisoners . . . 7 . . . . . . 5 . . . . 72 19
Total . . . 3527 . . . . . 2891 . . . . 5877 721

Total Casualties ⎧ Wounded   10242   Total casualties,
from   ⎪ Dead   2071   including prisoners
All Operations. ⎨ Prisoners   103   Wounded
                ⎩ Total   13016   Dead

Drawn by Lt. H.J. Lance

125

"The bands played as the troops marched through the towns."

CHAPTER XI.

The March to the Rhine.

ON November 17th, as one of the leading elements of the Third Army, the Division crossed what had been its front line on November 11th and started on its long march to the Rhine. On our right marched the First Division, veteran of many battles. On our left was the Second Division of regular doughboys and Marines. Behind us followed the 42nd Division, the famous Rainbows, who ŏn the Ourcq and in the Argonne had fought side by side with the 32nd. These four divisions, generally considered the flower of the American Army in France, were in the Third Army Corps, which had been through all the major offensives where American troops were employed, and was regarded as the elite corps of the Army. In this brilliant company it is no wonder that our men stepped off toward Germany with their heads high and the pride of good soldiers in their hearts.

·The Division took to the roads at the hour set, marching in two columns. There were no ceremonies, though the bands played the 32nd Division March and other triumphant pieces as the various regiments got under way. Except for the bands, the march was conducted at all times as in the presence of the enemy. The attitude of higher authority was that war conditions still prevailed, and the field orders issued by the Third Corps always prescribed advance guards, indicated out-post zones and lines of resistance to be established at the end of each day, and ordered that adequate measures be taken for the security of the command, both on the front and on the flanks. Cavalry was provided for advance scouting and maintaining liaison with the divisions on either flank of the 32nd, which were going forward about the same distance each day, and on parallel roads.

The roads used by the Division were charted as first class, but showed hard usage and little recent repair, so that the going was not easy. For some units the day's march was rather long, but the average distance marched by the foot troops was 20 kilometers. The first villages encountered were practically uninhabited; the country through which we marched was desolate and shot up by the artillery fire of the last days of the war.

After the first two hours of progress, signs of life in the villages became evident, regimental colors and standards were displayed, and the bands played as the troops marched through the towns at attention. Otherwise the movement was much like an ordinary practice march. Excellent discipline was maintained on this as well as on every succeeding day of the hike, and the movement was executed in each instance exactly as ordered. .

FRENCH CIVILIANS WELCOME DELIVERERS.

In some of the towns a few French civilians were encountered. These inhabitants, most of whom had remained in their homes during the German occupation, decorated their houses with flags which had survived four years of Teuton intolerance. Nowhere was there a boisterous welcome or anything in the nature of a carnival spirit. The people seemed to have been subdued and blunted by their four years of bondage, but their relief and joy in their deliverance was very impressive; it was expressed in their faces, their voices and their words of welcome. In Marville a modest ceremony was prepared for the arrival of the Division Commander. When his car entered the main street in the early afternoon and drew up in front of the building selected for his Headquarters, all the people of the town, dressed in their best and headed by the Mayor, met him with flags and flowers in their hands. The crowd, which had been waiting for two hours for General Haan's appearance, was mostly composed of women and little children, nearly all in black, with a few old men and some released French prisoners among them. The Mayor made an address of welcome, and a young girl, Mme. Marie Louise Desaux, read a testimonial in the name of her dear compatriots, which she afterwards presented to the General with a bouquet of flowers bound about with the French tri-color.

The plan for the march to the Rhine contemplated that the forward movement of the Americans should be by "bounds"—a "bound" to consist of two or three days' marching, followed by a rest of two or three days. Longwy, a considerable manufacturing town in the iron and steel district of Lorraine, was the objective of the first "bound" of the 32nd, and was reached on November 18th. The town was the largest in which the Division P. C. had ever been located. There were adequate billeting facilities there, and officers and a considerable number of men experienced the luxury of sleeping in comfortable beds for the first time in many months. The town had been relinquished but two weeks before by the Headquarters of General von Galliwitz, commander of the Third German Army Group, whose many divisions during the past two months of hard fighting had opposed the advance of the First American Army on both banks of the Meuse. The entire town was en fete through the day of the arrival of the Red Arrows. In the afternoon the Mayor read an address of welcome to General Haan and his command in the central square of the city, where the chief participants in the ceremony were surrounded by a remarkable crowd, consisting of the entire civil population of the city and over 2,000 released Italian and Russian prisoners and French *poilus*.

The day after the signing of the Armistice some captured Americans had returned through our lines, a few of them being men who had been taken when the advance guard of the 128th Infantry got into trouble on November 10th. During the following days prisoners of every allied country continued to pour into our lines as they were turned loose by the Germans. Feeding and handling these prisoners and the homeless civilians became a serious problem to our supply service, harassed by the necessity of getting up supplies without adequate facilities. A large number of German soldiers also gave themselves up, but were treated as prisoners of war and sent back to the prison camps. Many of them were Alsatians and natives of Lorraine, who claimed they had deserted or had been discharged from the German Army and were hurrying back to their liberated homes.

After one day's rest at Longwy the march was resumed, and on November 20th the Americans crossed the border into Luxemburg.

"The day after the Armistice some captured Americans had returned through our lines."

GENERAL HAAN LEAVES DIVISION.

At Longwy General Haan learned that he had been selected to command the Seventh Army Corps, which had been formed to go into Germany as the reserve Corps of the Army of Occupation. That same day Major General Wm. Lassiter, formerly chief of First Army Artillery and a veteran artilleryman who had seen action on all of the American fronts of France, arrived under orders to take command of the 32nd. General Haan accompanied the Division across the Luxemburg border, and then relinquished command to General Lassiter. On account of the imperative necessity of General Haan's reporting at once at the headquarters of his new corps at Dun-sur-Meuse, there were few farewells. The Staff congratulated the leader of Les Terribles on his promotion and wished him luck; but the General, while no doubt appreciating the honor that had been accorded him in recognition of the great qualities of leadership which he had displayed, seemed to have some doubt about the exact status of the luck that separated him from his beloved Division. With him, apparently, the 32nd Division ranked about as high as an Army Corps.

"C'est la guerre," said the General. "Never mind, I won't be far away from you. Tell the men I'll keep an eye on them and see them often, no doubt, when we get up there and reach the goal of our desire."

He kept an eye on "his" men. Frequently, in the months that followed, sorrowing parents in the United States wrote to General Haan for news of their loved ones. The General wrote to the proper units for the information and answered the letters himself. And when officers from the 32nd Division met officers from Seventh

Corps Headquarters and asked "How's the General?" the answer always was, "He seems sort of homesick." When the General came up across the Rhine to visit the 32nd, as he did on occasion, he always admitted his homesickness. That was a common malady in those days, though the General's ailment was different from that suffered by the rest of us—he wanted to get back to his Division; we wanted to get back to the U. S. A.

The change of command did not interrupt the progress of the business at hand. General Lassiter took hold immediately, and proved himself to be an admirable commander, handling the problems which subsequently arose in the administration of affairs in the Army of Occupation with rare tact and skill.

On November 21st General Pershing made a triumphant entry into the City of Luxemburg, with a part of the First Division as an escort, while the 32nd Division marched through the suburbs of the town in two columns to reach its billeting areas in the vicinity of the capital. Though the Red Arrows took no part in the formal entry into Luxemburg, which was witnessed by the Grand Duchess and the American Commander-in-Chief, it came about that each of our columns had a sort of private ceremony all its own in passing through the outskirts of the city. Colors and standards were uncased, and the men marched to the cadence of the regimental bands. The 127th Infantry received a considerable ovation from the Luxemburgers, who lined the streets as Colonel Langdon's command passed through. The Division P. C. that day was located in a chateau owned by the Grand Duchess, who had directed her retainers to invite the American Commander to occupy her property.

GERMAN BORDER REACHED.

On November 23rd the Division reached the German border on the Saar river. We had overtaken the retiring Germany Army. Across the river, enemy troops could be seen, apparently having cleared the bridges but a few hours in advance of our front line elements. It was announced by the Corps that the movement would halt on the German frontier until December 1st, as required by the terms of the armistice. The time intervening was to be devoted to cleaning up, the issuing of such equipment as could be secured, and the inevitable and hated training schedule.

The rest was very welcome for several reasons. Having started the march after participation in one of the toughest campaigns in military history, men and animals were far from being in prime condition. The period between the signing of the armistice and the beginning of the march had not been sufficient to transfer to the Division the supplies necessary to fully equip the troops for an operation of the character they were undertaking. Arrangements were made for bringing up the supplies during the halt on the German frontier, and it was thought that when the march was resumed and German territory actually invaded the material required would be on hand.

During the week's halt every effort was made to fill requisitions which had been submitted. As the result of the untiring endeavors of all Staff Departments, particularly the G-1 Section, a noticeable improvement was made. Every day, time was devoted to cleaning up and to disciplinary drills. Some equipment was drawn and distributed.

ON GERMAN SOIL AGAIN.

On December 1st the march was resumed, the Division using three bridges crossing the Saar into German territory. For some of our men the experience of setting foot on German soil was a new thrill, but for the veterans of the Division it was

"On December 1st the march was resumed, the Division using three bridges crossing the Saar into German territory."

CROSSING INTO GERMANY FROM ECHTERNACH, LUXEMBURG.

131

"old stuff." The doughboys who had been among those present in Alsace remarked that they were back where they started from—in Germany. That had been over six months ago. Well, it had been a long, hard trip. "So this is Germany." Let's go!

Our second crossing of the pre-war Germany frontier was as unostentatious as was the first, down in Alsace, and far less impressive. There was the usual American lack of ceremonies of any sort.

The columns moved out in the same formation that had previously prevailed, taking the precautions usual in the presence of the enemy. With the advance guards marched a detachment of G-2 observers and intelligence officers, charged with collecting early information concerning the attitude of the civilian population. Their first reports were to the effect that the citizens exhibited only the expected measure of curiosity, and that their general attitude seemed to be one of restraint. Later reports indicated that the civilians were more or less in doubt as to the treatment that would be accorded them by the Americans, and the restraint which had been noticed was due to fear of our soldiers. When they discovered that no harm was to be done to their persons or property, they became more affable. When the military representatives met the civil authorities for the purpose of arranging for billets for the troops, the matter was handled without the slightest friction. There was, of course, an absence of the cordial greeting which was accorded the Americans wherever they went in Luxemburg, but otherwise there was small difference in the attitude of the inhabitants. They seemed to do everything possible to make the soldiers comfortable, and the civil authorities promptly responded to both the letter and the spirit of any requests made of them.

GERMANS LOOKED WELL FED.

The soldiers' first impression of Germany was one of surprise at the well-fed appearance of the civil population, and the excellent condition of the livestock. Upon investigation it developed that barns were well stocked with forage, and the country immediately east of the Saar seemed very well provisioned.

On the first day's march on German soil, the Division advanced approximately 15 kilometers on an air line, the troops marching on an average of 20 kilometers. As a considerable part of this march was over a hilly country, men and horses arrived in the new billeting area quite tired, but apparently in fair condition, and undoubtedly able to continue the march prescribed for the following day. The motor transportation also found the going difficult, owing to the narrow, winding roads. However, by 3:00 o'clock all organizations were in the billeting areas assigned.

December 2nd we advanced the front line another 10 kilometers; but when the front line advanced 10 kilometers, that means on an air line, the troops themselves being forced to march twice that distance, and over an extremely rugged country, on roads which were ruinous to even the tough sole leather of Uncle Sam's shoes.

The march was continued on December 3rd. On the 4th we rested and on the 5th started out again on a three-day hike.

HARDEST DAY OF LONG HIKE.

On December 5th the advance was resumed. The movement still was over a very hilly country—the roads were winding, narrow and slippery from the prevailing wet weather. The march was by far the hardest the Division ever had attempted, and the fact that all units reached the objectives which had been assigned, proved that the 32nd Division could claim distinction as a hiking as well as a fighting organiza-

"The roads were winding, narrow and slippery."
NEAR DAUN, GERMANY

tion. The 125th and 128th Infantry Regiments had the longest distance to travel. In addition to the unusually long march required, the 128th Infantry was compelled to use some very bad roads. The men of these two regiments were on the road from daylight until dark, and it was long after the sun had set before the 128th reached its billeting area. The 125th Infantry covered a distance of 40 kilometers. The 128th covered an equal distance, but over a more difficult terrain. The men were on the road for fourteen hours, marching almost continuously. The 126th Infantry also had a hard day's march, covering 32 kilometers. The 127th had a comparatively easy day, but, even so, marched 20 kilometers. Heavy marching also fell to the lot of the artillery units. The light regiments covered 35 kilometers and the heavies made 30.

Corps and Division Headquarters were fully cognizant of the extreme difficulties encountered during the day by horses and men, and considerable concern was felt regarding their ability to continue the march on the following day. In order to be sure of the exact condition of the troops, inspections were ordered and reports forwarded to Division Headquarters. These reports indicated that although the shoes of many of the men were in very bad condition, causing them to finish the march with bleeding feet, their morale was still excellent, and they had no desire but to continue to march forward as the leading element of the Army.

The Headquarters of the Division moved from Speicher to Daun. Daun was a fairly large city, and it was thought that on this account the attitude of the population might be somewhat different from that of the small towns through which the Division had previously passed. Such, however, was not the case. Daun also seemed to be fully as well provisioned as the small farming towns to the west.

REACH VALLEY OF RHINE.

The march was continued on December 6th. On December 7th the 32nd Division was the leading Division of the Corps, being one day's march in advance of the 2nd Division, and shoulder to shoulder with the 1st Division on our right. The day's march was through the usual hilly country, and a number of extremely difficult grades were encountered. Good roads were scarce, and the entire Division was forced to move over two main highways. One of these was used by the 63rd Brigade in the left sub-sector and by the 2nd Division after our troops had cleared. The 64th Brigade in the right sub-sector encountered one of the steepest hills that military traffic had passed over in the Third Army's march to the Rhine. The 128th Infantry led the way up this difficult grade, the doughboys lending a hand to pulling their transportation up after them. The work required all the energy and endurance that men and animals were capable of exerting, but there was never a moment when the morale broke down or when the spirit of the toiling troops was not as high as their efficiency in handling the trying situations they encountered.

While the front line was advanced to a depth of only 12 kilometers, the troops were forced to march on an average of twice that distance in order to reach the

"The horses were not in as bad shape as might have been expected in view of the heavy hauling that was required of them."

NEARING THE RHINE.

134

new objective. The 126th Infantry had the hardest hiking, its battalions marching from 23 to 30 kilometers. The 125th Infantry marched 18 kilometers, the 128th Infantry, 15 kilometers. One battalion of the 127th Infantry marched 27 kilometers and the other two battalions 18 kilometers. All troops arrived in fairly good condition, and the horses were not in as bad shape as might have been expected in view of the heavy hauling that was required of them. There had been an issue of what shoes were available to the most needy cases, and this improved the situation somewhat. There were some men, however, who were forced to make the day's march in footgear that was entirely unserviceable.

On December 8th, the Corps field orders announced that the march to the Rhine would be completed in three more days. The sector limits were changed slightly, making the Moselle river the boundary line between the 32nd and 1st Divisions. This put the 1st Division into Coblenz, which is west of the Rhine and south of the Moselle.

On December 9th the Division made its first day's march in the Valley of the Rhine, and at the end of the day the foremost elements were 10 kilometers closer to the final objective. On good roads and through a more level country the troops marched on an average of less than 15 kilometers. The hike was an easy one, compared with the difficult marches of previous days, and was completed before noon. Division Headquarters moved from Mullenbach to Mayen.

ADVANCE GUARDS ON RHINE.

The attitude of the civilian population of the Rhine country appeared no different from that of the inhabitants on the Western German border. Their long habit of obedience to authority caused them to readily assent to whatever orders the Allied military saw fit to issue. There seemed to be less fear of our troops than had previously been the case, and accordingly less restraint was noticed, in spite of the fact that it appeared that some German newspaper writers were urging the people to be more distant in their relations with the invading troops. It was evident that reports of the good conduct of our troops had preceded the advance, and this fact had a great deal to do with the ready acceptance of our soldiers by civilians with whom the men were billeted. Division Headquarters moved from Mayen to Ochtendung.

On December 11th, just one month after the signing of the armistice, the 32nd Division reached the Rhine. The final phase of the march was completed at 11:00 o'clock, when the 128th Infantry established its outposts at the junction of the Rhine and Moselle opposite Coblenz. The city itself was not entered by our troops, as it was outside the Corps sector. The three other Infantry regiments had previously arrived on the Rhine, the 127th completing its dispositions at 9:30 o'clock. The 63rd Brigade had arrived at the river on the 10th, and on the 11th moved but one battalion in order to establish outposts on the west bank.

TROOPS IN HIGH SPIRITS.

The troops arrived in the Rhine in high spirits and good physical condition. The animals showed the strain of the hard march to which they had been subjected. The equipment of the Division had not suffered seriously, but there were many shortages which existed when the march started, and many requisitions still remained to be filled. During the progress of the march efforts were made to secure needed supplies, and as the end of the operation approached plans were made for energetically con-

"The Corps designated the Engers bridge for the use of the 32nd Division in crossing the Rhine on December 13th."

ENGERS BRIDGE.

tinning the work of getting the Division fully equipped. On December 11th Division Headquarters moved to a beautiful chateau at Bassenheim..

December 12th was a day of rest. The Corps designated the Engers bridge for the use of the 32nd Division in crossing the Rhine on December 13th. The order which prescribed the movement gave us two days to move all elements of the Division across. Accordingly it was planned to cross all infantry and light artillery units on December 13th, and to bring the heavy artillery and auxiliary troops over on the following day. The bridge was to be at the disposal of the 2nd Division after 3 P. M., December 14th.

THE RED ARROWS CROSS THE RHINE.

The 32nd Division crossed the Rhine on Friday the 13th. Although this day and date combination is usually not considered auspicious for the beginning of any important undertaking, the fact that the Americans were directed to make their historic passage of Germany's famed river on what is popularly called a "hoodoo" day, caused little concern to the doughboys fortunate enough to have the privilege of being in the front line of the Army of Occupation. Always quick to attach significance to any omen, they made no exception in this case, but contented themselves by frequently repeating the assertion that it meant bad luck for the Germans. It must have been as the doughboys said, for the 32nd Division certainly encountered no misfortunes during the day. The crossing was conducted exactly according to schedule, and the movement went off like clockwork.

The 32nd Division and the 1st Division were the leading elements of the 3rd Army in the passage of the Rhine. These two divisions crossed at the same hour, and pushed forward side by side into the Coblenz Bridgehead. Elements of the 2nd Division crossed on the extreme left of their sector, cavalry and advanced patrols occupying the 2nd Division front. The remainder of the 2nd Division was held in support under orders to complete its crossing on December 14th.

The forward limit of the American sector in the Coblenz Bridgehead was announced in Field Order No. 83, 3rd Army Corps. The order directed that the front line be plainly marked by signs, and that passage beyond this line be forbidden except by proper authority.

The crossing of the river was accomplished without ceremony. The leading elements of the 64th Brigade were lined up at the approach to the Engers bridge, and at 7:00 A. M. the advance guards moved out in combat formation. To the 127th Infantry went the honor of being the first to cross. The remainder of the 64th Brigade followed. The Brigade Commander had estimated that his command would require a maximum of 3 hours and 15 minutes to make the crossing, and he was allowed this time in the march table. However, it developed that the time allowed for unforseen delays was excessive, as there were none, and the 64th Brigade completed its movement at 9:45. The 63rd Brigade was under orders to begin crossing the bridge at 10:15, and the Brigade march table did not bring the head of the column to the bridge before that hour. Accordingly there was a gap of half an hour during which there was no traffic over the bridge. The 63rd Brigade was given until 12:30 to complete its movement, but the tail of the column was clear of the bridge at 12:15. The light artillery was scheduled to begin its movement at 12:30, so advantage was taken of the gap between the end of the infantry and the head of the artillery column to cross a convoy of trucks carrying regimental, brigade and division headquarters equipment. This convoy cleared in time to permit the light

"Outposts were established on the American Army's front."

artillery to start at the appointed hour. The field order regulating the movement fixed 3 P. M. as the limit of the artillery passage. The last of the artillery column was clear of the bridge at 2:30. The movement of the infantry and light artillery was so well conducted that the six regiments crossed the bridge in one hour and a quarter less time than had been allowed.

Division Headquarters moved from Bassenheim to Sayn.

IN FRONT LINE AGAIN.

While the last elements were being brought across the river on December 14th, the troops which made the passage on December 13th, were being moved toward the front line of the Division Sector in the Coblenz Bridgehead. A corps field order issued on the day before had fixed the limits on the left and right, and gave to the 32nd Division a front line of approximately 30 kilometers. Our area was 20 kilometers in depth, and the Division occupied nearly 400 square kilometers of territory. The troops either were billeted in, or occupied as outposts, 63 towns.

Outposts were established on the American Army's front, and a preliminary disposition of troops on the line of resistance was made. In the left sub-sector the 125th Infantry took over the line of observation and established liaison with the 2nd Division. In the right sub-sector the 127th Infantry covered the line of observation on the Division's right flank, and the 128th Infantry established outposts in the center of the sector. The 323rd Field Artillery was disposed in support of the left sub-sector, and one battalion of the 322nd Field Artillery was in a position in support of the right sub-sector.

On December 15th the Division was disposed with elements of four regiments in the front line. The artillery regiments moved forward to positions in support

"Authority to move the Division P. C. from Sayn to Regensdorf also was secured, and orders were given to make this move on the following day."
DIVISION P. C. RENGSDORF, GERMANY.

139

of the infantry units. The work of reconnoitering for strong points and suitable observation posts was continued.

Every effort was made by a careful examination of the ground to take advantage of favorable terrain in the preparation of preliminary plans for the organization of the sector. After the movement of troops on December 15th, only slight readjustments remained to be made, and these were to be concluded on December 16th, under the direction of Brigade Commanders.

Based upon the reports of the various reconnoitering parties plans for the defense of the sector were prepared and submitted by the various commanders on December 16th. While the reconnaissances were going on, there were several minor changes in the disposition of troops, owing to the necessity of billeting units in the vicinity of the part of the line of resistance they were to occupy.

The Division Surgeon published an interesting memorandum which recorded the fact that the evacuations of the 32nd Division during the march to the Rhine were much lower than the Corps average.

On December 17th there were further slight changes in troop dispositions, and the Divisional plan of defense for the sector was completed and forwarded to Corps Headquarters on December 18th. Authority to move the Division P. C. from Sayn to Rengsdorf also was secured, and orders were given to make this move on the following day, thus completing the 32nd Division's march to the Rhine and occupation of an important front line position in the Coblenz Bridgehead.

MARCH TO THE RHINE—32ND DIVISION.
Table of Daily Distances Traveled.　(Kilometers.)

DATE.	INFANTRY.		ARTILLERY.	
	Minimum.	Maximum.	Minimum.	Maximum.
November 17, 1918	13	29	9	34
" 18, "	16	30	14	23
" 19, "	..	..	..	..
" 20, "	14	20	9	19
" 21, "	18	35	18	26
" 22, "	9	19	7	13
" 23, "	10	23	10	17
" 24, 30, "	..	..	..	..
December 1, "	15	30	18	28
" 2, "	5	25	6	17
" 3, "	7	25	8	20
" 4, "	2	15	..	..
" 5, "	21	40	30	35
" 6, "	11	25	25	30
" 7, "	14	29	8½	20
" 8, "	4	16	..	..
" 9, "	4	16	16	20
" 10, "	8	18	11	20
" 11, "	2	18	14	14
" 12, "	4	6	..	..
" 13, "	17	35	9	23

One kilometer equals six tenths of one mile.

32nd Division Historical Chart.

FRONT	Dates ENTRY	Dates WITHDRAWAL	SECTOR	ARTILLERY BRIGADE ATTACHED	Prisoners Captured OFFICERS	Prisoners Captured MEN	Prisoners Captured TOTAL	Material Captured Heavy Artillery	Material Captured Light Artillery	Material Captured Trench Mortars	Material Captured Machine Guns	Material Captured Rifles	Killed in Action	Died of Wounds	Missing in Action	Died from Other Causes	Severely Wounded and Gassed	Slightly Wounded and Gassed Undetermined	Prisoners Taken by Enemy	Injured	LOCATION of DIVISION HEADQUARTERS	DATES From	DATES to
DISEMBARKED																					LIVERPOOL, ENGLAND	16 Feb.	16 Feb.
																					WINCHESTER, ENGLAND	17 Feb.	19 Feb.
																					LE HAVRE, FRANCE	20 Feb.	22 Feb.
																					ENROUTE TO 10TH TRAINING AREA FRANCE	22 Feb.	24 Feb.
10TH TRAINING AREA																16					PRAUTHOY, FRANCE	24 Feb.	17 May
ALSACE	May 18	July 21	Oct 1	57 F.A.		7	8						56	2		25	82	215	6	39	LA CHAPELLE ALSACE	17 May	6 June
																					BOURGMONT	6 June	20 July
																					PEROUSE	20 July	22 July
AISNE-MARNE OFFENSIVE Reserve	July 24	July 29	Active	3rd F.A. Jul 30-31																	BETHLEY ST. MARTIN	23 July	26 July
Front-Line	July 30	Aug.7		57th F.A. July 31	1	95	97	4	5	10	28	400	777	12		6	1155	183	2009	6	CHATEAU THIERRY	27 July	28 July
Reserve	Aug. 7	Aug. 23		Aug. 7																	LA CHAPELLE CHATEAU	30 July	3 Aug.
																					CIERGES	3 Aug.	7 Aug.
																				39	VILLOME	7 Aug.	23 Aug.
OISE-AISNE Reserve	Aug. 24	Aug. 27	Active	57th F.A.	9	928	937	2	2	16	112	700	485	14		8	299	137	1253	3		CHATEAU CHENOTTE SAINT DIZARDVONDS	23 Aug.	27 Aug.
Front-Line	Aug. 28	Sept. 2																			PIERLES	27 Aug.	6 Sept.
Reserve	Sept. 2	Sept. 9																			CHATEAU CHENOTTE	6 Sept.	9 Sept.
Rest (Pannes lt Area)	Sept. 20	Sept. 22																			JOINVILLE (Rest)	10 Sept.	22 Sept.
MEUSE-ARGONNE Reserve	Sept. 22	Sept. 30	Active	55th F.A. Sept. 30-Oct. 8; 56th F.A. Oct. 8-20; 57th F.A. Oct. 8-20; 130th F.A.	2	6	8		1	3	10	30	800	1179	82		35	1000	330	3521	91	AUTRECOURT	22 Sept.	26 Sept.
Front-Line	Sept. 30	Oct. 20																			VERDUN-EN-HESSE	26 Sept.	29 Sept.
Reserve	Oct. 30	Nov. 9																			BOIS DE MONTAGNE	29 Sept.	2 Nov.
																					BOMAGNE	2 Nov.	4 Nov.
																					AINCREVILLE	4 Nov.	10 Nov.
MEUSE-ARGONNE Second Phase Front-Line	Nov. 10	Nov. 11	Active	130th F.A.	28	1067	1095	2	1	10	100	160	24			1	332	81	289	2	VILOSNES-SUR-MEUSE	10 Nov.	17 Nov.
MARCH TO the RHINE, Army of Occupation (Meuse to Rhine) Front-Line	Nov. 17	Dec. 12		130th																	DAMVILLE	17 Nov.	18 Nov.
																					LONGWY	18 Nov.	20 Nov.
																					PETANGE, LUXEMBURG	20 Nov.	21 Nov.
																					WALFERDANGE	21 Nov.	22 Nov.
																					NIEDER ARVEN	22 Nov.	23 Nov.
																					CONSDORF	23 Nov.	1 Dec.
																					WELCHENHAUS (Germany)	1 Dec.	2 Dec.
																					SINSHEIMER	2 Dec.	5 Dec.
																					DAUN	5 Dec.	7 Dec.
																					MULLTHOACK	7 Dec.	9 Dec.
																					MAYEN	9 Dec.	10 Dec.
																					OCHTENDUNG	10 Dec.	11 Dec.
																					BASSENHEIM	11 Dec.	13 Dec.
																					SAYN	13 Dec.	13 Dec.
COBLENZ Bridgehead Front-Line	Dec. 13	Apr. 23		158										3			31		12			RENGSDORF	13 Dec.	23 Apr.
TOTALS.				158	40	2193	2155	11	15	128	800	2000	2660	134		122	2992	736	7005	110	97			13,056 TOTAL CASUALTIES.

141

CHAPTER XII.

Die Wacht am Rhein.

IFE in the Coblenz bridge-head was, as the doughboys put it, "not at all hard to take." They had better billets than they had "enjoyed" in France. Most of them had beds. The food, while "army straight," was excellent. There was, of course, too much of the hateful "training" to suit anybody, but as the Third Army got "oriented," things took on a more pleasant aspect. There were athletics for all who desired outdoor recreation. For many who did not desire so to utilize what they thought was their leisure time, there were soldier shows, and the *Y.* M. C. A. furnished professional talent to while away the long evening hours.

Fraternization with the enemy was from the first sternly prohibited by all manner of orders, and these orders were strictly interpreted and rigidly enforced. The French "defendu" and the German "verboten" were easy words compared with the "Lay off!" which the American Military Police hissed when a *Y*ankee doughboy smiled, perchance, at a German "mädchen" of more or less surpassing loveliness, or slipped a bit of chocolate to a roly-poly German youngster, or passed a neighborly "Guten Abend" to the motherly German matron with whom he was billeted. No orders were needed to prevent fraternization with the full-grown German male of the species, but with the "wimmin and kids" it was different. The *Y*anks just couldn't get up any hate for them, and couldn't help showing their good nature.

But orders were orders, and the doughboys managed to get along pleasantly with the citizens of the Rhineland without becoming unduly chummy with anybody. However, the anti-fraternization order made for a lot of homesickness and more or less discontent. We all wanted to go home; wanted that trip across the ocean more than we wanted anything else; but the general sentiment was summed up by a stalwart sergeant of the 127th Infantry who wore a D. S. C., and who made a speech one night to some of his homesick comrades, which ran about as follows:

"I sure want to go home, but let me tell you fellows that right now I am just where I wanted to be when, back in 1917, just after war was declared, I enlisted in the National Guard. And I got here in a lot better shape than I expected, and a lot sooner than I expected. And the circumstances of my being here are just what my fondest hopes pictured. Of course, it may have been Berlin instead of Coblenz I was thinking of at that time, but that's a detail. Sure I want to go home, but I'm so blamed well satisfied about getting here at all that I'm willing to be patient with Uncle Sam and wait until he says the job is finished. Then I know he'll send us home."

"There were soldier shows."

SAILING DATE ANNOUNCED.

Early in the New Year there were rumors that certain Divisions in the Army of Occupation which had been over longest would soon be put upon the sailing list. That meant us. There were only four combat divisions in France ahead of us, and three of them were in the Army of Occupation—the 1st, 2nd and 42nd—and the first two were regulars and no doubt would have to stay until the end. About the middle of February the announcement was made that the 32nd would sail in May. Happy days! We could hardly wait for the long weeks to pass. At first it was planned to send the homeward bound Army of Occupation divisions down the Rhine to a Dutch port to embark from there, but finally it was decided that the scheme was impracticable.

On April 18th the 32nd Division started moving back from the Rhine, across France to Brest, on the first lap of the Homeward journey. At the same time the announcement was made that General Lassiter had asked to remain in France, and that General Haan was to take the Division home. General Lassiter was assigned to command of the Third Army artillery, and General Haan joined the Division at Brest, after making an automobile tour to the sections of the western front over which his division had fought.

At Brest the 57th Field Artillery Brigade also was assembled, the 32nd Division thus bringing home two artillery brigades, the 57th and 158th. On May 1st the first troops of the Division were on the Atlantic, and by May 15th all but the casuals had left France.

144

Arriving in the United States, largely in regimental detachments, a great reception was accorded Les Terribles. Delegations from Wisconsin and Michigan met the incoming steamers in the harbor. The various detachments debarked at New York and Boston, and went to Camps Devens, Mills, Merrit, Upton and Dix, where they were separated into detachments and sent to the camps nearest their homes. The largest parties, of course, were sent to Camp Custer, Mich., and Camp Grant, at Rockford Ill. The arriving Michigan troops informally paraded in Detroit, Grand Rapids, Port Huron, Kalamazoo and others of their "home towns" before being mustered out of the service.

In Wisconsin a Red Arrow Day was set aside, and on June 5th the returning Wisconsin warriors were given an enthusiastic formal welcome and parades in Milwaukee, the state metropolis;—Milwaukee, with its Teutonic accent—which had sent to war some of the bravest and best soldiers that ever carried the Stars and Stripes or any other flag to victory.

The 32nd Division was broken up—gone—but arrangements had been made for perpetuating its memory, for renewing its associations in the years to come. During the Armistice Days on the Rhine a "Thirty-second Division Veteran Association" was formed, officers elected, members recorded, and plans perfected for continuing during the years to come the spirit which led Les Terribles to success on the battlefields of France in the great year of 1918.

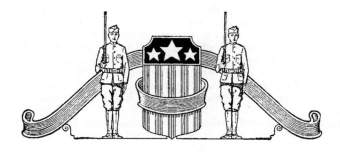

1. BRIGADIER GENERAL W. D. CONNOR, as Colonel, General Staff, Chief of Staff; Training Period; Occupation of
   Sector in Alsace; as Brigadier General commanded the 63rd Brigade, Aisne-Marne Offensive.
2. BRIGADIER GENERAL LOUIS C. COVELL, Commanded 63rd Infantry Brigade, Training Period; Occupation of
   Sector in Alsace; Oise-Aisne Offensive.
3. BRIGADIER GENERAL FRANK R. MCCOY, Commanded 63rd Brigade in Oisne-Aisne Offensive; Meuse-Argonne
   Offensive; March to the Rhine.
4. MAJOR GENERAL ROBERT ALEXANDER, as Brigadier General commanded 63rd Brigade, Aisne-Marne Offensive.
5. BRIGADIER GENERAL WILLIAM R. SMEDBERG, Commanded the 63rd Infantry Brigade; March to the Rhine; Army
   of Occupation.

146

CHAPTER XIII.

Leaders of Thirty-Second Division.

HE names of the officers assigned to command of the different units of the newly organized 32nd Division and the roster of the first Division Staff may be found in Chapter I. From the time the reorganization of the Division was completed at Camp Mac-Arthur in September, 1917, until its assembly in the Tenth Training Area in France there were, for one reason and another, several changes.

Upon arrival in the American Expeditionary Force the Division Staff was reorganized to conform to the requirements of overseas service. During the training period in France changes were necessitated by the drafting of Division Staff Officers for duty with higher units. Lieutenant Colonel E. H. De Armond was continued as Chief of Staff in the Overseas organization, with Major John H. Howard as G-1, Major C. S. Caffrey as G-2, Major Allen L. Briggs as G-3, Lieutenant Colonel Hjalmer Erickson as Division Quartermaster, Lieutenant Colonel Paul G. Hutton as Division Surgeon, Major Samuel D. Pepper as Division Judge Advocate, Major Geo. M. Russell as Division Inspector, Major Herbert L. Evans as Division Signal Officer, Captain Wm. A. Woodlief as Division Adjutant, Major John P. Smith as Division Ordnance Officer.

During the training period, Lieutenant Colonel De Armond was called to General Headquarters, and was succeeded as Chief of Staff by Colonel W. D. Connor, G. S. Major Caffrey was detailed on duty at Army General Staff College shortly after the Division entered the Alsace sector, and was succeeded by Major Paul B. Clemens, one of the original National Guard officers of the Division, who had been sent abroad before the Division left Camp MacArthur, to attend the American Expeditionary Force General Staff College at Langres, and who had graduated in May. Lieutenant Colonel Erickson was given a line command shortly after his arrival in France, and was succeeded as Division Quartermaster by Major Chas. R. Williams. Lieutenant Colonel Hutton also left the Division early in the training period in France and was succeeded as Division Surgeon by Lieutenant Colonel Gilbert E. Seaman. Major Russell was transferred to Fifth Corps headquarters as G-2, and for a time several different officers served as Division Inspector.

In the Alsace sector, Lieutenant Colonel Robert McC. Beck, Jr., relieved Lieutenant Colonel Briggs, who had been assigned to the Staff College at Langres. When Colonel Connor was promoted to the rank of Brigadier General and assigned to the 63rd Brigade, Lieutenant Colonel Beck became Acting Chief of Staff and Major Smith became Acting G-3.

GENERAL HAAN PLACED IN COMMAND.

General Haan was placed permanently in command of the Division in December, 1917, and the same War Department orders assigned Brigadier General E. F. McGlachlin, Jr., to the command of the 57th Field Artillery Brigade. General McGlachlin brought the brigade to France, but was transferred to more responsible duties almost immediately, and was succeeded a little later by Brigadier General G. Leroy Irwin, who commanded the brigade in all of its many actions.

General Haan was promoted to the rank of Major General on February 7th, 1918, just before he sailed for France.

Colonel Boucher, of the 125th Infantry, was found physically disqualified when he took his overseas examination at Camp MacArthur, and was relieved just before his regiment left for the Port of Embarkation. He was succeeded by Colonel Ambrose Pack, formerly of the 31st Michigan Infantry. Colonel Pack took his overseas physical examination at Camp Merritt, and was likewise disqualified, and the regiment was taken to France by Lieutenant Colonel Edward G. Heckel. After the 125th reached its training area in France, Colonel Peter F. Piasecki, formerly of the Fifth Wisconsin Infantry, was assigned to the regiment, but never assumed command, as a transfer was effected with Colonel Robt. B. McCoy of the 107th Trains, by which Colonel McCoy went to the 125th and Colonel Piasecki became commander of the Trains.

Colonel P. S. Bond took the 107th Engineers to France, but almost immediately upon his arrival was assigned to the American Expeditionary Force Engineer School, and Lieutenant Colonel L. H. Callan remained in command until Colonel H. C. Fisk joined the regiment.

Several changes were made in the organization of the machine gun units. The 119th Machine Gun Battalion was cut down to two companies, and was made the motorized machine gun battalion of the Division. Major Stanley Piasecki, who succeeded Major Percy C. Atkinson to the command of the battalion when the latter failed in his overseas physical examination, was transferred to the 121st Machine Gun Battalion when the 119th was motorized in April, 1918, and Major Frank H. Fowler of the 121st became commander of the 119th. Later Major Fowler was made Division Machine Gun Officer and promoted to the rank of Lieutenant Colonel. He was succeeded by Major Wm. A. McCullough in command of the 119th. Just before going into Alsace Major Piasecki was transferred to the infantry and Captain Daniel L. Remington assumed command of the 121st, later being promoted to Major and attaining the rank of Lieutenant Colonel after the armistice.

In the other organizations the commanding officers remained the same, the leaders who had trained the men in Waco taking them into the trenches in Alsace.

CHANGES ON FIRING LINE.

Once on the firing line, other changes occurred. At his own request, Brigadier General Charles R. Boardman was relieved of the command of the 64th Infantry Brigade, and was succeeded by Brigadier General Lejeune of the Marine Corps. General Lejeune commanded the Brigade until July 26th, just before the Chateau Thierry action, when he was promoted to the rank of Major General and placed in command of the 2nd Division. Brigadier General Edwin B. Winans succeeded to the command of the Brigade and held it until his "Les Terribles" were mustered out in 1919.

Colonel John Turner, who had commanded the 128th from its organization until the latter part of June, 1918, was at that time transferred to a school assignment, and was succeeded by Colonel Robt. B. McCoy of the 125th. Colonel McCoy commanded the 128th in all of its battles and during the latter part of its service in the Army of Occupation. He brought it back to the United States in 1919. Colonel McCoy was succeeded in command of the 125th by Colonel Wm. M. Morrow, U. S. A.

On July 22nd, 1918, just after the 63rd Brigade had been withdrawn from Alsace, Brigadier General Covell was ordered to a Field and General Officers' School and Brigadier General W. D. Connor was assigned to the command of the Brigade.

On July 12th Colonel Russel C. Langdon, U. S. A., succeeded Colonel Wilbur M. Lee in command of the 127th, and retained the command until the demobilization of the regiment.

The command of the 63rd Brigade changed again in the midst of the drive to the Vesle, Brigadier General Robt. Alexander succeeding General Connor on August 6th, when the brigade was engaged in firmly establishing itself on the Vesle and attempting to make a crossing of the river. General Connor was transferred to important duty elsewhere. There was only one change in the Division Staff during the Aisne-Marne offensive, Lieutenant Colonel Jerome G. Pillow reporting for duty as G-3 on August 31st, 1918. After the completion of the operation the Division Signal Officer, Herbert L. Evans, who had been promoted to Lieutenant Colonel, was given a Corps assignment and was succeeded by Major John Scott, promoted shortly afterwards to the rank of Lieutenant Colonel. At about the same time Lieutenant Colonel Glenn R. Garlock of the 128th Infantry, who had won recognition in the fight for Cierges, was transferred to the Division Staff and made Division Inspector. Major Amos T. Ashley became Division Ordnance Officer, and Major Smith, who had been acting G-3, was transferred to 5th Corps Headquarters.

The command of the 63rd Brigade changed again during the Oise-Aisne Offensive. On August 26th, the day before his brigade went into battle, Brigadier General Alexander was promoted to the rank of Major General and assigned to command of the 77th Division, where he was destined to win great fame. He was succeeded by Brigadier General Covell, who had been the first commanding general of the Brigade, and who at the time was on temporary duty with the Division. On August 29th, just as the Brigade was emerging from the front line to the support position, Brigadier General Frank R. McCoy reported with orders assigning him to command of the 63rd, and succeeded General Covell, who left the Division shortly after to command a depot brigade.

Colonel Morrow, of the 125th, was wounded at Juvigny on August 29th, and was succeeded by Lieutenant Colonel Heckel. Colonel Morrow returned to the Division on September 9th and was relieved on September 17th, going to the Third Division. Lieutenant Colonel Heckel again assumed command, was later promoted to the rank of Colonel, and commanded the regiment until its demobilization.

There were no changes in the Division Staff until just before the Argonne battle, when Lieutenant Colonel John H. Howard, G-1, was detailed to attend the General Staff College at Langres and was succeeded by Major Robert Connor, formerly of the Wisconsin National Guard, who had just returned from the Staff College.

CHANGES IN ARGONNE.

After the Argonne operation there were two changes in the Division Staff. Lieutenant Colonel Seaman was promoted to Corps Surgeon for the Fifth Corps, and was succeeded by Major James Scott, who later was promoted to Lieutenant

Colonel. Lieutenant Colonel Pepper was also transferred to the Fifth Corps and made Corps Judge Advocate, being succeeded as Division Judge Advocate by Major Fred S. Rogers.

While the Division was in reserve of the Fifth Corps after the breaking of the Kriemhilde Stellung, Colonel R. B. McCoy of the 128th was evacuated, sick, and when the regiment went into action in the Dun-sur-Meuse bridge-head early in November it was commanded by Lieutenant Colonel John B. Schneller. Lieutenant Colonel Schneller was relieved on November 9th, and the regiment fought during the last two days of the war under Lieutenant Colonel Henry Meyer, later promoted to Colonel. Lieutenant Colonel Meyer took the regiment to its position in the Coblenz bridge-head, where he was succeeded by Colonel Geo. T. Smith.

COLONEL WESTNEDGE DIES.

Colonel Joseph Westnedge of the 126th was evacuated, sick, just before the signing of the Armistice, and died in France. He was the only original regimental commander of the 32nd Division to retain his command from first to last. The regiment started the march to the Rhine under Lieutenant Colonel Caziarc, U. S. A. The latter was relieved at Longwy, and Major Guy Wilson brought the regiment to the Coblenz bridge-head. There Colonel Wm. A. Mollison reported with orders to take command, and he brought the regiment to the United States.

Lieutenant Colonel Chas. R. Williams, Division Quartermaster, was evacuated, sick, while the Division was on the Saar river, just before the march into Germany, and was succeeded by Major J. E. Barzynski, U. S. A. Lieutenant Colonel Howard returned from the Staff College in January and again resumed his duties as G-1. Major Rogers, Judge Advocate, was relieved in January. He was succeeded by Major Benjamin Chilton, and later by Major J. A. Howell, who was promoted to Lieutenant Colonel and remained with the Division until its demobilization. Just before the crossing of the Saar river General McCoy was transferred from the 63rd Brigade for important duty in the Service of Supply in connection with the homeward troop movement, and was succeeded in command in the Brigade by Brigadier General William R. Smedberg who continued in command until demobilization.

In February, 1919, Colonel McCoy returned to the Division. At that time General Winans of the 64th Brigade was away on special duty and Colonel Langdon of the 127th was commanding the Brigade. Accordingly Colonel McCoy was assigned to command of the 127th. Just before the homeward movement of the Division started Colonel McCoy was again transferred to the 128th, Colonel Smith taking charge of the troop movement.

Major Cleary, of the 120th Machine Gun Battalion, was sent to the States as an instructor while the Argonne battle was in progress. He was succeeded by Captain Sharp. On the march to the Rhine Major Rossow reported and took command.

Major McCullough, of the 119th Machine Gun Battalion, was wounded at Juvigny and evacuated. He joined the command again in time to take the battalion into the Argonne, where he was again wounded on the first day of the battle. Captain E. S. Reynolds then took command, retaining it during the balance of the Argonne battle. On the march to the Rhine Major Blossom reported and took command.

Lieutenant Colonel Remington remained in command of the 121st Machine Gun Battalion, except when on other temporary duty, when the battalion was commanded by Captain John A. McCullom.

LEADERS OF THIRTY-SECOND DIVISION

MANY PROMOTIONS MADE.

Most of the changes which from time to time took place in the commanding officers and staff officers of the Division were due to the transfer of officers to other duties which they were especially fitted to perform. Usually these changes were regarded by the authority issuing the orders as in the nature of promotions, but it is doubted if an officer ever left the 32nd Division for other work without a feeling of deep regret and a personal wish to remain.

This spirit, together with additional light on some of the changes that were made during the career of the 32nd Division, is perhaps well defined in a signed interview which General Haan gave at Seventh Corps Headquarters in Germany to E. A. Bachelor of the Detroit News, a newspaper correspondent who had been with the Division during its training period in the United States and later was accredited to the 32nd in France. The interview follows:

PRAISE FOR NATIONAL GUARD OFFICERS.

"The 32nd Division, as it went into battle, was composed of approximately three-fourths National Guard and one-fourth drafted men. The spirit of the Division was due entirely to the spirit that was built up in the Division when it was composed wholly of National Guard troops and before it left Camp MacArthur, Texas. In building up a Division spirit the Division Commander had most loyal support and assistance, particularly from the two Brigade Commanders in Infantry, Brigadier General C. R. Boardman from Wisconsin and Brigadier General L. C. Covell from Michigan. To these two officers must also be given credit for energetic work in training their units in accordance with the theory announced by the Division Commander and the schedules based upon War Department instructions.

"To these officers, as well as to other National Guard officers of high grade, must also be given credit for their conscientious assistance in eliminating officers unfit for war service. Nearly all such officers were eliminated upon the recommendations of National Guard officers, and, where that became necessary, went before Boards composed entirely of National Guard officers.

"The high spirit of the Division made itself felt even in those early days, because it seemed to me even then that the Division fully realized that we were not training merely in theory, but that we were training to actually go into battle, in consequence of which it became the more important that all officers unfit to lead men for any cause whatsoever had to be gotten rid of. Most of these officers recognized their own deficiencies and willingly quit. To their credit, it should be said that they quit with heavy hearts. Here again came in the spirit of loyalty in these men which was so manifest from the beginning and which grew day by day as the training progressed.

"Everyone knows what a heartsick feeling went through the Division upon arrival in France, when it was announced that it was to be a Replacement Division. The very heart seemed to drop out of it. Nevertheless the two Brigade Commanders stood firmly by the Division Commander, and told the men that some one had to do this work, and that, in order to do it well, the better trained organizations were, the better it would be for the Army as a whole. With this spirit the Division began to get ready replacements and send them forward.

SPIRIT OF AFFECTION.

"During the short period that the Division had been a replacement Division, nearly half of its infantry had been taken away, and consequently when it began training for a temporary combat Division again, many replacements had to be moulded into the organizations, including officers and men; but the old spirit of the Division predominated, and it was but a short time—a surprisingly short time—when these new troops, many of them but little trained, not only became efficient in their work, but came to like the Division, and, through a process which seemed almost contagious, never wanted to serve with any other Division. This is the spirit that has constantly existed in the 32nd Division. I have seen no such manifestation of personal liking for each other in any other organization, among men and among officers, as has always manifested itself in the 32nd Division. For these reasons naturally I have become greatly attached to the Division. I frequently feel more or less homesick to get back to it, and I certainly shall feel, if the Division goes home and I stay in France, as if I were an orphan far from home and friends.

"I have spoken of the spirit of the Division that was manifest before it entered into any of its great battles. Its conduct in these battles already has been published, but it cannot be too highly praised. Everywhere, always, the results were greater than I had expected, and in many cases equal to what I had hoped for. These successes of course added greatly to perhaps not the affection, but the pride, among the members of the Division, and particularly so with the Division Commander and the Division Staff and the higher commanders. It was this pride, together with the spirit of comradeship and liking for each other, that carried the front line troops many times into and over most difficult obstacles. It was this spirit that overcame the strong position of the Ourcq; it was this spirit that stormed Fismes and Juvigny; it was this spirit that carried the key position of the Kriemhilde Stellung, La Cote Dame Marie.

"My own personal liking for the Division on account of its fine response to my attempts for its training naturally grew as time passed, and grew even faster, I think, on account of the rewards that were handed to me by the higher authorities on account of the work of the 32nd Division. I feel very certain that I owe to this Division my promotion to Major General (temporary grade) and Brigadier General in the Regular Army, and Corps Commander. I have therefore personal reasons which alone would be sufficient to make me feel grateful to the men of this Division; but which are small in comparison to the feeling of admiration and pride that has manifested itself through the entire time, from its organization until the close of its last battle, and on its march to the Rhine."

1. MAJOR GENERAL JOHN A. LEJUENE, Marine Corps, as Brigadier General Commanded the 64th Infantry Brigade; Occupation of Sector in Alsace.
2. BRIGADIER GENERAL EDWIN B. WINANS, Commanded the 64th Infantry Brigade; Aisne-Marne Offensive; Oise Aisne Offensive; Meuse-Argonne Offensive; March to the Rhine; Army of Occupation. Occupation of
3. BR.GADIER GENERAL CHARLES R. BOARDMAN, Commanded 64th Infantry Brigade; Training Period; Sector in Alsace.

153

CHAPTER XIV.

Cited in Orders.

O F THE many words of commendation which the 32nd Division received during its career the expression of admiration which all ranks cherish most is a brief letter from ex-President Theodore Roosevelt to Major General Haan, written under date of September 13th, and received while the Division was battling its way through the Kriemhilde Stellung.

"I most heartily congratulate you, my dear Sir, on the great work of your Division," wrote Colonel Roosevelt.

"By George, your men have hit hard! Will you thank the Division for me?"

The letter from the former president was in answer to a note from General Haan, written in August, in which the 32nd Division commander reported that "Les Terribles" had conquered from the Germans the territory in which Lieutenant Quentin Roosevelt's grave was located. Near the little French village of Chamery this reminder of the brave son of a brave father was found by our doughboys. They passed it in their race from the Ourcq to the Vesle, and when they returned from the front line early in August the spot was in the reserve area to which they were assigned.

Reverently they replaced the plain marker erected by the Germans with a made-by-Americans cross. Flowers they brought from the woods near by, and a little fence was built around the grave. This General Haan reported to Colonel Roosevelt, and the ex-President replied, voicing his gratitude and his admiration for the 32nd Division.

When the first brief history of the 32nd Division was published during the Armistice days on the Rhine, the account contained only a few bald facts concerning the accomplishments of the Division, but a place of honor was given to Roosevelt's letter. Before and since, such noted persons as Clemenceau, the Tiger of France, great generals, governors and civic leaders, have said kind things about Les Terribles, but in their hearts they will always cherish above all else the simple, sincere appreciation of one great leader for the soldiers of another.

PREMIER CLEMENCEAU'S COMMENDATION.

Next to the commendation of Col. Roosevelt, the most highly regarded words of praise were perhaps those uttered by M. Clemenceau, prime minister of France. When the Division was at Brest late in March, 1919, M. Clemenceau sent to Admiral Moreau, commandant of the port, a letter to be read to Les Terribles on the occasion of presenting to General Haan and certain members of his immediate staff, the French medal of the Legion of Honor. The letter expressed the gratitude of

"The 32nd Division Commander reported that "Les Terribles" had conquered from the Germans the territory in which Lieutenant Quentin Roosevelt's grave was located."
NEAR CHAMERY, FRANCE.

1. MAJOR H. W. ROGERS, Adjutant 63rd Brigade; Army of Occupation.
2. LIEUTENANT COLONEL JOHN J. BURLEIGH, Infantry; as Major, Adjutant 63rd Infantry Brigade; Aisne-Marne
   Offensive; Oise-Aisne Offensive.
3. LIEUTENANT COLONEL JOHN B. JOHNSON, Cavalry, as Major, Adjutant 64th Infantry Brigade; Aisne-Marne
   Offensive; Oise-Aisne Offensive; Meuse-Argonne Offensive; March to the Rhine; Army of Occupation.
4. MAJOR EDGAR H. CAMPBELL, A. G. D., Adjutant, 63rd Brigade; Training Period; Occupation of Sector in Alsace.
5. MAJOR CHARLES A. GREEN, Infantry, Adjutant, 64th Brigade; Training Period; Occupation of Sector in Alsace.

the French Republic for the work of the 32nd Division and wished good luck to the officers and men.

On behalf of the French nation Admiral Moreau decorated General Haan with the rank of Commander in the Legion of Honor, Brigadier General G. LeRoy Irwin of the 57th Field Artillery Brigade and Colonel Robt. McC. Beck with the order of Officier, and Lieutenant Colonel Paul B. Clemens with the rank of Chevalier in the Legion of Honor. The rank of Officier was also awarded Brigadier General Edwin B. Winans of the 64th Brigade, Colonel Russell G. Langdon of the 127th Infantry, and Colonel H. B. Fiske of the 107th Engineers. Colonel Jerome G. Pillow of the G-3 Section, General Staff, Colonel Gilbert H. Seaman, formerly Division Surgeon, Lieutenant Colonel John H. Howard, G-1 of the Division, and Lieutenant Colonel John Scott, Division Signal Officer, were awarded the medal of Chevalier in the Legion of Honor. These officers were not present at Brest, and were decorated elsewhere later.

Premier Clemenceau's letter follows:

"Let me bid farewell to your division before it leaves France, and permit me to address to your unit a message of gratitude.

"When decorating your flags with the French War Cross, General Mangin enumerated some of your deeds and noted that the 64th Brigade had been given by its French brothers in arms the glorious name of the "BRIGADE LES TER-RIBLES."

"To that testimonial I wish to add a few remarks: From May to November the 32nd Division spent on the firing line one hundred and twenty days, thirty-five of which were during engagements in the hardest battles. Your losses from enemy fire were 14,268.

"In the spring you were holding the front line in Alsace. During the summer you fought from the Marne to the Vesle. In the autumn you were in the Mont-faucon Woods. On the eve of the armistice you were still delivering an attack. You have met successively twenty German divisions; you have never given up to them an inch of ground.

"I salute your glorious flag, I pay to your dead the homage of our thankfulness, and I say to those who leave: bon voyage, good luck in life; and do not forget your French friends."

PERSHING COMPLIMENTS 32ND.

When the 32nd Division had been placed on the sailing list and was preparing to leave France, General Pershing wrote a personal letter to Major General Lassiter, then in command of the Division, in which he spoke in the most complimentary terms of the great work of the Wisconsin and Michigan National Guardsmen. He briefly recited their accomplishments on the field of battle, and paid them a glowing tribute for their soldierly conduct in the Army of Occupation. General Pershing's letter follows:

"My dear General Lassiter:

"Please extend to the officers and men of the 32nd Division my sincere compliments upon their appearance and upon the splendid condition of the artillery and transportation at the review and inspection on March 15th. In fact, the condition of your command was what would be expected of a division with such a splendid fighting record.

CITED IN ORDERS

"After training for several months following its arrival in February, 1918, it entered the line in Alsace and held this sector until the time of the Aisne-Marne offensive, when it moved to that active front. On July 30th it entered the line on the Ourcq, and in the course of its action captured Cierges, Bellevue Farm and the Bois de la Planchette. The attack was resumed on August 1st; the Division captured Fismes and pushed ahead until it crossed the Vesle. On August 28th it again entered the line, and launched attacks which resulted in the capture of Juvigny at the cost of severe casualties. During the Meuse-Argonne Offensive the 32nd Division entered the line on September 30th, and by its persistence in that sector it penetrated the Kriemhilde Stellung, taking Romagne and following the enemy to the northeastern edge of the Bois de Bantheville. On November 8th, the Division took up the pursuit of the enemy east of the Meuse until the time when hostilities were suspended.

"Since the signing of the Armistice the 32nd Division has had the honor to act as a part of the Army of Occupation. For the way in which all ranks have performed their duties in this capacity, I have only the warmest praise and approval. The pride of your officers and men, justified by such a record, will insure the same high morale which has been present in the Division during its stay in France. I want each man to know my appreciation of the work he has done and of the admiration in which he is held by the rest of his comrades in the American Expeditionary Forces.

Sincerely yours,

(Signed) JOHN J. PERSHING."

General Pershing's letter was written after he had reviewed the 32nd Division in the Coblenz bridgehead in March. Previously, in December, he had made a flying trip through the 32nd area, where the troops were lined up on the roads in the vicinity of the villages which they occupied. Several times during the afternoon he left his car and passed along the line of paraded troops, looking them over very carefully. The General had last seen Les Terribles when they were in the thick of the Argonne fight and he came up one day to see how things were going. On that September day he had seen the Division for the first time since July, when he said he liked the snap of General Haan's men. When he visited the Division P. C. in the Argonne he expressed himself as satisfied with the way things were going.

HIGH REGARD FOR THE 32ND.

"I have regarded the 32nd Division highly since the day you took Hill 230 on the Ourcq when you first went into action," said the Commander-in-Chief. "I was anxious for you to make good, so we could prove to the French that all our divisions were made up of first class troops. You all know how well you fulfilled my expectations, and what an excellent impression you made upon the French.

"Then General Mangin wanted you to form the hammer-head of the blow he aimed to strike north of Soissons, and I sent you up there, and you again made good.

"Here in this battle you have had a hard task, and you are doing it well. I want ou to continue to strike and strike hard, as you have been doing, and I know you will."

After the Aisne-Marne Offensive General Pershing commended the work of the First and Third American Army Corps in General Headquarters General Orders

143, 1918, mentioning each division, including the 32nd. General Order 143 follows:

"It fills me with pride to record in General Orders a tribute to the service and achievements of the First and Third Corps, comprising the 1st, 2nd, 3rd, 4th, 26th, 28th, 32nd and 42nd Divisions of the American Expeditionary Forces.

"You came to the battlefield at the crucial hour of the Allied cause. For almost four years the most formidable army the world had as yet seen had pressed its invasion of France, and stood threatening its capital. At no time had that army been more powerful or menacing than when, on July 15th, it struck again to destroy in one great battle the brave men opposed to it, and to enforce its brutal will upon the world and civilization.

"Three days later, in conjunction with our Allies, you counter-attacked. The Allied Armies gained a brilliant victory that marks the turning point of the war. You did more than give our brave Allies the support to which as a nation our faith was pledged. You proved that our altruism, our pacific spirit, our sense of justice have not blunted our virility or our courage. You have shown that American initiative and energy are as fit for the test of war as for the pursuits of peace. You have justly won the unstinted praise of our Allies and the eternal gratitude of our countrymen.

"We have paid for our success in the lives of many of our brave comrades. We shall cherish their memory always, and claim for our history and literature their bravery, achievement and sacrifice.

"This order will be read to all organizations at the first assembly formation after its receipt. JOHN J. PERSHING,
General, Commander-in-Chief."

At the review of March 15th which was held for General Pershing in a big natural amphitheater about 20 kilometers east of the Rhine, near Dierdorf, Germany, General Pershing presented the Distinguished Service Medal to Major General Lassiter, Brigadier General Winans and Colonel R. McC. Beck. He presented Distinguished Service Crosses to over a score of officers and men of the Division to whom the honor had been awarded. After the presentation ceremonies and the parade which followed, General Pershing gathered the whole Division about him in a huge semi-circle and addressed the troops as follows:

"I cannot let the 32nd Division go home without taking this opportunity— without expressing to you in person my sincere thanks and appreciation for the splendid and efficient service you have rendered since you arrived in France. It may be that another opportunity may not come to me to say what I feel in my heart, and I am going to occupy a few minutes in your Division and say it now.

"When America entered the war we found our Allies in a very low state of morale. The leading men of those nations doubted very much whether they would be able to withstand another onslaught of the Armies of the Central Powers, but our entry gave them a new hope, filled them with fresh determination, and when in the Soissons-Chateau Thiery Offensive, which the 32nd Division aided in turning from a defensive into an offensive, they found that American stamina, American aggressiveness, American methods and training and American soldierly qualities were something to be considered worth while,—they were given new life and encouraged to assume a renewed spirit of aggressiveness. On the other hand: the enemy learned that he had a new force to contend with.

1. COLONEL E. G. HECKEL, Infantry, as Lieutenant Colonel of 125th Infantry (as Lieutenant Colonel Commanded 125th Infantry enroute to France) Training Period; Occupation of Sector in Alsace; Aisne-Marne Offensive; Oise-Aisne Offensive; as Colonel Commanded 125th Infantry; Meuse-Argonne Offensive; March to the Rhine; Army of Occupation.
2. COLONEL JOSEPH B. WESTNEDGE, Infantry, Commanded 126th Infantry; Training Period; Occupation of Sector in Alsace; Aisne-Marne Offensive; Oise-Aisne Offensive; Meuse-Argonne Offensive; Died in France, November 29th, 1918.
3. COLONEL R. B. McCOY, Infantry, Commanded Trains and Military Police; Training Area; Commanded 125th Infantry, Training Area; Occupation of Sector in Alsace; Commanded 128th Infantry, Occupation of Sector in Alsace; Aisne-Marne Offensive; Oise-Aisne Offensive; Meuse-Argonne Offensive; Commanded 127th Infantry, Army of Occupation; Commanded 128th Infantry, Army of Occupation.
4. COLONEL PETER F. PIASECKI, Infantry, Commanded Trains and Military Police; Training Area; Occupation of Sector in Alsace; Aisne-Marne Offensive; Oise-Aisne Offensive; Meuse-Argonne Offensive; March to the Rhine; Army of Occupation.
5. COLONEL RUSSELL C. LANGDON, Infantry, Commanded 127th Infantry; Occupation of Sector in Alsace; Aisne-Marne Offensive; Oise-Aisne Offensive; Meuse-Argonne Offensive; March to the Rhine; Army of Occupation.

161

"Where the troops were lined up on the roads in the vicinity of the villages which they occupied."

CITED IN ORDERS

"Beginning with Cantigny as a small example of what the American troops were able to do, on down through the Chateau Thierry and the Aisne-Marne Offensive, then at St. Mihiel where the First American Army first functioned, then in the last campaign carried through by the American Army alone, and the splendid final victory, American arms never met with a defeat. From the time they started there has been nothing but a continuous succession of victories to our credit.

"As to your services here in the enemy's country as a part of the Army of Occupation, I have none but words of praise. You have caught the idea of your superiors, and your conduct has been irreproachable. As I travel among the divisions of this army I find everywhere a record of humane conduct and fair treatment of a people whom you are entitled by the effects of your labors to regard as a conqueror regards the conquered. I congratulate your officers and you for the work you have done.

"When you return to your homes after having served here much will be expected of you, not only in your own locality as to policies there, but also in the nation at large as to higher policies; therefore, prepare to speak for your country's interest when you are asked for advice. A splendid indication of the worth of the principles you have shown here will be displayed when you go back into your old or your new positions if you show, in whatever job of whatever places you may be called upon to fill, the same industry and the same spirit you have shown here. It has been a very great honor for me to command an army composed of divisions like this, and now that the time has come for the divisions to break up and the men go to their homes, I can only hope that they will go back possessing the same spirit of idealism with which they fought. For this splendid work, I thank you. I thank you for the devotion you have shown; I thank you today in the name of your comrades of the American Expeditionary Force. I thank you, I may say, in the name of the American people, who will soon be able themselves to say to you what they think of you and of the work that you have done. I thank you sincerely."

GENERAL MANGIN DECORATES COLORS.

The review was a highly impressive ceremony, and was approached only by the military pageant held just before the Division left the Rhine on the occasion of the decoration of the colors of the 125th, 126th, 127th and 128th Infantry Regiments, and the 119th, 120th and 121st Machine Gun Battalions, with the Croix de Guerre. The same day over 200 officers and men of the Division were presented with the Croix de Guerre for gallantry in action, General Mangin himself pinning the medals on those cited in French Army orders. The honor of having all of its infantry and machine gun colors decorated with the French war cross by a French Army Commander was one of the greatest ever accorded an American military unit, and the significance of the occasion was not lost on the men of the 32nd.

In addition to the French decorations bestowed that day, Major General Dickman, of the Third Army, pinned battle ribbons on the colors of the various regiments and separate battalions, each ribbon recording a battle in which the unit so decorated had participated. General Haan, then commanding the Seventh Corps, pinned Distinguished Service Crosses on a number of men to whom the distinction had been awarded, and Major General Hines, of the Third Corps, pinned Belgian decorations on several officers and men whom the Belgian government saw fit to so honor.

After General Mangin had reverently kissed the colors on which he had pinned the French war cross, he stepped out in front of the assembled troops, and in a clear,

1. COLONEL CHESTER B. McCORMICK, F. A.; Commanded 119th Field Artillery, Training Period; Occupation of Sector in Alsace; Aisne-Marne Offensive; Oise-Aisne Offensive; Meuse-Argonne Offensive.
2. COLONEL CARL PENNER, F. A.; Commanded the 120th Field Artillery, Training Period; Occupation of Sector in Alsace; Aisne-Marne Offensive; Oise-Aisne Offensive; Meuse-Argonne Offensive.
3. LIEUTENANT COLONEL ROBERT ARTHUR, F. A,; Commanded 121st Field Artillery; Occupation of Sector in Alsace; Aisne-Marne Offensive; Oise-Aisne Offensive; Meuse-Argonne Offensive.
4. MAJOR GENERAL E. F. McGLACHLIN, as Brigadier General Commanded the 57th Field Artillery Brigade; Training Period.
5. BRIGADIER GENERAL G. LEROY IRWIN, Commanded the 57th Field Artillery Brigade, Training Period; Occupation of Sector in Alsace; Aisne-Marne Offensive; Oise-Aisne Offensive; Meuse-Argonne Offensive.
6. COLONEL PHILLIP WESTFAHL, F. A.; Commanded 121st Field Artillery, Training Period; Occupation of Sector in Alsace.
7. MAJOR JAMES GILSON, F. A.; Adjutant 57th Field Artillery Brigade; Occupation of Sector in Alsace; Aisne-Marne Offensive; Oise-Aisne Offensive; Meuse-Argonne Offensive.

ringing voice, easily heard by the thousands of officers and men present, he spoke in French, as follows:

"My dear American Comrades:

"I am very happy to be among you once more, and proud that this meeting of ours is taking place on the other side of the Rhine. The occasion of this reunion is to bestow upon you a few decorations, meager tokens of the gratitude which the French Republic, the People of France, and the soldiers feel towards you, for the brilliant conduct and the splendid courage you displayed in taking the town of Juvigny, the memory of which will remain forever intact with us, and which will place in history the glorious deeds of the 32nd Division and of its able and valiant Chief, General Haan.

"You are going back to your noble country, proud to have accomplished your task for its sake and for the sake of humanity.

"Take back with you the assurance of continued friendship and the eternal gratitude of France."

THE BRIGADE CITATIONS.

The citations on which the infantry regiments and machine gun battalions of the Division were decorated follow:

"63rd Infantry Brigade.

"The 63rd United States Infantry Brigade, composed of the 125th and 126th Infantry Regiments and the 120th Machine Gun Battalion, has acquired the most splendid titles of glory in the battle of August 28th, 1918, in the vicinity of Juvigny. Scarcely having entered the lines, it dashed forward into the assault; the enemy, surprised, became demoralized by the rapidity and vigor of the attack. It proved its superiority in a fierce hand-to-hand struggle where the 125th and 126th Regiments emerged victoriously despite counter-attacks by the enemy. It drove back the beaten enemy as far as the approach of Terny-Sorney, while efficaciously supporting the neighboring French troops during the attacks from August 31st to September 1st, 1918."

"64th Infantry Brigade.

"Magnificent brigade, to which the French soldiers fighting by its side have rendered the most beautiful homage in calling it the 'Brigade les Terribles.' Composed of the 127th and 128th Infantry Regiments and the 121st Machine Gun Battalion, it took, in a brilliant and irresistible attack, the village of Juvigny, the 30th August, 1918, and pursued its advance the 31st August and the 1st September, dominating constantly the enemy, in spite of heavy losses, sustaining without faltering the most violent enemy counter-attacks, fighting for three days without stopping, without rest, and almost without food."

CHEERING MESSAGES FROM THE STATES.

On several occasions while the Division was at grips with the enemy and after the American troops had pressed the war to a victorious conclusion, cheering messages came from the States.

On September 8th, after the 32nd Division had withdrawn from its second major offensive—the Oise-Aisne—the following cablegram addressed to General Haan was received from Governor Albert E. Sleeper of Michigan:

> "The newspapers recount heroic and daring exploits of Michigan men in our country's battles. Please convey to officers and men of your Division Michigan's thanks for their great work. Their deeds over there spur us over here. We salute them."

This brief cablegram was published in General Orders No. 88 of the 32nd Division and at the direction of General Haan was read to all officers and men as soon as they reached their rest area in the vicinity of Joinville.

On October 13th, while Les Terribles were battling for the Kriemhilde Stellung, the following cablegram was received by General Haan from Governor E. L. Philipp of Wisconsin:

> "The splendid work of your Division cheers our hearts. On behalf of the people of this state, I congratulate you, your officers and men, and ask you to express to our Wisconsin boys our deepest love and affection."

This cablegram was published in General Orders 94 of the Division, and was read to all officers and men.

WISCONSIN LEGISLATURE PAYS TRIBUTE.

While the Division was on the Rhine, a copy of Joint Resolution No. 36, "Commending the Wisconsin National Guard for its conspicuous part in the World War," was received by Major General Lassiter. The resolution was passed by the Wisconsin Legislature, then in session. General Lassiter published the resolution to the Division in General Orders No. 27, April 6th, 1919. The resolution follows:

> "WHEREAS, in the world war just brought to a victorious end, the Wisconsin National Guard, incorporated in the Thirty-second and Forty-second Army Divisions, were among the first American troops to land in France and confront the German enemy, and
> "WHEREAS, in Alsace, and in the advance from the Ourcq to the Vesle, at Soissons, at St. Mihiel, in the Argonne Forest, and the advance to Sedan and the Meuse, in fact in every major operation and victory of the American Army in France, these two Divisions had glorious and vital part, and
> "WHEREAS, the valor, the steadfast courage and fine soldiership of these Guardsmen has caused their Divisions to be rated and commended as among the five shock divisions of the American Army oftenest, longest and most severely tried of any, and
> "WHEREAS, Other thousands of Wisconsin soldiers on the battlefields of France and Russia and in camps and cantonments in Europe and this country have loyally done and are doing their full duty as soldiers of the Republic;
> "*Resolved* by the SENATE, the ASSEMBLY concurring. That the people of the State of Wisconsin, through their Legislature, extend their most sincere appreciation of the gallant soldiership of these Badger soldiers, who have blazoned high and bright in the constellation of states the star of Wisconsin as a loyal fighting member of this Republic, and be it further

CITED IN ORDERS

"*Resolved,* That a copy of these resolutions, signed by the presiding officers of both houses, and countersigned by their Chief Clerks, be forwarded to Major General William G. Haan, U. S. A., under whose leadership the Thirty-second Division (Wisconsin-Michigan National Guard) gained in its first great battle and advance the proud war title 'Les Terribles,' and that a further copy be forwarded to Major General William Lassiter, U. S. A., now commanding the Thirty-second Division, with the request that this message of appreciation be transmitted to officers and soldiers of Wisconsin residence, now assigned with the Army of Occupation in Germany."

That Waco had never forgotten the 32nd Division, but had eagerly followed the victorious career of the unit her citizens so fondly called "Waco's Own," was indicated by frequent newspaper clippings received by the men. On November 30th, when the Division was triumphantly marching toward the Rhine, the following cablegram from Jim Penland, President of the Waco Chamber of Commerce, was received by General Haan, who was then commanding the Seventh Corps. General Haan forwarded the message to General Lassiter, who published it in General Orders 111, 1918. The cablegram follows:

"In behalf of the people of Waco I congratulate you and your command. We hope you will be returned to Camp MacArthur for a demonstration of Waco's appreciation."

GENERAL HAAN'S WORDS OF PRAISE.

After each of the major offensives in which the Division participated, General Haan took occasion to comment, in General Orders, on the work accomplished. These General Orders recited the achievements of the troops, praised their fortitude and courage, and expressed the Division Commander's satisfaction with the results. That these General Orders were not mere matters of form, but were words of sincere appreciation, was indicated by the fact that General Haan often took occasion, while commending his men, to point out deficiencies the correction of which would make the 32nd even more efficient in battle.

The Division's first major operation in the Aisne-Marne Offensive was followed by General Orders 76, 1918, issued on August 7th, the day the troops were being withdrawn from the line. This order follows:

"In the first serious encounter of this Division with the enemy in offensive operations in open warfare, the work and conduct of the Division has been eminently satisfactory. In a campaign of eight days, during which there has been constant fighting or pursuit, the endurance of the men has been put to a severe strain. At no time during this period was there an indication of a lowering of the high spirit with which the Division started. The Division occupied the entire front of the Corps sector, and during the eight days threw the enemy back more than 18 kilometers, capturing in the neighborhood of 100 prisoners, 2 cannon and many machine guns, together with immense quantities of ammunition and other war supplies. The Division had a considerable number of casualties, but we have actually buried more of the enemy dead than our own total number in killed. This shows that the men have appreciated and understood the training in offensive spirit and war of movement that it was the policy to convey to them during the brief period of training in France.

1. COLONEL WILLIAM MOLLISON, Infantry; Commanded 126th Infantry; March to the Rhine; Army of Occupation.
2. COLONEL WILBUR M. LES, Infantry; Commanded 127th Infantry, Training Period; Occupation of Sector in Alsace.
3. COLONEL GEORGE T. SMITH, Infantry; Commanded 128th Infantry; Army of Occupation.
4. LIEUTENANT COLONEL JOHN B. SCHNELLER, Infantry; Division Inspector, Training Period; Occupation of Sector in Alsace; Commanded 128th Infantry in Meuse-Argonne Offensive.
5. COLONEL PAUL S. BOND, Engineers; Division Engineer, Training Period.
6. COLONEL HENRY A. MEYER, Cavalry; Commanded 128th Infantry; Meuse-Argonne Offensive; March to the Rhine; Army of Occupation.
7. COLONEL JOHN H. BOUCHEA, Infantry; Commanded 125th Infantry; Training Period; Camp MacArthur, Texas.
8. COLONEL AMBROSE C. PACK, Infantry; Commanded 125th Infantry, Port of Embarkation.
9. COLONEL JOHN TURNER, Infantry; Commanded 128th Infantry; Training Period; Occupation of Sector in Alsace.

CITED IN ORDERS

"The two strong positions captured in the first three days of the campaign were the center of resistance of the enemy's main line on the Ourcq, where a determined stand was made in order to permit him to withdraw as much of his war supplies between that river and the Vesle as possible. When these points were captured the entire line rapidly retired. The conduct of the men in capturing these two places was magnificent. The positions fell only after hard fighting which required courage, endurance and skill.

"We have yet many deficiencies, but the work already accomplished is one to be justly proud of, and the Division Commander, who has supervised the organization and training of the Division, is well satisfied with the work accomplished, and he feels confident that after a brief period of rest for equipment and a little training as to more scientific methods of attack, to minimize as much as possible our losses, this Division will be much better qualified to again take its place in the front line than it was July 29th.

"The Commander-in-Chief has expressed his desire that after an engagement prompt report be made of all casualties, and prompt report be also made of any heroic deeds performed by individuals which should be recognized by the awarding of Congressional medals. The Division Commander, therefore, desires that immediate steps be taken by all commanding officers to render reports in the form already prescribed (see Sec. 11, G. O. 67, current series, these headquarters). Great care must be taken in the preparation of these reports, in order that there may be as little delay as possible in getting action."

FRENCH CORPS COMMANDER CONGRATULATES 32ND.

After the first blow had been struck in the Oise-Aisne Offensive, General Haan, in Par. 2 of General Orders 84, 1918, published the following:

"The Division Commander desires that the congratulations of the French Corps Commander on the fine work that the Division has done be communicated to all officers and men of this command.

"The Corps Commander is very much pleased with the results accomplished, and has sent his personal congratulations to the Division, through the Division Commander, by an officer of the Corps Staff. The Commanding General desires that this order be communicated to all troops at as early a date as possible."

On September 5th, when the 32nd Division had been withdrawn from the Oise-Aisne Offensive after capturing Juvigny and driving through the enemy lines to a depth of 6 kilometers, General Haan expressed his satisfaction to his troops in General Orders 87, as follows:

"In the task accomplished by the 32nd Division with the Tenth French Army the Division has again demonstrated its fighting qualities, and has shown, more than in its previous operations, the results of scientific training, resulting in more perfect team work. I have never doubted the courage of the men of the Division, but I have wondered occasionally whether our training has been sufficiently complete to establish proper team-work between all its elements. The team-work in the recent operation worked immensely better than in the Second Battle of the Marne. There was much less straggling, and the Division Surgeon has reported officially from the hospitals and dressing stations that among the sick and wounded there were no quitters.

"The fighting spirit of the Division is as fine if not better than ever. The French Corps Commander and the French Army Commander have expressed their admiration of the work accomplished and of the spirit in which it was done. To this I desire to add my congratulations to every man in the Division. You had before you the very best of German troops, sent here fresh to hold the lines at all costs. These lines you succeeded in piercing, and at every point where you were ordered to go ahead you not only succeeded in going ahead, but during your brief period of action you have succeeded in capturing from the enemy's best troops 934 prisoners, 12 of whom are officers. You have made a record of which all the members of this Division will ever be proud and which will cheer our folks at home."

An example of the "common sense" advice that General Haan so frequently imparted to his men and officers on the occasions when he held informal conferences or inspections, both in and out of battle areas, is contained in General Orders 94, issued on October 15th, 1918, the day after the 32nd Division had broken through the Kriemhilde Stellung, advancing the front line some distance ahead of the farthermost gain made by divisions on the right and left. The Division on this occasion was very eager to press forward through the breach, and men and officers regarded it as unfortunate that the flanks could not move up.

LOVE THY NEIGHBOR AS THYSELF.

In General Orders 94, General Haan had the following to say about the comment that the situation developed:

"Bad habits are easily formed, and one of the worst that has come to the attention of the Division Commander is criticism of units that are fighting alongside of us. We frequently hear the remark that 'if the people on our right—or left—were able to go ahead, we could continue without any trouble.' Everyone must remember that everybody else is fighting as hard as he can, and if he could go ahead he would not wait for us to pull him along. Therefore, just put yourself in the other fellow's place, and make up your minds that he has just as hard a job as you have, and that he is trying just as hard to get ahead as you are, and perhaps by going ahead you can help him. Consequently, rather than to think of him, just try to get ahead yourself."

The same General Orders quoted a message from Capt. John McCullum, of Co. A, 121st Machine Gun Battalion, as "illustrating the kind of spirit that wins." General Pershing saw the message on September 15th when he came up to compliment the Division on breaking through the Kriemhilde Stellung. The Commander-in-Chief suggested its publication to the Division. Captain McCullum's field message, which was addressed to the C. O. 121st Machine Gun Battalion, and which was forwarded by the latter to the C. G. 64th Infantry Brigade, and then to Division Headquarters, follows:

"I am sending you a sketch showing my positions tonight. Have four guns in reserve. Corporal Jerry J. Jerabek went through the wire at 7 o'clock this morning, after he had fired 7,000 rounds into the woods west of Romagne, and went to the top of Hill 225 and stayed there until the infantry came through at 11 o'clock. He was ONLY 500 meters ahead of the infantry. He captured 22 prisoners and never lost a man. We are ahead so far, but will be a little more contented when the ammunition and grub get here. We fired 30,000 rounds today on Hill 246 and into the woods south of Hill 246 and Romagne. We sure can 'give them hell' in the morning, as we have good positions."

When Brigadier General Winans, of the 64th Brigade, received the message, he at once sent the following reply to Captain McCullum:

"The spirit of your message to your commanding officer appeals to me. Give Corporal Jerabek my personal congratulations, and tell him that his conduct will not be forgotten by me."

Another paragraph of the same General Orders is interesting as showing General Haan's attitude toward the "peace talk" which was heard now and then.

"The peace proposals of the enemy are another form of propaganda to affect the morale of the Allied Troops. Speculation thereon by officers and men is wholly out of place, and must be suppressed in this Division. The making of peace is not our job—which is defeating the enemy Armies.

· "The wireless news of the enemy's propositions should serve us in but one way, and that is to cause us to redouble our efforts to completely defeat him and so make him submit to the terms which the Allies will impose."

THE SPIRIT THAT NEVER FALTERED.

The last troops of the Division to be relieved in the first phase of the Argonne-Meuse Offensive came out of the line on October 20th, and the next day, when they were in bivouac in the Bois de Montfaucon, the following General Orders, No. 96, 1918, were issued and read to the officers and men:

"In its third effort in battle, the Thirty-second Division broke through the famous Kriemhilde Line, the last organized line of the enemy's defense on this front.

"During the nineteen days of almost continuous battle, not a day passed without some progress being made, and during this period a total advance of eight kilometers was accomplished. This in itself does not seem a great distance, but when it is considered that this progress was made through a well-organized position of great natural strength, at a key-point of that position, it is a task accomplished of which the Division can and should feel proud.

"The actual penetration of the famous Kriemhilde line was perhaps less difficult than the long approach to the wire of that position upon ground where the Division had to first work down a slope and then up another slope for from 3 to 4 kilometers, where it was constantly under observation and under artillery and machine gun fire. The excellent maneuvering of subordinate commanders, supported by the artillery, machine guns, stokes mortars, one-pounders, and all other auxiliary weapons all working together, permitted the accomplishment of our mission and the attaining of our objectives with a minimum of loss. The Corps Commander and the Commander-in-Chief have expressed to me personally their satisfaction at what the Division has accomplished, and I desire to add my hearty congratulations to all officers and men, one and all of whom have shown under the most difficult circumstances a spirit that never faltered under the most trying conditions." ·

1. COLONEL MORSE, Commanded 323rd Field Artillery; March to the Rhine.
2. BRIGADIER GENERAL A. S. FLEMING, Commanded 158th Field Artillery Brigade; Meuse-Argonne Offensive; March to the Rhine; Army of Occupation.
3. LIEUTENANT COLONEL S. R. HOPKINS, F. A.; Adjutant 158th Field Artillery Brigade; Army of Occupation.

CITED IN ORDERS

CHEERFUL TROOPS COMMENDED.

On the following day, October 22nd, after General Haan had been over the "billeting area" occupied by his troops, he issued the following General Order, No. 97, 1918:

> "In my general inspection of the infantry troops of the Division yesterday, I was more than pleased with the cheerful and wideawake spirit found everywhere; also by the well-formed habit of proper rendering of salutes.
>
> "The appearance of the uniform must be made the best possible under the difficult situation. Well-trained troops can make themselves look military even in old and badly used up uniforms, and nothing less is satisfactory in the 32nd Division.
>
> "We are to receive at once a considerable number of replacements, and every effort must be made to immediately inspire these new troops with the fine fighting spirit of the Division. All officers, non-commissioned officers and privates must unite in bringing the instruction, training and discipline of these troops up to the highest possible standard, and our Division will be a better fighting unit than ever before.
>
> "The enemy must be defeated, and wherever our Division is placed in the line it must accomplish its missions. This can only be done by the highest discipline, training and a proper development of the fighting spirit."

GENERAL SUMMERALL THANKS "LES TERRIBLES."

The same day, October 22nd, General Haan received from the Headquarters of the Fifth Army Corps a letter from Brigadier General W. B. Burt, Chief of Staff of the Corps, conveying the thanks of Major General Charles P. Summerall, the Corps Commander, for the work of the 32nd Division in breaking through the Kriemhilde Stellung and taking its objective. The letter of commendation follows:

> "The recent long service of the 32nd Division in the front line of the Fifth Army Corps has been characterized by such a fine example of soldierly effort that the Corps Commander commends you and your soldiers for it.
>
> "Under extremely difficult circumstances, and over a rough, hilly and wooded terrain, the Division broke through the enemy's strong lines, the Kriemhilde Stellung, and reached and took its objectives.
>
> "This effort and the result accomplished speak for themselves, but that you and your men may know that the Corps Commander appreciates their exertion, and acknowledges their success, he thanks each one."

This letter was published to the Division in a General Order.

It was for the strategy shown in this operation that General Haan was subsequently decorated with the Distinguished Service Medal.

"FIRST IN WAR AND FIRST IN PEACE."

Like the "Father of his Country," the 32nd Division was "first in war and first in peace." The conduct of "Les Terribles" in battle was no less excellent than the discipline and good order which they maintained on the dreary grind of the march to the Rhine. On December 10th when the first elements of the Division had reached the famous river which was the Third Army's goal, General Orders No. 114, 1918, were issued by command of Major General Lassiter:

"The Division has completed its march to the Rhine. Leaving the battlefields on the Meuse on November 17th it marched to and across the Grand Duchy of Luxemburg, and crossing into German territory on December 1st, it reached the Rhine on December 10th. Throughout this long march and its many difficulties the Division has kept closed up, prepared for action, and it now stands on the Rhine concentrated and ready for whatever may come. This feat will stand among the many memorable achievements of the Division. Hereafter, officers and men will recall it with pride.

"It is with sincere pleasure that the Division Commander records this accomplishment, and testifies to the fine spirit, characterizing all ranks, which has made it possible."

"ELITE" DIVISION COMPLIMENTED.

After General Pershing had inspected the 32nd Division on the Rhine in March he expressed his pleasure, in conversations with the Corps and Army Commander, at the condition in which he found the troops. The Commander-in-Chief inspected the First and Second Divisions, the other divisions in the Third (bridge-head) Corps, at the same time, and his remarks, after his visit to his elite divisions, resulted in the letters published in General Orders 22, Headquarters 32nd Division, March 24th, 1918, as follows:

No. 22.
  1. The following letter is published for the information of all concerned:

ARMY OF OCCUPATION,
THIRD U. S. ARMY.

Coblenz, Germany,
March 19th, 1919.

FROM: Chief of Staff, Third Army, American E. F
TO: Commanding General, Third Army Corps, American E. F.
SUBJECT: Commendation.
  1. The Army Commander desires me to congratulate the Commanding General of the Third Corps on the very satisfactory condition of the Third Corps troops and the Divisions of the Corps during the recent inspection of the Commander-in-Chief.
  2. The condition of your troops voices far more strongly than can be accomplished by any other means, the intelligent and successful labor which has been expended by all concerned in training and instruction since the occupation of the bridgehead.

By Command of Major General Dickman:
MALIN GRAIG.
Brigadier General, U. S. A.
Chief of Staff.

———

1st Ind.
Hq. Third Army Corps, American E. F., March 21, 1919—To Commanding General, 32nd Division, American E. F.
  1. For his information.
  2. The Corps Commander desires to express his keen appreciation of the high compliment paid the Third Corps troops and the Divisions of the Corps by the Army Commander.
By Command of Major General Hines:
CAMPBELL KING,
Chief of Staff.

By Command of Major General LASSITER:
R. M. BECK, Jr.,
Colonel, General Staff,
Chief of Staff.

FRENCH COMMENDATIONS NUMEROUS.

Commendatory letters from French commanders under whom the 32nd served during its earlier career in France are numerous. During their service in Alsace the conduct of the officers and men frequently inspired words of admiration from General Paulinier, of the 40th French Army Corps, which held the Haute Alsace sector. When the Division left the sector for sterner duty elsewhere General Paulinier ex-

"After General Pershing had inspected the 32nd Division on the Rhine in March he expressed his pleasure."
RENGSDORF, GERMANY.

pressed his appreciation in the following General Order No. 5, Headquarters 40th French Army Corps, July 25th, 1918:

"At the time when the 32nd U. S. Division leaves the zone of Haute Alsace, the Commanding General of the 40th Army Corps wishes to express to the Commanding General of the Division and to his troops, the great satisfaction he has experienced in having them under his command.

"By the courage, the excellent spirit, the perfect bearing, the zeal to gain knowledge, of which they have given proof in all circumstances, these troops have shown all that can be expected of them under a command such as that of General Haan.

"The 32nd U. S. Division leaves for coming battles, and our best wishes go with them. The General, the officers and the men, know that they are taking with them the affection and the esteem of the French troops of the zone with whom they have collaborated in a spirit of such cordial comradeship, and the gratitude of the people of Alsace, whom, together with their brothers in arms, they will contribute to return definitely to their country."

THE FIRST "CITATION."

During its tour of duty in Alsace the 32nd was closely associated with the 9th French Division, commanded by General Gamelin. On October 29th General Gamelin sent to General Haan, a brief of account of the operations of the 9th French Division after leaving the sector of Alsace. In transmitting the report General Gamelin wrote:

"Six months ago the 32nd U. S. Division and the 9th French Division were called upon to work together in the calm sector of Haute Alsace. That was at the time when the enemy was hurling divisions en masse upon the Anglo-French forces, in the hope of obtaining a decision before the great American Army could enter into action.

"Together we followed with anxiety the fortunes of the fight which others engaged in on the roads to Amiens and Paris; together we desired to be thrown into the great battle, side by side. But our desires could not be realized, and at the decisive hour, the 32nd U. S. and the 9th French entered the line separately.

"However, last August echoes of the splendid part played by your troops in the victorious offensive reached us. Personally, I had the great pleasure of meeting you and expressing my congratulations. The officers and soldiers of the 9th French Division were happy and proud to learn that their American comrades had, with them, taken part in the success upon the great battle-field whose name will always remain immortal—'The Marne.'

"Since that time the Divisions have followed their separate destinies. I have thought that you would be glad, in order to continue the chain of our cordial relations, to learn the history of our movements since we separated. This is the object of the modest account which I send you herewith, which will allow you to see that the 9th French Division endeavored whole-heartedly, and with all its energy, to accomplish its part of the common task.

"We entertain the hope that you will, in exchange, let us know the exploits of the 32nd U. S. in the great struggle which already the dawn of victory is beginning to light up.

"With my personal regards to you, my dear General, will you be good enough to accept for your officers, and for your soldiers, the ever faithful good wishes of the officers and soldiers of the 9th French Division."

PROUD TO COMMAND AMERICANS.

During and after the Aisne-Marne Offensive commendatory orders were frequently issued by the French Army and Corps commanders under whom served several American divisions in the great battle. As in General Pershing's order, the troops of the First and Third Corps were grouped for words of praise. Among the most cherished of these orders is a General Order of the 38th French Corps of the Sixth French Army, under which the 32nd gained its name of "Les Terribles." The order was signed by General L. de Mondesir, commanding the 38th Corps, and commended the 32nd and 28th (Pennsylvania National Guard) troops as follows:

"The time having come for him to turn over the zone of battle to General Bullard, commanding the Third Corps, American Expeditionary Force, General de Mondesir, commanding the 38th French Corps, addresses all his thanks to the splendid troops of the 28th and 32nd Divisions, American Expeditionary Force, who have proved during the pursuit, which is still being continued, not only their courage, but also their staying qualities.

"The casualties, the toils and the hardships due to the difficulties of bringing up rations during the marching and fighting of this period, were unable to break their high morale, their dash and their warlike spirit.

"General de Mondesir is proud to have had the opportunity to command them. He hopes that the day will come when he will have them next to him as comrades in our common fight."

CITED IN ORDERS

AMERICANS MADE VICTORY POSSIBLE.

The day the armistice went into effect, when the 32nd Division and the 15th French Colonial Division went in line side by side east of the Meuse, General Haan and General Guerin, who commanded the Colonials, exchanged felicitations. General Guerin's letter to General Haan follows:

"General Guerin, commander of the 15th French Division of Colonials, sends to the General Commanding the 32nd U. S. Division, his personal thanks, as well as those of his entire Division, for the kind letter of congratulations of November 11th, 1918, received by him.

"We are happy to celebrate victory in conjunction with the splendid soldiers of the United States.

"The indomitable energy and tenacity of the French troops, sustained without weakening for over four years, against a formidable enemy, prepared the way for victory.

"The entry into line of the American Army, coming out of the waves of the ocean like a miracle, and arriving with all the verve of its vigorous youth, with strength and dash which were irresistible, made victory rapid and decisive.

"This has cemented the union of the two great peoples, already bound by close ties, forever."

FRENCH OFFICER'S STORY OF FIGHT.

An interesting account of the Division's advance from the Ourcq to the Vesle, written by a French officer, was incorporated in the official report of the Aisne-Marne Offensive submitted by General Haan to the Commander-in-Chief. The author, Lieutenant de Tessan, was on duty as an instructor attached to the American forces, and his account of the battle was made in the form of a report to the Chief of the Information Section of French G. Q. G. His report went through the Headquarters of the Sixth French Army where it was marked "Seen and approved" by the Army Chief of Staff. Lieutenant de Tessan, who wrote under date of August 9th, entitled his account "The March of an American Division on Fismes." As in General Haan's official reports, Lieut. de Tessan had the advantage of writing while the facts, which he obtained from personal observation, were fresh in his mind. He wrote, from notes made on the ground, as follows:

"Forced to beat a general retreat, after our counter-offensive of 18th July, the Germans have tried to make a stand at the Ourcq, and, on the heights which overlook the river, have held some furious fights. However, under the repeated blows of our Allies, they were obliged to give way, and then, beginning on 30th July, the enemy commenced a falling back movement in the direction of the Vesle. Definitely thrown back from the heights of Seringes, and from Hill 230, northeast of Sergy, they were subjected to an energetic push on the part of American elements, fresh and in high spirits and ready to descend the slopes of Roncheres, while the French, on their right, were advancing through the Meuniere Woods.

"It is the action of the American Division, which marched from Roncheres to Fismes, progressing almost parallel with the road marked out by Coulonges, Cohan, the Longueville Farm, St. Gilles, that we are following from 30th July—date of its debut in the sector—until 5th August, when it entered Fismes.

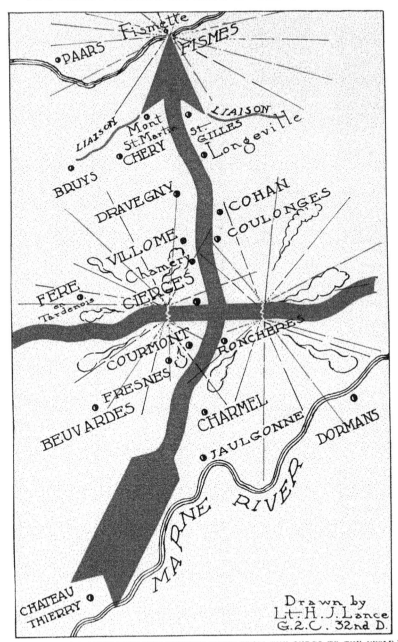

"THE RED ARROW PIERCING THE GERMAN LINES FROM THE OURCQ TO THE VESLE."

"It is interesing to note that in this Division were included regiments composed in majority of men originating from Wisconsin. This means that among them were large numbers of German-Americans, who, by giving their blood for the United States, gloriously affirmed their loyalty.

"On the 30th, they began their operations in the fighting sector, by attacking the Grimpettes Woods, after a short artillery preparation, and they attained the southeastern point of the woods. But the Germans were determined not to let go without a stubborn resistance. They soon counterattacked and pushed back the Americans' advanced elements. The fighting became extremely close, and some hand-to-hand fighting followed.

"It was not until the morrow, 31st, that the entire woods fell to the hands of the Americans.. The machine-gun nests which interdicted their march on Cierges had been smashed or reduced; the way was clear. Now installed in the Jomblettes woods, the enemy, by his well-fed fires, was trying to retard the advance of the Americans.

"Cierges is situated in a hollow. Therefore the Germans, after evacuating the village under a strong pressure, were showering it with gas shells. However, the Americans did not stop in Cierges. They passed this unfavorable position, and by a single rush they climbed up the inclines north of the village. Then, after a short pause, they partly cleared the Jomblettes Woods.

"In the meantime, the French were advancing on the right, and debouched from the Meuniere Woods, which they had thoroughly cleaned up.

KEEN AT INFANTRY MANEUVER.

"On the 1st of August, the Americans had a new series of obstacles to overcome, the most important of which were the Reddy Farm and Hill 230. In the course of the first engagements, they had already shown a keen sense of the infantry maneuver, seeking the tactical means most sure to attain their objective, and giving proof of precious qualities of initiative and imagination. Add to this the fact that they used with skill the machine guns, the automatic rifles, the light mortars of accompaniment. This is why they mastered the German defenses once again.

"Hill 230 was taken in a superb manner, and 70 prisoners were added to the tally.

"From then on, the enemy fled and opposed by feeble rear-guards the advance of the Americans. The latter swept them on their way, and took Chamery, Le Moncel, Villome, Cohan, without great difficulty. At Cohan, the Germans hung on for several hours, but were forced to give up toward the end of the day, the Americans having reached the heights north of Dravegny. Consequently a progress of 6 to 7 kilometers had been effected during that day of the 2nd of August. For 72 hours the infantry had been engaged in uninterrupted fighting, in spite of the difficulty of bringing up rations and supplies, there being but a single narrow road which could be used by the convoys, and heavy rains having rendered the roads very bad.

"In spite of the fatigue and privations of the leading units, the pursuit of the Germans was taken up again at day-break, on 3rd August. Easily enough, the line which passes through Les Bouleaux was reached. But then the enemy turned around and faced the Americans with numerous machine-gun sections and a powerful artillery, which showered the villages of the valley, the cross roads, the ravines.

"It became necessary to proceed with a methodical rolling back of the enemy, and maneuver around his strong points, which permitted the Americans to reach the slopes north of Mont Saint Martin and of St. Gilles. The Division had therefore added to its gains 7 kilometers in depth.

LAST SUPREME EFFORT.

"A last and supreme effort was to bring it to Fismes and the Vesle River.

"On 4th August, the infantry combats opened with unheard of bitterness. The outskirts of Fismes were strongly held by the Germans, whose advanced groups were very hard to take. The Americans persevered in their endeavors to reduce them with their light mortars and a few 37 mm. guns, and they succeeded, not without trouble, toward the end of the day; and, thanks to this slow and tenacious pressure, they were, at one kilometer of Fismes, masters of Villesavoye and of the Chazelle Farm.

"During the whole night the rain impeded their movements and rendered harder their task for the next day.

"On the right, by similar jumps, the French had conquered the series of woods and undulations of the Meuniere woods east of St. Gilles, and were then on the plateau of the Bonnemaison Farm. On the left, another American unit had succeeded in reaching the Vesle, to the east of Saint Thibaut.

"On 5th August, the artillery prepared the attack on Fismes by a well regulated bombardment, and the final assault was launched. The Americans penetrated in the city and began the very hard task of reducing the last remaining 'isles' of resistance. Evening saw the task nearly accomplished. We held the entire southern part of the city as far as the Reims road, and patrols were searching the northern part of the city. A few patrols even succeeded in crossing the Vesle, but they only made a simple reconnaissance, the Germans then occupying very strongly the right bank of the river. There then remained nothing but the complete cleaning up of Fismes and fortifying of ourselves therein, against an offensive return of the enemy.

"Such was the march of an American Division, which having started from Roncheres on 30th July, and having victoriously covered 18 kilometers, crowned its success by the taking of Fismes."

FRENCH NEWSPAPER PRAISE FOR "LES TERRIBLES."

Newspaper articles, both French and American, frequently referred to the exploits of the 32nd Division. The articles written by the American journalists were, of course, read by everybody at home, and came back, in magazines and newspapers and clippings from home, to the troops abroad. Some of the French articles, however, were not translated for publication in the United States.

In General Haan's personal files is a translation of an article published in "Le Petit Parisien" on August 16th, 1918, just after the 32nd Division had made its spectacular drive from the Ourcq to the Vesle. The article is entitled "La Brigade Terrible" and was published on the front page of the great French daily. The writer was a famous French war correspondent who had recently been the guest of the Division. His "story" follows:

"'The fighting, the wild, the terrible in combat' and 'savage'—thus has been called the 64th Brigade to which we had been conducted, while it was in support, after it had taken such a brilliant part in the recent operations against the villages which had been destroyed to such an extent that they were practically crumbling to pieces. The Brigade was encampd in a wood, the shattered trees of which showed only too plainly what havoc the shells had wrought.

"This 'savage' Brigade, composed of volunteers from Michigan and Wisconsin, is, as a matter of fact, made up of men of intellect to a very great extent, many of them being university students. To an air in which are mingled fragments of student songs, melodies dating from the days of the war against Spain, and a few notes of the 'Marseillaise', they have composed an attractive marching song, in which the Emperor of Germany is advised to look out for them,

> " 'The Kaiser has no chance
> " 'We'll shoot him in the pants'," etc.

"They have evidently amused themselves in composing pieces of this kind with the idea of giving the impression that they are old campaigners! As a matter of fact, the 64th Brigade, after a stay of six months in France, made a magnificent showing when under fire for the first time, and neither the French, who fought beside them, nor the enemy, whom they hurled aside, will dispute their right to the title of 'terrible.' This Brigade was engaged for a period of nine consecutive days. In order to proceed to the attack more quickly, these 'doughboys' as the Infantrymen are called, only took their ammunition along with them. During these nine days, they were only able to have small quantities of food three times. When relieved, their strength was exhausted but they had conquered a large area.

"Here they are today, still near the battle line, and they have completely regained their usual calm and serenity. After what they saw and what they did, the German aeroplanes, which only the previous evening had bombarded the wood—but luckily without success—do not bother them much. The charming cordiality of their welcome reminds us that there are young men of learning and of literary ability among these 'savages.'

" 'These aeroplanes are annoying, however,' one of them confessed to us. 'They deprive us of every form of amusement when we do not want to go to sleep. No noise, no light of any kind—that is the order. This idea, therefore occurred to us. In our company we have instituted this game: whoever can sing in the deepest voice—in one hardly audible, but in such a way that the tune and the words are recognizable—is the winner.'

"They have reminiscences in abundance. One of their officers recounted to us certain characteristics significant of the energy and decision of these fighters of yesterday.

"There were two men who, because of their enthusiasm, suddenly found themselves among the Germans. Without the least hesitancy, they sprang upon the machine gunners, killed them, and turning the machine gun around, one of them fired it while the other fed the strips. Thus they held the enemy at bay and cleared the way for their comrades. Liaison was established between companies with unbelievable boldness. Three patrols, which had lost their way, put an entire German platoon to flight. A doctor, who was proceeding under fire at the head of a group of stretcher-bearers, found a soldier entirely covered with blood, whose face no longer seemed like that of a human being.

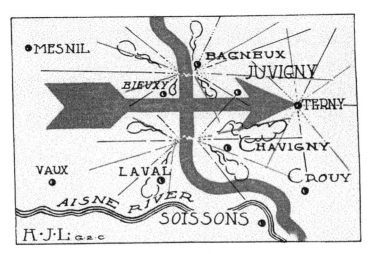

"THE RED ARROW PIERCING THE ENEMY LINES AT JUVIGNY."

" 'We must carry him back,' said the medical officer.

" 'Not on your life.' replied the soldier, who had heard the doctor's remark; 'I'm no softy—just show me the way.'

"These Yanks hold out on a position which they have reached until the very last, whether they are attacked in force or not, but their sacrifices permit their companions to arrive and maintain the position.

AMERICANS "UBER ALLES."

"There is a special point which I should like to bring out. In one of the regiments of this Brigade, there are a number of young men of German origin. Their attitude is one of the most characteristic manifestations of the thorough absorption by America of those who come to live under her laws. Atavism with them has ceased to exist, so to speak; they are first and last American citizens, and they think and act as such.

"Recently a reconnaissance had to be made by a man of determination, and at all costs. A volunteer came forward and asked that he might be allowed to carry out this honorable and perilous mission.

" 'So much the worse' said he laughing, 'if a Boche fires on a Boche.' The noble spirit of liberty with which they are saturated has removed from these soldiers all trace of similarity with the barbarians.

"In addition, the first American soldier killed on French soil was of German origin and name.

A CHILD AS MASCOT.

"Nearly every American regiment has a mascot, which is generally an animal of some kind. A regiment of Marines is greatly attached to an anteater which it brought from Mexico. Others have goats, curious looking dogs, or donkeys. The 64th Regiment outdoes these: its mascot is a young French boy, about twelve years old, whom it has adopted. The story of this youngster, the son of a French soldier killed in action, is an especially tragic one, for he had become lost and had suffered greatly until the Americans found him. Today he is the idol of all the soldiers. He has been given a khaki shirt, military breeches and wrapped leggings. The regiment act as his family, and they have decided to educate him. He has begun to learn English quickly in order to know his adopted fathers even better. He is devoted to them, endeavors to help them in every possible way, and boasts that he is already half American. He was angry only once; that was when he was compelled to remain behind, during an attack, when he insisted that he had the right to remain with the troops.

" 'The next time,' he told us, thinking that his big friends had not overheard him, 'I'll find a way of slipping in with them.' "

BRIGHTEST GEM OF AMERICAN ARMY.

Another French newspaper article by which General Haan sets great store was published in "Le Matin," one of the largest and most influential of the daily papers of Paris, on September 8th, just after the 32nd Division had been withdrawn from the Oise-Aisne Offensive. As the 32nd Division was the only American unit operating with the French army on this front at the time, the writer means the 32nd whenever he refers to the exploits of Americans in this battle. The statement of General Mangin, which he quotes, was made to a party of French and American correspondents, and was published in the United States, but the 32nd Division was, of course, not mentioned specifically at the time, because of the censorship regulations, although reference was made to Michigan and Wisconsin National Guardsmen being present on the front. In fact the War Department announced that it was General Haan's troops who took Juvigny and advanced to Terny-Sorny.

Le Matin's article follows:

"The results were very fine: all the Tardenois, a part of the Soissons, is recaptured, and the German forces shaken in such a way as to be hopelessly demoralized. But the retreat of the Boche and their pursuit did not take place everywhere at the same pace.

"North of Soissons, and between the Aisne and the Foret de Saint-Gobain, the Germans hung on tenaciously to all the strong points which constitute the advance posts of the Chemin des Dames, an indispensable buttress of their probable line of resistance. Therefore, one of the brightest gems in the history of the American Army is the conquest of the plateau of Juvigny and Terny-Sorny, which allowed our troops to penetrate into the Foret de Coucy.

"One can scarcely imagine the difficulties of the fighting in this country to the north of the Aisne, with deep valleys in between chalky crests, and honeycombed with holes making admirable machine-gun shelters. The artillery action against them was less efficacious than one would suppose. No matter how the terrain was churned by shell fire, it was always possible to move these light machine guns, which are capable of pouring down a deadly rain of bullets at 2,500 metres, along the communicating trenches. When in action these machine guns literally rain bullets, and when soldiers are called upon to cross this curtain of fire, those who have crossed the most dense artillery barrages hesitate and think twice before crossing such a deadly zone. Add to this, the fact that the gas which the Germans now send over is carried by shells which burst without making any noise. One does not die from the effects of this gas, but one is so suffocated or burned that it is humanly impossible to hold the line, and unfortunately the mask is not an absolute protection; the least opening in the mask allows the gas to penetrate to the skin, and, as it frequently happens, one is taken unawares by the silent bursting of the shell and intoxicated before one has had a chance to take precautions.

"The above will perhaps allow the readers to understand the immense efforts necessary to conquer these crests one after the other, after having destroyed the machine-gun nests by the use of the bayonet. The tanks, it is true, lend to the infantry a precious support, but it ofen happens that they cannot be used on such abrupt slopes.

AMERICAN DIVISION NEVER DAUNTED.

"Nevertheless, the keenness and fighting spirit of the American Division never was daunted. On the contrary, the difficulties seemed to stimulate them and the only reproach that can be adjudged them is that of an excess of young ardor. It is certain that their losses might have been much less had they been more patient and more prudent. Experience in war will teach them little by little to attain the same results without sacrificing so much heroism.

"The feats of bravery that might be cited are innumerable, but the 'doughboys' do not like to have one be astonished at what they do with such good humor and in such a natural way. Really, they go into combat as though it were a game, and if the game were not so terrible I might say that the relief of a regiment which leaves a line of fire to go into rest, with all these young men, tall and straight, wearing the flat cap of the soldiers of Cyrus, the brown shirt rolled back over their brawny arms, tired most certainly, but smiling and calm, is one of the most beautiful sporting spectacles that one could wish to see.

"Listen, however, to what General Mangin, who has seen them fight, thinks of them. This is the statement, word for word, which he gave to the War Correspondent who interviewed him:

GENERAL MANGIN'S GLOWING TRIBUTE.

" 'The American troops can be proud of what they accomplished on the plateau of Juvigny. They showed the same qualities of courage and tactical skill as those who fought at Chateau Thierry in the month of July. The American artillery acquitted itself well in the preparation before the attack, while the infantry displayed admirable courage and dash. Moreover, the General Staff made its strategic dispositions with consummate skill; it laid its plans before me prior to the attack and I accepted them without any change or additions. The enemy attached great importance to this battle of the plateau. He concentrated there his best troops and reinforced them with Guard Divisions, the 1st, the 4th, the Chasseurs and elements of dismounted cavalry. He considered the plateau of Juvigny as the keystone of his line of defense on the west. The Americans carried it like a whirlwind. America has a right to be proud of its children, and I also am proud to have them in my Army.' "

COMMENDATIONS FOR ARTILLERY BRIGADE.

Whenever the 32nd Division was commended, all of the elements of the 32nd Division, including the 57th Field Artillery Brigade, were included in the commendation, as every unit of the Division was present in each of the major actions in which the Division participated. In addition to sharing in the words of praise uttered on behalf of their Division, the four regiments in the 57th Field Artillery Brigade—the 119th, 120th, 121st and 147th—also were especially commended on several occasions by the commanders of other Divisions to whom the artillery brigade of Les Terribles was from time to time attached.

In the Aisne-Marne Offensive the 57th Brigade served the 28th and 77th Divisions after the 32nd had been withdrawn from the line, and sustained a number of casualties in the incessant artillery duel which the German and Allied guns carried on during the period of stabilization on the Ourcq. For the assistance given, the commanders of the 28th and 77th Divisions expressed their gratitude, which was indorsed by General Bullard, the American Corps Commander.

After the 32nd had taken Juvigny and had been relieved by the Second Moroccan Division, which included as one of its units the famous Foreign Legion, the 57th Brigade remained in line and supported the Moroccans in their attack, blasting a way for the charge of the Foreign Legion in the salient which the Red Arrows had

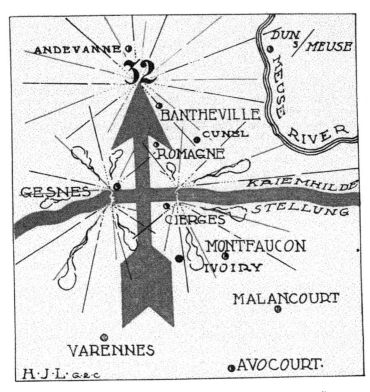

"THE RED ARROW PIERCING THE KRIEMHILDE-STELLUNG."

formed. The entire brigade was congratulated by the Commanding General of the Moroccan division, by General Penet, the French Corps Commander and by General Mangin. The Moroccan commander was especially delighted with the work of the men of the 147th Field Artillery, and recommended a number of them for the Croix de Guerre. The P. C.'s of the 147th and the Moroccan Division were located in the same cave, and the Staffs got to know each other intimately during the few days that they were close neighbors.

The Commanding General of the 79th U. S. Division, whose troops were supported by the 57th Field Artillery Brigade when the Division jumped off on the opening day of the Meuse-Argonne Offensive, praised the brigade for its wonderful work in literally dragging its guns across No Man's Land to follow in close support of the victorious infantry. This was an effort which put to the test the best that was in the artilleryman, and be it said to the credit of the 57th Brigade that it was among the first to get its guns across and again into action.

When the Brigade became a unit of the artillery of the First Army, after participating in the opening of the attack on November 1st, the Army Commander made it known that he appreciated the spirit with which the 57th "carried on" until the last ounce of its material was used up. Its guns were worn out, it had not sufficient horse-flesh left to move, but the personnel, tired and weary as the men were, remained, in the expressive parlance of both doughboy and red-leg, "rarin' to go."

But to go was impossible, and the Brigade was left behind the while the First Army swept on, across the Meuse and to Sedan. And when the 32nd Division was designated to go forward to the Rhine, the 57th Field Artillery was forced to bear, with the best grace possible under the circumstances, the knowledge that another had taken its place in the ranks of "Les Terribles." The 57th was finally moved back to the Service of Supply, and assigned to the 9th Army Corps. There, when at last relieved to rejoin the homeward-bound 32nd, the following letter of commendation was sent to Brigadier General G. Leroy Irwin by Major General Chas. P. Summerall, then commanding the Ninth Corps:

COMPLIMENTS OF 9th CORPS COMMANDER.

"Upon the relief of the 57th Field Artillery Brigade from the 9th Army Corps, in compliance with orders from higher authority, the Corps Commander desires to convey to the officers and soldiers of this Brigade his appreciation and commendation of the services rendered by the command, not only during its presence with the Corps, but throughout its participation in the campaigns of the American Expeditionary Forces. The review of this Brigade for the Corps Commander, which was held on April 7th, presented an excellent appearance and gave abundant testimony of the high morale and soldierly spirit that now animates the command.

"The Brigade is composed of the 119th, 120th, 121st and 147th Field Artillery Regiments. The records show that the Brigade arrived in France during March, 1918, and trained at Camp Coetquidan. Firing batteries from this Brigade were furnished to the Artillery Training Camps at Saumur and at Montigny-sur-Aube during the succeeding year. The 119th and 147th Regiments served in the Toul Sector from June 5th to June 22nd, 1918, in support of the 26th Division. The entire Brigade served in the Haute Alsace sector from June 12th to July 22nd, supporting the 32nd Division. It participated in the Aisne-Marne Offensive from August 1st to August 25th, supporting the 32nd, the 28th and the 77th Divisions, and advanced against resistance 20 kilometers. Without rest, it made a forced march to the Oise-Aisne Offensive, and supported the 32nd American Division and the First Moroccan Division from August 28th to September 6th. It participated in the capture of Juvigny and Terny Sorny, advancing 8 kilometers. After five days rest at Wassy, the Brigade marched to the Meuse-Argonne Offensive, where it supported the 79th, the 3rd, the 32nd and the 89th Divisions, serving continuously, without relief, from September 26th to November 8th. During this period, it advanced 26 kilometers and suffered severely from the campaign. It was then withdrawn to a rest area, where it served with the 40th Division at Revigny, and later with the 88th Division in the Gondrecourt area.

"Not only has the Brigade performed its full share of duty in the 32nd Division, to which it originally belonged, but it has contributed by its efforts and its sacrifices to the success of other divisions of the American Army. The work of the training batteries at the centers of artillery instruction has been no less valuable in contributing to the success of our arms than that of the batteries engaged in combat, and they are entitled to a full share of the credit which is due the command.

"Every officer and soldier may well cherish with pride the privilege of having participated in the momentous events of the campaigns with this Brigade, and its history will be a lasting inheritance to the Army and to the American people. The good wishes and the abiding interest of the Corps Commander will remain with the members of the Brigade in their future careers."

INVOLVED IN NO CONTROVERSIES.

It is worthy of note that all the commendatory statements which have been enumerated in this Chapter, as well as many others, which, being of no particular historical significance, have not been reproduced, failed to "turn the head" of the Division. In the controversy on "Who Won the War," which raged after the Armistice, and in which champions of a number of Divisions presented their claims in the columns of the American press published in *Europe*, the 32nd Division took no part. A few of the commendations, especially those of Clemenceau, Mangin and Pershing, were given to the correspondents by the headquarters issuing the orders, and were published in France and America. However, all newspaper articles dealing with the exploits of the 32nd Division were published under the names of the correspondents writing them, and were not—nor did they appear to be—inspired by anybody connected with the Division.

This policy of remaining aloof from the various controversies in which many Divisions participated was adhered to by the individual officers and men of the 32nd as well as those in authority on the Staff. The result of this policy, plus the amicable relations which always existed between the 32nd and its neighbors at the front, resulted in The Red Arrows leaving France with the high regard of their comrades in the American Expeditionary Force. As an Embarkation official remarked, at Brest:

"Nobody has anything on the 32nd."

This was literally true. In the Army of Occupation the 32nd was "neighbors" to the 1st, 2nd and 42nd Divisions, by common consent the "elite" of the American Expeditionary Force. With all of these proud and spirited organizations the most friendly relations were maintained. This was due in part, no doubt, to the fact that in the 1st Division were many officers and men who formerly had belonged to the 128th Infantry, in the 42nd Division was a battalion of the Wisconsin National Guard and an Ambulance Company from Michigan, and in the Second Division were many firm friends of the 32nd. To quote from an after-dinner speech made by Colonel Snyder of the famous Fifth Marines, who were on our left in the Coblenz bridge-head:

> "One of the greatest sources of personal satisfaction to me is the friendship which has sprung up between these two units of brave fighting men—the 32nd Division and the 5th Marines. Each is a proud outfit with a proud record, and each has for the other a sincere respect and admiration, born of a thorough knowledge and understanding of the accomplishments which have made us equal sharers in the glory that is ours."

The 32nd Division had the more or less unique distinction of having never claimed to be the best division in the American Army, nor, for that matter, to be better than any other of the combat divisions, although that latter claim was made for it by no less an authority than Colonel Frederick Palmer, known as the "war correspondent of the American Expeditionary Force," in his series of articles on the Meuse-Argonne Offensive. No word of detraction for any other division was ever written by anyone in the 32nd Division, and few, if any, were ever uttered. Perhaps this is why, with its wonderful record of achievement, which might well inspire envy in those less fortunate, the Embarkation official at Brest was able to put form to one of the most significant compliments ever paid the Red Arrows when he said:

> "Nobody has anything on the 32nd."

Home-coming encomiums, of course, were multitudinous, with home-town newspapers and welcome-home orators reviewing the accomplishments of the Division and speaking high words of praise for its men.

THE SKIPPER'S PRAISE.

At a banquet of 32nd Division officers on board the George Washington, homeward bound early in May, addresses were made by Secretary of War Newton D. Baker, Mr. Raymond B. Fosdick, Congressman Madden, Bishop Brent, and Captain McCauley of the "President's Ship." In his speech, Captain McCauley paid a compliment to the 32nd Division which those present will no doubt remember as one of the finest ever spoken. His appreciation of Les Terribles was based upon his personal observations, and his estimate of the Division's excellence was made after comparisons with other troops which the steamship commander had had many opportunities to make. Early in the troop movement to Europe in 1918, the George Washington took a regiment of the 32nd Division to France, and on that voyage Captain McCauley and his crew first became acquainted with the Michigan and Wisconsin Guardsmen.

"I am very glad to have the opportunity of saying what I am going to say in the presence of your Secretary of War and in the presence of your Division Commander," said Captain McCauley in closing his talk. "In no voyage which the George Washington has made, carrying troops to Europe or carrying them home, have we had on board a contingent which has been the equal of the present one in discipline, adaptability and efficiency, from the point of view of ship organization,

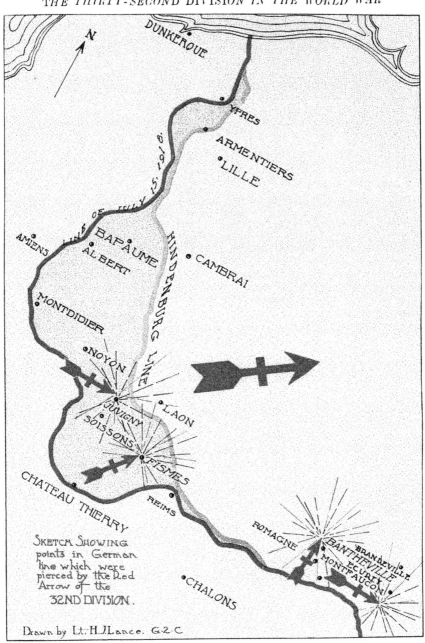

N

DUNKERQUE

YPRES

ARMENTIERS

LILLE

LINE OF JULY 15, 1918

AMIENS

BAPAUME

ALBERT

CAMBRAI

HINDENBURG LINE

MONTDIDIER

NOYON

JUIGNY

LAON

SOISSONS

FISMES

CHATEAU THIERRY

REIMS

ROMAGNE

BRANDEVILLE

BANTHEVILLE

ECUREY

MONTFAUCON

Sketch Showing
points in German
line which were
pierced by the Red
Arrow of the
32ND DIVISION.

CHALONS

Drawn by Lt. H. J. Lance. G-2-C

"THE RED ARROW ON THE BATTLE-FIELDS OF FRANCE."

190

cleanliness and upkeep. It has been my experience that when men—soldiers or sailors—are organized, controlled or constituted as the officers and men of this contingent have shown themselves to be, those officers and men are also the best when the real business of war is to be done. The record of the 32nd Division has demonstrated this to be true.

"I have heard from my officers, from my petty officers and men, and I have myself been impressed by the fact that this contingent of officers and men has more quickly assumed the habits and daily routine of life on board ship, has learned more readily and observed more carefully the ship's regulations and customs, than any other troops we have ever had on board. It has been more eager to co-operate with our officers, to accept and carry out suggestions. In short, I cannot imagine a body of officers and troops who could have done their part better than have the men now on board. As I said to the *E*xecutive Officer, Commander Perkins, this morning, after an inspection in which your Secretary of War, your Division Commander and your Commanding Officer of Troops did us the honor to accompany us:

" 'Perkins, to my mind, from what we have seen this morning, this ship has become an ideal troop transport,' and that is what all the naval officers and men on this ship have been working for. And now the 32nd Division has come on board and enabled us to accomplish our aim. We could not have realized our ambition without your efficient co-operation, or without the training, experience and discipline which you must have had as a part of the 32nd Division under Major General *H*aan."

"*LIVEST WIRE WITH TWO STARS*."

Mr. Fosdick, in his speech, told of a tour which he made of the Army of Occupation as a representative of the Training Camp Activities Committee.

"I distinctly remember my meeting with General *H*aan on that occasion at the headquarters of the Seventh Corps which he was then commanding," said Mr. Fosdick. "I asked him about the welfare work in his Corps. *H*e not only told me what was being accomplished but told me the number of workers and spoke their names in connection with their several activities. At that time I made an entry in my note-book which I shall read to you:

" 'The Livest Wire with two stars that I have seen on this trip.'

"And in view of my first impression I was glad to hear Colonel Beck, your Chief of Staff, say in a conversation on the boat the other day:

" 'General *H*aan from the start had, as a matter of course, the loyalty of his officers and men. Then he gained their confidence, their respect, their admiration, and now he has their affection.'

"That indeed is a matter of congratulation: to have the loyalty, confidence, respect, admiration and affection of a victorious Division with as proud a record as yours!"

CHAPTER XV.

Reading the General's Mail.

UPPLEMENTING his formal reports of the exploits of his Division, the semi-official reports (as General Haan calls certain letters which he wrote to his friends, in and out of the military service, during the stirring days of the summer of 1918,) contain a large amount of interesting material. General Haan made copies of these letters to his friends which he sent to Mrs. Haan in New York to preserve for future reference, and at the request of the Division historian the letters were made available for such use as might be made of them to amplify the more formal reports sent through military channels.

In his formal reports of the engagements in which his Division participated, General Haan discussed only the strategy of the immediate front with which his mind was occupied. In his letters to his friends, particularly those to Major General Enoch H. Crowder, the famous soldier who was known as the man who "put over the draft," General Haan took a larger view of the situation, and discussed the strategy of the whole front, as affecting the probable employment of his Division. Some of his estimates of the situation show an astonishing insight into the German plan of battle and express a constantly growing confidence in the ultimate success of the allied arms.

General Haan's first letter to General Crowder after the former's arrival in France was written on April 7th, 1918. The letter was not written in a prophetic vein, but gave a very clear estimate of what General Haan then considered to be the objective of the German Offensive. The letter was given considerable circulation among General Crowder's personal friends and associates in official Washington; in fact it is reported that the President saw it and was interested and pleased with the views it expressed.

In view of subsequent developments General Haan's grasp of the situation in April, 1918, is regarded by military men as truly remarkable. In a number of his later letters he refers to his first estimate, and up to the day of the Armistice when Germany was "licked"—not starved—he saw no reason to change the idea formed when he first came to France and which he put in writing in the following letter:

"My dear Crowder:

"This sure is some war, but it differs in no essential features from what my estimate had been when I left the United States. Of course, I had formed in my mind a pretty careful picture of what I thought we were going to meet when we got here.

"I do not know how you size up the situation at long range, but from my point of view things look far better than I expected to see them after the fourth day of the German drive. The spirit of the French and British soldiers and of our own I don't believe has ever been as good as it is now, and it will take a great deal more effort to break that spirit.

"The reports that have come from America about the seizure of Dutch ships, the procurement of ships from Japan and the number of new ships turned over is the best tonic that has struck the Allied armies.

"The Germans have an undoubted superiority in numbers at the present time, but this will not last long if our troops come over as fast as they should under the present arrangements, and once we catch up in numbers we soon will pass them, and then it will only be a question of time before we will get such a superiority that we will be able to take the offensive and keep it up until the war is over.

"We do not believe here that Germany can be starved, but we do believe it has to be licked, and furthermore it can be done provided decision does not come in favor of Germany in its present effort, and that I do not believe will happen.

"She has not sufficient superiority in numbers, and her losses must be terrific. What we hope is she will fritter away her present superiority in numbers.

"Evidently her progress is not in accordance with her plans, which we have every reason to believe were as follows, in three phases:

"1.—To break through the Allied line and practically separate the British and French armies.

"2.—To place as thin a line as possible in front of the French army and then crush the British army.

"3.—To then turn on the French army, offer them peace again, and if they did not accept it, to crush the French army and perhaps occupy Paris.

"The first phase of the battle appears to be over; at least she expected before this time to accomplish the first phase, and if she is unable to accomplish this first she will not be able to accomplish either of the others, and it looks to me now, as it did when the battle started, that it would be the decisive battle of the war and that Germany could only be successful if she won a complete victory in the first phase.

"It may be she considers the first phase still on, but I hope and believe she never will be able to accomplish this first phase, in which case it must be decided the battle was in favor of the Allies, because, as a result of such failure to accomplish the first phase, I believe the Allies will win the war and it will be won by the weight America can put into it in addition to what England can still put in.

"I think the length of the war will depend on the length of time it will take America to get from 1,500,000 to 2,000,000 men in France, or, in other words, to get 1,000,000 on the fighting line.

194

"I estimate that to put 1,000,000 on the fighting line we will have to have 1,800,000 here, and that will mean replacements of at least 50,000 a month thereafter to maintain that force.

"Very sincerely, (Signed) W. G. *Haan*."

Writing to General Crowder under date of July 29th, when his Division was going into battle for the first time, General *Haan* calmly discussed the success so far attained by the allied counter-attack.

"The French counter-attack in the west which began on July 18th was a fine stroke of strategy," he wrote. "Their present attack (referring to the assault planned on the German position on the Ourcq) does not seem to me to be so strategically well planned. It is merely driving in the salient without accomplishing anything much either in the way of capturing munitions or prisoners. It strikes me that if a greater effort had been made to the south of *R*eims that part of the salient might have been pushed in and more disastrous results accomplished for the Germans.

"The progress in the attacks from the south have been surprisingly successful so far. It looks now as if the Germans were attempting at stabilization in the vicinity of the Ourcq. The French appear to think the enemy can be driven further back. * * * * * "

"*R*eports of prisoners received from widely different parts of the line seem to confirm the view that many of the German divisions are getting quite short in men, and that the Germans are using more and more machine guns to save personnel. They handle their machine guns well, particularly on the defensive. This the American troops have not learned much about, but they are learning every day. * * * "

"On the whole, I think the Germans are beginning to realize that the first phase of their great offensive of March 21st cannot be realized, and consequently the second and third phase, as given in my first estimate of the situation, cannot even be attempted. They are beginning to realize that the American forces will cut a large figure in this war from now on, and this figure will be increasing in size as time goes on. This they know, and they also know that our air service will be rapidly expanding in the future. All this will not give them any particularly great pleasure."

On August 6th, when his Division was firmly established on the *V*esle and in Fismes, General *Haan* wrote:

EXPRESSES PRIDE IN HIS DIVISION.

"The 32nd Division has been put to the test and has made good." (He then gives a detailed account of the salient features of the fighting and adds) :

"The conduct of the soldiers of the 32nd Division was all that could be asked of any soldiers. They never faltered in their attack on any position, no matter what difficulties they encountered. When they were ordered to go in, they went in.

"I had received word from General Bullard, who, at the time, was not yet in command of the Corps, that General Pershing was exceedingly anxious for our Division to take *H*ill 230, which we were at that moment attacking. The Commander-in-Chief wanted to demonstrate to the French that our

National Guard Divisions were fighting Divisions, as well as our Regulars. I think we have succeeded in convincing everyone that the 32nd Division is a real fighting division and has the fighting spirit.

"At some places on the field of battle the dead lay very thick. Our losses have been very heavy but not heavier than should be expected from the work that has been done. The Division is going into camp, and it is my opinion that it will rapidly recuperate. If we get our replacements quickly, we will be ready to make another, and even better, fight, inside of two weeks.

"I think it can now be stated that the last attempt of the German Army, begun on the morning of July 15th, has not only been a failure, but that the Germans have been signally defeated in open warfare, which is the kind of fighting they have been looking for. The American troops, fortunately, have not had much trench warfare to contend with, and therefore the only warfare they know is open warfare. This has been the kind of warfare for which we have been training under instructions issued by the Commander-in-Chief, and it looks to me as if his policy were the correct one. Undoubtedly the greatest effort in this drive was made by the French, but the American Divisions, with their greater strength, have been able to take over a sector about double the front of the French divisions. Our men are fresher, they are enthusiastic, whereas the French are, naturally, much exhausted. The young Americans will recuperate quickly and will be ready for another battle before the Germans can recuperate the divisions which have opposed us.

"The 32nd has had in front of it, nearly the entire distance, one of the best of the German Guard divisions, but at no place have they shown any superiority over our men in actual open combat.

APPROVES ALLIED UNITY OF COMMAND.

"I am more than ever convinced that my first estimate of the situation of the German intention on the 21st of March was correct. They never have succeeded in accomplishing the first phase of the offensive, which was the separation of the French and British forces, and then beating them in detail. The American troops have been wisely thrown to the support of both flanks and the entire Allied Army placed under one head. This latter, in my opinion, is the only thing that could have made the present Allied offensive successful."

On August 19th, when his Division was recuperating, as he had predicted, but with its ranks still depleted by the absence of replacements, General Haan again wrote to General Crowder. General Haan told about being busy completing his formal report and said:

"It is about as much of a job to write the report as it was to fight the battle. * * * The weather has lately been perfectly beautiful and my men are now all right again. We are still greatly reduced in numbers, and many of the men are mourning the loss of comrades. However, I can have no feeling of sadness because we lost so many men; they died bravely and in a noble cause. Those young men who gave up their lives have at least left honorable names for their families, and since it will be only a comparatively short time before the rest of us have to give up our lives too, in one way or another, I am not sure but what these youngsters who fought for the whole human race should not be considered more fortunate than those who still have to trudge along. Their troubles are over, and perhaps their past misdeeds have been forgiven by the sacrifice they made.

"I don't think the German is feeling very good. I think he is beginning to realize that he made one hell of a big mistake in getting the United States into this war. Old Hindenburg seems to have given up the job and Ludendorff, I think, is getting a little tired himself. Just what the Turk is thinking of I don't know but I feel certain that the Bulgarians and the Austrians are beginning to wish they were out of it. I look to see Bulgaria try to get into the band-wagon before long.

THE GENERAL PLAYS HIS LUCK.

"We are living here in a little hunting lodge, and they have built me a dug-out nearby, but so far I have not gone into it, on account of the bombs. I have always thought I was lucky, so I stay in bed and let the damn bombs drop, which they do every night. I don't believe they can hit this little house anyway.

"By the way the German has been in complete control of the air in this sector ever since my Division has been here. However, I hear that some machines may be expected here some time, but they are not in evidence yet. We have one American squadron here, but they have observation machines and the Allies have no fighting planes to protect them in their observation flights. Our aviators are brave lads; they go over in spite of the lack of protection, but many of them are shot down. Their time will come soon, I hope. I believe we have good aviators here, if they can only get good machines.

"The Germans have been pretty busy with their night bombing in our area and I suppose they think they have inflicted a lot of punishment on our Division. But so far—and I just knocked wood—they have not killed a single one of my men in their night bombing.

"In the day time when observation planes are over us we hang our laundry in woods we are not using, and when the raiders come over at night they drop their eggs in these woods, while the men are sleeping—or trying to—under their shelter tents in other woods. So far the trick has fooled him. I don't think the German is so very cunning. I think the Americans are going to fool him in more ways than one.

"One thing I feel more certain of now than ever before, and that is that we are going to lick him. I told you at the beginning that we were going to lick him, but I did not feel anywhere near as certain about it as I do now. We are going to have lots of work to do yet, and lots of hard fighting, but I think it will generally be on the winning side, because I think that the German has lost his punch and pretty soon will lose his nerve. I should not be surprised to find that the German is not a very good loser and once we get him going—I think we have him going right now—then we may get him demoralized. We have not succeeded in doing that yet. He has made some good retreats, but in some places we have got a good deal of his ammunition, in which, if I am not mistaken, he is not at present overloaded."

PRAISE FOR STRATEGY OF MARSHALL FOCH.

General Haan wrote that he thoroughly approved of the discontinuation of the pressure of the Vesle front.

"Marshal Foch, instead, decided to hit the enemy in the Amiens front, where he took a slice out of them in quick order," wrote General Haan. "This was fine strategy, and much more was accomplished there, perhaps, than if he had given us sufficient force to continue the offensive here.

"Everyone I have talked to lately has expressed growing confidence in Marshal Foch's ability and strategy, and I think that Ludendorff is beginning to think that maybe the French Commander has not only some knowledge of strategy, but also that he has some punch left in his Armies.

"It appears that the American troops are being concentrated elsewhere. Possibly Foch has a mission for them. I hope they will hit the Boche unexpectedly somewhere. If General Pershing once gets through his lines with a lot of fresh American divisions, I am thinking he will give them a staggering blow. I hope I will get my Division into it, because it has recovered its old fighting spirit again, although yet too depleted in numbers. We have been out of the line now 11 days and have received practically no replacements, either in officers or men. I do not quite understand what this means. It may mean that we are to remain in this sector and help hold this front while other divisions are being filled up and prepared for offensive operations. My Division is not a good Division to sit on a quiet front—I think it prefers active operations. It is full of ginger, and the enemy has found that out. However, other divisions must have their chance, and I am sure most of them will give a good account of themselves. I want to see what our National Army divisions will do when they get a chance in open work. I hear that they have a lot of ginger, too. Well, if they have any more than the 32nd they will be going some!

REGRETS HEAVY LOSS OF OFFICERS.

"I have looked into our recent losses and have found that the reports show a larger percentage of casualties among the officers than among the men. This speaks well for our officers, but too many good ones were lost. However, many of them will soon be back, and they will be better for carrying a few scars with them.

"The training of our Division is now going on in a very satisfactory manner, but it is unfortunate that we must carry on this training so shorthanded in officers and men. If we only could get the men this would be a fine time to give them the necessary training for the next operation, but there is no use kicking—we cannot make officers and men out of nothing. So we will have to wait until we get some, and in the meantime, if we cannot smile, we will not weep either.

"The effort that has been made by America is marvelous. No one can say that a Republic cannot make war when it has good cause for doing so. I believe that there is today no man in the world who has such wide power as the President of the United States, and the best of it is that he has this power because the spirit of the American people is such that he must take it."

General Haan wrote a great deal, in this as well as in other letters, of about the same period, of the success of the Division liaison during the Aisne-Marne Offensive.

"Our liaison worked so much better than I ever hoped for that I am satisfied that in our next fight our liaison will be as good as the best in any veteran French or British division. The success of our liaison I attribute mainly to Major Lobez, chief of the French Mission attached to our Division. I detailed him as a personal staff officer with specific instructions to suggest to me continuously any improvements that we might make in getting information, and he has not been backward in coming forward with suggestions."

During the brief training period after the battle, General Haan delivered a series of lectures on the lessons of the operation, to officers and men, wherever it was possible to get them together for an informal talk. In his letters he discusses these lectures and writes:

ENEMY HEAVILY PUNISHED.

"I have found but little to criticize in the manner in which our infantry worked; they did splendidly. They attacked positions which, when examined afterward, seemed almost impossible to carry. The most satisfactory feature in connection with our attacks on several very strong machine gun nests was that we lost fewer men in killed in each case than the enemy dead found on the spot, which I think rather remarkable. It shows that our soldiers had profited much by their experiences in training in the Belfort sector. Our losses were heavy, but General Bullard told me that he had compared our losses with the casualties of the French on our right, who were in his Corps, and in comparison to what we did our losses were no heavier than theirs. General Bullard expressed himself as being satisfied with the manner in which our men behaved in this attack."

General Haan wrote of the Oise-Aisne Offensive in practically the same language as he wrote his official report. In regard to the commendation of the Division by General Penet, commanding the French Corps, General Haan wrote:

"The Corps commander sent an officer to my Headquarters, who stated to me that the Corps Commander had sent him especially to congratulate the 32nd Division on the excellent work that was done by it in the capture of the most difficult position which had been holding up the line for some time."

In a letter to a friend in his old home town of Hammond, Ill., General Haan, on October 5th, when the Division was struggling against the enemy between the Argonne and the Meuse, said:

"I have lost a good many men in killed and wounded, but that cannot be helped; I knew that would happen if we got into the war, that is, into the real fighting, and we are right in the midst of the real fighting now." * * *

General Haan then gave some facts concerning the length of the Division's service in actual combat and added:

BOASTING NOT FASHIONABLE.

"I don't want this published, because it might be construed as boasting, and no one here boasts; it is out of fashion. Everybody is doing the best he can and we are accomplishing something."

"The French are fine fighters—I like them more than ever."

General *Haan* told of visiting the observation post on the lofty crest of Mont-faucon and of the citadel which the Crown Prince of Germany had built there.

"The French lost 15,000 men trying to take the position," said General Haan. "The Americans lost some, too, but took it. Of course, the French had more troops opposing them when they made the attack, or perhaps they had a lesser force than we used. The French are fine fighters, they gain ground all the time and know the game. I like them more than ever, and after the war the American people will know much more about the French and they will like them, too."

In a letter written to Senator *Harry S. New*, on October 5th, General *Haan* made the following statement regarding the *Y. M. C. A.*:

"*THERE*'S NO SUCH THING AS A *REST* CAMP."

"The Y. M. C. A. does a fine work when we are in what is called 'Rest Camp,' though there is really no such thing as a '*Rest* Camp.' To be in a '*Rest* Area' merely means that we are training instead of fighting. The men and officers work hard every day. However, in these so-called *Rest* Camps the Y. M. C. A. serves the men very well. I suppose in the quiet sectors they do pretty good work, but in campaigns like the ones the 32nd Division has been in the Y. M. C. A. organization is hopelessly inadequate. Nor do I think that it should be expected to do so much."

When Major Generals write personal letters to each other they use language about like the rest of us; to judge from the following quotation from a letter written by General *Haan* on October 15th, to his friend, Major General *E. F. McGlachlin, Jr.*, then Chief of the First Army Artillery:

"My Division is in fine spirits though tired as hell. This has been by far the fiercest fight we have ever been in. Yesterday morning we went through a trench system (the Kriemhilde Stellung), protected in front by three bands of wire. It seemed almost prohibitive, and we would not have gotten through had it not been for perfect artillery fire, so well in hand that where the infantry got through the barrage went on, and where it didn't get through the fire was dropped back on the trenches. We got through with two battalions, but were held up with the other two; but the artillery, from good observation points which had been found, was recalled to the points where the infantry didn't get through and supported the infantry there until they did get through.

"KICKING 'EM IN THE TAILS."

"Some day I want you to come out and look at the positions my Division took yesterday morning. It is a veritable Gibraltar. And remember that the Division had been fighting in the open in front of this trench system for 13 days, during which time it was continuously under enemy observation and subjected to perfectly controlled artillery fire. Nevertheless we kept on approaching the position until we were in front of the wire, and then we went over and got it. And we are going to keep it, and we are going to kick them in the tails until they get further away; but we can't kick very hard any more. Some of my battalions are down to 6 officers and 250 men, but there is ginger in them yet."

201

Writing under date of October 19th, General Haan had more to say about the wonderful work of his Division in penetrating the Kriemhilde Stellung.

"It has been a terrific strain on the men who have been in continuous battle for 20 days," he wrote. "I am more than pleased at the work the Division has done and the ground it has gained, but I am more pleased at the way in which it was done. * * * I examined the German position—the Kriemhilde Stellung—in the vicinity of Cote Dame Marie today, and I don't believe any troops in the world could take it if it were held by our men."

On October 20th, just after the Division had been withdrawn from the front line, General Haan wrote as follows to General Crowder:

HIS MEN ALL SMILING.

"I have just returned from an inspection of my Division, which is huddled in a wood, covering about 4 square miles. I visited all of the Infantry regiments, which are the ones that suffered most of the casualties. This morning we had three or four hours of intermittent sunshine, and I am glad to find that my men are all smiling. Every one of them is lousy, but even this does not have any immediate bad effects on them. I know that my Division is going to recuperate in a very short time, and it will soon be ready for another scrap even if we have to stay in the damnable hole.

"I had pictured war as hell, but never quite so much like hell as this. I don't want any more war—but I want to stay in this one until it is finished, and moreover I want to stay with my Division. It's a peach. I believe there is no better Division here; in fact I don't believe there is as good a one. I have fine Brigadier Generals and fine Colonels and fine men with a spirit that can't be beaten."

The last letter of the file to General Crowder was written December 12th, just before the Third Army crossed the Rhine.

"In Germany, among the people as you see them on the streets," wrote General Haan, "they look perfectly healthy, and there is no indication of underfeeding. I think, again, that my estimate of the situation, made 'way last April, that the German people could not be starved out, but that the German Army had to be licked, is entirely correct. The German Army was licked—if the armistice had held off 10 days longer, it would have been destroyed. Of course we would have lost a good many men, and it is probably better as it is."

In a decidedly lighter vein, but none the less interesting, are General Haan's letters to Mrs. Haan, written at various times during the 32nd Division's career in France. These letters were secured from Mrs. Haan by a reporter for the Detroit Free Press, shortly after Les Terribles returned from France, and were published while the country was welcoming home the famous Wisconsin and Michigan warriors.

General Haan wrote his wife under the nickname of "Bunker," by which he has been known to his intimates since his West Point days. When the letters were published General Haan was in Battle Creek, Mich., commanding Camp Custer. Mrs. Haan had written him from New York that she had "given a reporter some letters." When he read them in the paper, a year after he had written them, far from the turmoil in which the words were penned, he smiled, and his only comment was:

"I am quite astonished at some of the statements I made."

In the same camp were a number of men of the 32nd Division, being demobilized. They read the letters with more interest than anyone else. They smiled, too, and a veteran officer remarked:

"Guess the Old Man is just like the rest of us. I've censored many a letter that reads like those to 'Margaret.' The General writes just like a doughboy."

And the Editor of the Free Press in his comment introducing the letters to his readers said:

"The outstanding feature running through the letters is that General Haan is revealed as 'human'—vitally interested in exactly the things that interested the men who fought under him."

It is a military principle that an organization tends to pattern itself after its commanding officer. No Division could be commanded for the length of time General Haan commanded the 32nd without assimilating many of the personal characteristics of its chief. "Bunker to Margaret" letters which General Haan has permitted the Division historians to republish demonstrate this fact more clearly, perhaps, than anything else.

If any one feature of the morale of Les Terribles was more evident than another, the cheerfulness with which the officers and men accepted whatever came their way was perhaps the most impressive characteristic of the Division. Many of General Haan's letters to his wife were written at times his men will remember as not being conducive to light-heartedness, but there was hardly a time when he couldn't find something to joke about. If it wasn't his rubber tub, which was the envy of his staff officers, it was the Kaiser's bed, in which he refused to sleep.

"We were billeted in the ex-emperor's house," he wrote, "but I couldn't bring myself to sleep in the old lobster's bed."

In the early training days in France before the Division went into the trenches in Alsace, the General was just as restless to go forward as any of his men— perhaps a bit more so. His letters exemplify the Division spirit of "Let's go." Many of his letters were written while the Division was under action or just coming out of a victorious fight. In these the spirit of pride in the glorious achievements of his men is always uppermost.

The natural beauty of France interested him, too, just as it interested all the fighters from America, and the spirit of the French women working in the fields tugged at his heartstrings, just as it tugged at the heartstrings of every American mother's son over there.

The General's first letter tells of his voyage across the Atlantic. It reads:

March 5, 1918.

"Dear Margaret: Here we are, safe and sound after an interesting trip. Had one fake 'sub' attack in mid-ocean; some one had dropped a barrel overboard, our lookouts signalled 'Submarine,' and we had some nice target practice.

"The last two nights the strain was a little wearing, but when we sailed into this beautiful French port, with bright sunshine on the hills and city, it was grand. The Cadillac is now being unloaded and we will use it to go to our headquarters.

"I do not detect the hopeless feeling among the French of which I have heard so much. We will give the German pirates a run for their money before we finish.   Lots of love,   BUNKER."

A week later General Haan wrote:

"Dear Margaret: It seems a long time since we landed, yet it is only a week. The sun has been shining beautifully every day, and all over France the farms are being plowed and planted. The season is earlier than in the United States.

"Apparently there is ample food; no meatless days in France, and you can buy anything you need cheaper than in the United States. I was surprised. Butter is very scarce. The bread is black, but good. Sugar is not plentiful, but more so than in New York.

"I have seen many old friends, and soon will see some more. We are billeted in 30 different quaint old villages, but quite comfortable. I have a chateau, or rather a large room in a big stone house, and eight officers are with me.

"I have a fine bed, good mattresses, sheets and blankets and towels all furnished, bed made and sheets and towels laundered for half a franc (10 cents) a day. Too much! No bath in the chateau. Too bad! But then I have my rubber tub, which is O. K., for I get a bucket of hot water now and then.

"Things are most interesting here, and I am glad I am in the thick of it. In a few days I expect to have a look at the enemy. They are rather active, but our men are full of confidence and pep, and we are getting more in all the time. I think our navy is going to get the better of the 'subs,' too.

"I don't know what to think yet of the end of the war. I can't see any way but to keep on scrapping for a long time."

The General's third letter was written on St. Patrick's day, and sets forth how he worked to get his Division together after the units had been separated by powers higher up:

"Dear Margaret: This has been a most beautiful day, and I have had a ride up front; not very near the front yet, but I shall get nearer next week.

"My Division is still all scattered and helping in the supply line, but I will get it together soon, I think. I have been after them hard with the big stick.

"I am feeling fine as silk. We don't get much news, although I take a French morning paper, Le Matin, and an English evening paper, the Daily Mail. Our American papers have better news.

"I am gradually getting acquainted with the general organization of things here and it is intensely interesting. The Secretary passed through here today. He is being taken on a personally conducted tour and seems to enjoy it.

"I am very comfortable, and like my work even better than at Waco."

A letter written by General Haan March 29th, reflects the spirit of unrest that spread over the Allied world during the German offensive in the north of France:

"Dear Margaret: Things are 'sizzling' here, and at the moment there is grave doubt as to whether our lines will finally hold, but the French are quite optimistic.

"A terrible battle is in progress. We hope to stem the onslaught, which was expected just where it came. If we are able to bring them to bay now, and I think we will, then we will get them in the end.

"Things are looking a little better today, and our British friends certainly are doing themselves proud.

"I hope soon to get a more active part in the doings."

April 2.

"Dear Margaret: The Germans seem to be stopped, and I feel certain we are going to get them in the end. Our troops are coming over much faster now and they will come faster soon.

"Our people must all realize that the enemy cannot be talked to death or starved out. He must be licked, and that will require some heavy fighting.

"I feel sure now that we will by fall get control or at least great superiority in the air, and that will give our armies a big advantage. By that time we also should have more soldiers than the Germans, and we will be able again to take the offensive, which we will do with a vengeance.

"I am quite comfortable in my chateau, where I come for a sponge bath now and then. That rubber tub is the envy of my staff.

"Ever since the Germans shot into the Paris church on Good Friday they have been in bad luck. The spirit of the Allied armies is fine—never better, and that is much."

In a letter of April 8th the General writes:

"Dear Margaret: All the general officers in France, except those in my Division, have been ordered to take another examination. We were ordered too, but when I told them we had been examined so often in the United States that whenever we met a medical officer we began to unbutton our clothes, they let us off. I hope I don't have any more physical examinations until the war is over; not that I am afraid of them, because I never felt better, but they are a nuisance.

"The troops of the Division are anxious to get to the front. A few of them are up there now.

"You tell any good people who are wondering what they could do to help, that they should use all their influence to do what General March asks. *He* is now Chief of Staff; he has been over here and he knows just what is needed.

"We have a nice 'mess,' although we have just lost our cook. We are promised a French chef, and then we will start all over again.

"I went to the movies Saturday night, saw Fatty Arbuckle and felt quite at home."

A trip to the front lines, and his views on the perilous situation with the British in the north, are set forth in the General's next letter:

April 13.

"Dear Margaret: War is even 'Heller' than we used to think it was. The British are now under a frightful strain. As I am writing, the battle is at its height. I hope and believe the British again will stop them before it is too late.

205

"I have just returned from the front trenches, where I have been studying the modern methods of trench warfare. I went into the middle of No Man's Land, into a listening post within 50 yards of the German trenches.

"Our soldiers are going to be fine. Where we are weak is in our older or rather our field officers, that is colonels and majors and most captains. They are too old to get into the full spirit of the strenuous training required.

"The French have become quite used to the war. They live in the villages 10 miles from the front and go on planting (the women), and carry on just as if nothing were happening. Shells drop in their fields, but that doesn't worry them. They do not go until they are ordered away by the military authorities, and then they go reluctantly. Practically all the work of planting the fields is done by the women. A few old men are seen now and then, but they don't seem to be able to do much work, except on the roads, which are kept in fine shape.

"This is Saturday night and I feel a little lonesome. Tomorrow I am running up to General Pershing's headquarters in a new car—made in Detroit. It's a peach, and the roads around here are in fine shape."

The General's next letter, dated May 1st, tells of the artistic beauties of France.

"Dear Margaret: France in the springtime, among the hills, is beautiful. I wish you could be here to enjoy it, as you surely would, and rummage around some of those quaint old country villages—marvelous specimens of unsanitary conditions, but artistic by their very nature—pictures to make the artists dance and drink the wine coming from the hillside vineyards."

That Thirty-second Division spirit of "Let's Go" is set forth in a letter of May 11th, as follows:

"Dear Margaret: Good for you for wanting to be a man and a soldier. You are doing good work, and will continue to do so as long as you feel that way. We have a tremendous job on our hands, but if we all pull together we'll put it over.

"Got me a new uniform today—a peach. Am going up front tomorrow.

"My sports are ready for a tour in the trenches. They are 'fed up' on training, as the Scotch say, and are all eager to get a try at the foe. Me, too, Pete!"

A letter written May 14th takes the Division up one step nearer the front. The General writes:

"Dear Margaret: We are moving today, but it is not like Texas. We get the order, and zip, in two hours we report ready. Good training!

"I had a nice trip to the front Sunday; lunched with a French General. He is quite comfortable, and so will we be when we get into the line (in a quiet sector).

"We are not to be in the thick of the battle for some time yet."

206

"Dear Margaret: We have just completed a 100-mile movement without a hitch and exactly on schedule time—not like the Texas movement. We are now in another locality, but not on an active front yet. Plenty of shooting and bombing and fights in the air. My men are learning by contact, and my officers are, many of them, improving fast.

"The enemy seems to be threatening another drive. Well, he will get another crack in the nose, and before long some more cracks, and then some more. It looks to me now as if we might spend next winter here, but one can never tell. I am not expecting a speedy decision, and he is trying his best to turn *R*ussian soldiers against us through his tools, Trotzky and Lenine, but I don't think he will succeed.

"We are quite comfortable here. I am writing this in my 'office' under an electric light."

A little touch of homesickness is evident in a letter dated May 24th:

"Dear Margaret: Things are not much different than I expected. Lots of details we are learning every day, and the French Officers are simply fine in giving us the benefit of their experience. We have much to learn yet, but not nearly as much as when we started.

"Being 'in contact' adds much zest to our work and keeps up the interest. And the days are nice and long now—plenty of daylight so that we don't miss the lightless nights so much.

"But, ye gods, how I would enjoy the lights on Broadway.

"One of my men was killed yesterday by machine-gun fire and two were wounded today by artillery fire—also some civilians.

"It has turned cool today, but the weather is generally fine, with plenty of sunshine and flowers, mostly yellow and blue."

General Haan's pride in the first two men in the Division to win the French Croix de Guerre, and his concern over his first wounded, are set forth in letters of May 29th and June 2nd:

"Dear Margaret: This war is some hell, but we are going to come out on top in the end; I feel sure of that.

"Have had a few men killed and some wounded; not many. Two of my men have won the Croix de Guerre. One was killed and the other shot through the lungs. The latter was Sergeant Sanford, 126th Infantry, who met a German patrol of five and attacked them single-handed. They fired at him and fled. He pursued them after he was shot and emptied his pistol into them. *H*e brought in grenades and a wire cutter they dropped in their flight. *H*e is very seriously ill in a hospital, but I think he will recover."

"Dear Margaret: I visited the hospitals today. The sergeant is still alive and has a good chance of recovery.

"We made a raid last night and caught two German prisoners; others were killed, number not known. All we wanted was to find out who was in front of us, and we have identified them.

"The Germans surely hit a soft spot in the Allied line in their last drive. I hope we will be able to hold at Soissons and Reims, which should force the enemy to withdraw. I hope further that they may push in at these points and make a disaster for the Germans.

"We are too short of men. The Germans have some 50 divisions more than the Allies, and they are a single command, and they are better trained. But our troops are coming over faster every day now, and already they are giving a great deal of help."

More impressions of the French Army are set forth in a letter dated June 24th. It reads:

"Dear Margaret: I guess you haven't had your mails crowded by my letters lately; things have been rather rushed with us the past month and I have not been troubled as to how to kill time.

"I have the great honor of commanding a French division in addition to my own. This is the first time an American Officer has commanded a French division. The French are doing everything they possibly can to help us along. I never believed such perfect relations could be established by troops of different nations serving together.

"The weather has been rather raw here, and tonight I am only fairly warm with a heavy overcoat on as I am writing.

"I noticed by the evening paper we have 300,000 men over here now. That's fine. I am glad they have decided to publish the numbers, because it will cheer up the French and British and will make the Germans weep. We flattened out four of their sports yesterday that we know of and will get more soon.

"Inclosed is a program for concert given by an American and French band playing as one band."

The General's next letter, dated July 24th, was written after he and the Thirty-second had moved from Alsace to the vicinity of Chateau Thierry. It follows:

"Dear Margaret: We are a long way from our old station. I expect you may have located us before you get this; anyhow, if you have not I can't help you. We are all O. K. and doing our best and will continue to do that to the end.

"The losses in our Division have not as yet been heavy, but no one can tell what will happen in the near future. All is uncertainty, but we are preparing as best we can for eventualities.

"Be that as it may we shall smite the enemy as hard as we can."

The next letter, written August 3rd, tells of the Division's first battle in its drive from the Ourcq to the Vesle. It reads:

"Dear Margaret: I have been with my Division for four days and nights in a terrific battle. My men have done excellent work and I am well satisfied.

"The men are about exhausted. We have beaten the German in 'open warfare,' where he thought himself invincible, and Berlin is not rejoicing overmuch. We have many casualties, but we have actually counted more than twice as many dead Germans on the ground as our dead numbered. I think tomorrow my Division will be replaced by a fresh one, but if not my men can fight more yet. Some of them have had nothing to eat for two days, but tonight they will be fed.

"We have driven the enemy across a river and he has blown up the bridges in his flight—so we have to stop over night. That gives us a chance to get food to the very front troops.

"I am starting out to inspect the front at 4 tomorrow morning. I would forever have regretted it had I missed this battle."

More about this same battle is contained in the General's next letter.

"August 7.

"Dear Margaret: Just a word now that our first real battle, lasting eight days, is over.

"We had many wounded, but only about 500 killed in the eight days of terrific fighting in the middle of the big push.

"One of my regiments took Fismes by storm and killed many Germans.

"On the battlefield of our first fight, lasting part of two days, more than 500 enemy corpses have been buried by our men. War is getting to be hell for the Germans, but it's nothing to what it's going to be.

"My men are having three days' rest now and they are reported very cheerful and in high spirits. Tomorrow I am going to visit all of them."

Capture by his troops of the town near which Quentin Roosevelt is buried is one of the outstanding features in a letter dated August 17th, which says:

"Dear Margaret: Tomorrow we will put on our first gold service stripe (six months on big war service).

"My Division has had a good rest and is about ready for another scrap, but we are very short in officers and men and I hope I will get replacements soon.

"I have been busier since the battle ended than I was during it—in getting matters in hand again. Battles are very discouraging even when you are winning.

"What do you think of our stunts? I told you we would get the Germans in the end. Well, the end is not yet, but I think the foe wishes it were. We are just beginning. I hope we don't dash in too boldly; we might get pinched a little—but anyway, we will lick the Kaiser before we come back.

"We don't want peace. We want to lick him to a frazzle.

"We captured the town near which Quentin Roosevelt is buried and found his grave alongside the remains of his aeroplane. I wrote to Teddy about it.

"Well, about four staff officers are waiting for me, so good-night."

The General found less time to write letters in the days of the Juvigny battle that followed the writing of this last one, but October 5th, he wrote:

"Dear Margaret: Yesterday I put in 24 hours' work and the time was too short. My Division was in a terrific battle all day and most of the night and again all today, but it has stopped now. They are good fighters, every one of them.

"I am quite well and glad we are on the offensive. Now for a little sleep."

A letter written twelve days later shows General Haan exceedingly proud of his Michigan and Wisconsin fighters. It reads:

"October 17th.

"Dear Margaret: The fighting here has been terrible and my fine Division has again pointed its nose straight through the enemy's Kriemhilde line, his last organized line on this front. My Division is the only one that got through on this front and now they are going (I hope) to push a fresh Division through the hole we made, which we are still enlarging.

"It's been frightful and the losses very heavy, but the men are in magnificent spirit and still going to it.

"We are to be taken out for a rest tomorrow night.

"I am proud of my Division."

On the morning of November 11th, when the Armistice went into effect, General Haan sent a brief cablegram to his wife.

"Happy days!" was all he said.

In the evening of Armistice Day, the General wrote:

"November 11.

"Dear Margaret: This is a day of celebration. Even in the wilds of the finish of the great war on our last battlefield we have been able today to have a banquet—perhaps the happiest of our lives.

"This morning we resumed the attack at 6:30 which we had stopped last night after dark. At 7 we received orders to stop the battle. That was some job, too. We got it stopped entirely at 10:45, just 15 minutes before the armistice went into effect. One of my chaplains was killed at 10:40. Hard luck!

"Day before yesterday we went back into the fight again, and yesterday we pounded them all day, driving them back everywhere. But they fought like the very devil still—had a new division in front of us and parts of two other divisions, but we punched them.

"I am glad the war is over. We are now waiting for the enemy to get a little start and then we will follow him and before long we will establish 'Die Wacht am Rhein.' Isn't that grand?

"Anyhow, we licked the foe to a frazzle and the Hohenzollerns and the Hapsburgs are out of business for keeps."

210

"Here at Longwy 5,000 French people were on the main square to greet me."

Three days later, General *H*aan wrote:

"Dear Margaret: Now that the fighting is over and we can have lights at night, the world seems different—a whole lot of improvement.

"My Division has been selected to move forward in the advance guard to establish a 'Wacht am *R*hein' and that tickles me most to death. We start after the Germans day after tomorrow. My Division is one of six (elite,) selected for a station on the *R*hine, probably at Coblenz. We march through *L*uxemburg and Treves. You remember our visit there? Isn't that grand?

"*N*othing doing but cleaning up and getting new clothes."

How it feels to sleep in a real bed is described in a letter from Chateau *L*ongwy dated *N*ovember 18th, as follows:

"Dear Margaret: Fine business this living in '*K*aiser *H*ouse' and 'Baron Chateau.' Things are improving.

"Had grand reception at Marville yesterday, and today here at Longwy 5,000 French people were on the main square to greet me when I arrived with the Division. We are now on the border of Luxemburg.

"I had a fine bed to sleep in last night—my first night in a real bed in more than three months, and a bath too. Too much! Afraid I'll get sick.

"The baroness called on me today and apologized for the filthy condition of the chateau, but explained that today was the first time she had been permitted to get inside for four years.

"Ye gods, but these people are happy to get rid of the invaders, who are beasts. Nothing less!   Lots of Love,   *B*UNKER."

In a letter dated November 22nd, the General tells about losing his "good old Thirty-second" and being promoted to command the Seventh Corps, and later, on November 28th, he writes:

"I occupied one of the Kaiser's houses the other night, but I couldn't bring myself to sleep in the old lobster's bed."

———————

Most of his subsequent letters have to do with the Seventh Corps, although now and then there is a touch of sadness at being away from "his boys" in the Thirty-second.

That he was overjoyed at being transferred back to the Red Arrows is well known by all General Haan's friends.

CHAPTER XVI.

Constitution of Thirty-Second Division Veteran Association.

1. The name of this Association shall be: THIRTY-SECOND DIVISION VETERAN ASSOCIATION.

2. The object of this Association shall be: To foster and perpetuate the spirit of comradeship which has been the greatest single factor in the success of the Division and to perpetuate in act and deed, by strong Americanism, the memory of our dead comrades, who by their supreme sacrifice have permitted us to return in honor.

3. The Active Members of the Association shall be: All persons of the military forces of the United States who honorably served with the 32nd Division at any time from the date of embarkation until the 8th of April, 1919, or any other persons who similarly served with the Division in any other official capacity during the time specified.

The Associate Members of this Association shall be: All persons who honorably served as members of the 32nd Division from July 15th, 1917, and who through no effort of their own were prevented from serving with the 32nd Division of the American Expeditionary Forces. The Executive Committee, hereinafter formed, is empowered to admit as Association Member, upon the personal application, any person entitled to such membership.

Honorary Members may be elected by a majority vote of the members of the Association present at a regular convention of the Association, upon the recommendation of the Executive Committee, for valuable services rendered to the Spirit of the Arrow. In addition the next of kin of all former members of the Thirty-second Division who were killed in action, or who died from other causes and whose status at the time of death was such as to warrant them memberships, may be admitted as Honorary Members under like conditions. .

4. The initial fee for Active and Associate Membership shall be ten (10) francs if paid in France and Two Dollars ($2.00)˙ if paid in the United States and will carry with it a life membership.

5. The annual convention shall rotate between the States of Wisconsin and Michigan, provided, however, either State may at any time waive its right to the convention in favor of one of the Middle West States. The first regular convention will be held in the year 1920 at Milwaukee, Wisconsin, and the second annual meeting in the year 1921 at Detroit, Michigan, at a time and place to be designated by the Executive Committee. The Executive Committee is also authorized to arrange for auxiliary Divisional Meetings in such place suitable for the members who find the regular Convention not available.

6. The term of office shall be for one year until their successors are elected and qualified.

The officers of the Association will be, a President, Senior Vice-President, Junior Vice-President, Senior Secretary, Junior Secretary, Treasurer, Chaplain, Historian and Assistant Historian. There shall also be an Executive Committee consisting of one member from each of the following organizations:

125th, 126th, 127th and 128th Infantry Regiments;
119th, 120th, 121st, 147th, 322nd, 323rd, 324th Artillery Regiments;
107th Engineers, 107th Ammunition Train, 107th Sanitary Train and 107th Supply Train;
119th, 120th, 121st Machine Gun Battalions, to be considered as a regiment and entitled to one representative. Each Machine Gun Battalion to be entitled to have its representative chosen from its members each third term.

All other units not otherwise mentioned to be entitled to one representative at large. The President, Vice-President, Secretary, Treasurer, Historian and the retiring President shall be *ex-officio* members of the Executive Committee with full power to vote at all its meetings. There will also be selected an Honorary President and Honorary Vice-Presidents, whose duties are to preside at all Memorial Meetings of the Association.

The Executive Committee shall have power to fill vacancies occurring between Conventions.

7. The Executive Committee shall have full control of all the affairs of this Association, between the times of its Conventions, and may act through duly delegated Sub-Committees selected by them. They shall make annual printed reports to the President at each Convention of their individual official activity and the collective Association activities since the last regular Convention.

8. Associate and Honorary Members shall be eligible to all the benefits of this Association but shall not hold office therein or have any voice or vote on the changes or additions to the Constitution, or of the Association By-Laws.

9. The membership fees of the Association shall be placed in a trust fund under the terms of a trust to be prepared and executed by the Finance Committee for and on behalf of the Association and a trust company designated by the Executive Committee, to the end that the income therefrom and limited amounts of the principal sum only are available for current Association expenses.

The Finance Committee shall consist of three members of the Association appointed by the Executive Committee for one, two and three years and their successors to be appointed for terms of three years each.

10. The Executive Committee shall designate a depository for the funds of the Association and they shall be paid out only upon warrants signed by the President and Secretary and countersigned by the Treasurer.

11. The Association adopts as its official name "The 32nd Division Veteran Association" with the sub-title "*Les Terribles.*" The official button and seal shall be a bronze circlet, with the official emblem, the Barred Red Arrow, imposed on two gold service chevrons and the Association directs that the Executive Committee protect all the above by copyright.

12. The Association directs that the Executive Committee be organized into a non-profit-making voluntary corporation under the Laws of the State of Wisconsin.

13. This Constitution may be amended by two-thirds vote of all the members present at a regular Convention of the Association.

A Duty

MONTHS after the tragic days of 1918 when the men whose names appear on the Thirty-Second Division's Roll of Honor gave their lives for their country on the battlefields of France, sorrowing parents, relatives and friends are still longing for details of the last days of their loved ones.

Many men who read this list of heroic names will recall incidents of the service of their dead comrades. Some, perhaps, were with them in the fatal hour of their passing. To these men is given the opportunity, and it should be considered in the light of a duty, to communicate whatever facts are in their possession to the next of kin whose names and addresses appear opposite those of the dead in the appended roll. There are many mothers and fathers who do not yet know from authentic sources of the manner in which their sons paid the supreme sacrifice. They are deeply grateful for each word from former comrades of their boys, and the Division Historians urgently request that those who have information concerning any of the Division's fatalities, write at once to the next of kin, giving the fullest accounts possible.

The casualty lists of the A. E. F. were prepared under the stress of combat, and in spite of efforts to fully correct the unavoidable errors, there are still many mistakes and much missing information. These lists can be made complete and correct only by details supplied by men who have first-hand knowledge of the facts, and these men are requested to correspond with the Secretary of the Thirty-Second Division Veteran Association to the end that our Roll of Honor may finally be made into a full and accurate record.

ROLL OF HONOR

OFFICERS

Name	Rank	Organization	Cause	Date	Address—Next of Kin
Abele, William H.	1st Lt.	Sup. Co. 324 F. A.	KIA	10/27/18	1620 Walnut St., Toledo, Ohio. Mrs. William H. Abele.
Amberlang, Lisle P.	1st Lt.	Med. Dept. 125 Inf.	KIA	8/8/18	Cascade, Wis. Mrs. Magdalene Amberlang.
Anderson, Orville L.	Captain	Co. E. 128 Inf.	KIA	8/1/18	Verdon, Manitoba, Canada. Mrs. Orville L. Anderson.
Arnold, Orville L.	Captain	Reg. Adjt. 128 Inf.	KIA	10/7/18	211 Chester St., Sparta, Wis. Mrs. Orville Arnold.
Atkins, Arthur K.	2nd Lt.	Co. C. 126 Inf.	DW	8/31/18	31 State St., Boston. c/o Frank B. Blair & Co. Mr. Astley Atkins.
Barlow, Francis A.	Captain	Co. H. 125 Inf.	KIA	10/7/18	202 Western Ave., Cheboygan, Mich. Mrs. Eva Audrey Barlow.
Beal, William John	1st Lt.	Co. L. 126 Inf.	KIA	8/29/18	101 Beirdler St., Muskegon, Mich. Mrs. William Beal.
Beaton, Lloyd Orendorff	2nd Lt.	Hq. Co. 119 F. A.	KIA	8/30/18	Baldwin, Kas. Mrs. John Beaton.
Beaudry, Frederick W.	Captain	Co. H, 126 Inf.	KIA	8/1/18	419 McDougall Ave., Detroit, Mich. Mrs. Elizabeth Beaudry.
Blomberg, Henry S.	1st Lt.	Co. D. 127 Inf.	KIA	10/4/18	2612 22nd St., Superior, Wis. Mrs. C. Blomberg.
Bostick, Ray E.	2nd Lt.	Co. C. 126 Inf.	KIA	8/1/18	Mantau, Mich. Mrs. Charles H. Bostick.
Brigham, Stephen O.	1st Lt.	Co. G. 127 Inf.	DW	8/1/18	Madison, Wis., R. F. D. 2. Mrs. J. J. Brigham.
Buck, Charles C.	2nd Lt.	119 Mg. Bn.	KIA	10/18/18	94 Prospect St., Dover, N. J. Mrs. A. G. Buck.
Burton, Edward A.	2nd Lt.	Co. D. 128 Inf.	KIA	8/2/18	Hillsboro, Wis. Mrs. Jessie L. Burton.
Canary, James H.	2nd Lt.	Co. I. 125 Inf.	KIA	7/31/18	Canary, Kas. S. C. Canary.
Champagne, John C.	2nd Lt.	Co. I. 125 Inf.	KIA	7/31/18	Elm St., Lake Charles, La. Mrs. Rena Champagne.
Chapman, John Arthur	1st Lt.	Co. C. 120 Mg. Bn.	DW	9/12/18	44 Puritan Ave., Detroit, Mich. Carlos Wintenmeyer.
Chatterton, Iden E.	1st Lt.	126 Inf.	KIA	10/6/18	1112 Wellington Ct., Ann Arbor, Mich. Mrs. Nora Chatterton.
Clarke, Bruce W.	2nd Lt.	Co. G. 127 Inf.	KIA	8/6/18	Augusta, Wis. Mrs. Frank L. Clarke.
Colvin, Delancy J.	2nd Lt.	1st Bn. 127 Inf.	KIA	10/14/18	428 West Mason St., Jackson, Mich. Harriet Colvin.
Cook, James	2nd Lt.	Co. H. 126 Inf.	KIA	7/30/18	103 Wayne St., Pontiac, Mich. Mrs. James Cook.
Cook, Richard E.	2nd Lt.	Co. H. 126 Inf.	KIA	8/4/18	204 E. 36th St., Minneapolis, Minn. Mrs. Eva R. Cook.
Cottrell, Erk M.	2nd Lt.	Co. F. 126 Inf.	KIA	10/9/18	232 E. 4th St., Greenville, Ohio. James A. Cottrell.
Cranefield, Marion C.	2nd Lt.	Co. G. 127 Inf.	KIA	7/31/18	304 N. Orchard St., Madison, Wis. Frederic Cranefield.
Crowell, Fleming M.	2nd Lt.	Co. G. 127 Inf.	KIA	10/15/18	2297 Baxter St., Los Angeles, Calif. Mrs. Daisy M. Crowell.
Daniels, Charles R.	2nd Lt.	Co. D 127 Inf.	DW	11/23/18	352 Gooding St., Lockport, N. Y. Mrs. H. E. Daniels.
Davis, Bryce E.	1st Lt.	125 Inf.	KIA	10/7/18	456 Goshin St., Salt Lake City, Utah. Mrs. Amelia Davis.
Davitt, William F.	1st Lt.	125 Inf.	KIA	11/11/18	842 Chicopee St., Willimansett, Mass. Mrs. Lawrence Davitt.
Devenny, James V.	2nd Lt.	Co. E. 126 Inf.	KIA	10/9/18	146 W. Chelton Ave., Philadelphia, Pa. Mrs. C. F. Devenny.
Dickop, Ray C.	1st Lt.	Co. L. 127 Inf.	KIA	8/4/18	West Bend, Wis. Mrs. Lena Schiller.

NAME	RANK	ORGANIZATION	CAUSE	DATE	ADDRESS - NEXT OF KIN
Dole, Sanford B.	2nd Lt.	Co. E. 128 Inf.	KIA	10/18/18	Lewiston, Idaho. Fred A. Dole.
Duff, Joseph M.	2nd Lt.	125 Inf.	KIA	10/11/18	564 Washington Ave., Carnegie, Ga. Rev. Joseph M. Duff.
Falk, Oscar	Captain	Co. F. 125 Inf.	DW	8/1/18	Menominee, Mich. Mrs. Oscar Falk.
Fenelon, Harry W.	1st Lt.	Co. L. 127 Inf.	DW	8/18/18	115 E. Frederick St., Rhinelander, Wis. Mrs. Mary Fenelon.
Feustel, William B.	2nd Lt.	Bat. B. 147 F. A.	DW	8/7/18	1070 E. Lincoln St., Portland, Ore. Mrs. Emma Feustel.
Ebert, Raphael P.	1st Lt.	Hq. Tr. 32 Div.	DD	2/19/18	Superior, Wis. Mrs. R. P. Ebert.
Fick, Everett S.	1st Lt.	Co. K. 125 Inf.	KIA	8/1/18	Winnifield, La. Mrs. Helen Fick.
Fielding, Donald M.	2nd Lt.	Co. G. 126 Inf.	DW	10/9/18	....
Frierson, Meade, Jr.	Captain	125 Inf. Att.	KIA	8/29/18	513 Broadway, Nashville, Tenn. Meade Frierson, Sr.
Gaartz, Alfred E.	Captain	Co. D. 120 Mg. Bn	KIA	8/29/18	Van Buren St., Milwaukee, Wis. Mrs. A. E. Gaartz.
Gerald, George M.	2nd Lt.	Co. D. 127 Inf.	KIA	7/31/18	2307 N. Church St., Beloit, Wis. Mrs. George N. Gerald.
Girard, John F.	Captain	Co. D. 126 Inf.	KIA	10/5/18	439 W. Washington St., Tonia, Mich. Mrs. Catherine Girard.
Godfrey, Frank C.	2nd Lt.	Co. D. 128 Inf.	KIA	8/30/18	8 Warren St., Norwalk, Conn. Mrs. B. A. Comstock.
Grassold, Randolph O.	2nd Lt.	Co. C. 127 Inf.	DW	7/21/18	Chilton, Wis. Joseph Grassold.
Hammond, Charles A.	1st Lt.	Co. L. 125 Inf.	KIA	7/31/18	785 15th St., Detroit, Mich. John J. Hammond.
Hanger, Fred L.	2nd Lt.	Co. A. 127 Inf.	KIA	10/14/18	Waupun, Wis. Mrs. Chas. Hanger.
Harding, Stacy L.	2nd Lt.	Bat. B. 120 F. A.	KIA	10/11/18	Antioch, Calif. Mrs. J. S. Harding.
Harris, Clifford O.	2nd Lt.	128 Inf.	KIA	9/1/18	95 E. 72nd St., Portland, Ore. Mrs. W. R. Harris.
Harris, George W.	2nd Lt.	Bat. A. 120 F. A.	DW	10/13/18	307 W. Cedar St., Franklin, Ky. George C. Harris.
Harrison, Little	Captain	Co. E. 119 F. A.	DW	7/15/18	215½ Dennis St., Houston, Texas. Dr. R. H. Harrison.
Hastings, Walcott B.	1st Lt.	127 Inf.	KIA	10/18/18	....
Hawkes, Milburn H.	Captain	Co. D. 125 Inf.	KIA	9/30/18	201 N. Ferry St., Ludington, Mich. Mrs. Milburn H. Hawkes.
Hefferan, Thomas E. M.	1st Lt.	Co. M. 126 Inf.	KIA	8/1/18	Ashland Block Bldg., Chicago, Ill. Mr. W. S. Hefferan.
Hill, Henry Robt.	Major	128 Inf.	KIA	10/16/18	516 Main St., Quincy, Ill. Mrs. Cecelia R. Hill.
Hoffman, Edward Aubrey	2nd Lt.	125 Inf.	DW	10/10/18	1121 Ford Bldg., Detroit, Mich. J. G. Hoffman.
Hyland, Harold W.	2nd Lt.	Co. F. 127 Inf.	DW	9/7/18	....
Johnson, Carl A.	1st Lt.	Co. M. 126 Inf.	KIA	6/23/18	356 Cherry St., Grand Rapids, Mich. Mr. A. P. Johnson.
Johnson, Henry G.	2nd Lt.	Co. C. 121 Mg. Bn.	KIA	10/4/18	Pepin, Wis. Frank Johnson.
Jones, Edwin Llewellyn	1st Lt.	Mg. Co. 128 Inf.	DW	8/3/18	Oconomowoc, Wis. Mrs. Oscar T. Jones.
Joyce, Harold H.	1st Lt.	Co. I. 128 Inf.	KIA	8/30/18	218 Power Block, Helena, Mont. George J. Joyce.
Kanter, Benjamin W.	2nd Lt.	Co. L. 127 Inf.	DW	8/21/18	....
Kearn, Lester W.	2nd Lt.	Co. K. 127 Inf.	KIA	8/31/18	551 W. 160th St., New York City. Mrs. Kearn.
Keiser, Harry Mase	1st Lt.	Att. 125 Inf.	KIA	7/31/18	4641 Lake Park Ave., Chicago, Ill. Mrs. Florence Mase Keiser.
Keller, Arthur I.	2nd Lt.	Co. I. 126 Inf.	KIA	8/1/18	250 St. Goodridge Ave., Riverdale on Hudson, N. J. Mr. Arthur T. Keller.
Kelly, Roy W.	2nd Lt.	Mg. Co. 127 Inf.	KIA	8/31/18	912 Beaser Ave., Ashland, Wis. Mrs. Otilia L. Kelly.
King, Harold J.	1st Lt.	F. & S. 126 Inf.	KIA	10/10/18	Manistee, Mich. Dr. James A. King.
Lamb, Merritt Udell.	Captain	Hq. 125 Inf.	KIA	8/29/18	Rockford, Mich. T. K. Lamb.
Learned, Charles A.	Captain	Co. A. 125 Inf.	KIA	8/5/18	446 Highland Ave., Detroit, Mich. Mrs. Charles A. Learned.
Le Baron, Paul K.	2nd Lt.	Sup. Co. 120 F. A.	DD	10/14/18	Berwyn, Ill. Mrs. Paul K. Le Baron.
Lietemeyer, Irenaeus J.	1st Lt.	Co. F. 127 Inf.	DW	8/6/18	New Iberia, La. Fred M. Lietemeyer.
Lindberg, Wendell A.	2nd Lt.	Co. H. 126 Inf.	KIA	10/18/18	....
Locke, Edward H.	2nd Lt.	128 Inf.	KIA	10/18/18	Madison, Maine. Mrs. Edward H. Locke.
McElderry, Augustus B.	2nd Lt.	Bat. C. 120 F. A.	DD	....	859 Park Ave., Baltimore, Md. Mrs. J. Jarok (Sister).

Name	Rank	Organization	Cause	Date	Address—Next of Kin
McLachlan, Ira D.	Captain	Mg. Co. 125 Inf.	DW	10/31/18	313 Spruce St., Sault Ste. Marie, Mich. Mrs. Helen McLachlan.
McGee, Archie D.	1st Lt.	127 Inf.	KIA	10/18/18	4243 Hudson Blvd., No. Bugen, N. J. Mrs. Stelle M. McGee.
Macheska, William J.	1st Lt.	Co. D. 128 Inf.	KIA	10/15/18	177 Woodruff Ave., Brooklyn, N. Y. Mrs. W. J. Macheska.
Mackay, William R.	1st Lt.	127 Inf.	DW	10/18/18	2446 10th Ave. N., Seattle, Wash. Mrs. John C. Mackay.
Maddox, Joe G.	2nd Lt.	Co. I. 125 Inf.	KIA	8/29/18	129 Ga. Ave., Baisville, Ga. Mrs. E. F. Maddox.
Malloy, Frederick Fagg	1st Lt.	Hq. Tr. 32 Div.	DD	10/18/18	Ashville, N. C. Mrs. Ella Fagg Malloy.
Mattern, Henry	2nd Lt.	Co. D. 128 Inf.	KIA	10/16/18	198 Easten Ave., New Brunswick, N. J Mrs. Mary Mattern.
Mauger, Harry B.	2nd Lt.	Co. A. 127 Inf.	KIA	10/18/18	5800 Rising Sun Av., Philadelphia, Pa. Mrs. Ida B. Mauger.
Mehl, Wm. F.	Major	1 Inf.	DD	10/22/17	1229 National Ave., Milwaukee, Wis. Dr. Hugo F. Mehl.
Morgan, William D.	2nd Lt.	Co. E. 128 Inf.	KIA	11/9/18	Tangiphahoa, La. Mr. Morgan.
Mulcahy, Richard W.	1st Lt.	Co. F. 128 Inf.	KIA	11/10/18	Jefferson St., Portage, Wis. Mr. Dan. Mulcahy.
Miller, William	1st Lt.	Amb. Co. 128 Inf.	DD	5/28/18	....
Miller, Raymond E.	2nd Lt.	Co. B. 120 Mg. Bn.	KIA	7/31/18	778 Lothrop Ave., Detroit, Mich. Mrs. C. J. Miller.
Murry, Sent W.	2nd Lt.	Co. I. 127 Inf.	DW	10/13/18	825 28th St., Newport News, Va. Mrs. Lucy W. Murray.
Nelson, Elmer Burdett	1st Lt.	Co. A. 120 Mg. Bn.	KIA	7/30/18	R. F. D. 4, Pontiac, Mich. Albert A. Nelson.
Nelson, John Bastian	2nd Lt.	Co. A. 127 Inf.	KIA	10/18/18	822 Main St., Eau Claire, Wis. Mrs. John B. Nelson.
Noble, Clarence G.	1st Lt.	Co. G. 128 Inf.	DW	8/4/18	1026 S. Webster Ave., Green Bay, Wis. Mrs. Wilhelmina B. Noble.
Oas, Otto	1st Lt.	127 Inf.	DW	1/3/19	Manitowoc, Wis. Mr. Otto Oas.
Oates, Morley S.	2nd Lt.	Bat. F. 119 F. A.	KIA	8/22/18	Detroit, Mich. W. R. Oates .
Osthaus, Robert Axford	2nd Lt.	Co. E. 126 Inf.	DW	10/15/18	330 Wheeler Ave., Scranton, Pa. Mrs. Alice Osthaus.
Perry, Ralph H.	Captain	Co. B. 128 Inf.	DW	11/22/18	Algoma, Wis. Mrs. Melvin W. Perry.
Peters, Harry B.	2nd Lt.	Co. B. 128 Inf.	KIA	10/15/18	Osceola Mills, Pa. Mrs. Ida May Peters.
Post, Dana C.	1st Lt.	125 Inf.	KIA	8/6/18	Benton Harbor, Mich. Dr. E. J. Post.
Redner, Joseph H.	1st Lt.	Hq. Co. 119 F. A.	DD	10/18/18	2547 28th St., San Francisco, Calif. Mrs. Fred P. Redner.
Regan, John M.	2nd Lt.	Co. D. 128 Inf.	KIA	8/4/18	1009 Warm Springs Av., Boise, Idaho. W. V. Regan.
Rhodes, Edward Byron	2nd Lt.	Co. E. 125 Inf.	KIA	10/10/18	701 N. J. St., Tacoma, Wash. Mrs. Edward B. Rhodes.
Rice, Bernard L.	1st Lt.	Hq. 128 Inf.	KIA	8/3/18	Sparta, Wis. Thomas P. Rice.
Rit, Maurice	Lt.	Terr. 127 Inf.	DW	10/18/18	....
Roberts, John Basil	1st Lt.	Reg. Int. Officer	DW	8/4/18	509 Edgewood Ave., Madison, Wis. Mrs. Mary Roberts.
Ross, Albert H.	2nd Lt.	Co. K. 125 Inf.	KIA	10/9/18	1627 12th Ave., S. Birmingham, Ala. Chas. W. Ross.
Rowles, William J.	Captain	Co. M. 128 Inf.	KIA	8/30/18	Davenport, Iowa. Mrs. W. T. Rowles.
Rust, William H.	1st Lt.	Co. K. 125 Inf.	DW	8/29/18	Merrill, Mich. Edward Rust.
Schwartz, Charles, Jr.	2nd Lt.	Co. D. 127 Inf.	KIA	10/18/18	1003 Currie St., Marinette, Wis. Mr. Chas. Schwartz.
Seif, Louis E.	2nd Lt.	Co. M. 127 Inf.	KIA	8/4/18	Neillsville, Wis. Mr. Fred Seif, Sr.
Settle, Paul T.	2nd Lt.	Co. A. 120 Mg. Bn.	DW	11/14/18	Unadilla, Ga. Edward G. Settle.
Sheldon, Herbert J.	2nd Lt.	F. & S. 125 Inf.	KIA	10/10/18	124 W. Bilhorn St., Lansing, Mich. Mrs. H. J. Sheldon.
Shelly, P. M.	2nd Lt.	Co. F. 125 Inf.	KIA	10/10/18	2516 Colfax Av., S. Minneapolis, Minn. Mrs. B. M. Shelly.
Shiells, Alexander E.	1st Lt.	Co. E. 107 Eng.	DD	2/17/19	240 6th Ave., Wauwatosa, Wis. Mrs. Emma Shiells.
Slade, John P.	1st Lt.	Bat. D. 121 F. A.	DD	9/17/18	1603 N. 5th St., Clay Center, Kans. Mrs. John P. Slade.
Slesinger, Albert	2nd Lt.	Co. H. 125 Inf.	KIA	8/18/18	....
Smith, Harvey F.	2nd Lt.	Co. K. 125 Inf.	KIA	10/13/18	208 Pingree Ave., Detroit, Mich. Miss R. G. Smith.
Smith, Homer R.	2nd Lt.	Co. F. 127 Inf.	KIA	8/29/18	3 West 3rd St., Fulton, N. Y. Mr. F. G. Smith.
Smith, Richard Fredrick	Captain	Co. F. 126 Inf.	KIA	8/5/18	410 Francis Court, Jackson, Mich. Catherine B. Smith.

Name	Rank	Organization	Cause	Date	Address—Next of Kin
Sperbeck, George E.	Major	147 F. A.	DW	10/11/18	Parker, S. Dakota. Mrs. George Sperbeck.
Steen, John Houston	1st Lt.	M. D. 125 Inf.	KIA	8/6/18	Vaughan, Miss. Mrs. John H. Steen.
Street, J. A.	Major	1st Bn. 128 Inf.	KIA	10/18/18	Fort Sam Houston, Texas. Mrs. John A. Street. Care Col. Alonzo Gray.
Stubbs, David	1st Lt.	Co. A. 127 Inf.	KIA	8/6/18	119 S. West 42nd St., Des Moines, Ia. Mr. V. R. Stubbs.
Sturtevant, Frank A.	2nd Lt.	Co. H. 128 Inf.	KIA	10/9/18	412 Wesley Ave., Oak Park, Ill. Mrs. Ruth K. Sturtevant.
Sugg, A. I.	2nd Lt.	121 F. A.	DD	....	....
Taylor, Douglas Arthur	2nd Lt.	Co. B. 127 Inf.	KIA	8/30/18	214 Clark St., Rhinelander, Wis. Mr. Arthur Taylor.
Taylor, Herbert Jones	1st Lt.	Co. M. 125 Inf.	DW	9/2/18	739 Jefferson Ave., Memphis, Tenn. Mrs. F. G. Taylor.
Terhune, Elmer S.	1st Lt.	Bat. B. 121 F. A.	KIA	10/8/18	670 Mt. Prospect Ave., Newark, N. J. Frank A. Terhune.
Thomas, Ottis B.	2nd Lt.	Co. A. 126 Inf.	DW	8/3/18	70 Radford St., Yonkers, N. Y. Mrs. F. R. Thomas.
Thompson, Carl	2nd Lt.	Co. E. 126 Inf.	KIA	8/31/18	Curtiss, Wis. Miss Anna Thompson.
Thompson, Edward W.	Major	F. & S. 119 F. A.	DW	10/18/18	933 Phoenix St., South Haven, Mich. Mrs. Edward W. Thompson.
Thorsen, Edwin B.	2nd Lt.	Mg. Co. 127 Inf.	DW	8/2/18	615 12th Ave. West, Ashland, Wis. Mrs. Bertha Thorsen.
Togstad, Morris	2nd Lt.	Hq. Co. 127 Inf.	KIA	11/10/18	337 W. Mifflin St., Madison, Wis. Mrs. O. C. Togstad.
Toole, Charles M.	1st Lt.	Co. B. 107 F. S.	DW	10/1/18	68 Weld Hill St., Forest Hills, Boston. Mr. John Toole.
Trier, Adolph M.	Major	C. O. Hq. 127 Inf., 2nd Bn.	KIA	7/30/18	325 Doty St., Fond du Lac, Wis. Mrs. Rose Trier.
Verney, Everett L.	2nd Lt.	127 Inf.	DW	10/19/18	406 West B. St., Marshfield, Wis. Mrs. A. F. Verney.
Vogel, Theodore K.	2nd Lt.	128 Inf.	KIA	11/10/18	169 Hillside St., Asheville, N. C. Mrs. Mary Vogel.
Wall, Lee N.	2nd Lt.	Co. M. 125 Inf.	KIA	7/31/18	2001 College Ave., St. Louis, Mo. N. Wall.
Wallber, Hilbert C.	1st Lt.	Bat. A. 120 F. A.	KIA	8/19/18	298 29th St., Milwaukee, Wis. Carl Wallber.
Ward, George A.	1st Lt.	Co. C. 107 F. S. Bn.	DD	3/26/18	....
West, Myron Chester	Captain	Hq. Co. 127 Inf.	DW	8/5/18	613 St. Lawrence Ave., Beloit, Wis. Mrs. Myron C. West.
Westnedge, Joseph B.	Colonel	126 Inf.	DD	11/29/18	R. F. D. 5, Kalamazoo, Mich. Mrs. Eva May Westnedge.
Wheeler, Tolman D.	1st Lt.	Co. G. 127 Inf.	DW	9/6/18	New York City, N. Y. H. R. Wheeler.
Wilber, Charles Raymond.	2nd Lt.	Co. B. 126 Inf.	KIA	10/3/18	Walpole, Mass. Mrs. Charles H. Wilber.

ENLISTED MEN

Name	Rank	Organization	Cause	Date	Address—Next of Kin
Abbott, Henry G.	Pvt.	Co. L. 125 Inf.	KIA	10/21/18	Vardaman, Miss. L. L. Abbott (Father).
Abe, Edward A.	Corp.	Co. F. 127 Inf.	KIA	8/4/18	187 Villard Ave., Milwaukee, Wis. August J. Abe (Father).
Abegg, Alfred	Pvt.	Co. B. 163 Inf.	DW	10/11/18	....
Abendroth, Franklin L.	Pvt.	Co. B. 127 Inf.	KIA	10/19/18	Markesan, Wis. Mr. Fred Abendroth (Father).
Abernathy, Joseph	Pvt.	Co. C. 126 Inf.	DW	10/5/18	Richards, Buffalo Co., So. Dakota. Mr. Wm. H. Abernathy.
Abrams, Glen R.	Corp.	Co. I. 125 Inf.	DW	10/11/18	1010 Essex St., Portland, Ore. Maud Daisy Beckley (Mother).
Ackley, Harry	Pvt. 1cl.	Co. I. 128 Inf.	KIA	9/1/18	166 E. 38th St., Portland, Ore. Ralph Ackley.
Adair, John	Pvt.	Mg. Co. 125 Inf.	KIA	9/1/18	Sandusky, Mich. James Adair.
Adamick, John	Pvt.	Co. M. 125 Inf.	KIA	10/20/18	....
Adams, George F.	Corp.	Co. B. 127 Inf.	KIA	10/11/18	1500 Ohio St., Oshkosh, Wis. Mrs. Nellie Adams.
Adams, Joseph	Pvt.	Co. A. 128 Inf.	KIA	8/1/18	1438 Mohawk St., Chicago, Ill. Mrs. Anna Adams (Mother).
Adamson, Bob	Pvt.	Co. B. 127 Inf.	KIA	10/11/18	Liberty, Tenn. A. C. Adamson (Father).
Agaires, Theodore	Pvt.	Co. H. 126 Inf.	KIA	10/9/18	Violet, La. Lucy Agaires.
Ahlf, Ben	Pvt.	Co. G. 125 Inf.	KIA	10/13/18	R. F. D. 4, Centralia, Ill. Claus Ahlf (Father).
Akin, Webster E.	Pvt.	Co. L. 128 Inf.	KIA	11/7/18	Lovergene, Tenn. Mr. John W. Akin (Father).
Albrecht, Herbert H.	Sgt.	Co. B. 128 Inf.	KIA	8/31/18	1410 Washington, Berlin, Wis. Mrs. Emma Albrecht.

ROLL OF HONOR

NAME	RANK	ORGANIZATION	CAUSE	DATE	ADDRESS—NEXT OF KIN
Aldereta, Leopold	Pvt.	Co. B. 128 Inf.	KIA	10/14/18	Cantillo, Texas. Bernardo Aldereta (Brother).
Alderman, Claude W.	Corp.	Co. A. 126 Inf.	KIA	7/31/18	Bronson, Mich. William Alderman (Father).
Alderman, Fredrick	Pvt.	Co. K. 127 Inf.	KIA	10/14/18	Wills, Va. Homer Alderman (Father).
Alderman, Hartzel	Sgt.	Co. K. 128 Inf.	KIA	11/7/18	Excelsior, Wis. Mrs. Florence Alderman.
Alexander, Harold J.	Pvt.	Co. E. 128 Inf.	KIA	11/10/18	4th & Clara Sts., New Orleans, La. Mary Alexander.
Alexander, John R.	Mech.	Co. G. 126 Inf.	KIA	8/27/18	....
Alexander, James	Pvt.	Co. B. 125 Inf.	KIA	9/14/18	R. F. D. 1, Lebanon, Va. John B. Alexander.
Alfano, Frank	Pvt.	Co. M. 127 Inf.	KIA	10/20/18	112 12th St., Ft. Smith, Ark. Joe Alfano (Father).
Alft, Joe	Pvt.	107 T. M. B.	ACC	7/8/18	Shawano, Wis. Mrs. John Alft (Mother).
Allen, Frank H.	Pvt. 1cl.	Co. L. 125 Inf.	KIA	7/31/18	North-Street, Mich. Mrs. Nettie Allen (Mother).
Allen, George W.	Pvt.	Co. L. 125 Inf.	KIA	7/31/18	R.F.D. 4, Washington Court House, O. Mrs. J. N. Beatty.
Allen, Leon E.	Pvt.	Co. A. 120 Mg. Bn.	KIA	8/4/18	Hartland, Mich. John Allen.
Allen, Miles D.	Corp.	Co. L. 127 Inf.	DW	10/12/18	Fair Oaks, Beloit, Wis. Mrs. J. L. Allen (Mother).
Allen, Ralph H.	Pvt.	Co. D. 126 Inf.	KIA	8/1/18	Elmdale, Mich. Mrs. Flora Allen (Mother).
Allen, Raymond	Sgt.	Mg. Co. 125 Inf.	KIA	9/2/18	Millington, Mich. Charles Allen (Father).
Allinson, Claude C.	Pvt.	Co. M. 125 Inf.	KIA	10/9/18	R. F. D. 2, Box 51, Rockville, Mo. William Allinson (Father).
Altman, John	Pvt.	Co. C. 127 Inf.	KIA	10/10/18	R. F. D. 1, White Lake, S. Dakota. Elizabeth Altman.
Ammarell, Louis E.	Corp.	Co. A. 125 Inf.	KIA	10/3/18	2028 Pitkin Ave., Brooklyn, N. Y. Emil Christian Ammarell.
Amstutz, Fred	Sgt.	Co. H. 127 Inf.	KIA	8/5/18	Monticello, Wis. Mrs. Samuel Amstutz (Mother).
Anderson, Adolph	Pvt. 1cl.	Co. M. 127 Inf.	KIA	10/13/18	Oconto, Wis. Mrs. O. Oldson (Mother).
Anderson, Albert H.	Pvt.	Co. G. 128 Inf.	KIA	9/1/18	....
Anderson, Anthony C.	Pvt.	Co. K. 126 Inf.	KIA	9/1/18	R. F. D. 3, Altok, Mich. Mr. Julius Wester (Friend).
Anderson, Arvid	Pvt.	Co. G. 127 Inf.	DW	9/5/18	....
Anderson, Charles O.	Sgt.	Co. F. 126 Inf.	KIA	10/9/18	708 Appinwald St., Elkart, Ind. Mrs. Catherine Elmer (Mother).
Anderson, Einar	Pvt.	Co. K. 126 Inf.	KIA	10/29/18	619 Broadway Av., Gd. Rapids, Mich. Mr. G. Anderson (Father).
Anderson, Fred R.	1st Sgt.	Co. L. 127 Inf.	KIA	9/2/18	1003 Keenan St., Rhinelander, Wis. Mrs. Oliver Anderson (Mother).
Anderson, George D.	Pvt.	Co. G. 128 Inf.	KIA	8/29/18	Fish Creek, Wis. A. C. Anderson.
Anderson, Gustaf H.	Pvt.	Co. D. 128 Inf.	KIA	8/3/18	512 East 44th St., Chicago, Ill. Charles Anderson (Brother).
Anderson, Harold C.	Pvt.	Hdqs. Co. 128 Inf.	DW	10/13/18	418 6th St., Crandon, Wis. Mrs. Otto Peterson.
Anderson, John M.	Pvt. 1cl.	Hdq. 110 Inf.	KIA	8/1/18	....
Anderson, Lewis	Pvt.	Co. B. 127 Inf.	DW	10/6/18	227 S. W. 13th St., Washington, D. C. Martha J. Anderson (Mother).
Anderson, Walter H.	Pvt.	Co. C. 126 Inf.	KIA	10/5/18	R. F. D. 1, Box 25, Vermillion, S. D. Ole Anderson.
Andres, Carl	Pvt. 1cl.	Co. G. 128 Inf.	DD	4/13/18	....
Andrews, Jeff	Pvt.	Co. C. 128 Inf.	KIA	10/12/18	R. 2, Millette, S. Dakota. Mr. Williard Sweeten.
Andrykowski, Victor	Pvt.	Co. G. 125 Inf.	KIA	7/31/18	....
Antczak, Louis F.	Sgt.	Co. G. 125 Inf.	KIA	8/29/18	738 Wesson Ave., Detroit, Mich. John Antczak.
Antico, Jack	Pvt.	Co. L. 128 Inf.	KIA	11/7/18	149 Columbia St., Brooklyn, N. Y. John Antico (Father).
Aravanis, Angelo	Pvt.	Co. E. 126 Inf.	KIA	8/3/18	....
Arbutz, Ledwig.	Pvt. 1cl.	Co. G. 126 Inf.	KIA	8/4/18	Lepa, Russian Poland. Andrew Arbutz (Father).
Arlt, George	Pvt. 1cl.	Co. H. 126 Inf.	KIA	10/9/18	Bird Island, Minn. Mrs. Christ Arlt.
Arlt, Louis H.	Pvt. 1cl.	Co. E. 125 Inf.	KIA	7/31/18	....
Armes, Tommie R.	Pvt.	Co. E. 125 Inf.	KIA	10/9/18	R. F. D. 4, Box 7, Keyville, Va. Robert J. Armes (Father).
Armijo, Marcus B.	Pvt.	Co. C. 125 Inf.	DW	8/5/18	....

221

Name	Rank	Organization	Cause	Date	Address—Next of Kin
Arms, James W.	Pvt.	Co. K. 128 Inf.	KIA	11/7/18	Licking, Mo. Mrs. Mary M. Arms.
Armstrong, Clyde L.	Pvt.	Co. B. 125 Inf.	KIA	10/4/18	Belleville, W. Va. Mrs. Anna Armstrong (Mother).
Armstrong, David W.	Pvt. 1cl.	Co. I. 125 Inf.	KIA	10/9/18	Centralia, Kansas. Mr. W. E. Armstrong (Father).
Armstrong, Homer A.	Pvt.	Co. D. 127 Inf.	KIA	8/5/18	Odell, Neb. John M. Armstrong (Brother).
Armstrong, John E.	Corp.	Co. F. 125 Inf.	KIA	8/5/18	....
Arnett, George	Pvt.	Bat. E. 120 F. A.	DD	....	....
Arnett, William	Pvt.	Co. A. 127 Inf.	ACC	8/15/18	612 E. 3rd St., Marshfield, Wis. John Arnett (Father).
Arnold, Charles	Pvt.	Co. M. 128 Inf.	KIA	11/10/18	R. F. D. 1, Palvel Station, Tenn. Pole Arnold (Father).
Arnold, Glenn H.	Pvt.	Hq. Co. 119 F. A.	KIA	10/3/18	Perry, Mich. Elmer N. Arnold.
Arnold, William M.	Pvt.	Hq. Co. 127 Inf.	KIA	9/3/18	27 K St., N. E., Washington, D. C. Mrs. T. E. Arnold (Aunt).
Arvig, Raymond O.	Corp.	Co. K. 125 Inf.	KIA	8/30/18	111 E. Bismark Av., Fergus Falls, Minn. Louis J. Arvig (Father).
Asch, Frank	Pvt. 1cl.	Co. F. 126 Inf.	KIA	8/5/18	....
Asmundsen, Celborn C.	Pvt.	San. Det. 121 Mg. Bn.	KIA	10/4/18	Rhinelander, Wis. Charles Asmundsen.
Astarita, Alphonsus	Pvt.	Co. C. 121 Mg. Bn.	KIA	10/4/18	197 22nd St., Brooklyn, N. Y. Ralph Astarita (Brother).
Atkinson, Wilmer	Corp.	Co. M. 126 Inf.	KIA	10/10/18	Empire, Mich. Helen Atkinson (Wife).
Augustine, Arthur	Corp.	Co. F. 127 Inf.	KIA	9/2/18	742 27th St., Milwaukee, Wis. Viola Augustine (Wife).
Ausems, Thomas	Pvt.	Co. E. 128 Inf.	KIA	10/21/18	Chasm, Holland. Cornelius Ausems.
Austin, Edwin	Pvt.	Co. F. 127 Inf.	KIA	7/31/18	Shawano, Wis. George Austin (Father).
Austin, Leslie B.	Pvt.	Co. M. 125 Inf.	KIA	7/31/18	....
Ayatte, Napallen	Pvt.	Co. G. 125 Inf.	KIA	7/31/18	....
Babin, Bennett J.	Pvt.	Co. G. 125 Inf.	KIA	8/29/18	Donaldsonville, La. Louise Babin (Mother).
Baca, Frederick	Pvt.	Co. K. 125 Inf.	KIA	10/13/18	1112 National Ave., Elas Vegas, New Mexico. Mrs. Lucis Garcia Baca.
Back, Joseph E.	Pvt.	Co. M. 125 Inf.	KIA	10/9/18	Appleton, Minn. Mary Mattson (Mother).
Bacon, John	Corp.	Co. L. 125 Inf.	KIA	10/3/18	80 W. Division St., Fond du Lac, Wis. Geraldine Bacon (Aunt).
Badke, Arthur	Sgt.	Co. B. 128 Inf.	KIA	10/10/18	Picketts, Wis. Rudolph Badke.
Baggett, Monroe J.	Pvt.	Co. F. 127 Inf.	DD	10/18/18	Garford, Texas. Mr. S. Baggett (Father).
Baggio, Michael	Pvt.	Co. I. 128 Inf.	KIA	10/12/18	217 Ave. B, New York City, N. Y. Antonio Baggio.
Bailey, Vurt	Pvt.	Co. E. 125 Inf.	KIA	7/31/18	....
Bailey, Elder	Sgt.	Co. I. 126 Inf.	KIA	10/9/18	Big Rapids, Mich. Alex Bailey.
Baily, John M.	Pvt. 1cl.	Co. M. 125 Inf.	KIA	7/31/18	....
Baird, George	Pvt.	Co. B. 125 Inf.	KIA	10/10/18	Montezuma, Ind. Mrs. Emma Baird (Mother).
Baird, John J.	Corp.	Co. K. 126 Inf.	DD	2/12/18	Ginseng, Ky. Mrs. Laura Baird (Mother).
Baker, Joseph J.	Pvt.	Co. C. 126 Inf.	KIA	10/5/18	R. F. D. 2, Station B, Locus Co., Toledo, Ohio. Walter J. Baker (Father).
Baker, Lee E.	Pvt. 1cl.	Co. L. 128 Inf.	KIA	11/7/18	Copperdale, Ohio. Isabell Dickinson Baker.
Baker, Peter	Pvt. 1cl.	Co. K. 126 Inf.	KIA	8/29/18	832 Crosby St., Gd. Rapids, Mich. Henry Baker.
Baker, William	Pvt.	Co. L. 125 Inf.	KIA	7/31/18	Lake View St., Menominee, Mich. Mrs. Levina Baker (Mother).
Baldridge, Ambrose H.	Pvt.	Co. F. 127 Inf.	KIA	10/7/18	Stonington, Ill. Mrs. Abbie Baldridge (Mother).
Baldwin, William	Not on Div. records.		KIA	10/5/18	....
Ball, Elihu F.	Sgt.	Co. F. 126 Inf.	DW	10/9/18	Kalkaska, Mich. Cornelius D. Hall.
Ballard, William T.	Pvt.	107 T. M. B.	ACC	8/1/18	White Lake, Wis. Mrs. Dora Ballard (Mother).
Ballman, Charles	Pvt.	Co. B. 121 Mg. Bn.	KIA	10/11/18	R. F. D. 1, McClive, Ohio. Helena Domer (Sister).
Bamm, Harry W.	Sgt.	Co. D. 125 Inf.	KIA	10/11/18	Dundee, Mich. F. Bamm (Father).

1. FIRST LIEUTENANT CHARLES M. TOOLE, Company B, 107th Field Signal Battalion. Died October 1st, 1918, of wounds received in action during the Meuse-Argonne Offensive.
2. CAPTAIN LITTLE HARRISON, Battery E, 119th Field Artillery. Died July 15th, 1918, of wounds received in Alsace.
3. FIRST LIEUTENANT ELMER BURDETT NELSON, Company A, 120th Machine Gun Battalion. Killed in action July 30th, 1918, during the Aisne-Marne Offensive.
4. SECOND LIEUTENANT EDWARD BYRON RHODES, Company E, 125th Infantry. Killed in action October 10th, 1918, during the Meuse-Argonne Offensive.
5. MAJOR EDWARD W. THOMPSON, 119th Field Artillery. Died October 18th, 1918, of wounds received in action during the Meuse-Argonne Offensive.
6. SECOND LIEUTENANT RAYMOND E. MILLER, Company B, 120th Machine Gun Battalion. Killed in action July 31st, 1918, during the Aisne-Marne Offensive.
7. SECOND LIEUTENANT MORLEY S. OATES, Battery F, 119th Field Artillery. Killed in action August 22nd, 1918, during the Aisne-Marne Offensive.
8. SECOND LIEUTENANT HENRY G. JOHNSON, Company C, 121st Machine Gun Battalion. Killed in action October 4th, 1918, during the Meuse-Argonne Offensive.
9. SECOND LIEUTENANT EDWARD AUBREY HOFFMAN, 125th Infantry. Died of wounds October 10th, 1918.

NAME	RANK	ORGANIZATION	CAUSE	DATE	ADDRESS—NEXT OF KIN
Banholzer, Albert A.	Pvt.	Co. M. 128 Inf.	KIA	11/10/18	Sewanee, Tenn. John Banholzer.
Banks, Charles E.	Corp.	Co. B. 125 Inf.	KIA	8/29/18	207 Emanuel St., Mobile, Ala. James A. Banks.
Bannister, Robert	Pvt.	Co. L. 125 Inf.	KIA	7/31/18	Capac, Mich. Mrs. Minnie Harvey (Mother).
Bannworth, Clarence J	Pvt.	Co. E. 126 Inf.	KIA	8/30/18	R. F. D. 2, Box 64, Belleview, Ohio. Mrs. Barbara Bannworth (Mother).
Baranouski, Gustave	Pvt.	Co. G. 126 Inf.	KIA	8/28/18	222 Perent St., Royal Oak, Mich. Peter Baranouski (Brother).
Barclay, Ernest	Corp.	Hq. C. 126 Inf.	KIA	8/29/18	108 Haifley St., Gd. Rapids, Mich. A. E. Barclay.
Barg, Joseph	Pvt.	Co. H. 128 Inf.	DW	9/2/18	....
Barkley, Millard O.	Pvt.	Co. L. 128 Inf.	KIA	11/7/18	Carrolton, Ark. Geoanna Barkley (Mother).
Barlow, Wilfred W.	Corp.	Co. B. 127 Inf.	KIA	2/14/18	....
Barnaby, Horace	Corp.	Co. K. 126 Inf.	KIA	10/14/18	1844 Horton Ave. S. E., Gd. Rapids. Horace F. Barnaby.
Barnard, Minor	Pvt. 1cl.	Co. B. 127 Inf.	KIA	8/4/18	Lohriville, Wis. Mrs. J. Murray (Sister).
Barnes, Harvey A.	Pvt.	Co. F. 127 Inf.	KIA	7/31/18	224 Brady St., Milwaukee, Wis. Mrs. A. L. Barnes (Mother).
Barnett, George W.	Pvt.	Co. L. 126 Inf.	KIA	10/9/18	Colmer, Ky. Mr. Henry Barnett (Father).
Barnett, James H.	Pvt.	Co. C. 128 Inf.	KIA	10/17/18	Allison, Kansas. Mr. J. M. Barnett.
Barr, Oscar	Pvt.	Co. M. 126 Inf.	KIA	10/10/18	Hanson, Ky. Mistern Jone Barr.
Barrett, Henry	Pvt.	Co. M. 128 Inf.	KIA	10/12/18	104 Sweet St., Gr. Rapids, Mich. Mrs. George B. Hall.
Bartels, Herman J.	Pvt. 1cl.	Co. D. 126 Inf.	KIA	8/30/18	R. F. D. 11, Holland, Mich. John Bartels.
Bartelt, Ernest	Pvt.	Co. H. 127 Inf.	KIA	10/13/18	Tripoli, Iowa. August Bartelt (Father).
Bartlett, Ellsworth H.	Bugler	Co. L. 125 Inf.	KIA	7/31/18	264 N. Johnson St., Pontiac, Mich. Mrs. Marguert Bartlett (Wife).
Bartlette, Orville	Pvt. 1cl.	Co. E. 127 Inf.	KIA	10/5/18	Appelson, Ark. A. G. Bartlett (Father).
Bartolino, Maris	Pvt. 1cl.	Co. G. 126 Inf.	KIA	8/28/18	Grocevien Prov., Trapani, Italy. Mr. Vito Bartolino (Father).
Bartusiak, Andrew E.	Corp.	Co. A. 128 Inf.	KIA	11/10/18	Elyria, Neb. Peter Bartusiak (Father).
Basel, Otto A.	Pvt.	Co. E. 127 Inf.	KIA	8/1/18	1257 19th St., Milwaukee, Wis. William Basel (Father).
Basford, Roy M.	Pvt.	Co. D. 128 Inf.	KIA	10/13/18	Ree, No. Dakota. William O. Basford (Father).
Bashore, Henry F.	Pvt. 1cl.	Co. A. 126 Inf.	KIA	7/31/18	818 4th St., Marine City, Mich. Morris Bashore.
Basom, Ransford B.	Pvt. 1cl.	Co. D. 126 Inf.	KIA	8/29/18	Sparta, Mich. Edward A. Basom.
Bass, John F.	Sgt.	Co. C. 126 Inf.	KIA	10/9/18	2142 Portage St., Kalamazoo, Mich. Mrs. Lucy Bass.
Basta, Guiseppe	Pvt.	Co. B. 121 Mg. Bn.	KIA	11/11/18	Auffizzio, Italy. Mrs. Clarina Basta (Mother).
Bastian, Anton	Pvt. 1cl.	Co. B. 121 Mg. Bn.	KIA	9/1/18	Wayne, Neb. C. C. Bastian (Father).
Bates, Clarence F.	Pvt.	Bat. C. 120 F. A.	DD	....	R. F. D. 1, Eau Claire, Wis. Mrs. I. A. Bates (Mother).
Batista, Sbodio	Pvt.	Bat. F. 147 F. A.	DD	9/30/18	Angera per Jaho Maggiore, Caprona, Italy. Miss Rose Shodio.
Battiste, Isidor	Pvt.	Co. F. 127 Inf.	KIA	9/1/18	501 Broadway, San Francisco, Calif. Joe Battiste (Brother).
Bausam, Oran R.	Pvt.	Co. E. 125 Inf.	KIA	10/9/18	North Jackson St., Magnolia, Ark. Besse Bausam (Wife).
Bauer, George	Pvt. 1cl.	Co. H. 126 Inf.	KIA	8/28/18	Racine, Wis. John Bauer (Father).
Baughey, Ward B.	Corp.	Co. B. 126 Inf.	KIA	8/28/18	149 S. Winter St., Adrian, Mich. William H. Baughey.
Bauley, Lafayette P.	Pvt. 1cl.	Mg. Co. 125 Inf.	KIA	7/31/18	Newport, Mich. Louis Bauley.
Bayhem, Ovedo O.	Pvt.	Co. K. 128 Inf.	KIA	10/8/18	Montpelier, Iowa. Aymantha Bayhem.
Bayons, Peter	Sgt.	Co. C. 127 Inf.	KIA	7/31/18	522 Spensor Court, Sheboygan, Wis. Mrs. C. Bayons (Mother).
Bazzarre, Roy	Pvt.	Co. K. 128 Inf.	KIA	10/6/18	Lawmoor, Va. Thomas M. Bazzarre.
Beam, William C.	Pvt.	Co. I. 128 Inf.	KIA	10/12/18	Limestone, Ark. Mrs. Laura Ogden.
Beard Tommy L.	Pvt.	Co. B. 128 Inf.	KIA	10/9/18	Talley Station, Tenn. Mrs. Ida Beard.
Beardsley, Floyd C.	Pvt. 1cl.	Co. D. 126 Inf.	KIA	10/31/18	1905 E. Main St., Jackson, Mich. W. J. Beardsley (Father).
Beavers, Maurice	Pvt.	Co. C. 125 Inf.	KIA	10/22/18	Bristow, Va. Magie Beavers (Mother).

Name	Rank	Organization	Cause	Date	Address—Next of Kin
Bebout, Charles A.	Pvt.	Co. C. 126 Inf.	ACC	7/30/18	West Finley, Pa. John L. Finley (Uncle).
Beck, William E.	Pvt. 1cl.	Co. G. 126 Inf.	KIA	8/4/18	Lansing, Iowa. Joseph B. Beck (Father).
Becker, Clarence	Pvt. 1cl.	Co. B. 128 Inf.	KIA	8/31/18	R. F. D. 2, Williamstown, Mo. George Becker.
Becker, Gustave G.	Pvt. 1cl.	Co. A. 126 Inf.	KIA	10/17/18	242 William St. S. W., Gd. Rapids, Mich. Mrs. Fred Becker.
Bedford, Walter	Pvt.	Co. H. 127 Inf.	DW	about 8/1/18	423 N 8th St., Manitowoc, Wis. Bedford Arthur (Father).
Beebe, Harold V.	Sgt.	Co. G. 127 Inf.	KIA	8/4/18	314 Railroad St., Woodstock Ill. Mrs. E. Reynolds (Mother).
Beechley, Artyur	Pvt.	Co. E. 125 Inf.	KIA	7/31/18	....
Beer, William F.	Pvt.	Co. E. 125 Inf.	KIA	10/9/18	90 3rd St., N., Minneapolis, Minn. Dodson-Fisher-Brockman Co., N. D. Beer (Uncle).
Besaw, Leonard	Corp.	Co. F. 127 Inf.	KIA	8/4/18	Shawano, Wis. Alex Besaw (Father).
Beldon, Harry O.	Pvt.	Co. B. 127 Inf.	KIA	10/19/18	Rush City, Minn. Mrs. Mattie Belden (Mother).
Bell, Harry T.	Pvt.	Mg. Co. 126 Inf.	KIA	about 10/11/18	Copperville, Va. Thomas B. Bell.
Bell, Newton	Corp.	Co. M. 126 Inf.	KIA	10/10/18	Muses Mills, Ky. Mrs. Rebecca Bell.
Bell, Pascal P.	Pvt.	Co. I. 125 Inf.	KIA	10/9/18	R. F. D. 1, Bedford, Ky. Mrs. P. P. Bell.
Bellis, Clell	Pvt.	Co. I. 127 Inf.	KIA	10/12/18	Baker, Mont. Fred Bellis (Father).
Beloungea, William A.	Sgt.	Co. M. 125 Inf.	KIA	10/8/18	Could City, Mich. Mrs. Frank Sly (Sister).
Benedict, Frank, Jr.	Corp.	Co. L. 125 Inf.	KIA	8/2/18	St. Clair, Mich. Mrs. Frank Benedict (Mother).
Bennett, Clyde J.	Pvt. 1cl.	Co. A. 128 Inf.	KIA	about 9/6/18	R. F. D. 3, Reedsburg, Wis. D. J. Bennett (Father).
Bennett, Earl C.	Corp.	Bat. D. 147 F. A.	KIA	8/13/18	Lester, Iowa. W. L. Bennett (Father).
Bennett, Jasper	Pvt.	Co. I. 126 Inf.	DW	10/11/18	R. F. D. 4, Waynesburg, Ky. J. D. Bennett (Father).
Bennetts, Harry	Pvt. 1cl.	Co. E. 125 Inf.	KIA	8/7/18	8 Duke St., St. Anstell, Cornwall, Eng. W. Bennetts.
Benoit, Steven	Pvt.	Co. I. 127 Inf.	KIA	9/1/18	2207 Thomas St., Marinette, Wis. Felix Menor (Friend).
Benson, Edward W.	Corp.	Co. M. 127 Inf.	KIA	8/6/18	6215 Aplin St., Chicago, Ill. Mrs. Elizabeth Benson.
Beranek, Joseph B.	Pvt.	Md. Dept. 128 Inf.	KIA	11/6/18	1303 Caladonia St., La Crosse, Wis. Mrs. Barbra Beranek.
Bereal, Anthony C.	Pvt.	Co. M. 125 Inf.	KIA	7/31/18	....
Berg, Alex.	Pvt.	Co. B. 128 Inf.	DD	3/13/18	....
Bergann, Frich A.	Sgt.	Co. I. 128 Inf.	KIA	10/9/18	746 Center St., Lansing, Mich. Wm. Bergann (Father).
Berge, Williard	Pvt.	Co. B. 127 Inf.	KIA	10/6/18	Cambridge, Wis. Mrs. Wm. Berge (Mother).
Bergmann, Fred W.	Pvt.	Co. D. 120 Mg. Bn	DW	10/6/18	310 N. 8th St., Watertown, Wis. Mrs. Fred Bergmann.
Bergquist, Rudolph W	Pvt.	Co. C. 127 Inf.	KIA	8/3/18	1010 7th St., Rockford, Ill. Mrs. Hilma Bergquist (Mother).
Berkompas, Olius	Bugler	Co. I. 125 Inf.	KIA	10/14/18	Rudyard, Mich. F. A. Berkompas (Father).
Berry, Floyd E.	Pvt. 1cl.	Co. F. 126 Inf.	KIA	8/2/18	106 Dryo Alley, Jackson, Mich. Mrs. Muntley Greg (Mother).
Bertram, William	Pvt.	Co. H. 127 Inf.	DW	8/27/18	....
Bertz, Joseph	Pvt.	Co. G. 127 Inf.	KIA	8/3/18	136 E 115th St., Chicago, Ill. Lena Bertz (Mother).
Best, Everett	Pvt.	Co. I. 128 Inf.	KIA	10/20/18	Hennessey, Okla. Mrs. Hannah Best (Mother).
Beuthin, Clarence	Pvt.	Med. Det. 125 Inf.	KIA	8/6/18	419 S. 13th St., Saginaw, Mich. Mrs. Lena Beuthin (Mother).
Bevier, James J.	Pvt.	Co. D. 128 Inf.	KIA	10/13/18	4430 Blaisdale Av., Minneapolis, Minn. Mrs. Hanna Bevier.
Bezio, Joseph	Pvt. 1cl.	Co. I. 127 Inf.	KIA	10/14/18	1007 Main St., Marinette, Wis. Edward Bezio (Father).
Biavaschi, Martin	Pvt.	Co. G. 127 Inf.	KIA	10/4/18	Sodria, North Italy. Barney Biavaschi (Brother).
Bicker, George C.	Pvt.	Co. C. 128 Inf.	KIA	8/1/18	Washington, Mo. Mrs. Mary Bicker (Mother).
Bierschbach, William Tony	Corp.	Co. E. 125 Inf.	KIA	10/9/18	R. F. D. 1, Mt. Pleasant, Mich. Sam Bierschbach (Uncle).
Bigelow, Gordon	Pvt. 1cl.	F. H. Co. 128 Inf. 107 San. Tr.	KIA	10/19/18	R. F. D. 2, Box 131, Anaheim, Calif. Mrs. Orilla Bigelow.

Name	Rank	Organization	Cause	Date	Address—Next of Kin
Bilets, Peter	Pvt.	Co. A. 121 Mg. Bn.	KIA	8/6/18	Krevlin Volyhsk, Russia. Mrs. Feodonia Bilets (Wife).
Bills, Claude W.	Pvt.	Co. B. 120 Mg. Bn.	KIA	7/31/18	Mills, Neb. Mrs. Emilia Irolson (Mother).
Rishell, Alfred	Corp.	Co. H. 127 Inf.	ACC	6/14/18	Darlington, Wis. Polete Bishell (Father).
Bissonnette, Charles J.	Corp.	Co. L. 127 Inf.	KIA	11/9/18	Rhinelander, Wis. George Bissonnette (Brother).
Bissonnette, Harold F	Corp.	Bat. C. 120 F. A.	DD	....	Charles City, Iowa. Wm. Bissonnette.
Bjerken, Helmer L.	Pvt.	Co. K. 125 Inf.	KIA	8/28/18	Germantown, Minn. Lars B. Bjerken (Father).
Bjorbeck, Lars	Pvt.	Co. G. 128 Inf.	KIA	10/5/18	Clear Brook, Minn. Mrs. Ole Bjorbeck.
Bjordal, John H.	Pvt.	Co. G. 128 Inf.	KIA	10/6/18	Hendrun, Minn. Mrs. J. N. Bjordal.
Black, Charles M.	Corp.	Co. L. 126 Inf.	DW	8/31/18	R. F. D. 1, Everett, Wash. Mrs. Ida Black (Mother).
Black, Morris	Pvt.	Co. H. 126 Inf.	KIA	8/28/18	518 S. Robinson St., Baltimore, Md. Mrs. Fannie Peltz (Sister).
Black, Thomas J.	Pvt.	Bat. I. 119 F. A.	KIA	9/29/18	195 Midland Av., Highland Park, Mich. Mrs. S. J. Houghton (Sister).
Blackmar, Maurice R.	Pvt.	Co. D. 125 Inf.	KIA	10/1/18	Santa Fe, Calif. Mrs. Mary I. Wheeler (Mother).
Blackwood, Bertin E.	Sgt.	Co. B. 121 Mg. Bn.	KIA	10/6/18	Tomah, Wis. Mrs. B. E. Blackwood (Wife).
Bladyka, James	Pvt.	Co. A. 128 Inf.	DW	8/30/18	864 Chene St., Detroit, Mich. Casmer Bladyka.
Blair, Charley	Pvt.	Co. E. 125 Inf.	KIA	10/18/18 about	2011 E. 4th St., Chattanooga, Tenn. Winnie Blair (Sister).
Blake, John P.	Pvt. 1cl.	Co. A. 128 Inf.	KIA	9/1/18 about	Boscobel, Wis. Mrs. Della Blake.
Blakeslee, Frank J.	Pvt.	Co. B. 128 Inf.	KIA	10/13/18	Conifer, Colo. Mrs. H. S. Blakeslee.
Blanford, Robert	Pvt.	Co. A. 128 Inf.	KIA	11/11/18	West Louisville, Ky. Mrs. Victorine Blanford (Mother).
Blankertz, Walter T.	Sgt.	Co. C. 120 Mg. Bn.	KIA	8/1/18	Dearborn, Mich. Mrs. Carrie Blankertz.
Blaschka, Frank A.	Pvt.	Co. L. 127 Inf.	DW	10/15/18	6 Lake St., Rhinelander, Wis. Mrs. Rose Blaschka (Mother).
Blase, Edward H.	Pvt.	Co. D. 125 Inf.	KIA	7/31/18	R. F. D. 4, Mexico, Mo. Mrs. August H. Blase.
Blevins, Willie	Pvt.	Co. A. 128 Inf.	KIA	11/11/18	Incline, Ky. George W. Blevins (Father).
Blixt, Gustave F.	Pvt.	Co. A. 126 Inf.	KIA	10/16/18	1921 Warren Ave. Mrs. Anna Nyberg (Mother).
Block, Frank A.	Pvt. 1cl.	Co. F. 127 Inf.	KIA	8/1/18	1381 30th St., Milwaukee, Wis. Otto Block (Father).
Blockside, John E.	Pvt.	Co. G. 127 Inf.	KIA	9/2/18	37 Atlantic Ave., Swampscot, Mass. Harry Blockside (Father).
Bloedorn, Arno	Corp.	Co. H. 127 Inf.	KIA	10/7/18	Brillion, Wis. Fred Bloedorn (Father).
Blumenthal, Alabel	Pvt.	Med. Det. 128 Inf.	KIA	8/3/18	6130 Evans Ave., Chicago, Ill. Mrs. Lena L. Blumenthal.
Bodell, Lloyd	Corp.	Co. I. 125 Inf.	DW	8/6/18	....
Bodin, August	Pvt. 1cl.	Co. B. 107 M. P.	KIA	8/31/18	Washburn, Wis. Mrs. Elizabeth Bodin (Mother).
Bodstuebner, Frank A	Pvt. 1cl.	Co. K. 125 Inf.	KIA	7/31/18	59 West St., Rockville, Conn. Oscar Bodstuebner (Father).
Boerner, Edward	Mech.	Hq. Co. 128 Inf.	KIA	10/17/18	Antigo, Wis. Mrs. Elizabeth Boerner.
Boog, Homer H.	Pvt.	Co. L. 128 Inf.	KIA	10/7/18	R. F. D. 1, Holly Springs, Ga. William A. Keeter.
Bohanon, Jesse	Pvt.	Co. I. 127 Inf.	KIA	10/21/18	Central City, Ky. Mrs. Perl B. Bohanon (Wife).
Bolcom, Frederick	Pvt.	Co. E. 125 Inf.	KIA	7/31/18	....
Bolin, Eugene H.	Pvt.	Co. D. 126 Inf.	KIA	10/4/18	Cannelton, Ind. Willis J. Bolin (Father).
Bohacz, Joe W.	Corp.	Co. A. 126 Inf.	KIA	8/2/18	Walker St., Bronson, Mich. Stanley Bonacz.
Bonue, Frank W.	Pvt. 1cl	Co. D. 127 Inf.	KIA	8/2/18	Mayville, Wis. Ferdinand Bonau (Father).
Bond, James	Pvt.	Co. F. 126 Inf.	KIA	7/31/18	....
Boneburg, George	Corp.	Co. K. 126 Inf.	KIA	10/16/18	Hudsonville, Mich. J. Boneburg.
Bonnevie, Christian	Pvt.	Co. A. 121 Mg. Bn	KIA	10/10/18	193 Menahan St., Brooklyn, N. Y. Mrs. Gertrude Bonnevie (Mother).
Boone, Charles E.	Pvt.	Co. D. 127 Inf.	KIA	10/14/18	428 S. Washington Av., Etowah, Tenn. Mrs. James T. Boone (Mother).
Boraback, Charles H.	Pvt. 1cl.	Bat. A. 119 F. A.	KIA	8/12/18	Bancroft, Mich. Mrs. Elizabeth Boraback (Mother).
Boraschi, Gelindo	Pvt.	Co. H. 125 Inf.	KIA	7/31/18	Palanzane Parana, Italy. Alexandro Barasche.

ROLL OF HONOR

Name	Rank	Organization	Cause	Date	Address—Next of Kin
Borle, Omer	Sgt.	Co. D. 126 Inf.	KIA	10/5/18	R. F. D. 4, Mount Pleasant, Mich. Throphile Borle (Father).
Borondo, Phillip R.	Pvt.	Co. D. 127 Inf.	KIA	10/12/18	King, Calif., Lucy Borondo (Mother).
Borst, James R.	Pvt. 1cl.	Co. I. 126 Inf.	KIA	10/9/18	147 Mechanic St., Big Rapids, Mich. J. H. Borst.
Bosnett, Alfred	Corp.	Co. E. 125 Inf.	KIA	7/31/18	....
Boswell, Giles D.	Pvt. 1cl.	Co. H. 126 Inf.	KIA	8/28/18	Chatham, Va. Mrs. Dave Boswell (Mother).
Bouder, Samuel	Pvt.	Co. K. 125 Inf.	KIA	10/9/18	R. F. D. 2, Powell, Ohio. Dave B. Bouder (Father).
Boursaw, Isaac V.	Corp.	Co. D. 126 Inf.	DW	6/23/18	....
Bovin, Peter	Corp.	Co. L. 125 Inf.	KIA	7/31/18	511 Bellvue St., Menominee, Mich. Mrs. A. Bovin (Mother).
Bovyn, Camiel	Pvt.	Co. H. 126 Inf.	KIA	10/9/18	Box 15, Marshall, Minn. Mrs. Phil Burse.
Boyer, Carl M.	Pvt.	Co. I. 127 Inf.	KIA	10/21/18	Box 12, Franklin, Ill. Mrs. Hettie E. Boyer.
Bowman, Alex J.	Pvt.	Co. A. 147 F. A.	DW	10/15/18	R. F. D. 1, Haywood, Calif. Kate Bowman (Mother).
Boyd, Harley	Pvt.	Co. E. 125 Inf.	KIA	10/17/18	R. F. D. 2, McMinnville, Tenn. Miss Eliza Boyd (Sister).
Boyer, Frank	Mus. 3cl.	Hd. Co. 127 Inf.	DW	10/14/18	Fifield, Wis. James Boyer (Father).
Boyett, Earl W.	Pvt.	Co. E. 128 Inf.	KIA	11/10/18	Sallis, Miss. Joe Boyett.
Boykin, Robert B.	Pvt.	Co. I. 126 Inf.	KIA	10/6/18	Mist, Ark. G. A. Boykin.
Brabazon, Vernon	Pvt.	Co. B. 127 Inf.	KIA	8/1/18	159 Harrison St., Oshkosh, Wis. Mrs. Brabazon (Mother).
Brackin, Gib.	Pvt.	Co. M. 126 Inf.	KIA	10/10/18	Bevear, Ky. Mrs. Sallie L. Brackin.
Bradburry, Henry E.	Pvt.	Co. M. 128 Inf.	KIA	8/30/18	....
Bradbury, Lester E.	Pvt.	Co. H. 128 Inf.	DW	8/4/18	....
Braden, John G.	Pvt.	Co. L. 126 Inf.	KIA	10/9/18	Rickreall, Oregon. James Braden (Father).
Bradley, Clarence	Corp.	Co. G. 127 Inf	DW	8/7/18	....
Bradley, Frank S.	Pvt.	Co. G. 128 Inf.	KIA	8/29/18	Red Bluff, Calif. James H. Bradley.
Bradley, Gaylord A.	Mus. 3cl.	Hdq. Co. 128 Inf.	DW	11/11/18	Mauston, Wis. E. W. Bradley.
Bradley, John H.	Cook	Bat. E. 147 F. A.	KIA	8/14/18	Barnes, N. Y. James Bradley, Jr. (Brother).
Bradley, Thomas J.	Pvt.	Co. B. 120 Mg. Bn.	KIA	6/16/18	308 Commonwealth Av., Boston, Mass. Miss Mary E. Bradley (Sister).
Bradshaw, Benjamin	Cook	Co. H. 128 Inf.	DW	10/5/18	Erskine, Minn. Mrs. B. J. Bradshaw.
Brady, Emory	Pvt.	Co. H. 125 Inf.	KIA	7/31/18	Unionville, Mich. William H. Brady.
Brady, Loren J.	Pvt.	Med. Det. 125 Inf.	KIA	8/6/18	R. F. D. 5, Marlin, Ont., Canada. Mrs. James Brady (Mother).
Bragvatne, Ole A. J.	Pvt.	Co. C. 126 Inf.	KIA	10/5/18	R. F. D. 2, Box 46, Urberg, S. Dak. Markus B. Johnson.
Branchini, Alfred	Pvt.	Co. L. 125 Inf.	KIA	7/31/18	Box 654, Iron River, Mich. Willma Branchini (Sister).
Branch, Clifford J.	Pvt. 1cl.	Co. I. 128 Inf.	DW	9/4/18	R. F. D. 2, Tekonisha, Mich. Mrs. William Slighley.
Brandt, Herman A.	Pvt. 1cl.	Co. L. 126 Inf.	KIA	10/6/18	Box 138, White Cloud, Mich. Edward Brandt.
Branigan, Frank E.	Pvt.	Co. L. 126 Inf.	KIA	10/9/18	16 Spencer Court, Brooklyn, N. Y. Mrs. Adam Branigan.
Bray, Earl L.	Pvt.	Co. C. 125 Inf.	KIA	10/7/18	Velma, Nebraska. Mr. S. E. Bray (Father).
Brazean, Joseph	Pvt.	Co. H. 125 Inf.	KIA	10/12/18	206 Julian St., Providence, R. I. Charles Brazeau (Father).
Brebout, Charles A.	Pvt.	Co. C. 126 Inf.	KIA	7/30/18	West Finley, Pa. John L. Finley (Uncle).
Brehl, John A.	Pvt. 1cl.	308 Btry., Tr. Art.	KIA	10/23/18	439 S. 5th St., Columbus, Ohio. Mrs. Theresa Brehl (Mother).
Breit, Joseph M.	Pvt. 1cl.	Co. M. 125 Inf.	KIA	7/31/18	....
Bremaiyer, William	Pvt.	Co. M. 126 Inf.	KIA	10/10/18	Fort Recovery, Ohio. Michael Bremaiyer.
Breningsthull, George	Pvt. 1cl.	Co. M. 128 Inf.	KIA	11/8/18	Milan, Mich. Will Greene (Uncle).
Brittenham, Floyd E.	Pvt.	Co. F. 127 Inf.	KIA	10/15/18	Brady Island, Neb. L. S. Brittenham (Father).
Brisendine, Ottie D.	Pvt.	Co. M. 128 Inf.	KIA	10/6/18	R. F. D. 1, Hunt, W. Va. Mary C. Brisendine.
Brewer, George	Pvt.	Co. G. 128 Inf.	KIA	10/18/18	Wilhurst, Ky. Taylor Brewer (Father).

Name	Rank	Organization	Cause	Date	Address—Next of Kin
Brewer, James W.	Pvt.	Co. I. 125 Inf.	KIA	7/31/18	....
Brewer, Jasper C.	Pvt.	Co. H. 128 Inf.	KIA	11/10/18	R. F. D. 3, Burnsville, Miss. Miss Pearl Brewer.
Briggs, Oscar T.	Corp.	Co. C. 126 Inf.	KIA	10/26/18	R. F. D. 2, Allegan, Mich. Mrs. Josephine Briggs.
Brigham, Albert E.	Pvt.	Hdq. Co. 128 Inf.	KIA	10/7/18	222 N. Bassett St., Madison, Wis. Mrs. A. E. Brigham.
Bright, Lewis A.	Pvt.	Co. I. 128 Inf.	KIA	9/1/18	Red Cloud, Neb. A. H. Bright (Father).
Brill, Clifford W.	Pvt.	Co. F. 126 Inf.	KIA	10/9/18	3439 Jay St., Avondale, Cincinnati, O. Mr. Daniel Brill (Father).
Brodie, John M.	Pvt. 1cl.	Co. C. 125 Inf.	KIA	10/22/18	Gaylord, Mich. John M. Brodie (Father).
Bronsted, Henry E.	Pvt. 1cl.	Co. A. 119 F. A.	KIA	8/31/18	Tomahawk, Wis. J. N. Bronsted.
Brontsena, Peter	Pvt.	Co. L. 128 Inf.	DS	9/16/18	75 Orchard St., Muskegon, Mich. Jennie Brontsena.
Brooks, Beverly F.	Pvt.	Co. G. 126 Inf.	KIA	10/26/18	Logan, Va. Mr. Tom Brooks (Father).
Brooks, Charles	Corp.	Co. I. 126 Inf.	DW	8/30/18	Cheboygan, Mich. James Brooks.
Brooks, Gale S.	Corp.	Co. E. 128 Inf.	DW	8/31/18	167 Nelson St., Battle Creek, Mich. Mrs. Ella Marie Brooks.
Brooks, Lloyd W.	Pvt.	Co. D. 127 Inf.	DW	10/9/18	Philip, S. Dak. Robert E. Brooks (Father).
Brougher, Edgar C.	Pvt.	Bat. D. 147 F. A.	DW	10/29/18	P. O. Box 11, Cokeville, Pa. Mrs. Elizabeth Brougher.
Brower, LaFay	Pvt.	Co. C. 127 Inf.	KIA	10/8/18	Ashton, Idaho. Mrs. Sarah Brower (Mother).
Brown, Albert	Pvt. 1cl.	Hdq. Co. 127 Inf.	KIA	8/30/18	....
Brown, Charles E.	Pvt.	Bat. D. 322 F. A.	KIA	11/4/18	....
Brown, Clarence E.	Pvt.	Co. A. 126 Inf.	DD	4/13/18	....
Brown, David A.	Pvt.	Co. E. 127 Inf.	KIA	10/18/18	R. F. D. 1, Union, Miss. R. A. Brown (Father).
Brown, James A. E.	Pvt.	Bat. A. 120 F. A.	ACC	....	132 Smith St., No. Attleboro, Mass. Mrs. Samuel Brown (Mother).
Brown, Lloyd E.	Pvt.	Co. M. 128 Inf.	KIA	10/13/18	R. F. D. 6, Fairmont, West Va.
Brown, Orley C.	Pvt. 1cl.	Co. B. 107 F. S. Bn.	KIA	10/10/18	825 Newhall St., Milwaukee, Wis. Mrs. Mary L. Brown (Mother).
Brown, Orville	Pvt.	Co. K. 125 Inf.	KIA	10/10/18	R. F. D. 7, Decatur, Ill. Thomas Brown (Father).
Brown, Solomon H.	Pvt.	Co. M. 128 Inf.	KIA	11/8/18	R. F. D. 2, Orlando, W. Va. Homer Brown (Father).
Brown, Walter B.	Pvt.	Co. K. 125 Inf.	KIA	10/10/18	Brainard, Minn. Mr. Andrew Brown (Father).
Brown, Wilbert C.	Pvt. 1cl.	Co. K. 125 Inf.	KIA	10/9/18	Ripling, Mich. Mrs. Anna Houghlin (Mother).
Browne, Joseph	Corp.	Co. C. 127 Inf.	DW	9/1/18	1705 S. 10th St., Sheboygan, Wis. Chas. Browne (Father).
Browning, Frank R.	Corp.	147 F. A.	DW	10/18/18	....
Browning, Lewis A.	Pvt. 1cl.	Co. A. 128 Inf.	KIA	10/20/18	Siloam Springs, Ark. Jacob Browning.
Brayles, William C.	Pvt.	Co. I. 125 Inf.	DW	11/18/18	....
Bruno, Peter	Pvt.	Co. E. 128 Inf.	KIA	10/21/18	Udena, Italy. Mr. Antonio Bruno.
Bruce, Daniel H.	Pvt.	Co. F. 128 Inf.	KIA	11/10/18	Lake Providence, La. James Wilburn.
Bruce, Lloyd G.	Pvt.	Co. G. 127 Inf.	KIA	9/1/18	Big Sandy, Mont. Mrs. F. C. Bruce (Wife).
Bruhn, Arent A.	Pvt.	Co. D. 127 Inf.	KIA	10/19/18	Enumclaw, Washington. Otto Bruhn (Father).
Brunner, Mike	Pvt.	Co. F. 127 Inf.	DW	8/8/18	Manitowoc, Wis. Frank Brunner (Father).
Bryan, Guy M.	Corp.	Co. I. 128 Inf.	KIA	9/1/18	908 Princeton Ave., Spokane, Wash. Mrs. Josephine Bryan.
Bryan, Leroy	Pvt.	Co. G. 126 Inf.	DW	10/5/18	Royalton, Pa. Anna Bryan (Mother).
Bryant, Clyff A.	Pvt. 1cl.	Co. H. 127 Inf.	KIA	8/5/18	142 Cape St., Oshkosh, Wis. Mrs. Mabel Bryant (Wife).
Brzozwski, Jacob	Mech.	Co. L. 125 Inf.	KIA	7/31/18	931 Kirby St., Detroit, Mich. Frank Brzozwski (Father).
Brzozwski, Walter	Pvt.	Co. H. 125 Inf.	KIA	7/31/18	122 Darford St., Hamtramck, Mich. Jove Brzozwski (Brother).
Buck, John H.	Mech.	Sup. Co. 119 F. A.	KIA	9/1/18	Holt, Mich. John Buck (Father).
Budd, Bert	Pvt.	Co. F. 125 Inf.	KIA	8/29/18	R. F. D. 1, Gustavus, Ohio. Mrs. Senna Budd (Mother).

1. SECOND LIEUTENANT DOUGLAS ARTHUR TAYLOR, Company B, 127th Infantry. Killed in action August 30th, 1918, during the Oise-Aisne Offensive.
2. FIRST LIEUTENANT RAPHAEL P. EBERT, Headquarters Troop, 32nd Division. Died at Coblenz, Germany, February 19th, 1919.
3. SECOND LIEUTENANT EDWIN B. THORSON, Machine Gun Company, 127th Infantry. Died of wounds August 2nd, 1918.
4. FIRST LIEUTENANT JOHN P. SLADE, Battery D, 121st Field Artillery. Died in France, September 17th, 1918.
5. CAPTAIN WILLIAM J. ROWLES, Company M, 128th Infantry. Killed in action August 30th, 1918, during Oise-Aisne Offensive.
6. FIRST LIEUTENANT HILBERT C. WALLBER, Battery C, 120th Field Artillery. Killed in action August 19th, 1918, during Aisne-Marne Offensive.
7. SECOND LIEUTENANT CHARLES C. BUCK, 119th Machine Gun Battalion. Killed in action October 18th, 1918, during the Meuse-Argonne Offensive.
8. FIRST LIEUTENANT FREDERICK FAGO MALLOY, Headquarters Troop, 32nd Division. Died in France October 18th, 1918, during Meuse-Argonne Offensive.
9. FIRST LIEUTENANT WILLIAM H. ABELE, Supply Company, 324th Field Artillery. Killed in action October 27th, 1918, during the Meuse-Argonne Offensive.

NAME	RANK	ORGANIZATION	CAUSE	DATE	ADDRESS—NEXT OF KIN
Buettner, Victor	Pvt.	Co. I. 125 Inf.	KIA	10/9/18	Waterloo, Monroe Co., Ill. Mr. Joseph Buettner.
Bumgarner, William A	Corp.	Co. M. 128 Inf.	KIA	8/30/18	611 N. Santa Fe Ave., Tulsa, Okla. R. Bumgarner.
Burbey, Paul	Pvt. 1cl.	Co. M. 127 Inf.	DW	8/4/18	Lena, Wis. Mrs. Paul Burbey (Mother).
Burch, Jesse C.	Pvt.	Co. K. 125 Inf.	KIA	7/31/18	R. F. D. 2, Coleman, Mich. Mrs. Julia Burch (Mother).
Burch, John D.	Pvt.	Mg. Co. 125 Inf.	DW	8/31/18	....
Burch, Verland	Pvt.	Co. H. 126 Inf.	KIA	10/9/18	Perry, Ark. H. W. Burch.
Burdick, Earl	Pvt. 1cl.	Co. D. 126 Inf.	KIA	7/31/18	159 W. River St., Otsego, Mich. Mrs. Velma Burdick.
Burk, James	Pvt.	Co. C. 126 Inf.	KIA	8/1/18	Crescent, Ohio. Mrs. Addie Burk (Mother).
Burke, Abie L.	Pvt.	Co. M. 128 Inf.	KIA	10/13/18	Montana, W. Va. Isabelle Burke.
Burke, John	Mech.	Co. L. 128 Inf.	KIA	11/6/18	Route 7, Box 59, Sparta, Wis. Daniel Burke (Father).
Burke, John	Pvt.	Co. K. 128 Inf.	KIA	11/9/18	648 June St., Cincinnati, Ohio. Mrs. Mary Burke.
Burkett, Alexander	Pvt.	Co. B. 127 Inf.	KIA	10/11/18	Glenn Lyon, Pa. Frank Burkett (Father).
Burkett, Dallis	Pvt.	Co. K. 125 Inf.	KIA	10/10/18	R. F. D. 4, Inka, Ill. Mrs. Marsh Burkett (Mother).
Burkland, Fred A.	Pvt. 1cl.	Co. C. 120 Mg. Bn.	KIA	8/29/18	R. F. D. 3, Cumberland, Wis. Gust Burkland.
Burns, Frank C.	Corp.	Co. E. 128 Inf.	DW	8/30/18	Candon, Ore. James D. Burns.
Burns, Robert E.	Sgt.	Co. H. 127 Inf.	DW	10/9/18	Main St., Cold Spring, N. Y. Mrs. M. V. Rogee.
Burton, Everett	Pvt.	Co. K. 127 Inf.	DW	10/24/18	R. F. D. 1, Waggoner, Ill. Walter W. Burton (Father).
Burwill, William C.	Pvt.	Co. I. 128 Inf.	KIA	11/9/18	Shenandoah, Va. Christina Burwill.
Bush, Maurice J.	Pvt. 1cl.	Co. B. 126 Inf.	KIA	10/5/18	111 Maple Ave., Adrian, Mich. Joseph Bush.
Buskirk, Ceal	Pvt.	Co. K. 128 Inf.	KIA	11/10/18	R. 4, Stanton, Mich. Mr. William Buskirk.
Butler, Frank T.	Pvt. 1cl.	Co. C. 120 Mg. Bn	KIA	8/1/18	237 Bishop St., Waterbury, Conn. Mrs. J. C. Butler.
Butler, John	Corp.	Co. C. 120 Mg. Bn	DW	8/28/18	1414 8th St., Superior, Wis. Mrs. John J. Butler.
Butler, Lester F.	Corp.	Co. L. 127 Inf.	KIA	8/4/18	Shapiers, Wis. Mrs. Mary Butler.
Butterfield George R.	Corp.	Hdq. Co. 126 Inf.	KIA	10/2/18	17 W. 9th St., Holland, Mich. Mrs. Stella Clark.
Bychinski, Nick J.	Pvt. 1cl.	Co. G. 128 Inf.	KIA	8/4/18	Wausaw, Wis. Tofili Bychinski (Mother).
Byers, John S.	Pvt.	Co. G. 126 Inf.	KIA	10/22/18	Bumpass, Louisa Co., Va. Mrs. A. C. Richardson (Sister).
Cabai, Louis	Pvt.	Co. D. 128 Inf.	KIA	8/4/18	....
Cairns, William B.	Sgt.	Co. G. 127 Inf.	KIA	7/30/18	2010 Madison St., Madison, Wis. William B. Cairns (Father).
Caldie, Thomas D.	Pvt. 1cl.	Co. A. 121 Mg. Bn.	KIA	10/7/18	Stiles, Wis. Mrs. Thomas D. Caldie (Mother).
Call, Ernest J.	Pvt.	Co. H. 127 Inf.	KIA	9/3/18	728 Lake Ave., Manchester, N. H. Silas W. Call (Father).
Caloni, Victor	Pvt.	Co. G. 126 Inf.	KIA	10/28/18	1251 Penn Ave., Pitt, Pa. John Culoni.
Cameron, Fred L.	Pvt. 1cl.	Bat. A. 120 F. A.	KIA	8/14/18	Bessemer, Ala. C. B. Cameron.
Camors, Arnold W.	Pvt.	Co. K. 125 Inf.	KIA	10/10/18	1527 Melpomene St., New Orleans, La. Mrs. Josephine Camors.
Campbell, Cecil E.	Pvt.	Bat. A. 119 F. A.	ACC	7/4/18	2097 Hamilton Blvd., Lansing, Mich. Mrs. O. G. Campbell (Mother).
Campbell, Ernest	Pvt.	Co. D. 126 Inf.	KIA	8/2/18	Monroe, Va. Mrs. Rachael A. Campbell.
Campbell, Fred E.	Pvt.	Co. H. 125 Inf.	KIA	10/7/18	222 S. 2nd St., Onaway, Mich. Mrs. Mary Campbell.
Campbell, John H.	Pvt. 1cl.	Co. I. 128 Inf.	KIA	10/16/18	510 Hamlin St., Jackson, Mich. Henry H. Campbell.
Campbell, Robert H.	Pvt.	Co. I. 126 Inf.	KIA	10/5/18	R. F. D. 1, Wichita, Kans. Mrs. Sue Campbell.
Campbell, William	Pvt.	Co. E. 125 Inf.	KIA	7/31/18	....
Canavan, Roy	Pvt. 1cl.	Co. C. 126 Inf.	KIA	8/1/18	Vicksburg, Mich. Mrs. Anna Canavan.
Cantanszei, Pometo	Pvt.	Co. I. 126 Inf.	DW	8/30/18	....
Canuteson, Otto	Pvt.	Co. M. 126 Inf.	DW	10/19/18	Sterling, Mich. C. Canuteson.
Cappelleti, Amedeo	Pvt.	Co. C. 126 Inf.	DW	8/30/18	Norma Room, Italy. Mrs. Orsolo Camandra (Mother).

Name	Rank	Organization	Cause	Date	Address—Next of Kin
Caradine, John G.	Corp.	Co. H. 127 Inf.	DW	8/12/18	Monroe, Wis. H. N. B. Caradine (Father).
Carboneau, Arthur L.	Pvt. 1cl.	Hdq. Co. 125 Inf.	KIA	10/10/18	East Lake, Mich. James Carboneau (Father).
Card, Glenn H.	Pvt. 1cl.	Bat. C. 120 F. A.	DW	10/29/18	639 Woodlawn, Owosso, Mich. Mrs. Mayme Card.
Carignan, Charles F.	Pvt.	Co. E. 126 Inf.	KIA	8/29/18	Avondale, Mont. Joseph Carignan.
Carlisle, Norman	Pvt. 1cl.	Co. K. 125 Inf.	KIA	10/9/18	Elkton, Ohio. William Carlisle (Father). .
Carlson, Carl	Pvt.	Co. E. 128 Inf.	KIA	10/6/18	Barrett, Minn. Emil Carlson.
Carnehan, George T.	Pvt.	Co. H. 126 Inf.	KIA	10/9/18	Snells P. O., Spottsylvania, Va. Mrs. Eva Brown.
Carps, Joseph	Pvt.	Co. B. 125 Inf.	KIA	10/4/18	Carnegie, Pa. Lawrence Carps (Brother).
Carr, Barnell	Pvt.	Co. K. 126 Inf.	KIA	8/28/18	Albany, Ky. T. R. Carr.
Carretto, Joe	Pvt.	Co. A. 362 Inf.	DW	10/2/18	....
Carrico, Edd.	Pvt.	Co. A. 128 Inf.	KIA	8/1/18	Davis City, Iowa. Mrs. Emily Carrico (Mother).
Carroll, Frank L.	Sgt.	Co. G. 127 Inf.	DW	10/8/18	Lynch, Neb. R. F. Carroll (Father).
Carter, Allen B.	Pvt.	Co. H. 126 Inf.	KIA	10/9/18	615 Kate Ave., Hattiesburg, Miss. Mrs. M. J. Carter.
Carter, George.	Pvt.	Hq. Co. 126 Inf.	KIA	10/4/18	St. Joseph, Mich. John Lysaght (Friend).
Carvounis, James J.	Pvt.	Co. M. 125 Inf.	KIA	10/11/18	Souvilleas, Phiotidos, Greece. John D. Carvounis (Father)
Case, Fred T.	Pvt. 1cl.	Co. G. 128 Inf.	KIA	10/4/18 about	Tomahawk, Wis. P. A. Case.
Casford, Earl	Pvt.	Co. D. 120 Mg. Bu	KIA	8/30/18	237 Division St., Oshkosh; Wis. Miss Millie Casford.
Casper, Orvel N.	Pvt.	Med. Dept. 120 F. A	DR	....	605 28th St., Milwaukee, Wis. Joseph H. Casper (Father).
Cassens, Herman	Pvt.	Co. F. 128 Inf.	KIA	about 8/4/18	....
Cason, William L.	Pvt.	Co. F. 125 Inf.	KIA	10/9/18	Atlanta, Ark. Albert C. Cason (Father).
Catilini, Bambino	Pvt.	Co. E. 127 Inf.	KIA	7/31/18	Crockett, Calif. Angelo Catilini (Brother).
Catlin, Samuel L.	Corp.	Co. B. 121 Mg. Bn	KIA	10/3/18	Kingsburg, Calif. James H. Catlin (Brother).
Catlow, Clarence E.	Pvt.	Hq. Co. 127 Inf.	KIA	10/16/18	Barrington, Ill. Mrs. John E. Catlow (Mother).
Caton, Guy L.	Pvt.	Co. F. 125 Inf.	DW	13/12/18	R. F. D. 1, Goshen, Ind. Mrs. Mary Caton (Mother).
Caulkins, Clifford M	Pvt.	Hq. Co. 127 Inf.	KIA	10/16/18 about	New Auburn, Wis. Calvin Caulkins (Grandfather).
Cayo, Edward J.	Sgt.	Co. G. 128 Inf.	KIA	10/17/18	416 Steward Ave., Wausau, Wis. Elsie Helen Cayo.
Calmer, Alexandria.	Pvt.	Co. D. 128 Inf.	KIA	9/1/18	4104 E 7th St., Cleveland, Ohio. Stanley Calmer.
Cescato, Vittorio	Pvt.	Co. F. 127 Inf.	DW	10/13/18	Latauche, Alaska. Angelo Cescato (Brother).
Chamberlain, Harry A	Pvt.	Hq. Co. 128 Inf.	DW	10/7/18	Mauston, Wis. Roy Chamberlain.
Champagne, Wilfred J	Pvt.	Co. H. 127 Inf.	KIA	10/4/18	53 Waterville St., Waterbury, Conn. Alfred J. Champagne (Father).
Champion, Horace R.	Sgt.	Co. D. 127 Inf.	KIA	10/10/18	7 Vauxhall St., St. Heliers, Jersey, Eng. Mrs. Lillian Dale (Sister).
Chaney, Walter T.	Pvt.	Mg. Co. 125 Inf.	KIA	10/9/18	R. F. D. 4, Horse Cave, Ky. Mrs. W. E. Chaney.
Chapman, George W.	Corp.	Co. L. 127 Inf.	KIA	8/4/18	Edgar, Wis. Louis Chapman (Father).
Chaplain, Louis H.	Pvt.	Co. F. 128 Inf.	KIA	11/8/18	2107 Art. St., New Orleans, La. Mrs. Frank Chaplain (Mother).
Chapman, Leslie K.	Mech.	Co. D. 126 Inf.	KIA	9/1/18	18 Orchard St., Auburn, N. Y. Mrs. A. H. Chapman.
Chapman, Wilbur R.	Sgt.	Co. E. 126 Inf.	KIA	8/28/18	Mesa, Arizona. Mrs. A. R. Chapman.
Chatfield, Wallace	Pvt. 1cl.	Co. G. 128 Inf.	KIA	10/6/18	....
Cherry, Joseph T.	Pvt.	Co. M. 125 Inf.	KIA	10/11/18	Saratoga, Texas. Mrs. Olmar Crow (Sister).
Chipchase, Roy	Corp.	Co. C. 125 Inf.	KIA	9/30/18	455 17th St., Detroit, Mich. Mrs. Clara Chipchase.
Choate, Hazael S.	Sgt.	Co. G. 126 Inf.	KIA	8/28/18	Cement City, Mexico. Mrs. W. H. Choate (Mother).
Cherney, Jack	Pvt.	Co. A. 125 Inf.	DW	8/29/18	Podolskoy, Huberni, Russia. Mike Cherney (Brother).
Christanson, Toward	Corp.	Co. M. 125 Inf.	DW	9/3/18	Soo Junction, Mich. Ed. Christanson (Father).
Christenson, Christ W	Pvt.	Co. G. 127 Inf.	KIA	8/4/18	R. F. D. 1, Box 82½, Gillett, Wis. Martin Christenson (Father).

NAME	RANK	ORGANIZATION	CAUSE	DATE	ADDRESS—NEXT OF KIN
Christensen, Jacob	Pvt. .	Co. C. 126 Inf.	KIA	10/11/18	R. F. D. 2, Hurley, So. Dakota. Miss Anna Christensen.
Christianson, Charles	Pvt.	Co. K. 125 Inf.	KIA	8/31/18	Hamilton, Texas. Mr. John Christianson (Father).
Christie, Maynard L.	Pvt. 1cl.	Co. L. 128 Inf.	KIA	9/1/18	2 Park Ave., Helena, Mont. Mrs. Agnes Christie.
Ciniglio, Andrew	Pvt.	Co. H. 127 Inf.	KIA	8/30/18	21 Frederick St., Grays Inn Road, London, England. Andrew Ciniglio (Father).
Cirwyski, Pete	Pvt.	Hq. Co. 126 Inf.	DW	10/6/18	46 Indiana Ave., Gd. Rapids, Mich. Izydor Cirwyski (Uncle).
Clancy, Dan B.	Pvt.	Co. H. 127 Inf.	KIA	7/31/18 about	2210 Harvard Ave., Butte, Mont. John Clancy (Father).
Clark, Budd W.	Pvt.	Co. M. 128 Inf.	KIA	9/1/18	R. F. D. 2, Blanchard, Mich. W. E. Clark.
Clark, Otis F.	Pvt. 1cl.	Co. A. 128 Inf.	KIA	11/10/18	Wonewoc, Wis. Mrs. Zetta F. Clark.
Clark, Roy F.	Pvt.	Co. F. 127 Inf.	DD	10/27/18	Moorefield, Nebr. C. G. Clark (Father).
Clarke, James H.	Corp.	Co. M. 128 Inf.	KIA	11/8/18	R. F. D. 1, Proctor, W. Va. David C. Clarke (Father).
Clarkson, William	Pvt. 1cl.	Bat. E. 308 Tren. M	DD	1/13/19	South Euclid, Ohio. Alice Clarkson (Mother).
Clegg, John T.	Pvt.	Co. F. 127 Inf.	KIA	10/10/18	Dubois, Idaho. Mrs. Walter Clegg.
Cleightman, Paul	Pvt.	Co. M. 128 Inf.	KIA	8/6/18	Albion, Ill. Mrs. Minnie Cleightman.
Clemens, Ralph B.	Sgt.	Bat. A. 322 F. A.	KIA	11/11/18	1625 Wyoming St., Dayton Ohio. D. D. Clemens (Father).
Cline, David E.	Corp.	Co. L. 125 Inf.	KIA	8/31/18	2337 Cherry St., Pt. Huron, Mich. Leonard Cline (Father).
Clinefelter, Clyde C.	Sgt.	Co. A. 126 Inf.	KIA	7/31/18	111 Elm St., Coldwater, Mich. Mrs. Addie Clinefelter (Mother).
Clinefelter, Robert O.	Pvt. 1cl.	Co. A. 126 Inf.	KIA	8/4/18	....
Clszek, Joseph F.	Pvt. 1cl.	Co. F. 128 Inf.	DD	8/14/18	....
Coates, Archie F.	Corp.	Co. A. 121 Mg. Bn.	KIA	10/10/18	404 Hatten Ave., Rice Lake, Wis. Mrs. Geneva Coates (Mother).
Cochren, Floyd B.	Pvt.	Bat. B. 147 F. A.	KIA	8/5/18	15 Central Ave., Batavia, N. Y. Mrs. Floyd B. Cochren.
Cody, Claude T.	Corp.	Co. H. 126 Inf.	DW	8/30/18	.... Mrs. Florence E. Cody (Mother).
Cody, Henry E.	Pvt.	Co. B. 125 Inf.	KIA	8/4/18	Billings, Mont. Mrs. Agnes Valenzula (Mother).
Coffee, Robert L.	Pvt.	Co. M. 128 Inf.	KIA	11/10/18	Chester, W. Va. Frank Coffee.
Coffin, Hiram W.	Pvt.	Co. D. 125 Inf.	KIA	8/29/18	Steuben Ave., Herkimer, N. Y. Mrs. Charles Bluett (Sister).
Cofran, Edward	Pvt.	Co. G. 127 Inf.	KIA	10/14/18	Silver Springs, Maryland. Miss Alice Leitch.
Cohen, Louis	Pvt.	Co. A. 121 Mg. Bn.	KIA	8/5/18	63 2nd Ave., New York. Mrs. Anna Cohen (Mother).
Cohen, Phillip	Pvt.	Co. M. 125 Inf.	KIA	10/11/18	19 Henry St., New York City, N. Y. Sam Ldowski (Friend).
Colbert, Donald C.	Pvt.	Co. C. 126 Inf.	KIA	8/1/18	Neoga, Ill. Mrs. Laura Cross (Godmother).
Cole, Elmer	Corp.	Co. K. 125 Inf.	KIA	8/30/18	Adrian, Mich. Miss Alice Cole (Sister).
Cole, Glenn	Reg. Sgt Mjr	Hq. 128 Inf.	KIA	10/7/18	317 Roosevelt St., Beloit, Wis. Mrs. Ben Cole.
Cole, James M.	Pvt.	Co. L. 128 Inf.	KIA	10/6/18	Marks, Miss. J. M. Stafford.
Coleman, Aron	Pvt.	Co. I. 128 Inf.	KIA	10/11/18	Adamstown, Pa. John Coleman (Father).
Colenso, Herbert H.	Sgt.	Co. G. 125 Inf.	KIA	10/7/18	Lock Box 403, Houghton, Mich. Capt. Edwin Colenso (Father).
Collins, Claude	Pvt. 1cl.	Co. C. 128 Inf.	KIA	8/7/18	R. F. D. 2, Fenwick, Mich. Ren Collins.
Collins, Edward	Pvt.	Mg. Co. 126 Inf.	KIA	8/29/18	760 11th Ave., New York City, N. Y. Kate Collins.
Collins, Edward A.	Sgt.	Co. L. 125 Inf.	KIA	7/31/18	1207 Division St., Pt. Huron, Mich. Mrs. Augusta M. Collins (Wife).
Collins, Herbert B.	Sgt.	Co. F. 125 Inf.	DW	10/9/18	222 Crapo St., Alpena, Mich. Bruce Collins (Father).
Collins, Lawrence R.	Corp.	Co. H. 126 Inf.	KIA	8/4/18	364 Vicksburg Ave., Detroit, Mich. Mr. Roy W. Collins (Father).
Collins, William N.	Pvt.	Co. F. 127 Inf.	KIA	10/7/18	Moonshine Hill, Humble, Texas. Mrs. Myrtle Dunn (Sister).
Combs, Sherman	Pvt. 1cl.	Co. F. 107 Engrs.	DW	11/24/18	.... Mrs. Lanna Combs (Wife).
Compana, Thomas	Pvt.	Co. M. 125 Inf.	DW	10/10/18	....
Comiska, Charles F.	Pvt. 1cl.	Co. L. 126 Inf.	KIA	8/28/18	R. F. D. 2, Alpena, Mich. Mrs. Anna Comiska.
Compton, John R.	Corp.	Co. K. 126 Inf.	KIA	8/28/18	2398 Clyde Park Ave., Gd. Rapids, Mich. John N. Compton, Sr.

Name	Rank	Organization	Cause	Date	Address—Next of Kin
Conley, Earl J.	Pvt. 1cl.	Bat. A. 120 F. A.	KIA	8/6/18	Apollonia, Wis. Peter Conley.
Conley, John P.	Pvt.	Co. F. 126 Inf.	KIA	10/9/18	Levi, West Va. Mr. James Lewis Conley.
Conley, Leonard	Pvt.	Co. C. 128 Inf.	KIA	10/17/18	4211 S. 20th St., Omaha, Neb. Mr. Viret E. Conley.
Conlin, Edward	Pvt.	Co. H. 125 Inf.	KIA	10/14/18	....
Conroy, George C.	Pvt.	Co. E. 127 Inf.	DW	8/3/18	Clinton, Wis. Mrs. Alice Ritsman (Sister).
Conti, Ernest F.	Pvt. 1cl.	Co. E. 125 Inf.	DW	10/9/18 about	Grottollela, Province Avellino, Italy. Mary Machia Conti (Mother).
Cook, George	Pvt.	Co. F. 127 Inf.	KIA	10/18/18	Frankfort, Ky. Mrs. Nettie Cook (Mother).
Cook, Lewis C.	Sgt.	Co. L. 128 Inf.	KIA	10/18/18	North Kansas City, Mo. Mr. Lewis L. Cook.
Colley, Jess B.	Pvt. 1cl.	Co. E. 126 Inf.	KIA	8/1/18	Brighton, Mich. Mrs. Francis Colley.
Cooper, Abraham	Pvt.	Co. C. 127 Inf.	KIA	8/3/18	....
Cooper, Clare	Pvt. 1cl.	Co. A. 128 Inf.	KIA	8/1/18	R. F. D. 5, Birch Run, Mich. Manford Cooper (Father).
Cooper, Jacob	Corp.	Co. L. 128 Inf.	KIA	11/7/18	Ferrysburg, Mich. Mrs. H. Cooper (Mother).
Cooper, Walter	Pvt.	Co. G. 126 Inf.	KIA	8/3/18	1816 3rd St., Superior, Wis. Joe Cooper.
Cooper, Willie B.	Pvt. 1cl.	Co. K. 126 Inf.	KIA	8/28/18	Cooper, Ky. Minnie Cooper.
Cooperider, Luke	Pvt.	Mg. Co. 125 Inf.	KIA	7/31/18	R. F. D. 1, Siloam Springs, Ark. E. Cooperider.
Cornal, Earl E.	Wag.	Hdq. Co. 126 Inf.	DW	10/10/18	2010 St. Charles St., Gd. Rapids, Mich. Mrs. E. M. Cornal (Mother).
Cornice, Joseph	Pvt. 1cl.	308 Bat. Tr. Art.	KIA	10/23/18	506 Rhodes Ave., Akron, Ohio. Mary Cornice (Mother)
Coryell, Stanley	Pvt.	Co. D. 128 Inf.	KIA	8/2/18	Browntown, Wis. John Coryell (Brother).
Cossette, Edward L.	Corp.	Mg. Co. 127 Inf.	DW	7/3/18	Box 11, Pence, Wis. Prosper Cossette.
Costa, Joe	Pvt.	Co. B. 127 Inf.	KIA	10/19/18	314 21st St., Windber, Penn. Mrs. Armello Conom (Sister).
Counter, Kenneth E.	Pvt.	Co. I. 127 Inf.	DW	5/27/18	....
Corwell, Charles L.	Pvt.	Co. K. 127 Inf.	KIA	10/14/18	R. 1, Danville, Ark. Frank Corwell (Father).
Coutu, Joseph R.	Pvt.	Co. G. 125 Inf.	KIA	8/29/18	298 Park Place, Woonsocket, R. I. Champ Coutu (Father).
Covert, Richard	Mess Sgt.	Co. K. 126 Inf.	KIA	10/14/18	540 Grand Ave., Grand Rapids, Mich. R. L. Covert.
Cowen, Earl	Pvt.	Co. C. 126 Inf.	KIA	10/4/18	Burford, N. Dak. Mr. Robert M. Cowen (Father).
Cowley, Joseph R.	Pvt.	Co. F. 126 Inf.	KIA	8/2/18	107 Van Dorn St., Jackson, Mich. Mrs. Emma Cowley (Mother).
Cox, Aubrey	Pvt.	Co. A. 128 Inf.	DW	8/5/18	Greenwood, Wis. Sidney Cox (Father).
Cox, Homer M.	Pvt.	Co. K. 128 Inf.	KIA	10/7/18	....
Cox, John W.	Pvt.	Co. G, 6 Inf.	DW	10/15/18	....
Craidge, Robert E.	Corp.	Co. I. 125 Inf.	KIA	7/31/18 about	611 Polk St., Bay City, Mich. Mrs. Mary Craidge.
Craig, Robert	Pvt.	Co. M. 126 Inf.	KIA	8/5/18	Centralia, Wash. Mrs. Robert Craig (Mother).
Crain, Albert	Pvt.	Bat. C. 120 F. A.	DD	....	Elmwood, Wis. Mrs. Della Crain (Mother).
Crane, Lester	Pvt. 1cl.	Co. M. 127 Inf.	KIA	7/1/18	....
Crawford, Henry B.	Pvt.	Co. H. 126 Inf.	KIA	10/9/18	Fairmont City, Pa. Mrs. Ella Crawford.
Crawford, Henry J.	Pvt.	Co. C. 128 Inf.	KIA	10/17/18	Alpena, Mich. Mrs. John Crawford.
Crawford, Walter	Pvt.	Co. H. 128 Inf.	KIA	10/5/18	Corydon, Ky. Mr. A. J. Crawford (Father).
Creasey, Walter H.	Pvt.	Co. A. 127 Inf.	KIA	7/31/18	Custer, Washington. William Creasey.
Creech, Phelix	Pvt.	Co. F. 127 Inf.	KIA	10/4/18	.... Mrs. Henry J. Creech (Mother).
Cripps, William H.	Pvt. 1cl.	Co. H. 128 Inf.	KIA	11/10/18	R. F. D. 3, Liberty, Tenn. Mrs. Nola Caroline Cripps (Wife).
Crist, Jessie	Corp.	Co. G. 126 Inf.	KIA	10/5/18	410 Michigan Ave., Detroit, Mich. John Allen (Friend).
Crocos, Angel	Pvt.	Co. D. 121 Mg. Bn.	KIA	6/13/18	200 W. Johnston St., Fond du Lac, Wis. John Paper (Cousin).
Croff, Clarence	Pvt.	Co. D. 126 Inf.	KIA	10/20/18	Osceola, Ark. Sallie Groff.
Croninger, Dewey C.	Pvt.	Co. D. 127 Inf.	DW	9/1/18	Washburn, N. Dakota. Mamie Evans (Sister).

Name	Rank	Organization	Cause	Date	Address—Next of Kin
Crosby, Harry	Pvt.	Hdqs. 125 Inf.	DW	10/8/18	26 Sunnyside St., Burnside, Conn. Mrs. Ella Crosby (Mother).
Cross, Archie B.	Pvt.	Co. C. 128 Inf.	KIA	10/14/18	....
Crothers, Gordon M.	Corp.	Co. M. 126 Inf.	KIA	8/2/18	P. O. Box 374, Rockford, Mich. Mrs. Hazel Crothers (Wife).
Crystal, William L.	Wag.	Co. C. 120 F. A.	DW	6/27/18	Rigby, Idaho. Mrs. Mary E. Crystal.
Cudworth, Alonzo R.	Corp.	Bat. C. 120 F. A.	KIA	8/29/18 about	387 Prospect Ave., Milwaukee, Wis. Wm. H. Cudworth.
Cummings, Edwin L.	Pvt.	Co. A, 128 Inf.	KIA	10/20/18	402 Vine St., Baraboo, Wis. Mrs. N. Cummings.
Cunningham, Charles	Sgt.	Co. K. 126 Inf.	DD	7/3/18	1317 LaFayette Av., Gd. Rap'ds, Mich. Augusta Bangboune (Mother).
Cunningham, Walter	Pvt.	Co. A. 121 Mg. Bn.	DW	10/11/18	Sturgeon Bay, Wis. Robert Cunningham (Father).
Cupast, August	Pvt.	Co. M. 128 Inf.	KIA	10/15/18	Box 39, Burnside, Conn. Mrs. Pezin.
Curb, James M.	Corp.	Co. I. 125 Inf.	KIA	10/9/18	Myra, Texas. J. W. Curb (Father).
Curran, John J.	Pvt.	Co. A. 121 Mg. Bn.	KIA	8/4/18	Brooklyn, N. Y. Mary Curran (Aunt).
Curwen, Harry T.	Corp.	Co. G. 127 Inf.	KIA	8/3/18	R. F. D. 2, St. Croix Falls, Wis. Thomas Curwen (Father).
Cushing, Benjamin.	Pvt. 1cl.	Co. C. 120 Mg. Bn.	KIA	8/28/18 about	R. F. D. 2, Marion, Mass Mrs. Amy R. Cushing.
Cusick, Jay N.	Corp.	Co. H. 128 Inf.	KIA	10/5/18	Tiltonville, Ohio. Mrs. Sarah E. Cusick (Mother).
Custer, Earl J.	Pvt.	Co. B. 121 Mg. Bn.	KIA	10/10/18	Bolivar, Ohio. Mrs. M. Custer (Mother).
Cutright, Amon	Pvt.	Co. E. 128 Inf.	KIA	10/5/18	Ozar, W. Va. Mr. Job. A. Cutright.
Cutsinger, William	Pvt.	Co. G. 126 Inf.	DW	10/14/18	Taylorsville, Ky. Mr. Martin Cutsinger.
Cuza, Nick	Pvt.	Co. D. 128 Inf.	KIA	8/3/18	Palaggo Adriano, Provingia Parlemo, Via Colegio, Italy. Vincenjo Cuza.
Czyziewski, Marion	Pvt.	Co. E. 128 Inf.	KIA	10/5/18	2 Wallicki Place, Detroit, Mich. Mrs. Pollie Lysczewska (Sister).
Dadison, Andrus P.	Pvt.	Co. M. 125 Inf.	KIA	7/31/18	....
Dahl, Arthur	Pvt.	Co. C. 120 Mg. Bn.	KIA	8/1/18	R. F. D. 1, Galesville, Wis. Mrs. Andrew Dahl.
Dahl, Oscar	Pvt.	Co. E. 128 Inf.	KIA	10/11/18	608 Arnold Av. N., Thief River Falls, Mrs. Clara Dahl (Mother). Minn.
Dahlberg, Abner F.	Pvt.	Co. L. 127 Inf.	KIA	8/4/18	R. F. D. 41, Rhinelander, Wis. Mrs. Lydia Wernstram (Mother).
Dahlem, Glenn G.	Corp.	Co. G. 127 Inf.	KIA	8/3/18	427 N. Murray St., Madison, Wis. A. W. Dahlem.
Dalen, Arnold	Pvt.	Co. I. 127 Inf.	DW	9/1/18	R. F. D. 1, Box 40, Starbuck, Minn. Mrs. Bertha Dalen (Mother).
Daley, Michael J.	Pvt.	Co. I. 119 F. A.	DW	9/2/18	Andover, Mass. Mrs. Patrick Daley (Mother).
Dally, Theodore J.	Pvt.	Co. E. 127 Inf.	KIA	10/10/18	Reno, Minn. Mrs. Augustus Dally (Mother).
Daly, Bernard J.	Mech.	Co. I. 125 Inf.	DW	7/31/18	....
Dambuk, Jake	Pvt.	Co. B. 125 Inf.	KIA	8/6/18	....
Daniels, Charles	Pvt.	Co. I. 127 Inf.	KIA	10/16/18	Buyck, Minn. Mrs. Johanna Dnniels (Mother).
Daniliuk, Vasily	Pvt.	Co. K. 127 Inf.	KIA	8/4/18	Sawara, S. C. J. D. Knel Sta., Russia. Mrs. Christiana Daniliuk (Wife).
Danner, Claude F.	Pvt.	Co. D. 126 Inf.	DW	10/4/18	Gardner, Ill. Mrs. Jacob F. Danner (Mother).
Dant, Taylor S.	Pvt.	Co. G. 126 Inf.	DW	10/5/18	R. F. D. 1, St. Joseph, Ky. Mr. William T. Dant (Father).
Dargo, Leo	Pvt.	Co. L. 125 Inf.	KIA	7/31/18	Beaver, Wis. Theodore Dargo (Father).
Daugherty, James D.	Pvt.	Co. F. 127 Inf.	KIA	10/7/18	R. F. D. 3, Englewood, Tenn. William T. Daugherty (Brother).
Dausman, Leroy L.	Sgt.	Co. D. 126 Inf.	KIA	10/4/18	Saranac, Mich. Samuel Dausman (Father).
Davenport, Lyle	Mech.	Co. F. 127 Inf.	KIA	8/6/18	....
Davenport, Millard E.	Mus.	Hq. 322 F. A.	DW	10/23/18	R. F. D. 1, Perrysburg, Ohio. Mrs. Rose E. Wellstead (Mother).
Davis, George F.	Pvt.	Co. I. 125 Inf.	DW	8/3/18	....
Davis, Henry	Pvt.	Co. M. 125 Inf.	KIA	7/31/18	....
Davis, Less F.	Pvt.	Co. A. 127 Inf.	KIA	10/7/18	Colesburg, Iowa. Thos. Davis (Father).
Davis, Joseph	Pvt.	Co. B. 121 Mg. Bn.	KIA	10/10/18	99 Cook St., Brooklyn, N. Y. Mrs. Annie Levj (Sister).
Davis, Russell R.	Sgt.	Mg. Co. 125 Inf.	KIA	10/10/18	Genesee, Mich. Mrs. Sarah A. Davis.

1. FIRST LIEUTENANT RICHARD W. MULCAHY, Company F, 128th Infantry. Killed in action November 10th, 1918, during Meuse-Argonne Offensive.
2. SECOND LIEUTENANT FRANK A. STURTEVANT, Company H, 128th Infantry. Killed in action October 9th, 1918, during Meuse-Argonne Offensive.
3. SECOND LIEUTENANT JOHN M. REGAN, Company D, 128th Infantry. Killed in action August 4th, 1918, during Aisne-Marne Offensive.
4. FIRST LIEUTENANT HAROLD H. JOYCE, Company I, 128th Infantry. Killed in action August 30th, 1918, during Oise-Aisne Offensive.
5. CAPTAIN ORVILLE L. ARNOLD, Adjutant, 128th Infantry. Killed in action October 7th, 1918, near Epinonville, France, during the Meuse-Argonne Offensive.
6. FIRST LIEUTENANT EDWIN LLEWELLYN JONES, Machine Gun Company, 128th Infantry. Died August 3rd, 1918, of wounds received during Aisne-Marne Offensive.
7. SECOND LIEUTENANT THEODORE K. VOGEL, JR., 128th Infantry. Killed in action November 10th, 1918, during the Meuse-Argonne Offensive.
8. SECOND LIEUTENANT HENRY MATTERN, Company D, 128th Infantry. Killed in action October 16th, 1918, during the Meuse-Argonne Offensive.
9. SECOND LIEUTENANT HARRY B. PETERS, Company B, 128th Infantry. Killed in action October 15th, 1918, during the Meuse-Argonne Offensive.

235

Name	Rank	Organization	Cause	Date	Address—Next of Kin
Davis, Thorman	Pvt.	Co. G. 58 Inf.	DW	8/5/18	....
Davis, Fallmer	Pvt.	Co. D. 127 Inf.	KIA	....	Leola, Ark. Mrs. L. A. Davis (Mother).
Davis, Warner	Pvt.	Co. M. 128 Inf.	KIA	11/8/18	R. F. D. 1, Box 17, Slate, W. Va. Mrs. Bill Davis (Mother).
Davis, William J.	Pvt.	Co. F. 126 Inf.	KIA	10/9/18	Sanma, W. Va. Mrs. M. C. Davis.
Davis, Willard	Pvt.	Co. I. 127 Inf.	KIA	8/31/18	Aberdeen, So. Dakota. John H. Davis (Father).
Daws, Harrison	Pvt.	Co. K. 127 Inf.	KIA	10/5/18	R. R. 4, Prospect, Tenn. Robert Daws (Father).
Dawson, Albert M.	Sgt.	Co. M. 125 Inf.	KIA	8/1/18	Owosso, Mich. ....
Dawson, Hollus E.	Corp.	Co. A. 121 Mg. Bn	DW	10/7/18	Barron, Wis. Miss Verne Dawson (Sister).
Day, Claude O.	Pvt.	Co. H. 128 Inf.	KIA	10/12/18	R. F. D. 2, Turner, Mich. Mrs. Melinda Day.
Day, Harry H.	Pvt. 1cl.	Co. M. 127 Inf.	KIA	9/1/18	St. Urain, New Mexico. Lydia Day (Mother).
Day, Robert J.	Pvt.	Co. D. 125 Inf.	DW	10/10/18	Aurora, Neb. Walter Day (Father).
Dearmond, Thomas	Pvt.	Co. C. 128 Inf.	Error	....	....
Debutts, Ray G.	Pvt. 1cl.	Co. K. 128 Inf.	KIA	9/3/18	Boyne City, Mich. H. Debutts.
Decaire, David	Pvt. 1cl.	Co. F. 125 Inf.	KIA	8/6/18	....
Decorah, Foster	Corp.	Co. D. 128 Inf.	KIA	8/2/18	Friendship, Mich. Mrs. Elizabeth Decorah (Mother).
Decorah, Robert	Pvt. 1cl.	Co. D. 128 Inf.	KIA	8/2/18	Mauston, Wis. John Wallace (Brother).
De Dominicis, Aristide	Pvt.	Bat. E. 322 F. A.	DD	12/24/18	....
Deeds, Kennie H.	Pvt.	Co. M. 126 Inf.	KIA	8/3/18	College Park, Maryland. Mrs. Lydia Deeds (Mother).
Doering, Herman	Pvt. 1cl.	Co. C. 128 Inf.	DW	7/2/18	....
Deeringer, Guy	Pvt.	Co. G. 127 Inf.	KIA	10/4/18	Saline, Mo. D. M. Deeringer (Father).
Deeringhoff, Ferdinand E	Corp.	Co. A. 127 Inf.	KIA	10/15/18	Mozee City, Washington Mrs. Verena Deeringhoff.
Deetz, Edwin H.	Corp.	Co. I. 126 Inf.	KIA	10/9/18	Aurora, Oregon. H. H. Deetz (Father).
Degiacomo, Nickolia	Pvt.	Co. B. 128 Inf.	KIA	8/31/18	Nenteodarisio Chieti, Italy. Rose Degiacomo.
DeGuerre, Ernest A.	Sgt.	Co. G. 126 Inf.	KIA	8/4/18	Toronto, Canada. M. T. DeGuerre.
Dehl, Herbert A.	Pvt. 1cl.	308 Batry. Tr. Art.	KIA	10/23/18	902 W. Mound St., Columbus, Ohio. Mrs. Christina Dehl (Mother).
Dekkinga, Mart	Pvt.	Co. I. 126 Inf.	KIA	10/9/18	R. F. D. 2, Husey, Mich. Klile Dekkinga.
Delaney, Forrest L.	Pvt.	Btry B. 147 F. A.	ACC	8/9/18	227 Linden Ave., Moundsville, W. Va. Mrs. Abbie Doty (Mother).
Delapp, Galbert F.	Pvt.	Co. L. 127 Inf.	KIA	9/2/18	412 Gardner St., Rhinelander, Wis. Charles Nitschke (Friend).
Delgoff, Rodney	Pvt.	Co. G. 127 Inf.	KIA	7/31/18	....
Delihant, Leslie E.	Clr. Sgt.	122 F. A.	DW	10/3/18	....
Dahlberg, Abner F.	Pvt.	Co. L. 127 Inf.	KIA	8/4/18	....
Demorest, Joe A.	Corp.	Co. A. 126 Inf.	KIA	8/1/18	8 Wood St., Quincey, Mich. D. A. Demorest.
Demund, Jacob H.	Corp.	Co. E. 125 Inf.	KIA	10/11/18	Gaines, Mich. Candance Demund (Mother).
Dencker, Henry W.	Pvt.	Co. F. 126 Inf.	DW	10/11/18	1827 Hawkins St., Cincinnati, Ohio. Mrs. Elizabeth Dencker.
Dennis, Joe H.	Pvt.	Co. M. 128 Inf.	KIA	11/8/18	Magnolia, Ark. Phil Dennis (Father).
Denno, Henry D.	Pvt.	Co. B. 128 Inf.	KIA	10/13/18	R. F. D. 5, Brandon, Vt. Mrs. Mary Denno.
Denouden, Dirk	Pvt.	Co. A. 126 Inf.	DW	10/4/18	Putten Gelderland, Holland. Antoni Denouden (Father).
Densmore, Fred L.	Pvt.	Co. L. 125 Inf.	KIA	10/17/18	Oswayo, Pa. Mrs. G. E. Densmore (Mother).
Denton, Gilford	Pvt.	Co. B. 127 Inf.	KIA	10/13/18	R. F. D. 4, Box 47, Bristol, Tenn. Mrs. Margaret L. Denton (Mother).
Derdowski, Omer	Pvt.	Co. I. 125 Inf.	DW	8/1/18	1411 Marsac St., Bay City, Mich. Mary Derdowski (Mother).
Dereuisseaux, Ralph	Pvt.	Co. C. 126 Inf.	KIA	10/5/18	Box 162, Hamilton, Mont. Matilda Bennett.
DeRonde, Edward J.	Corp.	Co. L. 125 Inf.	KIA	8/31/18	36 Taft Ave., Detroit, Mich. Leona DeRonde (Mother).
Desantis, Anibale	Pvt.	Co. D. 126 Inf.	KIA	10/18/18	Woodstock Postoffice, Portland, Ore. Mr. Louis Desantis (Brother).

Name	Rank	Organization	Cause	Date	Address—Next of Kin
Devries, Arthur	Sgt.	Co. M. 126 Inf.	KIA	8/2/18	1069 W. Bridge St., Gd. Rapids, Mich. Dr. W. Devries (Father).
Dewitt, Albert W.	Pvt.	Co. H. 127 Inf.	KIA	7/31/18	Box 122, Moore, Mont. John D. Dewitt (Father).
DeWitt, Morris B.	Sgt.	Co. B. 121 Mg. Bn.	KIA	10/6/18	185 Glessner St., Mansfield, Ohio. H. B. DeWitt (Father).
Deyo, Harold D.	Pvt.	Mg. Co. 126 Inf.	KIA	10/2/18	113 East Ward St., Urbana, Ohio. Mr. George Deyo (Father).
Diamond, Jack	Pvt.	Co. D. 127 Inf.	KIA	10/10/18	Farmington, Minn. Fred A. Thomas (Friend).
Deangelo, James J.	Pvt.	Co. K. 128 Inf.	KIA	8/3/18	414 S. Exter St., Baltimore, Md. Mrs. A. Deangelo.
Dick, Coy	Pvt.	Co. G. 125 Inf.	KIA	10/6/18	1222 S. West St., Indianapolis, Ind. Oliver M. Dick (Father).
Dickerson, George T.	Pvt.	Co. B. 127 Inf.	KIA	10/19/18	R. F. D. 1, Indian Valley, Va. Port Dickerson (Father).
Dickey, Irwin E.	Corp.	Co. C. 128 Inf.	DW	8/3/18	Hudson, Wis. Mrs. George Dickey.
Dickinson, Timothy	Corp.	Co. M. 128 Inf.	DW	11/4/18	Lisbon, New Hampshire. Mrs. Hattie L. Dickinson (Mother).
Dietrich, Alfred H.	Pvt.	Co. F. 127 Inf.	KIA	7/30/18	1717 Wright St., Milwaukee, Wis. Mrs. Mary Dietrich (Mother).
Dimassa, Alexandre	Pvt.	Co. E. 125 Inf.	KIA	7/31/18	....
Dinwiddie, Frank	Pvt.	Co. H. 127 Inf.	KIA	10/6/18	....
Dirrigl, Frank	Sgt.	Co. C. 128 Inf.	DW	8/31/18	Park Falls, Wis. Mr. Dirrigl.
Dicken, Clarence O.	Sgt.	Q. M. C. Att. Hq. 32 Div	DD	2/20/18	....
Distler, George	Pvt.	Co. E. 125 Inf.	KIA	8/29/18	R. F. D. 1, Jefferson City, Mo. Albert Distler.
Dixon, Maurice	Corp.	Bat. C. 119 F. A.	KIA	8/8/18	103 Lahana St., Lansing, Mich. Mrs. Emma Dixon (Mother).
Dodds, James M.	Pvt. 1cl.	Co. D. 126 Inf.	KIA	10/4/18	Panquitch, Utah. John Dodds (Brother).
Doerr, John	Pvt.	Co. I. 125 Inf.	KIA	7/31/18	Barnes, Kansas. Daniel Doerr (Father).
Dolan, Joe	Pvt.	Co. C. 121 Mg. Bn.	DW	9/2/18	734 Prospect Place, Brooklyn, N. Y. Mrs. Mary Callahan (Mother).
Dollinger, Abraham	Pvt.	Co. D. 126 Inf.	KIA	10/5/18	419 E. 5th St., New York, N. Y. Joseph Dellinger (Father).
Dombrowski, Joseph I	Pvt.	Co. E. 125 Inf.	DW	10/9/18	519 Isabell St. Alex. Dombrowski (Brother).
Doney, Everett	Corp.	Co. M. 127 Inf.	KIA	8/4/18	Oconto, Wis. Ira Doney (Godmother).
Donnelly, Michael J.	Pvt.	Co. H. 127 Inf.	KIA	10/16/18	36 Arlington St., N. Cambridge, Mass. Mary Donnelly (Sister).
Doran, George E.	Pvt. 1cl.	Co. D. 127 Inf.	KIA	6/17/18	764 14th St., Milwaukee, Wis. Daniel Doran (Father).
Dorcheus, John A.	Pvt.	Co. F. 127 Inf.	KIA	10/7/18	Ashton, Idaho. Mrs. Mary Dorcheus (Mother).
Dorenburg, Frank A.	Pvt.	Co. H. 127 Inf.	DW	10/13/18	318 June St., Carnegie, Pa. Catherine Dorenburg (Mother).
Dorey, Hugh	Pvt.	Co. H. 127 Inf.	DW	10/4/18	240½ Hibbard Ave., Detroit, Mich. Mrs. H. L. Dorey (Mother).
Dorfman, Alexander	Pvt.	Co. A. 121 Mg. Bn.	KIA	10/7/18	16 E. 7th St., New York City, N. Y. Miss Sarah Zuckeman (Cousin).
Doughert, Edward	Pvt. 1cl.	Co. F. 125 Inf.	KIA	7/31/18	....
Douglas, Arthur W.	Pvt.	Co. B. 128 Inf.	KIA	7/9/18	152 Terrace, Redlands, Calif. W. C. Douglas (Father).
Dow, Francis E.	Corp.	Co. H. 126 Inf.	KIA	8/3/18	377 Putman Ave., Detroit, Mich. Mrs. Mathilda Dow (Mother).
Dowling, Lawrence	Serg.	Co. D. 322 F. A.	KIA	10/15/18	R. F. D. 5, Dayton, Ohio. Mrs. Irene Louis Dowling (Mother).
Dowdy, Monroe	Pvt.	Co. G. 127 Inf.	KIA	10/10/18	Ingram, Texas. Mrs. Lee Ella Dowdy (Mother).
Dowty, Chancey P.	Pvt.	Co. C. 128 Inf.	KIA	8/1/18	Morlan, Kansas. Ella L. Dowty.
Dozier, Clifford	Pvt.	Co. I. 126 Inf.	KIA	10/9/18	Wallsend, Ky. Evin Dozier (Father).
Drabenstott, Alvia R.	Pvt.	Co. I. 126 Inf.	KIA	8/1/18	R. F. D. 3, Custer, Mich. Mrs. Flora Drabenstott.
Drake, Payne	Pvt.	Co. F. 127 Inf.	KIA	9/4/18	Shawano, Wis. Mrs. Mora Drake (Mother).
Draper, Frank M.	Pvt.	Co. L. 125 Inf.	KIA	7/31/18	2716 8th Blvd., Pt. Huron, Mich. Mrs. Elizabeth Draper (Mother).
Drennon, Merritt.	Pvt.	Co. K. 128 Inf.	DW	10/6/18	....
Dreps, Anthony	Pvt.	Co. C. 127 Inf.	KIA	8/3/18	1401 N. 8th St., Sheboygan, Wis. John A. Dreps (Father).
Dressell, Egerett C.	Corp.	Mg. Co. 125 Inf.	KIA	10/10/18	R. F. D. 4, So. Haven, Mich. Mr. Fred A. Dressell.

NAME	RANK	ORGANIZATION	CAUSE	DATE	ADDRESS—NEXT OF KIN
Dresser, Frank A.	Pvt. 1cl.	Co. B. 107 F. S. Bn.	KIA	10/18/18	Richland, Washington. Frank Dresser (Father).
Drill, Edward L.	Pvt.	Co. C. 107 F. S. Bn.	KIA	10/2/18	Princeton, Wis. Mr. Andrew Drill (Father).
Driver, Dib.	Pvt.	Co. B. 127 Inf.	KIA	10/11/18	Liberty, Tenn. Burrel Driver (Father).
Drury, John R.	Pvt. 1cl.	Amb. Co. 126, 107 San. Tr.	......	10/1/18	....
Dry, Wufford	Corp.	Co. C. 107 F. S. Bn.	KIA	8/29/18	Richfield, N. Carolina. James C. Dry (Father).
Duane, Mark S.	Pvt.	Co. D. 121 F. A.	KIA	8/5/18	Mellan, Wis. Mrs. Mary Duane.
Duckett, Gordon A.	Corp.	Co. H. 126 Inf.	......	8/30/18	160 Fireman Ave., Detroit, Mich. William B. Duckett.
Dudek, John	Pvt. 1cl.	Co. M. 125 Inf.	KIA	7/31/18	....
Dudley, Joe D.	Pvt. 1cl.	Co. K. 125 Inf.	DW	10/18/18	Madison, S. D. Mrs. Blanche Hegdahl.
Dudley, Newton	Pvt.	Co. A. 128 Inf.	KIA	....	Pleasant Hill, Mo. Mrs. Lula Bagshaw (Sister).
Dudzinski, Franciszak	Pvt.	Co. I. 125 Inf.	KIA	10/11/18	8813 23rd Ave., Brooklyn, N. Y. Mary Dudzinski (Sister).
Duerwearder, Alberic J	Corp.	Co. H. 125 Inf.	KIA	10/8/18	Cheboygan, Mich. Charles Van Hoorn Tannery.
Dufun, John	Pvt.	Co. F. 125 Inf.	KIA	10/12/18	5407 Carthage Ave., Norwood, Ohio. Mrs. Josephine Dufan (Mother).
Duffy, Edward	Pvt.	Co. L. 128 Inf.	DW	8/30/18	233 N. Fanfield Ave., Chicago, Ill. Patrick J. Duffy.
Duffy, Michael	Pvt.	Co. M. 127 Inf.	KIA	8/4/18	Phillipsburg, Mont. John W. Duffy (Father).
Dugan, Joseph P.	Pvt.	Co. D. 125 Inf.	KIA	5/25/18	....
Duhn, Arnie F.	Pvt.	Co. L. 127 Inf.	KIA	9/2/18	R. F. D. 32, Black Creek, Wis. August Duhn (Stepfather).
Dujoudin, Arthur	Pvt.	Co. B. 126 Inf.	KIA	8/29/18	Swevere Le Province, W. Vlawnderen, Belgium. Louise Dujoudin.
Duket, Stanley G.	Corp.	Co. I. 127 Inf.	KIA	11/10/18	1111 Minnesopolis St., Marinette, Wis. Mr. Chester Duket, Jr. (Father).
Dulepski, Stanley E.	Pvt.	Co. H. 127 Inf.	KIA	10/16/18	Etna St., Naugatuck, Conn. Mrs. Mary Rosgen (Sister).
Duncan, Clinton E.	Corp.	Co. L. 125 Inf.	KIA	10/9/18	903 Beard St., Port Huron, Mich. Mrs. J. W. Duncan (Mother).
Duncklee, Lester W.	Corp.	Co. B. 125 Inf.	KIA	8/29/18	928 Mt. Clair Ave., St. Clair Hts., Mich. Mrs. Wm. Cole Duncklee (Mother).
Dunham, Scott H.	Pvt.	Co. H. 126 Inf.	KIA	10/15/18	3003 E. Grand Blvd., Detroit, Mich. James F. Dunham (Father).
Dunigan, Luke B.	Corp.	Co. D. 120 Mg. Bn.	KIA	8/29/18	....
Dunken, Guy H.	Pvt.	Co. G. 127 Inf.	KIA	9/2/18	Peetz, Col. Walter Dunken (Father).
Dunn, Benjamin.	Pvt.	Co. M. 128 Inf.	KIA	10/11/18	Toledo, Ohio. Mrs. J. Burns.
Dupras, Eugene	Pvt.	Co. C. 127 Inf.	KIA	7/31/18	2012 E. River St., Two Rivers, Wis. Ray Dupras (Father).
Dupius, Ezra	Pvt. 1cl.	308 Btry. Tr. Art.	KIA	10/23/18	Box 189, Ashland, New Hampshire. Mrs. Amy Dupius (Mother).
Dupris, Joseph	Pvt. 1cl.	Bat. C. 147 F. A.	DD	9/2/18	....
Durbin, Lonnie	Pvt.	Co. K. 126 Inf.	KIA	8/28/18	Garfield, Ky. Hiram Durbin (Father).
Durka, Henry	Pvt.	Mg. Co. 126 Inf.	DW	8/30/18	643 Frankfort St., Detroit, Mich. John Pikora (Half Brother).
Durkee, Frank	Pvt. 1cl.	Co. B. 126 Inf.	DW	10/18/18	R. F. D. 1, Onsted, Mich. E. B. Durkee.
Durnberger, Peter O.	Sgt.	Mg. Co. 125 Inf.	KIA	10/11/18	R. F. D. 1, Okanogan, Washington. Mrs. Carrie Parks.
Duseld, Joseph	Pvt. 1cl.	Co. H. 127 Inf.	KIA	9/2/18	1111 S 9th St., Manitowoc, Wis. August Duseld (Father).
Dwyer, Leo M.	Pvt.	Bat. E. 322 F. A.	KIA	10/23/18	R. F. D. 8, Dayton, Ohio. Mrs. Glenn Mrlin (Sister).
Dyer, John M.	Corp.	Co. M. 128 Inf.	KIA	8/30/18	Reed City, Mich. Mrs. Jas. Dyer.
Dykes, Jesse M.	Pvt.	Co. F. 126 Inf.	KIA	10/4/18	314 2nd St., Richmond, Ky. Jesse Dykes (Father).
Easly, Luther B.	Corp.	Co. K. 126 Inf.	KIA	8/29/18	....
Eastlund, Ole A.	Pvt.	Co. E. 128 Inf.	KIA	....	Dalbo, Minn. Peter A. Eastlund (Father).
Eastman, Richard D.	Corp.	Co. M. 128 Inf.	KIA	8/30/18	Lawrence, Mich. Mrs. Velevia Eastman.
Eaton, Frank J.	Pvt. 1cl.	Co. L. 128 Inf.	KIA	10/18/18	R. 4, Box 48, Augusta, Wis. Mrs. Annie Eaton.
Eby, Daniel A.	Corp.	Co. F. 127 Inf.	DW	10/21/18	....

Name	Rank	Organization	Cause	Date	Address—Next of Kin
Edelson, Samuel M.	Pvt.	Co. C. 120 Mg. Bn.	KIA	10/1/18	63 Pike St., New York, N. Y. Harris Edelson.
Edmonson, William F.	Pvt.	Co. C. 125 Inf.	KIA	10/10/18	Strasburg, Va. Maggie Edmonson.
Edwards, George W.	Pvt. 1cl.	Co. K. 126 Inf.	KIA	8/29/18	Bengal, Ky. James Edwards (Father).
Egelhoff, Otto J.	Pvt.	Co. F. 127 Inf.	KIA	10/7/18	Raymond, Ill. William F. Egelhoff (Father).
Eggert Thomas W.	Pvt.	Co. G. 127 Inf.	KIA	9/1/18	3021 N. 30th St., Omaha, Neb. Paul Eggert (Father).
Egle, William.	Pvt.	Co. A. 128 Inf.	KIA	8/1/18	Palisade, Neb. Christian E. Egle (Brother).
Egleston, Lewis	Pvt. 1cl.	Co. E. 125 Inf.	DW	10/10/18	526 Norman St., Lansing, Mich. Henry Egleston (Father).
Ehlen, Fred	Pvt. 1cl.	Co. C. 127 Inf.	DW	10/6/18	Aurora, Oregon. Henry C. Ehlen (Father).
Eich, Peter J.	Pvt.	Co. F. 127 Inf.	DW	10/9/18	Prairie Du Rocher, Illinois. Peter Eich (Father).
Eick, George	Pvt. 1cl.	Co. M. 127 Inf.	......	9/1/18	Oconto Falls, Wis. August Eick (Father).
Elder, William W.	Pvt.	Co. M. 128 Inf.	KIA	10/9/18	Farmington, W. Va. Mrs. Agnes Beck.
Eldridge, Rix B.	Pvt.	Co. I. 126 Inf.	DW	10/11/18	Green Forest, Ark. John E. Eldridge.
Elefson, Edwin	Sgt.	Co. F. 127 Inf.	KIA	9/1/18	Shawano, Wis. Eli Elefson (Father).
Elias, Loman C.	Pvt.	Co. M. 125 Inf.	KIA	10/21/18	1914 Sarah St., Fresno, Calif. Mary Elias (Mother).
Elijah, Richard	Pvt.	Co. B. 128 Inf.	KIA	11/10/18	Kinder, La. Joseph Elijah.
Ellenberger, Franklin	Pvt.	Co. K. 128 Inf.	KIA	10/7/18	....
Elliott, John C.	Pvt.	Co. M. 128 Inf.	KIA	11/8/18	730 6th St., S. W., Roanoke, Va. Hilda Elliott.
Ellis, Ross R.	Corp.	Co. E. 128 Inf.	DW	8/31/18	Allouez, Mich. Mrs. Thomas Ellis.
Elmer, George	Pvt.	Sup. Co. 128 Inf.	DW	10/4/18	2829 Fletcher St., Chicago, Ill. Anna Elmer.
Embrey, Sidney E.	Pvt.	Co. A. 128 Inf.	KIA	8/1/18	Booneville, Mo. Andrew A. Embrey (Father).
Emerick, Clarence	Pvt.	Co. C. 120 Mg. Bn.	DD	9/14/18	....
Emfinger, James M.	Pvt.	Co. I. 126 Inf.	KIA	10/5/18	Bude, Miss. Edgar R. Emfinger.
Engle, Charles W.	Pvt. 1cl.	Co. C. 126 Inf.	KIA	10/5/18	R. F. D. 5, Kalamazoo, Mich. Mrs. C. F. Engle.
Englehardt, Carl	Pvt.	Co. C. 127 Inf.	DW	9/3/18	125 Park Ave., Sheboygan, Wis. William Englehardt (Father).
English, Cyrus J.	Corp.	Co. M. 125 Inf.	KIA	7/31/18	....
Enochs, Paul S.	Pvt. 1cl.	Co. M. 126 Inf.	DW	8/4/18	Puyallup, Wash. John A. Enochs (Father).
Epley, George P.	Pvt.	Co. G. 126 Inf.	KIA	10/22/18	Marlowe Ave., College Hill, Cincinnati, Ohio. Mrs. George P. Epley (Wife).
Erbe, Garret	Pvt.	Co. E. 125 Inf.	KIA	10/9/18	1121 Clinton St., St. Louis, Mo. Ruth Erbe (Wife).
Erickson, Carl	Pvt. 1cl.	Co. D. 125 Inf.	KIA	10/9/18	Bladen, Neb. Charles C. Erickson (Father).
Erickson, George	Corp.	Co. I. 127 Inf.	......	9/1/18	912 Holmes Ave., Menominee, Mich. G. Erickson (Father).
Erickson, Jens M.	Pvt.	Co. G. 128 Inf.	KIA	10/19/18	Flom, Minn. Mrs. J. Erickson.
Erickson, John V.	Corp.	Co. E. 119 F. A.	DW	10/14/18	P. O., Lacota, Mich. John V. Erickson (Father).
Erickson, Olaf	Pvt.	Co. A. 126 Inf.	DW	10/7/18	3119 No. 20th St., Tacoma, Wash. Irene Vosoba (Sister).
Ericson, John A.	Pvt. 1cl.	Co. C. 128 Inf.	KIA	8/1/18	....
Escuek, John	Pvt.	Med. Det. 128 Inf.	KIA	10/8/18	Dora, Ark. Miss Elsie English.
Essman, Alfred B.	Pvt. 1cl.	Co. A. 126 Inf.	KIA	7/31/18	R. F. D. 25, Waterford, Wis. Mrs. Elizabeth Essman.
Estabrook, Sylvester C	Pvt. 1cl.	Co. M. 127 Inf.	KIA	8/4/18	New London, Wis. Mrs. Pearl Seigle (Sister).
Etue, Walter F.	Pvt.	Co. A. 128 Inf.	KIA	8/1/18	513 Ketchum St., Bay City, Mich. Mrs. Mary Etue (Mother).
Ethier, Alfred	Corp.	Bat. A. 120 F. A.	DW	8/6/18	998 Island Ave., Milwaukee, Wis. A. D. Ethier.
Eustice, Raymond R.	Pvt. 1cl.	Co. E. 10 Am. Tr.	KIA	10/5/18	Rewey, Wis. Mrs. M. P. Eustice.
Euper, Clarence A.	Pvt.	Bat. C. 120 F. A.	......	....	R. F. D. 2, Woodland, Mich. Mrs. Christina Euper (Mother).
Euswiller Herman E.	Pvt.	Co. G. 126 Inf.	KIA	10/10/18	R. R. 4, Tippecanoe City, Ohio. John Z. Euswiller.
Eva, Harry	Sgt.	Co. G. 125 Inf.	KIA	8/29/18	....

NAME	RANK	ORGANIZATION	CAUSE	DATE	ADDRESS—NEXT OF KIN
Evans, LeRoy	Pvt. 1cl.	Co. E. 128 Inf.	KIA	8/31/18	Forbes, Tenn. Mr. Tham Evans.
Evans, Otis	Pvt. 1cl.	Co. F. 127 Inf.	DW	10/2/18	Gresham, Wis. Mrs. Marie Johnson (Mother).
Evans, Walter	Pvt. 1cl.	Co. L. 127 Inf.	DW	8/29/18	942 6th St., Beloit, Wis. Vera H. Evans (Sister).
Evens, Elgin	Pvt.	Co. E. 128 Inf.	KIA	11/10/18	Voss, N. Dak. Even Evens (Father).
Ewald, Edward A.	Pvt.	Co. D. 127 Inf.	KIA	10/11/18	Brownton, Minn. John Ewald (Father).
Ewing, Edwin H.	Corp.	Co. I. 126 Inf.	DW	8/5/18	104 Harris St., Ludington, Mich. F. C. Ewing.
Exline, Oscar	Pvt.	Co. K. 128 Inf.	KIA	11/7/18	Strange Creek, W. Va. Martha C. Exline.
Fahey, Matthew L.	Sgt.	Co. B. 127 Inf.	KIA	10/19/18	674 10th St., Brooklyn, N. Y. Miss Katherine Fahey (Sister).
Fair, Randolph W.	Pvt.	Co. M. 126 Inf.	KIA	10/17/18	R. F. D. 2, Manassas, Va. Mrs. Julia T. Fair (Mother).
Farmer, Joseph H.	Pvt.	Co. C. 128 Inf.	KIA	11/10/18	Dawnsville, La. Mrs. Sally Farmer.
Farnham, Dewitt E.	Sgt.	Co. L. 128 Inf.	KIA	11/7/18	Sparta, Wis. Matilda I. Farnham (Mother).
Farrand, Arthur D.	Pvt.	Co. F. 126 Inf.	DW	8/5/18	....
Farrell, Michael	Pvt.	Co. I. 126 Inf.	KIA	10/9/18	60 Fall St., Ashely, Pa. Mrs. Ed. Carry.
Ferris, William H.	Pvt.	Co. C. 127 Inf.	KIA	10/4/18	1408 Schiller Ave., Little Rock, Ak. Wayne Ferris (Brother).
Faunce, Charles	Pvt. 1cl.	Co. M. 128 Inf.	KIA	8/30/18	Plainwell, Mich. Mrs. Irwin Hamilton.
Fay, Ernest J.	Pvt.	Co. L. 127 Inf.	KIA	10/16/18	Rhinelander, Wis. Mrs. Ernest Fay.
Fehrs, Peter	Pvt.	Co. A. 128 Inf.	DW	8/4/18	Belgrade, Neb. John Fehrs (Father).
Felber, Frank	Pvt. 1cl.	Co. G. 126 Inf.	......	8/30/18	376 E. 1st St., Mansfield, Ohio. Frank Felber.
Felhefer, Henry	Pvt.	Co. G. 128 Inf.	KIA	10/18/18	Jacksonport, Wis. Frank Felhefer (Father).
Feltz, John A.	Pvt.	Co. G. 126 Inf.	KIA	10/9/18	16 Filmore St., Dayton, Ohio. Joe Feltz (Father).
Fergison, Francis B.	Pvt. 1cl.	Co. K. 128 Inf.	KIA	8/5/18	Onsted, Mich. Richard Morgan.
Ferguson, Eugene	Corp.	Co. H. 125 Inf.	KIA	8/31/18	Raco, Mich. Mrs. Ada Ferguson (Mother).
Ferguson, Lerey	Corp.	Co. K. 128 Inf.	KIA	10/6/18	Holden, W. Va. Miss Marie Ferguson.
Fessenden, Bert A.	Pvt.	Co. F. 127 Inf.	KIA	10/18/18	Edgehill, Montana. Albert B. Fessenden (Father).
Fetrow, Charles G.	Corp.	Co. K. 128 Inf.	KIA	11/5/18	R. F. D. 3, Dover, Pa. Mrs. Savilla Fetrow.
Fetscher, Valentine A.	Pvt. 1cl.	Co. L. 128 Inf.	DW	9/4/18	1101 Michigan Ave., Chicago, Ill. Valentine M. Fetscher.
Fett, Paul	Sgt.	Co. L. 126 Inf.	KIA	8/28/18	519 5th St., Grand Haven, Mich. Ernest Fett.
Fick, Everett S.	......	Error	......	....	....
Finley, John	Pvt.	Co. C. 125 Inf.	DW	10/3/18	....
Fischer, Edward	Pvt. 1cl.	Co. D. 127 Inf.	ACC	10/20/18	....
Fields, William	Pvt.	Co. D. 125 Inf.	KIA	8/31/18	St. Louis, Mich. Mrs. Helen Fields.
Fien, Julius	Pvt. 1cl.	Co. K. 125 Inf.	KIA	10/9/18	51 Morgan St., Hartford, Conn. Mrs. A. P. Fien (Mother).
Fikstad, Melvin P.	Pvt.	Co. I. 127 Inf.	KIA	....	Thornton, Idaho. Mrs. Frederica Pikstad (Mother).
Finnerty, Joseph J.	Corp.	Co. G. 127 Inf.	KIA	9/1/18	315 North Lake St., Madison, Wis. Mrs. E. Finnerty (Mother).
Finney, John	Pvt.	Co. G. 127 Inf.	KIA	8/3/18	1813 Winter St., Superior, Wis. Tony Burgraff (Friend).
Finstad, Carl K.	Pvt. 1cl.	Co. B. 120 M. P.	KIA	8/5/18	Washburn, Wis. Knude J. Finstad (Father).
Fintrilakis, Enanglos	Pvt.	Co. A. 127 Inf.	KIA	10/6/18	518 W. 2nd St., Salt Lake City, Utah. John Fintrilakis (Brother).
Fisher, Earl C.	Pvt.	Co. M. 128 Inf.	KIA	11/10/18	R. F. D. 1, Parkersburg, W. Va. James O. Fisher (Father).
Fisher, John	Corp.	Co. A. 127 Inf.	DW	10/15/18	R. F. D. 4, Marshfield, Wis. Mrs. Henry Schmidt (Mother).
Fisher, Peter W.	Pvt. 1cl.	Co. L. 128 Inf.	DW	9/3/18	206 Water St., Grand Haven, Mich. Mrs. Dena Fisher.
Fitzgerald, Chester	Corp.	Co. I. 125 Inf.	KIA	10/9/18	98 6th Ave., North Tonawanda, N. Y. Mrs. Peter Fitzgerald (Mother).
Fitzgerald, Rossetter S.	Pvt. 1cl.	Co. C. 128 Inf.	KIA	8/1/18	R. F. D. 2, Howard City, Mich. Ambrose Fitzgerald.
Fitzpatrick, Joseph	Pvt.	Co. C. 127 Inf.	DW	10/10/18	2432 So. 7th St., Sheboygan, Wis. Tom Fitzpatrick (Father).

1. SECOND LIEUTENANT ROY W. KELLY, Machine Gun Company, 127th Infantry. Killed in action August 31st, 1918, during the Oise-Aisne Offensive.
2. FIRST LIEUTENANT STEPHEN O. BRIGHAM, Company G, 127th Infantry. Died August 1st, 1918, of wounds received during the Aisne-Marne Offensive.
3. SECOND LIEUTENANT LESTER W. KEARN, Company K, 127th Infantry. Killed in action August 31st, 1918, during the Oise-Aisne Offensive.
4. SECOND LIEUTENANT JOHN BASTIAN NELSON, Company A, 127th Infantry. Killed in action October 18th, 1918, during the Meuse-Argonne Offensive.
5. MAJOR GEORGE E. SPERBECK, 147th F. A. Died of wounds October 11th, 1918.
6. SECOND LIEUTENANT EVERETT L. VARNEY, 127th Infantry. Died October 19th, 1918, of wounds received in action October 14th, 1918, during the Meuse-Argonne Offensive.
7. SECOND LIEUTENANT CHARLES SCHWARTZ, JR., Company D, 127th Infantry. Killed in action October 18th, 1918, during the Meuse-Argonne Offensive.
8. SECOND LIEUTENANT HOMER R. SMITH, Company F, 127th Infantry. Killed in action August 29th, 1918, during the Oise-Aisne Offensive.
9. SECOND LIEUTENANT E. SEIP, Company M, 127th Infantry. Killed in action August 4th, 1918, during the Aisne-Marne Offensive.

241

NAME	RANK	ORGANIZATION	CAUSE	DATE	ADDRESS—NEXT OF KIN
Flanery, Leo E.	Sgt.	Co. M. 128 Inf.	KIA	8/30/18	216 Racine St., Janesville, Wis. John Flanery.
Fleisner, Louis	Pvt. 1cl.	Co. A. 127 Inf.	DW	8/5/18	....
Fligg, Ray W.	Pvt.	Co. L. 127 Inf.	KIA	10/16/18	R. F. D. 2, Jacksonville, Ill. Mrs. George Fligg (Mother).
Flee, Lewis	Corp.	Co. H. 128 Inf.	DW	10/6/18	Eland, Wis. Mrs. Andrew Flee.
Florine, Paul F.	Pvt.	Co. D. 127 Inf.	DW	6/19/18	R. F. D. 4, Ft. Atkinson, Wis. G. Florine (Father).
Flynn, John J.	Sgt.	Co. M. 128 Inf.	KIA	10/15/18	....
French, John B.	Pvt.	Hq. Co. 127 Inf.	DD	10/6/18	....
Foley, Thomas L.	Pvt.	Co. H. 128 Inf.	DW	11/11/18	R. F. D. 5, Clinton, Mo. Miss Virgie Foley.
Folkener, Harry	Pvt.	Co. H. 125 Inf.	KIA	10/15/18	York, New Salem, Pa. Mrs. J. C. Folkener.
Folker, Dan	Pvt.	Co. C. 127 Inf.	KIA	10/15/18	Forsythe, Mont. Jake Leemhuis (Friend).
Foody, Joseph P.	Pvt.	Co. D. 127 Inf.	KIA	10/15/18	323 E. 2nd St., Xenia, Ohio. Nora Foody (Mother).
Forbes, James A.	Corp.	Co. E. 127 Inf.	KIA	9/2/18	Reno, Washington. James G. Halvorson (Father-in-Law)
Ford, Walter T.	Corp.	Mg. Co. 126 Inf.	KIA	8/29/18	Central Point, Ore. Miss Clara Shoemaker.
Forsberg, Lawrence	Pvt.	Co. I. 127 Inf.	KIA	8/31/18	1275 Logan St., Marinette, Wis. V. Forsberg (Father).
Forshee, Henry E.	Pvt.	Co. G. 125 Inf.	KIA	8/21/18	....
Forsman, Fritz	Pvt. 1cl.	Co. M. 125 Inf.	KIA	7/31/18	....
Fortenberry, Forest	Pvt.	Co. L. 128 Inf.	KIA	11/7/18	Route 1, Columbus, Miss. Conrad Fortenberry (Father).
Foss, Jerry S.	Pvt.	Co. C. 128 Inf.	KIA	10/12/18	Milbank, So. Dak. Charles Foss.
Fountain, William F.	Corp.	Co. D. 126 Inf.	KIA	8/1/18	R. F. D. 6, Ferry Road, Manchester, N. H. Agnes C. Fountain (Mother).
Fowers, Herbert F.	Pvt.	Co. K. 128 Inf.	DW	9/2/18	Hooper, Utah. Joseph Fowers.
Fowler, Arthur V.	Sgt.	Co. B. 125 Inf.	DW	8/29/18	Address unknown. Lillian Fowler (Mother).
Fowler, John W.	Pvt.	Co. E. 125 Inf.	KIA	8/29/18	R. F. D. 1, Box 14, Fleming, Mo. Mary C. French.
Fowler, Raleigh	Pvt.	Co. G. 127 Inf.	KIA	9/1/18	767 Brooks St., Beloit, Wis. C. W. Fowler (Father).
France, B. W.	Pvt.	Co. E. 125 Inf.	KIA	10/9/18	440 Putman Ave., Detroit, Mich. Hattie France (Mother).
France, George C.	Pvt.	Co. K. 126 Inf.	DW	9/10/18	R. F. D. 1, Byron Center, Mich. Mrs. Pedir France (Mother).
Francis, Oliver J.	Pvt.	Mg. 119 F. A.	DW	8/31/18	321 N. Normal St., Mt. Pleasant, Mich. Mrs. Alfred Francis (Mother).
Francovick, Peter	Pvt. 1cl.	Co. F. 127 Inf.	KIA	8/30/18	Crivitz, Wis. Mrs. John Kaishim (Sister).
Franek, Lewis	Pvt.	Co. C. 128 Inf.	KIA	8/1/18	Stanton, Neb. Mrs. Mary Franek.
Frank, Earl	Pvt.	Co. G. 125 Inf.	KIA	10/10/18	R. F. D. 1, Montezuma, Ohio. Albert Frank.
Frank, George A.	Pvt.	Co. F. 127 Inf.	KIA	8/1/18	Shawano, Wis. Charles W. Frank (Brother).
Franks, Amos B.	Pvt.	Co. C. 119 F. A.	DW	10/11/18	R. F. D. 2, Perry, Mich. Mrs. Amos B. Franks (Wife).
Franz, William C.	Pvt.	Co. L. 126 Inf.	KIA	8/2/18	11 Mt. Wood, Wheeling, W. Va. John Franz.
Frede, Arthur	Pvt.	Co. L. 125 Inf.	......	9/5/18	R. F. D. 3, Mt. Clemens, Mich. Mrs. Anna Frede (Mother).
Frederickson, Glenn S.	Pvt.	Hq. Co. 127 Inf.	KIA	11/11/18	Warsaw, Ind. Ray Frederickson (Brother).
Fredrichs, Ferdinand	Pvt.	Co. C. 127 Inf.	KIA	7/31/18	Sheboygan Falls, Wis. Arno Fredrichs (Father).
Freeman, Charles C.	Corp.	Co. M. 125 Inf.	KIA	10/11/18	R. F. D. 2, Box 88, Owosso, Mich. Wm. R. Freeman (Father).
Freshour, Daniel A.	Pvt. 1cl.	Co. C. 126 Inf.	......	8/30/18	Kibbie, Mich. Mrs. Maude Freshour.
Freyler, Victor H.	Pvt.	Co. A. 126 Inf.	KIA	10/10/18	316 Pine St., Helena, Mont. Hugo Freyler (Father).
Frink, Edward	Pvt.	Co. A. 128 Inf.	KIA	8/1/18	R. F. D. 5, Mt. Clemens, Mich. Edward Frink (Father).
Friske, Robert E.	Pvt. 1cl.	Mg. Co. 127 Inf.	KIA	10/5/18	1001 Beaser St., Ashland, Wis. Mrs. Minnie Friske (Mother).
Frith, Jesse T.	Pvt.	Co. G. 126 Inf.	KIA	10/27/18	Sydnorsville, Va. Mrs. E. T. Frith.
Fritz, Alfred J.	Pvt.	Co. A. 128 Inf.	KIA	10/16/18	2416 Griffith Ave., Louisville, Ky. Mrs. Charles E. Fritz.

Name	Rank	Organization	Cause	Date	Address—Next of Kin
Frest, Ernest F.	Pvt.	Co. C. 128 Inf.	KIA	8/1/18	Morland, Kans. M. P. Prest.
Fruend, Herman A.	Pvt.	Co. G. 125 Inf.	KIA	10/14/18	Hoffman, Ill. Fred W. Fruend (Father).
Frye, George E.	Sgt.	Co. D. 322 F. A.	KIA	11/4/18	....
Fuchs, John	Pvt. 1cl.	Co. B. 121 Mg. Bn.	KIA	8/4/18	Tomah, Wis. Frank Fuchs (Father).
Fuerback, Fred	Pvt.	Co. F. 127 Inf.	KIA	7/31/18	616 6th St., Milwaukee, Wis. Mrs. Mary Fuerback (Mother).
Fuller, Ralph	Pvt. 1cl.	Co. B. 127 Inf.	......	9/7/18	199 Ashland Ave., Oshkosh, Wis. Mrs. E. T. Fuller (Mother).
Fuller, Walter R.	Pvt.	Co. C. 126 Inf.	KIA	8/1/18	1407 Maton Ave., St. Joseph, Mich. Mrs. Rachel Fuller.
Fulton, Charles J.	Sgt.	Co. L. 125 Inf.	KIA	7/31/18	516 Vine St., St. Clair, Mich. Mrs. Louise Fulton (Mother)
Furmanski, Anthony	Pvt.	Co. M. 126 Inf.	KIA	10/10/18	Bessemer, Mich. Stanley Furmanski (Father).
Gaj, W.	Pvt.	Co. I. 127 Inf.	KIA	8/1/18	1308 Dubois St., Detroit, Mich. Wojciech Mackowski (Friend).
Galaska, Edward J.	Pvt.	Co. A. 121 Mg. Bn.	KIA	8/4/18	829 Garden St., Milwaukee, Wis. Albert Galaska.
Galvin, John L.	Pvt. 1cl.	Batry A. 121 F. A.	KIA	8/11/18	Cottage Grove, Wis. John Galvin (Father).
Gallus, John A.	Sgt.	Hq. Co. 128 Inf.	KIA	10/17/18	Independence, Wis. Frank Gallus.
Gamblin, Henry N.	Pvt.	Co. A. 127 Inf.	KIA	10/29/18	Mt. Vernon, Oregon. Mrs. Florence Bird (Mother).
Gample, Ethel	Pvt.	Co. F. 127 Inf.	KIA	10/7/18	R. F. D. 1, Edgemae, Tenn. Lena Gample (Brother).
Gander, William U.	Pvt.	Co. A. 128 Inf.	KIA	8/3/18	1415 Race St., Cincinnati, Ohio. Mrs. Emma Gander (Mother).
Gappa, Joseph	Pvt.	Co. G. 128 Inf.	KIA	8/3/18	....
Garcia, James	Pvt.	Co. E. 127 Inf.	KIA	10/23/18	Crescent, Calif. Eliza Donavan (Aunt).
Gardiner, Haral	Sgt.	Co. E. 126 Inf.	DW	10/14/18	Delta, Ohio. Mrs. Alice Gardiner.
Gariepy, Albert	Pvt.	Med. Det. 125 Inf.	KIA	10/15/18	Leroy, N. Dak. Joe Gariepy (Father).
Garrett, Stanley B.	Pvt.	Hq. Co. 127 Inf.	KIA	10/16/18	Nelsons Bridge, Pa. Charles E. Coy (Friend).
Garski, Nick L.	Pvt. 1cl.	Bat. F. 121 F. A.	KIA	10/15/18	1936 Mead St., Racine, Wis. Joe Garski (Father).
Gates, John O.	Pvt.	Co. A. 126 Inf.	KIA	7/31/18	309 Elm St., Eau Claire, Wis. Mrs. Anna Knees (Mother).
Gattis, Paul	Pvt.	Co. G. 126 Inf.	KIA	10/5/18	R. F. D. 2, Alabama City, Ala. Fannie G. Gattis.
Gebert, Joseph	Sgt.	Co. B. 128 Inf.	KIA	8/31/18	Box 67, Princeton, Wis. Mrs. Rose Gebert.
Gecowets, A. C.	Pvt.	Co. C. 127 Inf.	KIA	....	1039 Harrison St., Defiance, Ohio. Mrs. Fred Stahl (Sister).
Gehring, Thomas	Pvt.	Mg. Co. 126 Inf.	KIA	10/8/18	354 College Ave., Gd. Rapids, Mich. George Gehring.
Georgakis, James G.	Pvt.	Co. C. 127 Inf.	KIA	9/2/18	1334½ E. 1st St., Los Angeles, Calif. John Menegakis (Father).
George, Guy S.	Pvt. 1cl.	Co. F. 127 Inf.	KIA	8/4/18	Shawano, Wis. D. H. George (Father).
George, William	Pvt.	Co. L. 128 Inf.	DD	9/23/18	....
Gerald, Charles, Jr.	Sgt.	Co. D. 127 Inf.	KIA	8/4/18	845 St. Lawrence Ave., Beloit, Wis. Mrs. G. M. Gerald (Mother).
Gerbasi, Pasquale	Pvt.	Co. F. 125 Inf.	KIA	10/12/18	Belle Vernon, Pa. Saveus Oliverio (Friend).
Gerheim, Harry M.	Pvt. 1cl.	Mg. Co. 125 Inf.	KIA	10/13/18	P. O. 318, Salina, Pa. Phillip Henry Gerheim (Father).
Gerlach, William H.	Pvt.	Co. G. 128 Inf.	KIA	11/10/18	Sturgeon Bay, Wis. Henry Gerlach (Father).
Germann, William	Pvt.	Co. G. 125 Inf.	DW	10/9/18	Belleville, Ill. Fred J. Klemme (Uncle).
Gilligan, Earl	Pvt.	Co. F. 107 F. S. Bn.	DW	8/8/18	....
Germershausen, Leo J.	Pvt. 1cl.	Co. A. 120 F. A.	KIA	9/3/18	813 Oakland Ave., Milwaukee, Wis. Mrs. B. Germershausen.
Gerowx, David	Pvt.	Co. G. 125 Inf.	DW	10/6/18	Box 531, Lake Linden, Mich. Remi Gerowx (Father).
Getchel, Dan	Corp.	Co. B. 128 Inf.	KIA	8/31/18	24 Zimmerman St., Waupun, Wis. Charles Getchel.
Giacoma, Peter	Pvt.	Co. K. 126 Inf.	DW	8/28/18	1215 Bishop Ave., Milwaukee, Wis. Joe Oddone (Brother-in-Law).
Gibbons, Eba	Pvt.	Co. I. 126 Inf.	KIA	8/8/18	R. F. D. 2, Edmore, Mich. Edwin Gibbons.
Gielarowski, Joseph	Pvt. 1cl.	Mg. Co. 127 Inf.	KIA	9/1/18	34 Everett St. E., Hampton, Mass. Bartlomien Gielarowski (Father).
Gietzen, William	Corp.	Co. E. 128 Inf.	KIA	8/31/18	R. F. D. 2, Warren, Mich. Nicholas Gietzen.

Name	Rank	Organization	Cause	Date	Address—Next of Kin
Gilbert, Cornelius	Pvt.	Co. F. 127 Inf.	DW	....	Concord, Calif. Thomas Gilbert (Father).
Giles, Arthur E.	Pvt. 1cl.	Co. E. 107 Am. Tr.	KIA	9/29/18	532 W. Main St., Waukesha, Wis. William Bruhn.
Gillespie, Clyde	Corp.	Co. M. 126 Inf.	DD	6/26/18	59 Arthur Ave., Gd. Rapids, Mich. Nina E. Gillespie.
Gillette, William F.	Pvt.	Co. M. 128 Inf.	KIA	11/8/18	Mills St., Kalamazoo, Mich. Otha Gillette (Brother).
Green, Lloyd H.	Pvt. 1cl.	Co. C. 120 Mg. Bn	KIA	10/2/18	Northville, Mich. Frank Green.
Gilmette, Joseph	Bug.	Co. A. 125 Inf.	KIA	8/7/18	Onaway, Mich. Alfred Gilmette (Brother).
Gislasson, Charles	Sgt.	Co. G. 128 Inf.	KIA	10/6/18	Detroit Harbor, Wis. Lawrence Gislasson.
Glenn, Jay T.	Sgt.	Co. F. 126 Inf.	KIA	8/3/18	Gregory, Mich. E. L. Glenn (Father).
Glynn, George H.	Pvt.	Med. Det. 125 Inf.	DW	10/5/18	R. F. D. 1, Lansing, Iowa. Josephine Glynn.
Goddard, Lewis	Sgt.	Co. A. 119 Mg. Bn	DD	12/16/18	....
Godowski, Zighn	Pvt.	Co. G. 128 Inf.	KIA	10/8/18	Chappell Hill, Texas. Mary Godowski.
Godwin, Eli	Pvt.	Co. C. 127 Inf.	KIA	....	DeQueen, Ark. Joe F. Godwin (Father).
Golden, Horace F.	Pvt.	Co. H. 127 Inf.	KIA	10/7/18	Gothenburg, Neb. Charles Golden (Father).
Goltz, Herman D.	Pvt.	Co. F. 127 Inf.	KIA	10/10/18	2105 E. 37th St., Los Angeles, Calif. Mrs. Henrietta Goltz (Mother).
Goree, Jow	Pvt.	Co. F. 127 Inf.	KIA	8/1/18	Shawano, Wis. Mrs. Ida Goree (Mother).
Gorke, William G.	Sgt. 1cl.	Co. G. 107 F. S. Bn	KIA	8/29/18	1946 E. Main St., Madison, Wis. Mrs. Minnie Gorke (Mother).
Gortz, Bert D.	Pvt. 1cl.	308 Batry. Tr. Arty	KIA	10/23/18	4427 Ganna Ave., Cleveland, Ohio. Mrs. W. Lillian Gortz (Wife).
Gossett, Charles W.	Pvt.	Co. A. 128 Inf.	KIA	11/10/18	....
Gosswiller, Robert C.	Pvt.	Co. I. 127 Inf.	KIA	10/17/18	....
Gould, Lyle E.	Pvt.	Hq. Co. 125 Inf.	KIA	9/1/18	1119 Harker St., Port Huron, Mich. Mrs. Laura Gould (Mother).
Gowan, James	Pvt.	Co. F. 127 Inf.	DW	8/2/18	Shawano, Wis. William Erdman (Friend).
Gowers, R. H.	Sgt.	Co. M. 362 Inf.	DW	10/5/18	....
Grabowski, Leonard	Pvt. 1cl.	Co. K. 127 Inf.	KIA	9/1/18	1095 10th St., Milwaukee, Wis. Mrs. Francis Grabowski (Mother).
Grabowski, Paul	Pvt.	Co. H. 128 Inf.	KIA	10/20/18	510 Braddock, Braddock, Pa. William Arnowitz.
Graf, Ernest	Sgt.	Co. E. 126 Inf.	KIA	10/4/18	1223 Wright St., Ann Arbor, Mich. Mrs. Margaret Graf (Mother).
Graham, James H.	Sgt.	Co. G. 127 Inf.	KIA	8/6/18	1210 Williamson St., Madison, Wis. H. B. Graham.
Graham, William	Corp.	Co. K. 128 Inf.	KIA	8/2/18	202 Franklin St., Whitewater, Wis. Mrs. R. Graham.
Grammer, Joe	Corp.	Co. G. 127 Inf.	DW	10/9/18	Big Fork, Mont. Mrs. Emma L. Grammer (Wife).
Grams, August B.	Pvt.	Co. H. 125 Inf.	KIA	8/29/18	R. F. D. 2, Friesland, Minn. John F. Grams.
Granc, Joseph	Pvt.	Co. K. 125 Inf.	KIA	7/31/18	332 W. Elm St., Kent, Ohio. Edmund Granc (Brother).
Grave, Clarence C.	Pvt.	Co. I. 125 Inf.	KIA	10/29/18	Harpers Ferry, W. Va. Morris F. Grave.
Graves, Arthur T.	Pvt.	Co. H. 125 Inf.	KIA	10/14/18	Quitman, Mo. Mrs. Georgiana Graves.
Graves, Johnson	Pvt.	Co. G. 128 Inf.	DW	10/6/18	....
Gray, James S.	Pvt. 1cl.	Co. C. 126 Inf.	KIA	8/1/18	R. F. D. 4, Battle Creek, Mich. Mr. S. R. Gray.
Gray, Roscoe	Corp.	Co. M. 127 Inf.	KIA	8/4/18	Lima, Ohio. Elizabeth Gray (Mother).
Gray, Schyler	Pvt.	Co. K. 126 Inf.	DW	8/31/18	Cadiz, Ky. James Gray.
Greeley, Tim W.	Pvt. 1cl.	Co. F. 126 Inf.	......	8/29/18	86 S. efferson Av., Battle Creek, Mich. Ms. Dell Greeley (Mother).
Green, Carl	Corp.	Co. F. 128 Inf.	KIA	11/10/18	North Vendon, Ind. E Y. Green (Father).
Green, Donald E.	Pvt.	Co. M. 126 Inf.	KIA	10/10/18	927 Dorchester Av., Gd. Rapids, Mich. Mrs. E. Green (Mother).
Green, James L.	Pvt.	Co. F. 127 Inf.	KIA	10/7/18	Amissville, Va. James Green (Father).
Green, Roy A.	Pvt. 1cl.	Co. D. 126 Inf.	KIA	8/12/18	R. F. D. 2, Portland, Mich. Albert Green.
Greggs, Archie L.	Pvt.	Co. F. 125 Inf.	KIA	10/7/18	2006 Edna Ave., Scranton, Pa. Thomas Greggs (Father).
Grego, Dominick	Pvt.	Co. C. 107 Engrs.	KIA	8/9/18	716 Brown St., Sault Ste Marie, Mich. Ambrose Grego.

NAME	RANK	ORGANIZATION	CAUSE	DATE	ADDRESS—NEXT OF KIN
Greer, Glenn	Pvt.	Co. K. 128 Inf.	KIA	11/10/18	Laurel Bloomery, Tenn. Sam Greer.
Greskowiak, Bert S.	Corp.	Co. F. 125 Inf.	DW	8/10/18	1407 Mill St., Alpena, Mich. George Greskowski (Father).
Griffin, Fred H.	Pvt.	Co. M. 127 Inf.	KIA	10/13/18	316 So. Oakley, Kansas City, Mo. A. M. Griffin (Brother).
Griffin, Joe B.	Pvt.	Co. H. 128 Inf.	KIA	10/5/18	Earlington, Ky. Ella Griffin.
Grimes, George	Pvt. 1cl.	Co. C. 127 Inf.	KIA	8/4/18	415 Franconia Ave, San Francisco, Calif. John Grimes (Father).
Grimes, Harry L.	Pvt.	Med. Det. 128 Inf.	KIA	8/31/18	R. F. D. 2, Anocartes, Wash. Mrs. Leona Grimes.
Grimes, James F.	Corp.	Mg. Co. 125 Inf.	KIA	10/13/18	Melvin, Mich. Hobert Grimes.
Griswold, Frank M.	Sgt.	Co. L. 126 Inf.	KIA	8/3/18	40 Reynolds St., Muskegon, Mich. Mrs. R. A. Griswold.
Grooms, Robert	Pvt.	Co. A. 128 Inf.	KIA	8/1/18	R. F. D. 11, Rushville, Mo. James E. Grooms (Father).
Gross, Alfred	Pvt.	Co. F. 127 Inf.	KIA	7/31/18	R. F. D. 3, Shawano, Wis. Henry Gross (Father).
Gross, Merle F.	Pvt.	Co. A. 127 Inf.	KIA	10/15/18	Richmond, Ind. Mrs. Nora Gross.
Groves, Burtaw	Pvt.	Co. A. 125 Inf.	DW	8/7/18	....
Grubb, William T., J	Pvt.	Co. D. 127 Inf.	KIA	10/19/18	1462 9th St., San Francisco, Calif. Mrs. Nellie Grubb (Mother).
Guest, Donald A.	Pvt.	Co. M. 128 Inf.	KIA	8/20/18	1263 Franklin St., Otsego, Mich. Mrs. Nellie Guest.
Guide, Fred	Pvt.	Co. L. 128 Inf.	KIA	8/3/18	1452 S. Komensky Ave., Chicago, Ill. Mrs. Anna Gordon Guide.
Gullo, Sam	Pvt.	Co. A. 127 Inf.	DW	5/8/18	....
Gustafson, John	Pvt.	Co. I. 125 Inf.	DW	2/15/18	....
Gustafson, Alfred I.	Pvt.	Co. I. 125 Inf.	KIA	10/11/18	Cook, Minn. Theila Gustafson.
Guth, Carl E.	Pvt. 1cl.	Co. I. 126 Inf.	KIA	10/9/18	324 Moll St., Lockland, Ohio. Emil H. Guth (Father).
Guyton, Joseph W.	Pvt.	Co. I. 126 Inf.	KIA	5/24/18	Ebart, Mich. Mrs. Winona Guyton.
Guzal, Anthony J.	Pvt.	Co. I. 125 Inf.	KIA	7/31/18	R.F.D. 4, Box 126, Pinconning, Mich. Mrs. Mary Guzal (Mother).
Guzman, Jesus	Pvt.	Co. C. 125 Inf.	KIA	10/22/18	Corpus Christi, Texas. Mrs. J. Cortez (Sister).
Haas, Alvin A.	Pvt.	Bat. D. 322 F. A.	KIA	10/15/18	....
Hadtrath, Byron	Pvt.	Co. C. 128 Inf.	DW	10/10/18	Ortonville, Minn. Charles Hadtrath.
Hagan, John J.	Pvt.	Hdq. Co. 121 Mg. Bn.	KIA	10/27/18	....
Hagerstrom, Charles R	Pvt.	Bat. B. 120 F. A.	DW	8/7/18	549 10th Ave. S., Wisconsin Rapids, Wis. Wm. Hagerstrom.
Haines, Richard B.	Sgt. 1cl.	Med. Det. 125 Inf.	KIA	8/6/18	Aptos, Calif. Mr. W. W. Haines (Father).
Hall, Charles A.	Pvt.	Co. L. 125 Inf.	KIA	10/9/18	R. F. D., Weston, W. Va. Sarah D. Hall (Sister).
Hall, Floyd	Pvt.	Co. A. 128 Inf.	DW	8/2/18	Fenton, Mich. Mrs. Frank Hall (Mother).
Hall, Oliver	Pvt. 1cl.	Co. L. 125 Inf.	KIA	8/31/18	Turner, Mich. Mrs. Mary Nightingale (Mother).
Hatch, Harold F.	Pvt.	Co. G. 127 Inf.	DW	10/6/18	Cobbs Creek, Va. Mrs. Evelyn Hatch (Mother).
Hallopeter, Charles C.	Corp.	Co. L. 128 Inf.	KIA	11/7/18	Bruce, Wis. Curtin Hallopeter (Father).
Hamilton, Burr	Pvt.	Co. I. 126 Inf.	KIA	10/5/18	Alpena, Ark. Rosa Hamilton.
Hamilton, Ivan R.	Pvt.	Mg. Co. 126 Inf.	KIA	7/31/18	859 4th St., Gd. Rapids, Mich. Mrs. Hugh Thayer.
Halvorsen, John	Pvt.	Co. F. 127 Inf.	DW	10/7/18	Meridian, Wash. Erick Halvorsen (Father).
Hamilton, Nevel H.	Pvt.	Co. A. 126 Inf.	KIA	10/5/18	Enavesta, Va. Matt. Hamilton (Father).
Hammond, Mervin F	Pvt.	Co. B. 128 Inf.	KIA	8/2/18	Oregon City, Ore. T. J. Hammond (Father).
Hampton, Robert	Corp.	Co. H. 127 Inf.	DW	8/4/18	926 N. 10th St., Manitowoc, Wis. Harry Hampton (Father).
Hanlon, Patrick L.	Corp.	Co. G. 126 Inf.	KIA	8/28/18	813 Burr Oak St., Albion, Mich. Mr. P. H. Hanlon (Father).
Hanrahan, Martin	Pvt.	Co. M. 128 Inf.	KIA	10/5/18	23 James St., Providence, R. I. James L. Hanrahan.
Hamilton, Jay O.	Pvt.	Hdq. 119 F. A.	KIA	9/30/18	Decatur, Mich. Emmett Hamilton (Father).
Hansen, Frank R.	Pvt.	Hq. Co. 119 F. A.	DW	8/16/18	....
Hansen, Ray H.	Pvt. 1cl.	Co. C. 125 Inf.	KIA	8/29/18	851 Halcolm Ave., Detroit, Mich. Mrs. Clare Hansen (Sister-in-Law).

245

NAME	RANK	ORGANIZATION	CAUSE	DATE	ADDRESS—NEXT OF KIN
Hansford, Morie	Pvt. 1cl.	Co. E. 125 Inf.	KIA	7/31/18	....
Haralobas, Vasilian	Pvt.	Co. M. 125 Inf.	KIA	10/12/18	Isle of Cyprus. Vasilios Haralobas (Father).
Hargis, Marion D.	Pvt.	Co. F. 128 Inf.	DW	10/15/18	....
Harden, James	Pvt.	Co. D. 128 Inf.	KIA	10/15/18	Shelley, Idaho. William Harden.
Harder, Paul	Corp.	Co. B. 127 Inf.	DW	8/1/18	Ft. Atkinson, Wis. Guido Harder (Father).
Harding, Ward M.	Corp.	Co. M. 125 Inf.	KIA	7/31/18	....
Hardlicks, James	Pvt.	Co. E. 125 Inf.	KIA	8/29/18	Stewartville, Minn. Mrs. Nellie Hardlicks.
Harding, Lloyd	Corp.	Co. I. 125 Inf.	KIA	10/10/18	312 4th St., Bay City, Mich. Mrs. Jennie Harding.
Hardy, Arthur H.	Sgt.	Hdq. 125 Inf.	DW	10/5/18	Flint, Mich. Mrs. Wesley Conke (Sister).
Harem, Andrew	Pvt.	Co. A. 127 Inf.	KIA	10/15/18 about	Trondhjem, Norway. Mrs. Anna Harem.
Harmon, Frederick A	Pvt. 1cl.	Co. M. 125 Inf.	KIA	10/18/18	....
Harkins, James	Corp.	Co. H. 126 Inf.	KIA	8/29/18	1609 Sterling Place, Brooklyn, N. Y. Patrick Harkins (Brother).
Harridge, Elmer	Pvt.	Co. A. 107 Engineer	DD	2/15/18	Prairie Hill, Mo. Wilbert F. Harridge.
Harms, Ufkie	Pvt.	Co. I. 127 Inf.	KIA	9/3/18	R. F. D. 3, Humbolt, Mich. Harry H. Harms (Father).
Harper, Fred B.	Pvt. 1cl.	Co. A. 125 Inf.	KIA	9/3/18	....
Harper, Henry P.	Pvt.	Co. A. 128 Inf.	KIA	11/11/18	Scott, Ark. Mrs. Nancy Harper.
Harpham, Bert E.	Pvt. 1cl.	Co. C. 121 Mg. Bn.	KIA	8/31/18	Council, Idaho. Mrs. A. Harpham (Mother).
Harris, George	Pvt.	Co. H. 126 Inf.	DD	11/2/18	....
Harris, Clarence G.	Pvt.	Co. M. 126 Inf.	DW	8/1/18	R. F. D. 2, Oakley, Mich. Mrs. Ellen Harris (Mother).
Harris, Walter S.	Pvt.	Bat. A. 120 F. A.	DD	....	413 16th St., Milwaukee, Wis. Mrs. G. R. Cassidy (Mother).
Harris, William H.	Pvt.	Co. I. 127 Inf.	KIA	10/4/18	....
Hassell, Walter E.	Sgt.	Co. H. 125 Inf.	KIA	10/13/18	Stockholm, Wis. L. A. Hallell.
Harrison, Frank	Pvt.	Co. C. 128 Inf.	KIA	8/1/18	164 Northampton St., Easton, Pa. Mrs. Samuel Harrison.
Harrison, John	Pvt.	Co. B. 127 Inf.	KIA	10/7/18	Bleasdale Lane, Nr. Garstang, Eng. Margaret Harrison (Mother).
Harrison, Oscar B.	Pvt.	Co. C. 125 Inf.	KIA	10/22/18	Greeneville, Tenn. William B. Harrison (Father).
Hart, Joe H.	Pvt.	Co. F. 5 F. A.	DW	10/7/18	....
Hartman, Leland O.	Corp.	Co. I. 126 Inf.	KIA	10/2/18	R. F. D. 2, Stanwood, Mich. A. M. Hartman.
Harvey, Roy E.	Pvt.	Co. F. 125 Inf.	KIA	10/12/18 about	Walnut Ridge, Ark. Louise Harvey (Mother).
Haslick, Charles	Pvt.	Co. E. 125 Inf.	KIA	9/4/18	R. F. D. 1, Brown City, Mich. Clarence Haslick (Brother).
Haught, Thomas M.	Pvt.	Co. B. 128 Inf.	DW	10/15/18	Sincerity, W. Va. William Haught.
Hayden, Frank J.	Pvt.	Bat. C. 147 F. A.	KIA	9/29/18	4 Lowell St., Lawrence, Mass. Mrs. Catherine Hayden.
Haugen, Oscar O.	Pvt.	Co. E. 127 Inf.	KIA	10/17/18	Hanska, Minn. Ole J. Haugen (Father).
Hawes, Wiles T.	Pvt.	Hdq. Co. 128 Inf.	DW	10/23/18	141 Austin St., Cambridge, Mass. Minnie L. Hawes (Mother).
Hawks, Emery M.	Sgt.	Co. E. 125 Inf.	KIA	10/9/18	317 Pasadena Ave., Flint, Mich. Charles Hawks (Brother).
Hawkins, Marvin	Pvt.	Co. M. 126 Inf.	KIA	8/2/18	Davy, West Va. Floyd Hawkins (Father).
Hawkins, Roscoe	Pvt. 1cl.	Co. L. 127 Inf.	DW	11/11/18	R. F. D. 2, Murrayville, Ill. Levi Hawkins (Father).
Hawks, John	Pvt. 1cl.	Co. M. 126 Inf.	KIA	8/2/18	R. F. D. 3, S. Norwich, Wash. Mrs. Jos. Gardnier (Mother).
Hazelton, Patrick	Pvt.	Co. C. 128 Inf.	KIA	10/20/18	Eau Claire, Wis. Mrs. M. Hazelton.
Hayes, Harrison G.	Corp.	Co. C. 125 Inf.	KIA	6/30/18	....
Haynes, Lynn L.	Pvt. 1cl.	Hq. Co. 126 Inf.	KIA	10/10/18	1301 Lerry St., Jackson, Mich. Louis Haynes.
Hayton, Joseph K.	Pvt.	Co. L. 125 Inf.	KIA	10/9/18	R. F. D. 1, Bristol, Va. William Hayton (Father).
Hayword, Wayne	Pvt.	Co. M. 125 Inf.	KIA	10/21/18	....
Heier, Phillip P.	Pvt.	Co. D. 128 Inf.	KIA	10/15/18	Glenullin, N. D. Mr. Philip Heier.

1. First Lieutenant Iden E. Chatterton, Intelligence Officer, Second Battalion, 126th Infantry. Killed in action October 6th, 1918, during the Meuse-Argonne Offensive.
2. First Lieutenant Thomas E. M. Heffernan, Company M, 126th Infantry. Killed in action August 1st, 1918, during the Aisne-Marne Offensive.
3. First Lieutenant William John Beal, Company L, 126th Infantry. Killed in action August 29th, 1918, during the Oise-Aisne Offensive.
4. Captain John F. Girard, Company D, 126th Infantry. Killed in action October 5th, 1918, during the Meuse-Argonne Offensive.
5. Captain Richard Frederick Smith, Company F, 126th Infantry. Killed in action August 5th, 1918, during the Aisne-Marne Offensive.
6. Captain Frederick W. Beaudry, Company H, 126th Infantry. Killed in action August 1st, 1918, during the Aisne-Marne Offensive.
7. Second Lieutenant Arthur Kindred Atkins, Company C, 126th Infantry. Died of wounds August 31st, 1918.
8. Second Lieutenant Robert Axford Osthaus, Company E, 126th Infantry. Died of wounds October 15th, 1918, during the Meuse-Argonne Offensive.
9. Second Lieutenant Richard E. Cook, Company H, 126th Infantry. Killed in action August 4th, 1918, during the Aisne-Marne Offensive.

Name	Rank	Organization	Cause	Date	Address—Next of Kin
Healey, Charles G.	Pvt. 1cl.	Co. L. 126 Inf.	KIA	10/9/18	Churchview, Va. Mrs. Vashti Healey (Mother).
Heasley, Henry C.	Pvt.	Co. B. 127 Inf.	KIA	10/11/18	Ree Heights, S. Dak. Henry Heasley (Father).
Heffron, Peter J.	Pvt. 1cl.	Batt. A. 121 F. A.	DW	8/21/18	415 Grand Ave., Milwaukee, Wis. James J. Heffron (Brother).
Hegelan, Christ	Pvt.	Hdq. Co. 127 Inf.	KIA	10/10/18	Grandin, Mo. Mrs. Mary Haller (Cousin).
Hillery, John	Pvt.	Mg. Co. 126 Inf.	DW	2/18/18	650 S. Broadway, Akron, Ohio. Michael Hillery (Brother).
Heinecke, Frank H.	Pvt.	Co. E. 127 Inf.	KIA	10/4/18	New Athens, Ill. Henry Heinecke (Father).
Heis, Roman J.	Pvt.	Co. K. 127 Inf.	KIA	10/15/18	1432 Clay St., Cincinnati, Ohio. Mrs. Harriett Heis (Mother).
Helmke, William	Pvt.	Co. E. 125 Inf.	KIA	7/31/18	....
Hendrikson Henry B.	Pvt.	Co. A. 127 Inf.	KIA	8/5/18	R. F. D. 4, Verndale, Minn. John B. Hendrikson (Father).
Henning, William	Pvt.	Co. D. 126 Inf.	KIA	7/31/18	R. F. D. 3, Mt. Clemens, Mich. William Henning.
Henniger, George	Pvt.	Co. 128 Inf.	DW	11/11/18	....
Herber, August W.	Pvt.	Co. G. 126 Inf.	KIA	8/28/18	425 McGivan Ave., Akron, Ohio. Mrs. Elizabeth School.
Herbert, Leon S.	Corp.	Co. K. 126 Inf.	KIA	8/28/18	Perry, La. Renny S. Herbert (Father).
Herbst, Fred B.	Sgt.	Co. A. 125 Inf.	KIA	10/9/18	Park Ave., Bexley, Ohio. Celia Louise Herbst (Wife).
Herigstad, Nels	Pvt. 1cl.	Co. I. 126 Inf.	DW	8/29/18	Silverton, Oregon. Nels N. Herigstad (Father).
Herman, Irving E.	Sgt.	Co. M. 128 Inf.	KIA	8/30/18	421 River St., Janesville, Wis. Mrs. D. Herman.
Herrold, Carl E.	Pvt.	Mg. Co. 125 Inf.	KIA	8/29/18	R. F. D. 6, Seward, Neb. Raymond Herrold (Brother)
Hesterkind, Timmon	Corp	Mg. Co. 127 Inf.	KIA	8/4/18	Cedar Rapids, Neb. Mrs. Henry Ricken (Friend).
Hewitt, George E.	Pvt.	Co. G. 126 Inf.	KIA	8/5/18	122 Merrill St., Detroit, Mich. Mrs. Laura Hewitt.
Heyenga, Lubbert L.	Pvt.	Co. D. 127 Inf.	KIA	10/12/18	Ridott, Ill. Lubbert L. Heyenga (Grandfather).
Hibbard, Albert L.	Pvt.	Co. L. 127 Inf.	KIA	10/16/18	905 4th St., Beloit, Wis. Mrs. O. L. Hibbard (Mother).
Hickey, John J.	Pvt. 1cl.	Co. G. 127 Inf.	KIA	8/4/18	22 N. Bassett St., Madison, Wis. Mrs. Sophia Hickey.
Hieatt, Aaron C.	Pvt.	Co. M. 128 Inf.	KIA	11/8/18	Smithfield, Ky. Aaron Hieatt.
High, Willie D.	Pvt.	Co. E. 125 Inf.	KIA	10/9/18	R. F. D. 1, Crystal Hill, Va. Mary R. High (Mother).
Highfil, James G.	Pvt.	Co. M. 125 Inf.	KIA	10/21/18	....
Higley, Earl L.	Pvt.	Co. C. 6 Inf.	DW	10/15/18	....
Hildebrand, William F	Pvt.	Co. E. 127 Inf.	KIA	9/2/18	Guide Rock, Neb. A'ava H. Hildebrand (Father).
Hiler, Edward	Pvt. 1cl.	Co. L. 126 Inf.	DW	7/31/18	639 Jackson St., Gd. Haven, Mich. Mrs. G. P. Hiler.
Hilferink, Hubert	Pvt.	Sup. Co. 120 F. A.	DD	.... about	R. F. D. 11, Grand Rapids, Mich. Mrs. M. Hilferink.
Hill, James	Pvt.	Co. F. 128 Inf.	KIA	10/10/18	Van Buren, Ark. Quinn Hill.
Hill, Phillip	Pvt.	Co. B. 127 Inf.	KIA	10/19/18	6th & Arizona St., Huron, S. Dak. Mrs. Augusta Hill (Grandmother).
Hillman, Anton F.	Pvt.	Co. A. 128 Inf.	DD	3/13/18	....
Hilton, Robert I.	Pvt.	Hdq. Co. 128 Inf.	KIA	10/17/18	....
Hoff, Charles A.	Pvt.	Co. D. 128 Inf.	KIA	10/15/18	Ft. Ransom, N. D. Mr. Sam C. Hoff.
Hintz, Fred E.	Corp.	Co. A. 127 Inf.	KIA	10/7/18	901 S. Peach St., Marshfield, Wis. August Hintz (Father).
Hintz, John A.	Pvt. 1cl.	Co. B. 125 Inf.	KIA	8/31/18	....
His-horse-is-fast, Isaac	Pvt.	Co. C. 128 Inf.	KIA	8/1/18	White Horse, S. Dak. Robert His-horse-is-fast.
Hitchcock, Floyd M.	Pvt.	Co. M. 127 Inf.	KIA	10/20/18	Gillespie, Ill. Edward Hitchcock (Father).
Hix, James C.	Corp.	Co. F. 127 Inf.	KIA	10/7/18	136 Grave Ave., Detroit, Mich. H. W. Hix (Brother).
Hodder, Jesse C.	Mech.	Co. F. 125 Inf.	KIA	9/3/18	Tawas City, Mich. Sarah Navess (Mother).
Hodges, Fred	Pvt.	Co. D. 126 Inf.	KIA	10/16/18	Blythesville, Ark. Mrs. Fannie F. Hodges.
Hodson, Floyd F.	Pvt.	Co. A. 125 Inf.	DW	8/28/18	Bellaire, Mich. Velma Russel (Mother).
Hoefer, Michael	Corp.	Co. I. 127 Inf.	KIA	7/31/18	2102 Thomas St., Marinette, Wis. Matt Hoefer (Father).

Name	Rank	Organization	Cause	Date	Address—Next of Kin
Hoeppner, Herbert O.	Pvt.	Co. M. 127 Inf.	KIA	9/2/18	Desmond, Neb. Theodore Hoeppner (Father).
Hoffman, Russell L.	Pvt.	Co. D. 128 Inf.	DW	10/16/18	Clinton, Dewitt Co., Ill. Jacob Hoffman (Father).
Hoffman, Frank	Corp.	Co. C. 127 Inf.	KIA	9/1/18	1024 St. Clair St., Sheboygan, Wis. Mrs. Elizabeth Jackett (Mother).
Hollingsworth, Bane C.	Pvt.	Co. M. 126 Inf.	DW	10/6/18	Mineral, Ark. Helen H. Hollingsworth.
Hoffman, Theobald	Pvt. 1cl.	Co. C. 127 Inf.	DW	8/31/18	1423 So. 8th St., Sheboygan, Wis. Mrs. Isabel Hoffman (Wife).
Hoffner, Herman	Pvt.	Bat. E. 322 F. A.	KIA	10/10/18	....
Hohn, Joseph A.	Pvt.	Co. L. 125 Inf.	KIA	7/31/18	Westmoreland, Kan. John Hohn (Father).
Hokanson, Carl A.	Pvt.	Bat. D. 147 F. A.	KIA	8/31/18	Sioux Falls, S. Dak. Mrs. Victoria Munkvold (Sister).
Holcomb, Frank J.	Pvt.	Bat. D. 147 F. A.	KIA	8/4/18	Centerville, S. Dak. James H. Holcomb (Father).
Holland, Harold	Pvt. 1cl.	Co. D. 127 Inf.	KIA	10/6/18	1523 E. Jefferson St., Seattle, Wash. John Holland (Father).
Hollenberger, Floyd H.	Wag.	Sup. Co. 120 F. A.	DR	6/8/18	Plymouth, Wis. Mrs. F. Hollenberger.
Holewinski, Leo	Pvt.	Co. L. 127 Inf.	KIA	10/16/18	Roberts, Wis. Peter Holewinski (Father).
Hood, James W.	Pvt.	Co. K. 128 Inf.	KIA	10/10/18	....
Hollis, Charles	Pvt.	Co. D. 128 Inf.	KIA	11/10/18	Gravel Ridge, Ark. Henry Hines.
Hollonsbad, Hoyt	Corp.	Co. E. 125 Inf.	KIA	7/31/18	707 Prospect St., Flint, Mich. Mrs. Bessie Brady.
Holmes, Floyd D.	Corp.	Co. D. 125 Inf.	KIA	7/31/18	1133 W. 4th St., Marion, Ind. Wellington Holmes.
Holtke, Herbert	Pvt.	Co. E. 125 Inf.	KIA	7/31/18	....
Holton, Guy H.	Corp.	Mg. Co. 127 Inf.	DW	9/21/18	....
Holtz, Frank F.	Pvt.	Co. L. 127 Inf.	KIA	8/4/18	26 Lathrop Ave., Beloit, Wis. George Holtz (Brother).
Holub, Floyd C.	Sgt. F. H	Co. 128, 107 S. Tr.	KIA	10/19/18	998 14th St., Milwaukee, Wis. Mrs. Anna Holub.
Holzschuh, George	Pvt. 1cl.	Co. F. 125 Inf.	KIA	7/31/18	....
Honaker, Jason	Pvt. 1cl.	Hdq. Co. 125 Inf.	KIA	8/28/18	705 Fort St., Sault Ste. Marie, Mich.
Hood, Harold H.	Corp.	Co. E. 126 Inf.	KIA	8/1/18	120 W. Washington St., Ann Arbor, Mich. Mrs. Harold Hood (Wife).
Hurst, Karl	Pvt.	Co. B. 107 Sup. Tr.	DD	10/18/18	....
Hooker, Sam	Pvt.	Co. E. 125 Inf.	KIA	10/18/18	Prescott, Ark. J. Y. Hooker (Father).
Hooten, Floyd	Pvt.	Co. H. 125 Inf.	KIA	8/4/18	Burlington, Iowa. Minnie Hooten.
Hope, Charles E.	Pvt.	Bat. E. 322 F. A.	KIA	10/10/18	....
Hopkins, Albert	Pvt. 1cl.	308 Bat. Tr. Art.	KIA	10/23/18	7504 Claasn Ave., Cleveland, Ohio. Mrs. William Hopkins (Mother).
Hopkins, Arden	Pvt.	Co. M. 128 Inf.	KIA	11/8/18	R. F. D. 1, Giles, W. Va. Tobatha Hopkins (Father).
Hopkins, Harry	Pvt.	Co. H. 125 Inf.	KIA	10/12/18	Russell St., Saginaw, Mich. Mrs. Ela Freder.
Hopkins, Thomas R.	Pvt.	Co. C. 128 Inf.	KIA	8/1/18	Milan, Mo. Mrs. Mary E. Hopkins.
Hopeland, Obert	Pvt. 1cl.	Co. E. 127 Inf.	KIA	8/3/18	Eleva, Wis. E. O. Hopeland.
Hopp, Roy	Pvt.	Co. F. 127 Inf.	KIA	7/31/18	335 13th St., Milwaukee, Wis. Matt P. Hopp (Father).
Horn, Nelson J.	Pvt.	Co. M. 128 Inf.	KIA	8/30/18	551 Chatham St., Janesville, Wis. E. D. Horn.
Horn, William	Pvt.	Co. H. 125 Inf.	KIA	10/21/18	Green Spring, W. Va. Andy J. Horn.
Hornaday, Paul W.	Pvt.	Hq. 120 Mg. Bn.	DD	6/9/18	....
Hosier, Clifford C.	Pvt.	Co. H. 125 Inf.	KIA	10/9/18	East Jordan, Mich. Mrs. Kate Hosier.
Hottenstein, Lonnie	Pvt.	Co. D. 126 Inf.	KIA	10/3/18	Moore, Mont. P. S. Hottenstein (Father).
Hottinger, Benedict J.	Mech.	Co. G. 126 Inf.	KIA	8/28/18	243 E. Jefferson Ave., Detroit, Mich. George Mcgonegal.
Houshin, Ward W.	Pvt.	Mg. Co. 127 Inf.	KIA	10/2/18	Hosterman, W. Va. Thomas Houshin (Father).
Hourcaillou, Jean B.	Pvt.	Co. D. 127 Inf.	KIA	7/31/18	1055 Valencia, San Francisco, Calif. John Hourcaillou (Brother).
House, Forest G.	Bnd. Corp	Hdq. Co. 125 Inf.	KIA	8/6/18	Lee Center, N. Y. Mrs. Hettie House.
Houser, William M.	Pvt. 1cl.	126 Inf.	KIA	8/28/18	200 S. Main St., Keyser, W. Va. Forest Houser.

NAME	RANK	ORGANIZATION	CAUSE	DATE	ADDRESS—NEXT OF KIN
Hovercamp, John	Pvt.	Co. L. 125 Inf.	KIA	8/2/18	R. F. D. 1, Ensign, Mich. Charles Hovercamp (Brother).
Howard, Glenn L.	Pvt.	Co. A. 128 Inf.	KIA	8/1/18	Neillsville, Wis. John Howard (Father).
Howard, Ray A.	Corp.	Co. L. 127 Inf.	KIA	8/4/18	506 W. Washington St., Harvard, Ill. George A. Howard (Father).
Howe, Frank	Pvt.	Co. G. 127 Inf.	KIA	10/5/18	1203 Hamilton St., Saginaw, Mich. Ellen Howe (Mother).
Howell, Eldridge	Pvt.	Co. F. 125 Inf.	KIA	10/9/18	Grubbs, Ark. May Howell (Sister).
Holzhieter, Herbert A	Pvt.	Co. A. 125 Inf.	ACC	8/8/18	....
Hrdlicka, James L.	Pvt.	Co. E. 125 Inf.	KIA	8/31/18	Stewartville, Minn. Mrs. Nellie Hrdlicka (Mother).
Hubbard, Joseph J.	Sgt.	Co. I. 128 Inf.	KIA	11/1/18	Forest Ave., Neenah, Wis. Mrs. Mary A. Hubbard (Mother).
Hubert, Don	Pvt.	Co. A. 125 Inf.	KIA	8/29/18 about	Redford, Mich. M. Hubert (Father).
Hudson, Elza O.	Pvt.	Co. B. 128 Inf.	KIA	10/20/18	Midway, West Va. Mr. Albert Hudson.
Huff, Lawrence	Corp.	Batt. A. 323 F. A.	DD	1/1/19	....
Huff, William Mck.	Pvt.	Mg. Co. 126 Inf.	KIA	7/31/18	R. F. D. 2, Sand Lake, Mich. Mrs. Susan Huff.
Huggins, Robert C.	Pvt.	Co. M. 128 Inf.	KIA	10/5/18	R. R. 7, Owensboro, Ky. Milus Huggins (Father).
Hughes, Forrest	Pvt.	Co. H. 128 Inf.	KIA	8/3/18	....
Hughes, James D.	Pvt. 1cl.	Co. M. 127 Inf.	KIA	9/1/18	280½ Pearson St., Milwaukee, Wis. Jeanette Hughes (Sister).
Hughes, Richard C.	Pvt.	Co. C. 127 Inf.	KIA	7/31/18	Richard J. Hughes (Father).
Hulet, Moses A.	Pvt.	Co. L. 125 Inf.	KIA	10/9/18	....
Humphreys, Burey	Pvt.	Co. F. 128 Inf.	KIA	11/10/18	Trinity, Texas. Betty Humphreys.
Humphrey, Avery Collins	....	Co. F. 128 Inf.	KIA	11/10/18 about	....
Humphrey, David H.	Corp.	Co. F. 128 Inf.	KIA	10/23/18	Eugene, Oregon (Ctow Stage). Mrs. Pline E. Humphrey.
Hunsinger, William A.	Pvt.	Co. A. 127 Inf.	KIA	10/7/18	1423 West 60th St., Seattle, Wash. Mrs. Mary Hunsinger (Mother).
Hunt, Richard R.	Pvt.	Co. A. 128 Inf.	KIA	8/1/18	68 Foster St., Pontiac, Mich. Charles Hunt (Father).
Hunt, Willard	Pvt.	Co. F. 126 Inf.	KIA	10/9/18	209 N. Horton St., Jackson, Mich. Mrs. John Lacy (Friend).
Hunter, Alger R.	Corp.	Co. H. 126 Inf.	DW	8/22/18	Mt. Clemens, Mich. Mr. Albert Hunter (Father).
Hurst, Robert H.	Pvt.	Co. F. 128 Inf.	DW	10/7/18	Mackoy, Ky. Lucy Hurst (Mother).
Hurt, William J.	Pvt. 1cl	Co. B. 127 Inf.	KIA	10/19/18	R. R. 9, Paris, Tenn. John W. Hurt (Father).
Huschke, Bernard H.	Pvt.	Co. E. 103 Engrs.	DW	8/5/18	....
Hutcheson, Clarence E	Pvt.	Hq. Co. 121 F. A.	KIA	8/1/18	Bentonville, Ark. W. T. Hutcheson (Father).
Hutchison, Henry	Pvt.	Co. B. 120 Mg. Bn	DW	9/3/18	....
Ibbotson, George W.	Corp.	Co. C. 126 Inf.	KIA	10/18/18	R.F.D. 2, Box 17, Kalamazoo, Mich. George W. Ibbelson.
Igo, William	Pvt.	Co. G. 128 Inf.	KIA	10/6/18	Turner, Ariz. Mrs. M. A. Igo.
Ingram, Hamilton	Pvt.	Co. H. 125 Inf.	KIA	10/21/18	....
Ingram, Judson E.	Corp.	Co. G. 125 Inf.	KIA	8/4/18	....
Irish, Wallace J.	Corp.	Co. H. 125 Inf.	KIA	10/10/18	R. F. D. 5, Gaylord, Mich. Mr. George Irish.
Irons, Oliver	Pvt.	Co. H. 125 Inf.	KIA	10/11/18	Moberly, Mo. Mr. William A. Irons.
Irwin, Abram L.	Mech.	Co. D. 128 Inf.	KIA	10/13/18	655 Hanes Ave., Alliance, Ohio. Harry Irwin.
Irwin, Herbert W.	Pvt. 1ci.	Co. D. 126 Inf.	KIA	10/15/18	R. F. D. 1, Smyrna, Mich. Dudley M. Irwin (Father).
Isaacson, Victor S.	Pvt. 1cl.	Co. M. 128 Inf.	KIA	8/30/18	57 S. Jefferson Av., Kalamazoo, Mich. Mrs. Mary Isaacson.
Iverson, Ole	Pvt.	Co. B. 128 Inf.	DW	10/14/18	Carson, N. Dak. Mr. Peter Iverson.
Jack, Joe D.	Bug.	Co. I. 127 Inf.	KIA	11/10/18	Ticonderoga, N. Y. Mr. Tony D. Jack (Brother).
Jackola, Axel R.	Pvt. 1cl.	Co. C. 125 Inf.	KIA	7/31/18	Hancock, Mich. Mrs. Axel Jackola.
Jacks, Robert	Pvt.	Co. E. 125 Inf.	KIA	10/12/18	Plattsmouth, Neb. A. J. Jacks (Father).
Jackson, Brewster	Pvt.	Co. L. 128 Inf.	KIA	10/18/18	R. 2, Ellenwood, Ga. Mrs. Ollie Pope.

ROLL OF HONOR

Name	Rank	Organization	Cause	Date	Address—Next of Kin
Jackson, Charles B.	Sgt.	Co. A. 125 Inf.	DW	12/23/18	
Jackson, John	Pvt. 1cl.	Amb. Co. 126 Inf.	DW	7/31/18	
Jacobson, Arthur	Pvt.	Co. C. 128 Inf.	KIA	8/1/18	Calumet, Mich. Mrs. Kaisa Jacobson.
Jacobson, William A.	Pvt.	MD. 128 Inf.	KIA	10/7/18	Viroqua, Wis. Mr. Jacob Jacobson.
Jaeckel, Harold	Corp.	Co. A. 127 Inf.	KIA	9/1/18	500 N. Cherry St., Marshfield, Wis. Mrs. Louise Jaeckel (Mother).
Jager, John	Corp.	Co. L. 126 Inf.	DD	10/29/18	568 W. Western Av., Muskegon, Mich. Samuel W. Jager.
Janczyak, Stanislaw	Pvt.	Co. G. 126 Inf.	KIA	8/2/18	990 E. 57th St., Cleveland, Ohio. Jan Czekal (Friend).
Janke, Otto W.	Pvt.	Co. D. 127 Inf.	KIA	10/15/18	New Auburn, Minn. Mrs. Marvell G. Janke (Wife).
Jankowski, Leo	Pvt.	Bat. A. 147 F. A.	KIA	10/13/18	White Pigeon, Mich. Mrs. Mary Jankowski (Mother).
Jankowski, Walter	Pvt.	Co. D. 128 Inf.	KIA	8/1/18	Kalisz, Pomat Kolo Gmin Koscilec, Wils Gosdow, Russia, Poland. Mrs. Leona Jankowski (Wife).
Janssen, Fred R.	Pvt.	Co. E. 127 Inf.	DW	10/6/18	Nokomis, Ill. Ubbe Janssen (Father).
Jarkala, Axel R.	Pvt. 1cl.	Co. G. 125 Inf.	KIA	7/31/18	
Jatropulos, Gust. S.	Pvt.	Co. L. 128 Inf.	KIA	9/1/18	1201 Gratiot Ave., Detroit, Mich. W. A. Buerger.
Jaworski, Jacob	Pvt.	Co. L. 125 Inf.	KIA	8/31/18	129 Andrus St., Hamtramck, Mich. Joseph Jaworski (Father).
Joworski, Stephen	Pvt.	Co. G. 126 Inf.	KIA	8/3/18	127 31st St., Detroit, Mich. Frank Jaworski.
Jelbrer, Marcel	Pvt.	Co. A. 126 Inf.	KIA	8/1/18	
Jenkins, Melvin	Corp.	Co. A. 121 Mg. Bn.	DW	9/1/18	Sturgeon Bay, Wis. Mrs. Joseph Jenkins.
Jonnart, Leon	Bugler	Co. E. 119 F. A.	KIA	7/12/18	608 Heckel Ave., Spring City, Pa. Mrs. Anna Jonnart (Sister).
Jenson, Emil A.	Pvt.	Co. A. 128 Inf.	DW	10/12/18	R. F. D. 1, Erskine, Minn. Bethel Jensen.
Jeppson, Hilmer	Pvt.	Co. C. 128 Inf.	KIA	8/1/18	Chappell, Neb. H. Jeppson.
Jerred, Harry D.	Corp.	Co. D. 127 Inf.	DW	9/6/18 about	
Jerzakowski, Walter	1st Sgt.	Co. K. 127 Inf.	KIA	10/15/18	940 2nd Ave., Milwaukee, Wis. Jacob Jerzakowski (Father).
Jett, Jesse J.	Pvt. 1cl.	Co. D. 126 Inf.	DW	10/11/18	R. F. D. 2, Fredericksburg, Va. Mrs. Irene E. Jett (Mother).
Jewell, Carleton	Sgt.	Co. F. 125 Inf.	KIA	7/31/18	
Jewell, Harvey	Pvt.	Co. K. 127 Inf.	DW	10/29/18	37 So. 20th St., Louisville, Ky. Ed. Jewell (Father).
Jobe, Dera	Pvt.	Co. M. 126 Inf.	KIA	10/4/18	Slaughterville, Ky. Mrs. Clarence Jobe.
Johns, Herman		Hq. Co. 128 Inf.	DW	10/11/18	R. F. D. 1, La Crosse, Wis. Chas. Johns.
Johns, Lewis C.	Pvt.	Co. F. 125 Inf.	KIA	10/9/18	Bath, Mich. Mrs. Mary Johns (Mother).
Johnson, Albert	Pvt.	Co. L. 125 Inf.	KIA	7/31/18	P. O. Box 31, Olondo, Wis. Fred Johnson (Brother).
Johnson, Algot	Pvt.	Co. M. 128 Inf.	DW	8/30/18	Box 484, White Hall, Mich. Mrs. Clara Johnson.
Johnson, Andie J.	Corp.	Co. E. 125 Inf.	KIA	7/31/18	
Johnson, Andrew M.	Pvt.	Co. L. 125 Inf.	KIA	10/9/18	Scoffs Lamhull, Sweden. John M. Magnuson (Father).
Johnson, Anton	Pvt.	Co. J. 128 Inf.	KIA	8/3/18	Box 31, Oconto, Wis. Fred Johnson (Brother).
Johnson, Cecil	Pvt.	Hq. Co. 125 Inf.	DW	10/13/18	Bayfield, Wis. Effie Johnson (Wife).
Johnson, Clyde	Pvt.	Co. G. 125 Inf.	DW	8/29/18	Joy, Mich. John A. Johnson (Father).
Johnson, Edmund O.	Pvt. 1cl.	Co. F. 128 Inf.	DW	9/16/18	
Johnson, Ernest	Pvt.	Co. H. 128 Inf.	KIA	9/2/18	
Johnson, Forrest	Pvt.	Co. D. 128 Inf.	DW	10/9/18	R. F. D. 3, Box 17, Monticello, Ark. Mrs. Minnie Pevcy.
Johnson, Fred L.	Sgt.	Co. H. 128 Inf.	KIA	8/3/18	Farmington, Me. Mrs. Florice G. Johnson.
Johnson, Gilbert	Pvt.	Co. L. 128 Inf.	KIA	11/7/18	Viola, Ill. Lee William Johnson (Brother).
Johnson, Graves	Pvt.	Co. G. 128 Inf.	KIA	10/6/18	R. F. D. 7, McMinnville, Tenn. Will Johnson (Father).
Johnson, Harold	Sgt.	Co. L. 125 Inf.	KIA	7/31/18	Menominee, Mich. Mrs. Hilda Johnson (Mother).
Johnson, Harry	Corp.	Co. I. 127 Inf.	KIA	8/4/18	5917 Oakes Ave., Superior, Wis. Mr. C. L. Johnson (Father).

NAME	RANK	ORGANIZATION	CAUSE	DATE	ADDRESS—NEXT OF KIN
Johnson, William M.	Pvt.	Co. G. 125 Inf.	KIA	7/31/18	Standish, Mich. Mrs. Wm. M. Johnson (Mother).
Johnson, William H.	Pvt.	Co. I. 126 Inf.	DW	10/5/18	Sartori, Louisiana. Jeau Carpenter (Uncle).
Johnson, Herbert C.	Bug.	Co. B. 125 Inf.	KIA	10/12/18	92 Clifford St., Detroit, Mich. Julia Johnson (Mother).
Johnson, Jens A.	Corp.	Co. G. 127 Inf.	KIA	10/4/18	R. F. D. 30, Beloit, Wis. Jens S. Johnson (Father).
Johnson, John E.	Pvt.	120 Mg. Bn.	DD	10/11/18	....
Johnson, John S.	Pvt.	Co. S. 125 Inf.	KIA	7/31/18 about	....
Johnson, John W.	Pvt.	Co. D. 127 Inf.	KIA	10/10/18	Ruhl, Idaho. Mrs. Anna Brown (Sister).
Johnson, Malvin B.	Pvt.	Co. M. 127 Inf.	KIA	10/19/18	Clear Brook, Minn. Olivia Johnson (Mother).
Johnson, Oscar E.	Pvt.	Co. M. 125 Inf.	KIA	6/31/18	....
Johnson, Peter	Sgt.	Co. B. 127 Inf.	KIA	7/3/18	191 5th St., Oshkosh, Wis. James Johnson (Brother).
Johnson, Ralph C.	Pvt. 1cl.	Co. L. 127 Inf.	KIA	10/18/18	1111 Cummings Ave., Superior, Wis. J. Nelson (Father).
Johnson, Richard	Sgt.	Co. E. 127 Inf.	KIA	7/31/18	Putnam & Birch Sts., Eau Claire, Wis. Carl Johnson (Brother).
Johnson, Rollie	Pvt.	Co. E. 127 Inf.	KIA	10/4/18	Stamping Ground, Ky. Lenora Johnson.
Johnson, Victor E.	Pvt.	Bat. B. 120 F. A.	DD	....	Weyerhauser, Wis. (Mother).
Johnston, Percy L.	Pvt.	Bat. D. 119 F. A.	KIA	9/29/18	Lake, Miss. Alice Johnston (Mother).
Jones, Ben	Corp.	Co. D. 128 Inf.	KIA	9/1/18	Camp Douglas, Wis. Oliver Jones.
Jones, Charlie	Pvt.	Co. D. 128 Inf.	KIA	10/13/18	R. R. 2, Snyder, Okla. Mary Plumlee.
Jones, Clarence E.	Pvt.	Bat. F. 322 F. A.	DW	10/27/18	....
Jones, Harmon R.	Pvt.	Co. K. 126 Inf.	KIA	8/28/18	925 Burlingame Ave., Gd. Rapids, Mich. J. C. Zimmer (Father).
Jones, Harry R.	Pvt. 1cl.	Hq. Co. 126 Inf.	KIA	10/2/18	321 Conant Terrace, Gd. Rapids, Mich. F. E. Jones (Father).
Jonker, Alvin	Sgt.	Co. L. 126 Inf.	KIA	10/9/18	513 Columbus St., Gd. Haven, Mich. Mrs. Annie Jonker.
Jorgenson, Knute	Pvt.	Co. F. 128 Inf.	KIA	11/10/18	Thompson, N. Dak. Jergen Jnutson (Father).
Josephson, Edwin B.	Pvt.	Co. B. 127 Inf.	KIA	10/11/18	1417 Griffith St., Los Angeles, Calif. Jolianas A. M. Josephson (Father).
Joyner, Other	Pvt.	Co. F. 128 Inf.	KIA	11/10/18	Holum, Louisiana. Ebenzen Joyner.
Judkins, Aubrey	Pvt.	Co. B. 127 Inf.	DD	1/15/19	....
Judson, Ralph A.	Pvt.	Co. M. 125 Inf.	KIA	7/31/18	....
Jump, Eden W.	Pvt.	Co. L. 125 Inf.	KIA	10/18/18	Lewistown, Mont. Samuel Curtis (Friend).
Jung, Otto F.	Pvt.	Co. E. 128 Inf.	KIA	10/5/18	473 E. 143 St., Bronx, N. Y.
Kagibitang, Alex	Pvt.	Co. K. 125 Inf.	KIA	8/28/18	Cross Village, Mich. Mrs. Margeret Kagebitang (Mother).
Kah, Alonzo L.	Pvt.	Co. I. 128 Inf.	DW	10/5/18	R. F. D. 1, Anna, Ohio. Mrs. Emma Kah (Mother).
Kahn, Leo	Pvt. 1cl.	Co. G. 127 Inf.	DW	8/12/18	514 N. Troy St., Chicago, Ill. Mrs. Jennie Kahn (Mother).
Kahra, Reino	Pvt. 1cl.	Co. K. 125 Inf.	KIA	7/29/18	Iron River, Mich. Ely Kahra (Brother).
Kain, Frank M.	Wag. Sup	Co. 127 Inf.	DD	10/23/18	Maddock, N. Dak. Mrs. Jasper Kain (Mother).
Kalbes, John	Pvt. 1cl.	Co. M. 127 Inf.	KIA	8/4/18	Round, Wis. Adam Kalbes.
Kalkbrenner, Fred W.	Pvt. 1cl.	Co. I. 125 Inf.	KIA	7/31/18	301 W. Ross Ave., St. Bernard, Hamilton, Ohio. Walter Kalkbrenner.
Kapanke, Fred	Pvt. 1cl.	Co. F. 127 Inf.	KIA	8/4/18	Shawano, Wis. Fred Kapanke, Sr. (Father).
Kaparos, Nicolas P.	Pvt.	Co. C. 128 Inf.	KIA	8/1/18	10 N. 14th St., St. Louis, Mo. Louis Kaparos.
Kapczuk, Joseph	Pvt.	Co. K. 127 Inf.	KIA	8/31/18	....
Kaphan, Jerome	Pvt. 1cl.	Co. E. 127 Inf.	KIA	9/2/18	563 24th St., Oakland, Calif. George Kaphan (Father).
Karch, Karl	Pvt.	Co. B. 128 Inf.	KIA	11/10/18	R. F. D. 1, St. Joseph, N. Dak. Mr. Karl Karch.
Karolczak, John	Pvt.	Hdq. 126 Inf.	DW	10/6/18	302 Sero St., Heidlersburg, Pa. Stanley Karolczak (Brother).
Karston, Gilbert D.	Corp.	Co. M. 126 Inf.	KIA	8/2/18	Zeeland, Mich. Miss Martha Karston (Sister).
Karvola, William	Corp.	Co. A. 107 Eng.	KIA	10/21/18	232 1st St., Calumet, Mich. Matt Karvola.

1. First Lieutenant Bruce W. Clarke, Company G, 127th Infantry. Killed in action August 6th, 1918, during the Aisne-Marne Offensive.
2. First Lieutenant Henry. S. Blomberg, Company D, 127th Infantry. Killed in action October 4th, 1918, while directing the organization of important ground which had just been won by his company during the Meuse-Argonne Offensive.
3. First Lieutenant Ray C. Dickop, Company L, 127th Infantry. Killed in action August 4th, 1918, during the Aisne-Marne Offensive.
4. First Lieutenant John Basil Roberts, Regimental Intelligence Officer, 127th Infantry. Died August 4th, 1918, of wounds received during the Aisne-Marne Offensive.
5. Major Adolph Trier, Commanding Second Battalion, 127th Infantry. Killed in action July 30th, 1918, during the Aisne-Marne Offensive.
6. Captain Myron Chester West, Headquarters Company, 127th Infantry. Died August 5th, 1918, of wounds received during the Aisne-Marne Offensive.
7. First Lieutenant Archie D. McGee, 127th Infantry. Killed in action October 18th, 1918, during the Meuse-Argonne Offensive.
8. First Lieutenant Irenaeus J. Lietemeyer, 127th Infantry. Died of wounds August 6th, 1918, during the Aisne-Marne Offensive.
9. First Lieutenant Otto Oas, 127th Infantry. Died January 3rd, 1919, of wounds received in action August 4th, 1918, during the Aisne-Marne Offensive.

253

NAME	RANK	ORGANIZATION	CAUSE	DATE	ADDRESS—NEXT OF KIN
Kase, Harry	Pvt.	Co. I. 126 Inf.	KIA	8/29/18	Rugtown, Pa. Mrs. Luke Kase (Mother).
Katapodes, John	Corp.	Co. E. 126 Inf.	KIA	8/1/18	1003 Broadway Av., Ann Arbor, Mich. George Katapodes.
Katz, Morris	Pvt.	Co. B. 128 Inf.	DW	10/2/18	1895 Milwaukee Ave., Chicago, Ill. Max Katz.
Kaufman, Alex	Pvt.	Co. D 107 Eng.	KIA	9/6/18	776 Bow St., Milwaukee, Wis. Mrs. Mary Kaufman (Mother).
Keegan, Ray	Pvt.	Co. F. 125 Inf.	KIA	7/31/18	....
Keel, Edward H.	Pvt.	Co. A. 127 Inf.	KIA	8/4/18	809 14th St., So. Bellingham, Wash. C. O. Keel (Father).
Keener, William H.	Pvt.	Co. H. 126 Inf.	DW	10/9/18	Seymour, Tenn. Hannar Keener.
Keezel, William A.	Pvt.	Co. A. 127 Inf.	KIA	10/15/18	Limestone, Tenn. Lizzie Williams.
Keezer, Charles	Pvt.	Co. I. 125 Inf.	KIA	8/28/18	Erickson, Neb. Mrs. Clara A. Keezer.
Kegley, Charles	Pvt.	Hq. 125 Inf.	DW	10/8/18	789 6th St., Detroit, Mich. Charles Arbough (Brother-in-Law).
Keinarth, Conrad	Pvt.	Co. H. 126 Inf.	DW	10/6/18	3560 Vine St., Cincinnati, Ohio. Mrs. Martin Keinarth.
Keith, Lee	Pvt.	Co. L. 128 Inf.	KIA	11/7/18	1543 Galleger St., Louisville, Ky. John Keith (Brother).
Kelian, George L.	Corp.	Co. E. 127 Inf.	KIA	8/5/18	....
Kellar, Samuel W.	Pvt. 1cl.	Bat. E. 147 F. A.	KIA	8/24/18	Hurley, S. Dak. Ida M. Kellar (Mother).
Kelle, Fred	Pvt.	Co. B. 128 Inf.	KIA	10/17/18	R. F. D. 1, Napoleon, N. Dak. Jacob Kelle.
Keller, Ralph C.	Pvt.	Co. D. 127 Inf.	KIA	10/19/18	Monterey, Indiana. Martin Keller (Father).
Kelley, George W.	Cook	Co. E. 56 Coast Art.	ACC	10/15/18	....
Kelley, Raymond S.	Pvt.	Co. E. 128 Inf.	DW	11/15/18	R. R. 2, Opdyke, Ill. Dorothy Furn Kelley (Wife).
Kellis, Burnice B.	Pvt. 1cl.	Co. E. 128 Inf.	KIA	8/29/18	Wickenburg, Ariz. Mrs. Hattie J. Kellis.
Kelly, Dan C.	Pvt.	Co. F. 126 Inf.	KIA	8/29/18	Mazon, Ill. Wayne Carter (Friend).
Kelly, Harry E.	Pvt. 1cl.	Bat. F. 120 F. A.	DD	....	101 Broad St., Elkhorn, Wis. C. E. Kelly (Father).
Kelly, Nelson C.	Corp.	Co. H. 128 Inf.	DW	10/18/18	545 Parker Ave., Detroit, Mich. Mrs. Joe Freend.
Kempter, John B.	Sgt.	Co. E. 128 Inf.	KIA	11/10/18	1616 Prairie St., Milwaukee, Wis. Mr. John Kempter (Father).
Kennedy, Lyman J.	Pvt. 1cl.	Co. M. 128 Inf.	KIA	11/8/18	2116 Division Ave., Gd. Rapids, Mich. Mrs. Ada Kennedy (Mother).
Kent, Roscer H.	Pvt.	Co. B. 125 Inf.	KIA	10/4/18	40 E. Montgomery St., Baltimore, Md. Lida Kent (Wife).
Kerlin, Arthur A.	Pvt.	Bat. B. 120 F. A.	DW	8/5/18	801 Armour Ave., Cudahy, Wis. Gust Kerlin.
Kerns, Perry	Pvt.	Co. E. 125 Inf.	KIA	10/9/18	Washington St., Petersburg, Va. Mary Kearns (Wife).
Kerp, Christian N.	Pvt.	Co. C. 127 Inf.	KIA	8/3/18	Zortman, Mont. John Kerp (Brother).
Keske, Clarence H.	Pvt.	Co. M. 127 Inf.	KIA	10/19/18	R. F. D. 2, Beaver Dam, Wis. Charles Keske (Father).
Kesser, James C.	Pvt.	Co. K. 128 Inf.	KIA	11/10/18	2417 Ohio Ave., Parkersburg, W. Va. Mrs. Rose Bolser.
Kessler, Godfred	Pvt.	Co. F. 127 Inf.	KIA	9/1/18	754 10th St., Milwaukee, Wis. Fred Kessler (Father).
Keveney, Alfred	Pvt.	Co. A. 127 Inf.	KIA	10/15/18	921 Riverview Place, Cincinnati, Ohio. Mrs. Anna Keveney.
Kicklighter, Charlie	Pvt.	Co. 107 F. S. Bn.	KIA	10/2/18	Jesup, Georgia. Mark Kicklighter (Father).
Kidd, John	Pvt.	Co. E. 127 Inf.	KIA	10/16/18	....
Kidder, Albert M.	Sgt.	Co. B. 126 Inf.	DW	10/5/18	Raisin Tw., Adrian, Mich. Mrs. Rena Sanford (Mother).
Kiefer, Carl	Corp.	Co. B. 121 Mg. Bn.	KIA	8/7/18	Tunnel City, Wis. J. J. Keifer (Father).
Kierschke, Edward G.	Pvt.	Co. C. 128 Inf.	KIA	8/1/18	1143 McDougal Ave., Detroit, Mich. Mrs. Anna Kierschke.
Kilgore, Clyde B.	Pvt.	Co. B. 128 Inf.	DW	9/1/18	Council Bluffs, Iowa. Mrs. J. J. Kilgore.
Kimball, Herbert P.	Corp.	Co. L. 126 Inf.	DW	9/1/18	1954 France Ave., Gd. Rapids, Mich. Mrs. Alice Kimball.
Kimbel, Roy	Sgt.	Co. E. 125 Inf.	KIA	10/9/18	Round Lake, Minn. Fred Niennher (Friend).
Kimmel, Donald K.	Corp.	Co. G. 126 Inf.	KIA	8/27/18	360 Linewood Ave., Detroit, Mich. Mrs. Pauline Kimmel (Mother).
Kinard, Ray V.	Pvt.	Co. H. 126 Inf.	KIA	10/5/18	Eldorado, Ark. G. G. Kinard.
King, Eldridge G.	Pvt. 1cl.	Co. A. 126 Inf.	KIA	7/31/18	Westfield, Penn. Mrs. Etta Car.

Name	Rank	Organization	Cause	Date	Address—Next of Kin
King, George A.	Pvt. 1cl.	Co. D. 126 Inf.	DW	10/6/18	R. F. D. 3, White Pigeon, Mich. Charles W. King.
King, George H.	Corp.	Hq. Co. 119 F. A.	KIA	8/12/18	65 Ledyard Ave., Detroit, Mich. Mrs. George H. King (Wife).
King, William C.	Corp.	Co. G. 127 Inf.	KIA	10/17/18	2119 Corry St., Madison, Wis. John King (Father).
Kingsburg, Leo F.	Sgt.	Co. D. 125 Inf.	KIA	8/4/18	1410 Koswett Ave., Lansing, Mich. Mr. Edward M. Kingsbury (Father).
Kirkeman, Sofus P.	Pvt.	Co. B. 127 Inf.	KIA	10/7/18	Veiers Pr. Oksbol, Copenhagen, Denmark. Axsel Anderson (Half Brother).
Kirkpatrick, Roy	Corp.	Co. G. 126 Inf.	KIA	10/10/18	434 S. Cherrie St., Alatha, Kan. James Kirkpatrick (Father).
Kister, Harold T.	Corp.	Bat. F. 121 F. A.	KIA	8/30/18	1737 Erie St., Racine, Wis. Mrs. Anna Kister (Mother).
Klavanian, Guiegh	Pvt. 1cl.	Co. H. 128 Inf.	KIA	11/10/18	228 Ferdinand Ave., Detroit, Mich. Abgar Chanian (Brother-in-Law).
Klebba, August J.	Corp.	Co. F. 125 Inf.	KIA	10/9/18	904 Mill St., Alpena, Mich. Mrs. Julia Klebba (Mother).
Klemmer, Louis A.	Pvt.	Co. F. 127 Inf.	KIA	8/1/18	2605 Walnut St., Milwaukee, Wis. Mrs. Louis A. Klemmer (Wife).
Kline, Anthony	Pvt.	Co. E. 125 Inf.	DW	10/17/18	164 Jacob St., Detroit, Mich. Mrs. Mary Kleine (Mother).
Klingman, Alfred	Pvt.	Co. E. 362 Inf.	DW	10/12/18	....
Klinkner, Gilbert	Corp.	Co. I. 126 Inf.	DW	10/10/18	423 Washington Av., Muskegon, Mich. Mr. Jake Klinkner.
Klomstad, Fred O.	Pvt.	Co. B. 125 Inf.	KIA	8/29/18	Audubon, Minn. Ole Klomstad.
Klucka, Anthony	Pvt.	Co. F. 125 Inf.	KIA	7/31/18	....
Klusendorf, Rudolph	Pvt.	Co. A. 126 Inf.	KIA	10/4/18	R. F. D. 1, Welcome, Minn. Henry Klusendorf (Father).
Klykunas, Stipanes	Pvt.	Co. L. 128 Inf.	KIA	9/1/18	133 Dorchester Ave., Worcester, Mass. Mary Swedarski.
Knag, Edward J.	Pvt.	Co. F. 127 Inf.	KIA	10/18/18	Litchfield, Ill. Mrs. Lewis Knag (Mother).
Knapp, Roy	Pvt.	Co. G. 127 Inf.	KIA	10/15/18	Sidney, Mont. M. W. Knapp (Father).
Knarr, Donald C.	Pvt.	Co. A. 127 Inf.	DW	8/3/18	93 13th St., Portland, Oregon. Mrs. E. F. Knarr (Mother).
Kneer, Mathias	Pvt. 1cl.	Co. E. 127 Inf.	KIA	8/3/18	309 Elm St., Eau Claire, Wis. Mrs. Anna Kneer (Mother).
Knobloch, Louis	Pvt.	Co. I. 125 Inf.	DW	10/10/18	Prairie du Rocher, Illinois. Mrs. Ollie Knoblock.
Knoke, Harvey A.	Corp.	Co. B. 127 Inf.	KIA	10/11/18	844 Mt. Vernon St., Oshkosh, Wis. C. C. Wiederman (Friend).
Koblitz, Emil	Pvt. 1cl.	Co. B. 128 Inf.	KIA	8/31/18	1626 Market St., La Crosse, Wis. Mrs. G. Peterson.
Koca, Frank E.	Pvt.	Co. C. 128 Inf.	DW	8/29/18	Tobias, Neb. Miss Emily Koca.
Kochanik, John	Corp.	Co. K. 127 Inf.	KIA	8/4/18	1002 7th Ave., Milwaukee, Wis. Walter Kochanik (Brother).
Kocian, William	Corp.	Co. H. 127 Inf.	KIA	10/4/18	....
Kocklaun, Richard H.	Pvt. 1cl.	Mg. Co. 125 Inf.	KIA	10/11/18	2188 Fulton Road, Cleveland, Ohio. Mrs. Louise Kocklaun.
Kohlmeier, George	Pvt.	Co. B. 128 Inf.	KIA	7/9/18	Gen. Del., Linn, Kansas. Mr. Henry Kohlmeier (Father).
Koivupalo, Henry	Corp.	Co. D. 120 Mg. Bn.	KIA	10/9/18	15 N. Tamarack St., Calumet, Mich. Mrs. Emma Koivupalo.
Kokoska, Michael	Pvt.	Co. L. 127 Inf.	DW	6/27/18	2122 W. 18th St., Chicago, Ill. Joseph Kokoska (Father).
Kolche, Sylce	Pvt.	Co. C. 126 Inf.	KIA	10/16/18	Unlinski Gub, Russia (Szodrasz). Oprzinka Kolche.
Kolean, Geo. L.	Corp.	Co. E. 127 Inf.	KIA	8/3/18	River St., Chippewa Falls, Wis. Herman Kolean (Father).
Kolkana, Herman J.	Pvt. 1cl.	Co. K. 126 Inf.	KIA	8/2/18	725 E. 28th St., Portland, Ore. Nicholas Kolkana.
Kolling, William	Corp.	Co. 125 Inf.	DW	10/9/18	Hardy, Neb. William Kolling.
Kolodziejski, Albert F	Pvt. 1cl.	Co. E. 126 Inf.	KIA	8/30/18	78 Center Ave., Detroit, Mich. Mr. Frank Kolodziejski (Father).
Kominek, Frank	Pvt.	Co. A. 128 Inf.	DW	10/7/18	Cushing, Minn. Martin Kominek (Brother).
Kopchinski, Frank J.	Corp.	Co. H. 126 Inf.	KIA	8/2/18	109 Hair St., Detroit, Mich. Miss Anna Kopchinski (Sister).
Koperwicz, Anthony	Pvt.	Co. D. 126 Inf.	KIA	6/19/18	913 Willis Ave., Detroit, Mich. Francis Kreiaski.
Kopp, Clarence E.	Pvt.	Co. G. 125 Inf.	KIA	10/14/18	810 York St., Hanover, Pa. John Kopp (Father).
Kops, Otto Herman	Corp.	Co. F. 107 Sup. Tr	DW	10/3/18	Unity, Wis. Herman Kops.
Kordus, Paul F.	Pvt. 1cl.	Co. G. 128 Inf.	DW	8/24/18	....
Kores, John L.	Pvt. 1cl.	Co. E. 128 Inf.	KIA	10/5/18	506 S. Center St., Beaver Dam, Wis. Barney Jores.

NAME	RANK	ORGANIZATION	CAUSE	DATE	ADDRESS—NEXT OF KIN
Korinski, Adolph	Pvt.	Co. C. 53 Inf.	DW	10/12/18	....
Kornas, John C.	Pvt.	Co. L. 125 Inf.	KIA	7/31/18	11 Flower St., Detroit, Mich. Katherin Kornas (Sister).
Kosal, Eli	Pvt. 1cl.	Co. H. 125 Inf.	KIA	10/15/18	Ruth, Mich. Mr. Valentine Kosal (Father).
Koss, George J.	Sgt.	Co. C. 107 F. S. Bn.	KIA	8/28/18	343 18th St., Milwaukee, Wis. Mr. John Koss (Father).
Kossewski, Atnoni	Pvt.	Co. C. 127 Inf.	KIA	7/31/18	Wallace, Mich. Pete Kossewski (Brother).
Koster, Thomas	Pvt. 1cl.	Co. H. 125 Inf.	KIA	7/31/18	Butterfield, Mich. Mr. William Koster.
Kovasivick, Wasil	Pvt.	Co. M. 125 Inf.	KIA	7/31/18	....
Kovnat, Hyman	Pvt.	Co. M. 127 Inf.	KIA	10/5/18	1137 N. Oakley Blvd., Chicago, Ill. Alex Kovnat (Brother).
Kovich, Bosceo	Pvt.	Co. D. 127 Inf.	KIA	10/19/18	Bear Creek, Mont. Sam Somarreh (Friend).
Krause, John	Pvt. 1cl.	Co. M. 127 Inf.	KIA	8/4/18	Gillett, Wis. Mrs. Charles Krause (Mother).
Kovola, Oscar	Pvt.	Co. F. 126 Inf.	KIA	8/28/18	P. O. Box 661, Hancock, Mich. Fred Kovola.
Krawczyk, John	Pvt.	Co. D. 120 Mg. Bn.	DW	10/12/18	900 American Ave., Milwaukee, Wis. Mrs. Martha Krawczyk.
Krazewski, John	Pvt.	Co. B. 125 Inf.	Suicide	10/2/18 about	....
Kreitel, Glen	Pvt.	Co. B. 128 Inf.	KIA	10/11/18	R. F. D. 1, Box 25, Napoleon, N. D. Mrs. Clem Kreitel.
Krell, George	Pvt.	Co. I. 127 Inf.	DW	10/13/18	246 Benzinger St., Buffalo, N. Y. Mrs. Emma Schwartz (Aunt).
Kremer, John F.	Sgt.	Co. F. 126 Inf.	KIA	8/29/18	411 N. Blackstone St., Jackson, Mich. C. B. LaRue.
Kremetski, William	Pvt.	Co. E. 125 Inf.	KIA	10/18/18	717 N. 17th St., Springfield, Ill. William Kremetski (Father).
Kresen, Frank A.	Corp.	Bat. F. 120 F. A.	ACC	....	Williston, N. D. Mrs. Frank Kresen (Wife).
Kresowki, Adolph	Pvt.	Co. E. 128 Inf.	DD	9/23/18	....
Kristoferson, Alfred	Sgt.	Co. A. 126 Inf.	KIA	10/15/18	3710 High Lane, Seattle, Wash. Mrs. A. Kristoferson.
Kritt, Harry A.	Pvt.	Co. M. 125 Inf.	ACC	2/13/18	400 S. Saratoga St., Baltimore, Md. Mrs. Vera Kritt (Mother).
Kriz, Joseph F.	Corp.	Bat. E. 147 F. A.	DD	10/3/18 about	R. F. D. 2, Cedar Rapids, Iowa. Joseph A. Kriz (Father).
Kroepfel, Arthur J.	Sgt.	Co. E. 128 Inf.	DW	10/13/18	1810 Cold Spring Av., Milwaukee Wis. Arthur Kroepfel (Father).
Kronquist, Charles T.	Corp.	Co. I. 127 Inf.	KIA	10/17/18	R. F. D. Box 37, Marinette, Wis. Mrs. A. Kronquist (Mother).
Kromer, Bernard G.	Sgt.	Mg. 127 Inf.	DW	8/2/18	....
Krueger, William J.	1st Sgt.	Co. M. 127 Inf.	KIA	10/3/18	628 2nd St., Oconto, Wis. Mr. Albert Krueger (Father).
Krull, Reubin	Pvt.	Co. I. 126 Inf.	KIA	8/1/18	R. F. D. 4, Three Rivers, Mich. John H. Krull.
Kryscysyns, Stanley	Pvt.	Co. K. 127 Inf.	DW	5/29/18	Podulski, Russia. Frank Kryscysyns (Father).
Kubeck, James	Pvt.	308 Btry. Tr. Art.	KIA	10/23/18	4274 E. 128th St., Cleveland, Ohio. Mrs. Marie Kubeck (Mother).
Kucera, Jerry E.	Corp.	Co. C. 128 Inf.	KIA	8/1/18	....
Kudlinski, Joseph.	Pvt. 1cl.	Co. K. 127 Inf.	KIA	9/1/18	1026 1st Ave., Milwaukee, Wis. Anton Kudlinski (Father).
Kuhn, Russel C.	Corp.	308 Btry. Tr. Art.	KIA	10/23/18	258 Soucler Ave. Mrs. Florence W. Kuhn (Wife).
Kujawa, Walter	Pvt.	Med. Dept. 120 F. A.	DD	....	1008 Chicago Ave., Milwaukee, Wis. Michael Kujawa (Father).
Kujawski, Thomas	Pvt.	Co. K. 127 Inf.	KIA	10/24/18	8437 Brandon Ave., So. Chicago, Ill. John Kujawski (Brother).
Kulbacki, Witold	Pvt.	Co. F. 107 Am. Tr.	KIA	10/6/18	984 Grove St., Milwaukee, Wis. Theodora Kulbacki (Mother).
Kumbera, Albert	Pvt.	Co. F. 107 Am. Tr.	KIA	11/10/18	....
Kunes, Archie G.	Pvt.	Co. K. 125 Inf.	KIA	10/12/18	Crescent, Idaho. David Kunes (Grandfather).
Kunkel, Frank	Pvt. 1cl	Bat. A. 120 F. A.	DW	11/21/18	1027 29th St., Milwaukee, Wis. Frank Kunkel, Sr.
Kunz, William	Pvt.	Co. E. 121 F. A.	DR	9/14/18	....
Kunzie, Harry K.	Corp.	Co. I. 126 Inf.	DW	8/13/18	Hersey, Mich. Mrs. W. G. Kunzie (Mother).
Kurklietis, Joseph	Pvt.	Co. E. 126 Inf.	KIA	10/9/18	509 Pearl St., Toledo, Ohio. Laurimias Kurkietis (Friend).
Kvlet, Oscar B.	Pvt.	Co. G. 128 Inf.	DW	10/9/18	Lonneberge, Sweden. Louisa Kvist (Mother).
Kvikawskie, Barney J.	Pvt.	Hdqs. Co. 126 Inf.	DW	10/15/18	....

NAME	RANK	ORGANIZATION	CAUSE	DATE	ADDRESS—NEXT OF KIN
Kwyecinski, Wldyslaw	Pvt.	Co. K. 127 Inf.	DW	8/5/18	....
Labar, Harry V.	Pvt.	Hdq. Co. 119 F. A.	KIA	9/1/18	Clio, Mich. Mrs. Harry V. Labar.
Labelle, Eugene	Corp.	Co. L. 125 Inf.	KIA	8/29/18	494 Alma St., Montreal, Canada. Jule Labelle (Father).
Labudavitch, Savo	Pvt.	Co. B. 127 Inf.	KIA	10/19/18	Nicgich, Montenegro. Plara Lubudovich (Sister).
Labutsky, Charles A.	Pvt. 1cl.	Co. FH. 128 Inf.	DD	2/26/18	230 Terrace Av., SE., Gd.Rapids, Mich. Glen Whitney (Brother-in-Law).
Ladd, Alfred E.	Pvt. 1cl.	Med. Det. 125 Inf.	KIA	8/6/18	Cranberry Isles, Maine. Louis E. Ladd (Father).
Lade, Arthur	Pvt.	Co. B. 126 Inf.	KIA	10/15/18	Sherburn, Minn. Mr. Herman Lade (Brother).
Laffey, John H.	Pvt.	Co. E. 125 Inf.	DW	10/7/18	Williamsonville, Ill. Josephine Walsh Laffey (Wife).
LaFrania, Kenelm	Corp.	Co. E. 127 Inf.	KIA	7/31/18	Bloomer, Wis. Joseph LáFrania (Father).
Lagemarsino, Stefano L.	Pvt.	Co. B. 127 Inf.	KIA	10/18/18	38 Alert Alley, San Francisco, Calif. Mrs. Mary Creno (Sister).
Lair, John C.	Pvt.	Co. A. 128 Inf.	DW	10/8/18	1319 6th St. W., Canton, Ohio. Mr. Alois Lair (Father).
Laird, Floyd M.	Pvt. 1cl.	Co. A. 127 Inf.	KIA	7/31/18	Comstock, Wis. William Laird (Father).
LaJeunnesse, Henry J.	Pvt. 1cl.	Co. M. 128 Inf.	KIA	8/30/18	520 N. Taylor Ave., Oak Park, Ill. Mrs. Delia LaJaunnesse.
LaJiness, Harry W.	Corp.	Co. D. 125 Inf.	KIA	10/10/18	209 Elmira Ave., Monroe, Mich. Mrs. Agnes LaJiness (Mother).
Lajores, Louis	Pvt.	Co. E. 126 Inf.	DW	8/4/18	804 Monroe St., Toledo, Ohio. Peter Lajores (Brother).
LaLonde, Joseph	Pvt.	Co. G. 128 Inf.	DW	8/29/18	Gold City, Mich. Mrs. Philman LaLonde.
Lamb, Ernest A.	Pvt.	Co. D. 126 Inf.	DW	10/9/18	R. F. D. 5, Fulton, Ky. James Edd Lamb (Brother).
Lamberton, Harold	Pvt.	Co. K. 128 Inf.	KIA	11/10/18	Toledo, Ohio. Mrs. Edith Denman.
Lammerding, Joseph H	Pvt.	Co. D. 126 Inf.	KIA	10/4/18	Buffalo, Minn. Anthony Lammerding (Father).
Lamphere, Glenn	Corp.	Co. A. 119 Mg. Bn.	KIA	10/15/18	Stanley, Wis. Mrs. Charles Lamphere (Mother).
Lams, Albert	Pvt.	Co. G. 127 Inf.	KIA	8/3/18	Allouez, Wis. Victor Lams (Uncle).
Lander, Richard	Sgt.	Co. G. 126 Inf.	KIA	10/2/18	21 Trinwith Pl., Cornwall, England. Mrs. Richard Lander (Mother).
Landstrom, Axel E.	Pvt. 1cl.	Co. H. 128 Inf.	DD	9/28/18	Commonwealth, Wis. A. F. Lanstrom (Father).
Lane, Edward	Sgt.	Co. I. 125 Inf.	DW	9/1/18	436 Ford Ave., Highland Park, Mich. Lulu Oliphant (Fiancee).
Lane, William D.	Pvt.	Co. B. 125 Inf.	DW	10/9/18	R. F. D. 1, Murraysville, W. Va. Mrs. Camie Lane (Mother).
Lang, Frank J.	Pvt.	Co. F. 126 Inf.	KIA	8/28/18	641 W. German St., Baltimore, Md. Mrs. Anna Lang (Mother).
Lang, Michael J.	Sgt.	Co. G. 127 Inf.	KIA	8/3/18	1603 Sherman Ave., Madison, Wis. M. J. Lang (Father).
Lange, Albert	Pvt.	Co. F. 125 Inf.	KIA	8/5/18	....
Lange, Harry L.	Corp.	Co. D. 127 Inf.	DW	8/4/18	Horicon, Wis. Mrs. Anna Lange (Mother).
Lange, Otto R.	Corp.	Co. F. 127 Inf.	DD	10/13/18	Columbus, Wis. Julius S. Lange (Father).
Langehaug, Ole	Pvt.	Co. G. 128 Inf.	KIA	10/12/18	Bottineau, N. Dak. Halver Langehaug.
Langendorf, Charles W	Pvt. 1cl.	Mg. Co. 127 Inf.	DW	8/1/18	96 N. Dale St., St. Paul, Minn. Mrs. Margaret Langendorf (Mother).
Langford, Richard J.	Pvt.	Co. A. 128 Inf.	KIA	11/10/18	Osseo, Minn. Richard F. Langford (Father).
Laniesski, Victor	Pvt.	Co. A. 125 Inf.	KIA	10/10/18	Chicago, Ill. Frank Cuno (Half Brother).
LaPage, Dewey N.	Sgt.	Co. I. 127 Inf.	KIA	8/3/18	1511 12th St., Superior, Wis. Mr. Napoleon LaPage (Father).
LaPoint, Delbert	Pvt.	Mg. Co. 125 Inf.	KIA	8/4/18	Box 47, Linden, Wis. Mrs. Lizzie LaPoint.
Larges, Walter W.	Pvt.	Co. H. 126 Inf.	KIA	9/1/18	345 Moviell St., Detroit, Mich. Mrs. Anna Larges.
Larkin, Harold	Corp.	Co. F. 128 Inf.	KIA	about 9/1/18	Kilbourn, Wis. Miss Jessie Larkin.
Larkowski, Ted	Pvt.	Co. C. 128 Inf.	KIA	8/1/18	Dannebrog, Neb. John Larkowski.
Larm, Joseph R.	Unknown	....	DW	10/2/18	....
Larrick, Everett	Pvt.	Co. K. 128 Inf.	KIA	10/6/18	....
Larson, Axel	Pvt.	Co. L. 125 Inf.	KIA	10/5/18	499 Pettit St., St. Paul, Minn. Mrs. Betty Olson (Friend).
Larson, Enoch L.	Pvt.	Co. L. 127 Inf.	DD	1/19/19	....

NAME	RANK	ORGANIZATION	CAUSE	DATE	ADDRESS—NEXT OF KIN
Larson, Rudolph A.	Pvt.	Co. A. 128 Inf.	KIA	8/1/18 about	Box 112, National Mine, Mich. Mrs. Mary Larson (Mother).
LaReu, Thomas B.	Pvt. 1cl.	Co. A. 128 Inf.	KIA	9/1/.8	Ironton, Wis. Luke LaRue (Father).
Lathrope, Lowell D.	Pvt.	Co. M. 125 Inf.	KIA	10/12/18	Joplin, Mo. Mrs. Catherine F. Lathrope (Mother).
Law, Edward	Pvt.	Co. D. 128 Inf.	DW	10/12/18	....
Leach, Gaylord P.	Corp	Co. M. 125 Inf.	KIA	7/31/18	Manistique, Mich. Rev. Frederick R. Leach.
Leary, Leo F.	Pvt.	Co. G. 127 Inf.	KIA	8/3/18	Gratiot, Wis. Elmer J. Leary (Brother).
Le Buda, Emil	Pvt.	Co. G. 128 Inf.	DW	8/6/18	Sauk Rapids, Mich. Gotlieb Le Buda.
Lecher, John P.	Pvt.	Co. H. 128 Inf.	KIA	10/17/18	R. F. D. 1, Box 39, Venturia, N. D. Mrs. Kate Lecher.
Ledford, James E.	Pvt.	Co. E. 128 Inf.	KIA	10/14/18	Rome, Tenn. Mr. Mathew Mofield.
Lee, Harold	Sgt.	Co. E. 127 Inf.	DW	9/2/18	Wheeler, Wis. George Lee (Father).
Lee, Nels	Pvt.	Co. A. 128 Inf.	KIA	11/10/18	R. F. D. 2, Ogilvie, Minn. Mrs. Dagmar O. Lee (Wife).
Lee, William W.	Pvt.	Co. G. 127 Inf.	KIA	8/3/18	Fleming, Minn. Sware L. Lee (Father).
Leggett, Archie C.	Pvt.	Co. H. 126 Inf.	KIA	11/10/18	....
Lehmann, Wilford	Pvt.	Co. G. 127 Inf.	KIA	8/3/18	Montague, Mich. Mrs. Fred Lehmann (Mother).
Leistikow, Herman	Pvt.	Co. F. 127 Inf.	KIA	7/31/18	1024 25th St., Milwaukee, Wis. Herman Leistikow (Father).
Lesland, Edgar H.	Pvt.	Co. L. 125 Inf.	KIA	7/31/18	308 Linwood Ave., Detroit, Mich. Mrs. Fred S. Leland.
Lemanski, Roman	Corp.	Co. D. 127 Inf.	KIA	6/17/18	1053 Middleman Av., Milwaukee, Wis. John H. Lemanski (Father).
Lemaster, Homer W.	Pvt.	Co. K. 128 Inf.	KIA	11/7/18	....
Lemke, Gustav O.	Corp.	Co. K. 128 Inf.	KIA	11/7/18	R. 4, Weston, Mich. William Lemke.
Lemke, John W.	Mech.	Co. I. 128 Inf.	DD	3/26/18	....
Lemke, William C.	Corp.	Co. D. 126 Inf.	KIA	7/31/18	543 Cyrus St., Irma, Mich. Mr. Charles Lemke (Father).
Lendowsky, Lea J.	Sgt.	Co. G. 128 Inf.	DW	9/1/18	221 E. Jefferson St., Wausau, Wis. Mr. A. Lendowsky.
Lenig, Harvey	Pvt.	Co. C. 125 Inf.	DW	10/12/18	Lyons, Neb. Mrs. Menia Lenig.
Leonard, Harry J.	Sgt.	Co. E. 125 Inf.	KIA	7/31/18 about	....
Leonard, Leo L.	Pvt. 1cl.	Co. B. 128 Inf.	KIA	10/20/18	Westfield, Wis. c/o James Russell. Mrs. Mary Leonard.
Lesch, Charles	Pvt.	Co. D. 126 Inf.	KIA	6/19/18	174 Freeman St., Brooklyn, N. Y. Mrs. Mary Lesch (Mother).
Lerch, Henry	Pvt.	Co. F. 127 Inf.	KIA	10/18/18	R. F. D. 2, Valmeyer, Ill. Adam Lerch (Father).
Leschikaz, Emil	Pvt.	Co. I. 128 Inf.	KIA	10/16/18	New Ulm, Tex. Emil Leschikaz.
Lese, Jacob P.	Pvt. 1cl.	Co. B. 128 Inf.	KIA	8/31/18	Princeton, Wis. Mr. William Lese.
Leslie, Martin O.	Corp.	Co. B. 126 Inf.	KIA	10/6/18	Box 322, Kenmare, N. Dak. Anna Leslie (Mother).
Lesniak, Michael	Pvt.	Co. G. 126 Inf.	KIA	10/5/18	116 Charest St., Hamtramck, Minn. Steve Antoscsyk.
Lesselyoung, William	Sgt.	Co. A. 127 Inf.	KIA	8/2/18	200 Vine St., Marshfield, Wis. Mr. John Lesselyoung.
Leszczcinski, John	Pvt.	Co. H. 126 Inf.	DW	8/33/18	625 Main St., Detroit, Mich. Joseph Bristevicz (Friend).
Leszkievitch, Joseph	Pvt.	Hdq. 127 Inf.	DW	8/30/18	....
Leveaux, Cosmer M.	Corp.	Bat. A. 119 F. A.	KIA	8/10/18	Ludington, Mich. John Leveaux (Father).
Leverenz, Clarence R.	Sgt.	Co. E. 128 Inf.	KIA	8/4/18	274 10th St., Milwaukee, Wis. Miss Louise Leverenz.
Levesque, Joseph R.	Pvt.	Co. B. 128 Inf.	KIA	10/14/18	Salem, Mass. Mrs. Claudia Berceir.
Levesque, Leo	Pvt.	Co. G. 126 Inf.	DW	8/4/18	....
Levi, Sandy	Pvt.	Co. F. 125 Inf.	KIA	7/31/18	....
Lewis, Frank A.	Pvt. 1cl.	Co. I. 125 Inf.	KIA	10/11/18	Chavies, Alabama. Joseph W. Lewis.
Lewis, Harry	Pvt.	Co. E. 128 Inf.	DW	10/8/18	1111 Sherman Ave., Cincinnati, Ohio. Richard Lewis (Father).
Lewis, Jack	Pvt.	Co. C. 127 Inf.	DW	10/6/18	Franklin, Mo. J. T. Lewis (Father).
Leyanna, Francis	Pvt.	Co. I. 126 Inf.	KIA	10/9/18	R. F. D. 1, Muskegon, Mich. Mose Leyanna.

1. SECOND LIEUTENANT GEORGE M. GERALD, Company D, 127th Infantry. Killed in action July 31st, 1918, during the Aisne-Marne Offensive.
2. SECOND LIEUTENANT RANDOLPH O. GRASSOLD, Company C, 127th Infantry. Died July 21, 1918, of wounds received in Alsace.
3. SECOND LIEUTENANT FRED L. HANGER, Company A, 127th Infantry. Killed in action October 14th, 1918, during the Meuse-Argonne Offensive.
4. SECOND LIEUTENANT FLEMING M. CROWELL, Company G, 127th Infantry. Killed in action October 15th, 1918, during the Meuse-Argonne Offensive.
5. SECOND LIEUTENANT CHARLES R. DANIELS, Company D, 127 Infantry. Died of wounds November 23rd, 1918, during the Meuse-Argonne Offensive.
6. SECOND LIEUTENANT MARION C. CRANEFIELD, Company C, 127th Infantry. Killed in action July 31st, 1918, during the Aisne-Marne Offensive.
7. SECOND LIEUTENANT SETH W. MURRAY, Company I, 127th Infantry. Died of wounds October 13th, 1918, during the Meuse-Argonne Offensive.
8. SECOND LIEUTENANT DELANCY J. COLVIN, First Battalion, 127th Infantry. Killed in action October 14th, 1918, during the Meuse-Argonne Offensive.
9. SECOND LIEUTENANT MORRIS TOGSTAD, Headquarters Company, 127th Infantry. Killed in action November 10th, 1918, during the Meuse-Argonne Offensive.

259

Name	Rank	Organization	Cause	Date	Address—Next of Kin
Lichtfuss, Charles H.	Pvt. 1cl.	Hq. Co. 127 Inf.	KIA	9/9/18	....
Liedke, Albert	Pvt.	Co. D. 121 Mg. Bn.	ACC	7/31/18	507 Washington St., Fond du Lac, Wis. Mrs. Caroline Liedke.
Lien, Louis	Pvt.	Co. F. 128 Inf.	KIA	11/10/18	R. F. D. 1, Rothway, Minn. Alf Lien (Brother).
Likens, Arthur	Pvt.	Co. F. 127 Inf.	DW	10/5/18	Corn Land, Ill. John Likens (Brother).
Lillefloren, Ole	Pvt.	Co. G. 126 Inf.	ACC	10/10/18	Brucelyn, Minn. George Lillefloren (Brother).
Lindon, Curtis	Pvt.	Co. A. 125 Inf.	KIA	10/9/18	Taulbee, Ky. Sofia Lindon (Wife).
Lindsay, Henry B.	Sgt.	Mg. Co. 125 Inf.	KIA	10/11/18	1345 Fairview St., Flint, Mich. R. A. Lindsay.
Linar, Oscar R.	Pvt.	Co. D. 127 Inf.	DW	10/12/18	R. F. D. 1, Benton, Tenn. James S. Linar (Father).
Liniger, William	Sgt.	Co. I. 126 Inf.	KIA	10/9/18	153 W. Western Av., Muskegon, Mich. Mrs. E. Liniger.
Linn, Ralph E.	Pvt. 1cl.	Co. H. 127 Inf.	KIA	10/13/18	Three Forks, Mont. Leslie R. Linn (Father).
Linna, George H.	Pvt.	Co. G. 125 Inf.	KIA	10/14/18	Painesdale, Mich. George Linna (Father).
Linstrum, Clemens	....	Co. C. 128 Inf.	KIA	10/13/18	182 Alvarado Rd., Berkeley, Calif. Mrs. P. G. Betts (Cousin).
Lippert, William W.	Pvt.	Co. K. 126 Inf.	KIA	8/2/18	Nicholsville, Ky. W. M. Lippert.
Lipschitz, Isaac	Pvt.	Co. C. 120 Mg. Bn.	KIA	10/1/18	Lockhaven, Pa. Max Liply.
Littleton, William C.	Pvt.	Co. H. 128 Inf.	KIA	8/3/18	....
Livingston, Clyde D.	Pvt.	Bat. D. 324 F.A.Hvy.	ACC	11/25/18	R. F. D. 2, Louisville, Ohio. Mrs. Lue Livingston (Mother).
Lockhart, John I.	Pvt.	Co. H. 126 Inf.	DW	10/12/18	Linneus, Mo. John W. Lockhart.
Locke, Guy	Corp.	Co. B. 121 Mg. Bn.	KIA	10/11/18	221 E. Silver St., Wapakoneta, Ohio. Clyde Locke (Father).
Locke, Harrison	Pvt.	Bat. F. 322 F. A.	DW	11/3/18	....
Lodusire, Frank	Pvt.	Co. G. 128 Inf.	DW	10/11/18	Scofield, Wis. Albert Lodusire (Father).
Loeacono, Frank	Pvt.	Co. L. 125 Inf.	KIA	10/21/18	Triggiano Di Bari, Italy. Guiseppi Loeacono (Father).
Loftus, Glen E.	Pvt.	Bat. C. 120 F. A.	DD	....	1314 Blandina St., Utica, N. Y. Edward Loftus (Father).
Loibl, Anthony T.	Sgt.	Hq. Co. 126 Inf.	KIA	8/31/18	126 Franklin St., Gd. Rapids, Mich. Mrs. Thriesia Alberts (Mother).
Loicca, Joseph P.	Pvt.	Co. E. 127 Inf.	KIA	10/5/18	R. F. D. 4, Kankakee, Ill. Dominie P. Loicca (Brother).
Loomis, Clyde A.	Sgt.	Co. H. 126 Inf.	KIA	10/9/18	6 Palmer St,. Gd. Rapids, Mich. James N. Loomis (Father).
Lopez, Reducindo A.	Pvt.	Co. C. 128 Inf.	KIA	10/10/18	Casa Grande, Ariz. Mrs. Carmen A. Lopez.
Losciskie, Joseph	Pvt.	Co. M. 128 Inf.	KIA	10/5/18	Parsons, Pa. Martha Lapinski.
Lukeman, Joseph	Pvt. 1cl.	Bat. F. 119 F. A.	KIA	10/3/18 about	567 Patterson St., Flint, Mich. Herman D. Lukeman (Brother).
Lott, Peter M.	Pvt.	Co. C. 128 Inf.	KIA	9/1/18	Fairmont, Neb. Mrs. L. F. Lott.
Lovejoy, Philip	Pvt.	Co. H. 125 Inf.	DD	4/30/18	....
Lowall, Mikady N.	Pvt.	Co. C. 119 Mg. Bn.	DW	10/6/18	....
Lowder, Herbert	Pvt.	Co. G. 128 Inf.	KIA	11/9/18	Cohtopa, Ala. Harry Lowder (Father).
Lowe, George	Pvt. 1cl.	Co. F. 125 Inf.	KIA	10/9/18	R. F. D. 2, Snover, Mich. George Lowe, Sr. (Father).
Loxon, Carl W.	Pvt.	Co. L. 126 Inf.	DW	8/28/18	Grant, Mich. Peter L. Loxon.
Lucas, Everett	Pvt. 1cl.	Co. G. 120 Mg. Bn.	KIA	8/28/18	....
Luce, Fred E.	Corp.	Co. A. 126 Inf.	KIA	8/1/18	R. F. D. 3, Bronson, Mich. Wellington Luce.
Luciand, Bonbert	Pvt.	Co. L.	DW	10/10/18	.... Luciand, Bonbert.
Luduser, Clinton B.	Pvt.	Co. B. 128 Inf.	KIA	10/14/18	R. F. D. 1, Lyndonville, Vermont. Mrs. Cora Luduser.
Ludvigson, Earl	Wag.	Sup. Co. 120 F. A.	......	....	Elk Mound, Wis. Mrs. G. Ludvigson.
Luecke, Robert	Pvt.	Co. F. 127 Inf.	KIA	8/1/18	....
Lueskow, Arthur	Pvt.	Co. L. 125 Inf.	KIA	7/31/18	805 Martha Ave., Menominee, Mich. Bertha Lueskow (Mother).
Lumsden, Clarence	Pvt.	Co. G. 126 Inf.	KIA	10/2/18	....
Lund, Eddy G.	Pvt. 1cl.	Co. C. 128 Inf.	KIA	8/1/18	Frederick, Wis. Mrs. Lund.

Name	Rank	Organization	Cause	Date	Address—Next of Kin
Lund, Otto T.	Pvt.	Co. M. 126 Inf.	KIA	8/2/18	Blooming Prairie, Minn. Mr. C. L. Lund (Father).
Lungwitz, Theobald	Pvt.	Co. G. 128 Inf.	KIA	10/13/18	Wittenberg, Mo. Herman Lungwitz (Father).
Lutz, Anthony E.	Sgt.	Co. A. 125 Inf.	ACC	9/19/18	923 Livernois Ave., Detroit, Mich. Mrs. Elizabeth Lutz (Mother).
Lutz, William B.	Pvt. 1cl.	Bat. A. 119 F. A.	KIA	8/10/18	Saline, Mich. Mr. John Lutz (Father).
Lux, Jesse J.	Pvt.	Co. L. 125 Inf.	KIA	7/31/18	Encinitas, Calif. Peter Lux (Father).
Lyczkowski, Anthony	Pvt.	Co. L. 128 Inf.	DD	10/14/18	6 Winter St., Detroit, Mich. Albert Lyczkowski (Brother).
Lymburner, Robert H.	Pvt.	Mg. Co. 125 Inf.	KIA	8/4/18	602 Huron Av., Harbor Beach, Mich. Mr. Alfred Lymburner.
Lynch, John	Pvt.	Co. A. 128 Inf.	DW	10/11/18	Sevy, W. Va. Mrs. Minnie Lynch.
Lynge, Nels P. L.	Pvt.	Co. K. 127 Inf.	KIA	10/16/18	R. F. D. 1, Arlington, S. Dak. Martin P. Nelson (Friend).
Lyngen, George H.	Pvt.	Co. K. 125 Inf.	KIA	10/9/18	Milan, Minn. Mr. Andrew Lyngen (Father).
Lyons, Ivan B.	Pvt.	Co. M. 125 Inf.	DW	10/10/18	Wayne, Neb. Mrs. Lizzie Lyons (Mother).
Lyons, Joseph P.	Pvt.	Co. H. 127 Inf.	KIA	7/31/18	....
Maas, Peter J.	Pvt. 1cl.	Co. G. 127 Inf.	KIA	7/30/18	....
MacGregor, Robert	Corp.	Co. A. 128 Inf.	DW	....	Co. I. 3rd Oregon Inf. George Mayleer (Friend).
Machen, Raymond O.	Pvt. 1cl.	Co. H. 127 Inf.	KIA	7/5/18	89 Wisconsin St., Oshkosh, Wis. Mrs. Alice Machen (Mother).
Maciejewski, Joseph E	Pvt. 1cl.	Co. C. 128 Inf.	KIA	7/2/18	624 Broadway, Berlin, Wis. Mrs. Josephine Maciejewski.
Mackinder, Joseph	Pvt. 1cl.	Co. I. 128 Inf.	KIA	9/1/18	....
MacMillen, Ralph F.	Pvt.	Co. M. 126 Inf.	DD	6/14/18	119 Fuller Av. SE., Gd. Rapids, Mich. Mrs. Mary G. MacMillen (Mother).
Madera, Arthur	Pvt.	Co. C. 128 Inf.	DW	10/7/18	....
Madson, Peter A.	Pvt.	107 M. P.	DW	8/31/18	Iron River, Wis. Mrs. Anna L. Madson (Mother).
Mairsky, Peter	Pvt.	Co. C. 128 Inf.	KIA	8/1/18	Box 39, Butler, Pa. Oleck Maersky.
Mainard, Lawrence	Pvt.	Co. M. 127 Inf.	DW	8/16/18	523 4th St., Great Falls, Mont. Nancy Mainard (Mother).
Mainville, Lewis J.	Corp.	Co. F. 125 Inf.	KIA	10/9/18	324 Avery Ave., Alpena, Mich. Mrs. Lena M. Dove (Sister).
Maiorana, Marius	Pvt.	Co. C. 128 Inf.	DW	8/1/18	260 Antontom St., Detroit, Mich. Mrs. Josephine Ajosta.
Malinowski, Nikodym	Pvt.	Co. K. 127 Inf.	KIA	8/4/18	691 55th St., West Allis, Wis. Albert Malinowski (Brother).
Malinski, John	Pvt. 1cl.	Co. D. 128 Inf.	KIA	9/1/18	992 Greenbush St., Milwaukee, Wis. Frank Grajak.
Manecke, Erwin R.	Pvt. 1cl.	Co. D. 120 Mg. Bn.	KIA	10/9/18	506 State St., Merrill, Wis. August Manecke.
Mangan, Edmund	Corp.	Co. H. 125 Inf.	DW	8/29/18	Onaway, Mich. Mrs. James Daly (Sister).
Margold, Louis A.	Corp.	Co. F. 128 Inf.	KIA	8/4/18	1002 Cedar St., Milwaukee, Wis. Mrs. Anna Margold (Mother).
Manocke, Dommicke	Pvt. 1cl.	Co. A. 126 Inf.	KIA	8/5/18	....
Manriquez, William	Pvt.	Co. A. 128 Inf.	KIA	....	Whittier, Calif. Trinidad Burrul (Brother-in-Law).
Mansfield, Henry R.	Pvt.	Co. K. 128 Inf.	KIA	11/10/18	Greensville, Texas. H. A. Mansfield.
Manska, Harry W.	Pvt.	Co. D. 128 Inf.	KIA	....	Elroy, Wis. Albert Manska (Father).
Manson, Harvey D.	Corp.	Co. G. 127 Inf.	KIA	9/1/18	1013 Center Ave., Madison, Wis. Margaret Priest (Mother).
Manzella, Michael	Pvt. 1cl.	Co. G. 126 Inf.	KIA	8/28/18	Palermo, Italy. Guiseppe Manzella.
Mapes, Ray D.	Pvt.	Co. C. 128 Inf.	KIA	....	Wolbach, Neb. B. A. Mapes.
Marco, Deloir A.	Pvt.	Co. A. 126 Inf.	DW	8/1/18	8 Sunset Ave., Little Falls, N. Y. Mrs. Celia Marco (Mother).
Markel, George	Pvt.	Co. H. 125 Inf.	DW	9/1/18	R. F. D. 2, Gagetown, Mich. Mrs. Elizabeth Markel (Mother).
Markely, Frank	Pvt.	Co. G. 126 Inf.	KIA	10/9/18	Columbia Furnace, Va. Moses Markely (Father).
Markowski, John	Pvt. 1cl.	Co. C. 121 Mg. Bn.	KIA	8/31/18	201 S. 58th St., Superior, Wis. Mrs. J. O. Olenski (Sister).
Markowski, Lee	Pvt.	Co. L. 128 Inf.	KIA	8/31/18	1274 Chene St., Detroit, Mich. Verna Rogalski.
Marks, Arthur A.	Pvt. 1cl.	Co. B. 126 Inf.	KIA	10/4/18	R. F. D. 2, Palmyra, Mich. Will F. Marks.
Marks, Rex V.	Corp.	Co. M. 126 Inf.	KIA	8/2/18	Fennville, Mich. Mrs. Rose Marks (Mother).

NAME	RANK	ORGANIZATION	CAUSE	DATE	ADDRESS—NEXT OF KIN
Marler, E. D.	Pvt.	Co. M. 6 Inf.	DW	10/15/18	....
Marlin, Jesse	Corp.	Co. B. 127 Inf.	DW	10/5/18	Genl. Del., Billings, Mont. L. C. Hall (Friend).
Marquardt, Albert R.	Sgt.	Co. G. 127 Inf.	KIA	8/5/18	R. F. D 4, Baraboo, Wis. Mrs. Louis Marquardt.
Marsh, Beteen	Corp.	Co. F. 128 Inf.	KIA	11/10/18	Red Granite, Wis. Mrs. C. H. Cody.
Marshall, Peter	Pvt.	Co. L. 127 Inf.	KIA	10/16/18	R. F. D. 2, Dedham, Iowa. Mrs. Sarah Sagler (Aunt).
Marthaler, Otis C.	Pvt.	Co. M. 127 Inf.	DW	8/12/18	143 Vermont St., Beaver Dam, Wis. Mrs. E. Marthaler (Mother).
Martin, Carl	Pvt.	Co. F. 128 Inf.	KIA	11/10/18	Elliston, Ohio. John Martin.
Martin, Claude B.	Pvt.	Co. D. 125 Inf.	KIA	8/31/18	....
Martin, John W.	Pvt. 1cl.	Co. F. 125 Inf.	KIA	8/4/18	....
Martin, Joseph	Pvt.	Co. B. 128 Inf.	KIA	11/10/18	Coal Creek, Tenn. Miss Bonnie Martin (Sister).
Martin, Luce C.	Pvt.	Co. L. 125 Inf.	KIA	7/31/18	1755 Lincoln Ave., Pittsburg, Pa. Mrs. Hattie Martin (Mother).
Marvin, Melvin.	Pvt.	Bat. D. 147 F. A.	KIA	8/4/18	Sioux Falls, S. Dak. Mrs. Ida Marvin.
Mason, Chester M.	Pvt.	Hq. Co. 128 Inf.	DW	10/18/18	Whitmore, Ark. James L. Mason (Father).
Mason, Murry	Pvt. 1cl.	Co. H. 127 Inf.	KIA	7/30/18	Blanchardville, Wis. Mrs. Ella Mason (Mother).
Matchkiewicz, Stanley	Pvt.	Co. B. 127 Inf.	KIA	10/11/18	343 E. Grant St., Nanticoke, Pa. Joe Matchkiewicz (Brother).
Matenazyk, John	Pvt.	Co. D. 128 Inf.	KIA	8/5/18	3225 Fisk St., Chicago, Ill. George Sabloski (Cousin).
Mather, Harry	Pvt.	Co. D. 126 Inf.	DW	10/16/18	R. F. D. 2, Box 15, Shakopee, Minn. John Mather (Father).
Mathews, Burton Jay	Pvt. 1cl.	Co. E. 125 Inf.	KIA	10/9/18	R. F. D. 3, Caro, Mich. John Mathews.
Mathiot, Cyrus	Pvt.	Co. D. 110 Inf.	KIA	......	....
Mayer, John	Pvt.	Co. A. 128 Inf.	KIA	11/10/18	Gackle, N. Dak. John M. Mayer (Father).
Maynard, Mertaon	Pvt. 1cl.	Co. A. 128 Inf.	KIA	8/1/18	Lodi, Wis. John Maynard (Father).
Mazouski, Hendrick	Pvt.	Co. H. 126 Inf.	......	......	422 30th St., Detroit, Mich. Mary Mozonski.
McArthur, Charles R.	Corp.	Co. I. 127 Inf.	KIA	8/4/18	Hancock, Minn. A. F. McArthur (Father).
McCabe, Edward	Pvt.	Co. I. 128 Inf.	KIA	9/1/18	Lenna, Okla. William McCabem.
McCadam, Joseph J.	Pvt.	Co. L. 361 Inf.	DW	10/11/18	....
McCann, Fred	Pvt. 1cl.	Co. H. 127 Inf.	KIA	7/31/18	Shullsburg, Wis. James McCann (Father).
McCann, George	Corp.	Co. H. 127 Inf.	KIA	8/5/18	Shullsburg, Wis. James McCann (Father).
McCarter, Jesse	Pvt.	Co. G. 125 Inf.	KIA	13/14/18	R. A. Carlisle, Ind. Mrs. John McCarter (Mother).
McCarthy, Joseph D.	Pvt.	Bat. C. 119 F. A.	KIA	10/23/18	2 Howard Place, Dorchester, Mass. Margaret E. McCarthy (Mother).
McCarthy, Thornton	Pvt. 1cl.	Bat. B. 119 F. A.	KIA	8/12/18	Webberville, Mich. Charles McCarthy (Father).
McCloskey, Douglas K	Pvt.	Mg. Co. 125 Inf.	KIA	8/1/18	Carson City, Mich. Flora E. McCloskey.
Mathison, Melvin	Pvt. 1cl.	Co. A. 128 Inf.	DD	3/31/18	....
McCann, Frank A.	Pvt.	Co. A. 120 Mg. Bn.	DW	10/29/18	Jacksonville, Ohio. Mrs. Ella McCann (Mother).
McClurg, John H.	Pvt. 1cl.	Bat. B. 147 F. A.	KIA	9/30/18	Inkom, Idaho. Mrs. E. J. Mears (Mother).
McCormack, George R.	Corp.	Co. L. 125 Inf.	KIA	10/9/18	5726 Magnolia Ave., Chicago, Ill. Lilly McCormack (Mother).
McCormick, Charles W.	Corp.	Co. B. 128 Inf.	KIA	....	Soldiers Grove, Wis. Mrs. Frank McCormick (Mother).
McCormick, Everett	Sgt.	Co. M. 125 Inf.	DW	10/9/18	Cooks, Mich. Mrs. A. J. McCormick (Sister).
McCoy, Marion	Pvt. 1cl.	Co. A. 120 Mg. Bn.	ACC	7/16/18	Box 374, Ravenna, Neb. Mrs. Earl Harris (Mother).
McCracken, Charles	Corp.	Co. M. 128 Inf.	DW	9/24/18	....
McDermott, Albert	Corp.	Co. K. 128 Inf.	KIA	11/7/18	1009 Sibley St., Gd. Rapids, Mich. T. McDermott.
McDermott, Thomas W.	Pvt.	Mg. Co. 128 Inf.	ACC	5/27/18	R. F. D. 2, Albany, Wis. John McDermott (Father).
McDonald, Archie R.	Corp.	Co. C. 126 Inf.	DW	9/15/18	Box 55, Central Lake, Mich. Mrs. Anna McDonald.
McDonald, James	Pvt.	Co. D. 128 Inf.	DW	11/11/18	Box 572, Livingston, Ill. Mrs. Helen Hunter.

Name	Rank	Organization	Cause	Date	Address—Next of Kin
McDonnell, Peter	Pvt.	Mg. Co. 128 Inf.	DW	11/12/18	Baraboo, Wis. Peter McDonald.
McDowell, John H.	Pvt.	Co. A. 126 Inf.	DD	12/8/18	R. F. D. 3, Mendon, Mo. Orrin McDowell (Father).
McElfresh, Leon	Pvt.	Co. B. 127 Inf.	DW	9/1/18	Redmond, Oregon. Josephus McElfresh (Father).
McEvoy, John J.	Pvt. 1cl.	Co. B. 120 Mg. Bu.	DD	7/7/18	Station C, Detroit, Mich. Joseph McEvoy (Brother).
McFarling, George T.	Pvt. 1cl.	Co. E. 125 Inf.	KIA	7/31/18	....
McGaughey, Mathias	Pvt.	Co. E. 128 Inf.	DW	11/10/18	....
McGenley, Eddie Roy	Pvt.	Co. K. 126 Inf.	KIA	10/14/18	....
McGlue, William G.	Pvt. 1cl.	Hq. Co. 125 Inf.	KIA	8/6/18	L'Anse, Mich. William McGlue.
McGolerick, Judge	Pvt.	Co. K. 127 Inf.	KIA	10/15/18	Star Route, Point of Rocks, Md. Minerva McGolerick (Mother).
McGraw, Michael B.	Pvt. 1cl.	308 Btry. Tr. Arty.	KIA	10/23/18	817 Frank St., McKees Rocks, Pa. Miss Mary McGraw (Sister).
McGraw, Thomas	Pvt.	Co. F. 128 Inf.	DW	10/7/18	1016 Calumet Ave., Chicago, Ill. Mrs. Charlotte McGraw.
McGraw, Wilson L.	Pvt.	Co. M. 127 Inf.	KIA	11/8/18	Prairie, Miss. Lula Corter.
McGregor, Wayman J	Pvt. 1cl.	Co. M. 127 Inf.	KIA	11/11/18	Abrams, Wis. Mrs. Delia McGregor (Mother).
McGuinness, James W.	Corp.	Co. D. 127 Inf.	DW	8/2/18	....
McQuire, Michael	Pvt.	Co. E. 125 Inf.	KIA	7/31/18	....
McGushin, Christopher M	Pvt.	Co. K. 127 Inf.	KIA	....	1112 W. 63d St., New York City, N.Y. James McGushin (Brother).
McHugh, Kenneth L.	Corp.	Bat. A. 120 F. A.	KIA	10/4/18	71 31st St., Milwaukee, Wis. M. L. McHugh.
McIntyre, Harry	Pvt.	Co. F. 125 Inf.	KIA	10/9/18	616 W. Carpenter St., Springfield, Ill. Mrs. D. L. Hixon (Sister).
McKeehan, David A.	Pvt.	Co. M. 128 Inf.	KIA	11/8/18	King. Ky. Franklin McKeehan.
McKeehan, Henderson S	Pvt.	Co. M. 128 Inf.	KIA	11/8/18	King. Ky. Franklin McKeehan.
McKay, William W.	Pvt.	Mg. Co. 127 Inf.	DD	9/30/18	Ismay. Mont. Mrs. William McKay (Mother).
McKearn, Joseph A.	Corp.	Co. L. 127 Inf.	KIA	8/4/18	822 4th St., Beloit, Wis. Michael McKearn (Father).
McKeen, James	Pvt.	Co. C. 127 Inf.	KIA	10/5/18	2864 8th Ave., New York City, N. Y. Mrs. Susie McKeen (Mother).
McKinney, Hugh L.	Pvt.	Co. B. 127 Inf.	KIA	10/19/18	Douglas, Ariz. Earl McKinney (Brother).
McLaughlin, James F	Pvt.	Co. C. 120 Mg. Bn.	KIA	8/1/18	5 Rcbey St., Dorchester, Mass. Mrs. Nellie McLaughlin.
McLenahan, James	Pvt.	Co. F. 128 Inf.	KIA	11/10/18	Quiton, Okla. Mrs. Beulah McLenahan (Mother).
McLean, Donald	Pvt.	Co. E. 128 Inf.	KIA	10/5/18	Brighton, Colorado. Donald McLean (Father).
McLenden, Felix	Pvt.	Co. L. 128 Inf.	DW	11/14/18	R. 1, Atlanta, Ark. R. H. McLenden (Father).
McManus, Eugene N.	Pvt.	Hq. Co. 147 F. A.	DW	8/2/18	....
McMillan, Fred	Pvt.	Co. B. 128 Inf.	KIA	11/10/18	Richfield, Idaho. Miss Bertha McMillan.
McMullen, Howard	Pvt.	Co. M. 128 Inf.	KIA	11/8/18	Grandfit, Colo. Mrs. Elsie McIntire.
McNamara, Leon	Sgt.	Co. F. 128 Inf.	KIA	10/4/18	Cadillac, Mich. Mrs. T. McNamara (Mother).
McNeese, Walter L.	Co p.	Co. M. 128 Inf.	KIA	10/6/18	R. F. D. 3, Jonesboro, Tenn. John McNeese.
McPherson, Ivan	Corp.	Co. H. 125 Inf.	KIA	7/31/18	Onaway, Mich. John McPherson (Father).
McQuien, Walter H.	Pvt.	Co. C. 120 Mg. Bn	DW	8/28/18	Lau, Texas. Mrs. M. A. McQuien.
McRae, Orlo	Pvt.	Co. C. 120 Mg. Bn.	KIA	8/29/18	La Veta, Colo. J. W. McRae.
Meacham, Lawrence	Pvt.	Co. E. 128 Inf.	DW	10/12/18	Port Allegheny, Pa. George Meacham.
Mead, James F.	Pvt. 1cl.	Co. A. 128 Inf.	KIA	8/1/18	Sandusky, Wis. William Mead (Father).
Meadows, Lee C.	Pvt.	Co. A. 127 Inf.	KIA	8/5/18	51 E. 72nd St., Portland, Oregon. C. W. Meadows (Father).
Meier, Walter E.	Pvt.	Co. H. 126 Inf.	KIA	10/9/18	Knox, Pa. Mrs. J. J. Meier.
Meinhart, John L.	Pvt.	Co. M. 126 Inf.	KIA	11/8/18	R. 1, Jewett, Ill. Muichen Meinhart.
Meiser, Julius	Pvt.	Co. H. 127 Inf.	KIA	10/15/18	240 Vine St., Reading, Ohio. Mayme Meiser (Sister).

263

Name	Rank	Organization	Cause	Date	Address—Next of Kin
Melcher, Edward	Sgt.	Co. C. 120 Mg. Bn.	KIA	8/28/18	43 Williams Ave., Detroit, Mich. Mrs. Emma Melcher.
Melnichuk, Samuel	Pvt.	Co. C. 128 Inf.	KIA	8/1/18	
Melosh, Eugene	Pvt. 1cl.	Co. G. 128 Inf.	KIA	....	R. 1, Ellsworth, Mich. Bert Melosh.
Melvin, Frank	Cook	Bat. C. 120 F. A.	DW	10/31/18	8338 N. Phillyss St., Philadelphia, Pa. Mrs. Kity Melvin.
Mercer, Bruce A.	Pvt. 1cl.	Co. F. 126 Inf.	KIA	10/4/18	421 W. 9th Ave., Puyallupp, Wash. Mrs. C. N. Mercer (Mother).
Merrill, Percy E.	Pvt. 1cl.	Co. F. 107 Sup. Tr.	DD	12/24/18	
Merry, Clarence F.	Corp.	Co. K. 126 Inf.	KIA	8/28/18	548 Giddings St., Gd. Rapids, Mich. Harry L. Merry.
Messner, Fred	Pvt.	Co. G. 125 Inf.	KIA	10/8/18	Trimountain, Mich. Oscar Steinheld (Brother-in-Law).
Metzenbauger, Claire	Corp.	107 Sup. Tr.	KIA	2/5/18	
Metzler, Harry	Pvt.	Co. A. 121 Mg. Bn.	KIA	10/10/18	R. F. D. 3, Oak Hill, Ohio. Charles Metzler (Father).
Meuli, Michael	Corp.	Co. E. 127 Inf.	......	9/2/18	212 Rurla St., Chippewa Falls, Wis. Joseph Meuli (Father).
Meyer, Frank	Pvt.	Hq. 127 Inf.	KIA	7/31/18	1032 N. Hickory St., Janesville, Wis. Henry F. Meyer (Father).
Michel, Henry A.	Mech.	Co. A. 125 Inf.	KIA	8/6/18	Lapeer, Mich. Anna Michel (Mother).
Michell, Carl A.	Pvt.	Co. L. 126 Inf.	KIA	10/9/18	R. F. D. 1, Emmett, Ark. A. F. Jahanke (Father).
Michel, John A.	Pvt.	Co. M. 128 Inf.	KIA	11/8/18	1304 Huntington Ave., Sandusky, O. Wm. Michel.
Michelson, Heimer	Horseshr	Co. B. 107 M. P.	DW	8/2/18	
Mienkwicz, Frank P.	Pvt.	Co. A. 18 Inf.	......	9/1/18	1306 Michigan Ave., Bay City, Mich. Mrs. Julia Mienkwicz.
Mierzwinski, Peter W.	Pvt.	Hq. Co. 126 Inf.	KIA	10/2/18	2429 Walton Ave., Chicago, Ill. Mieczislaw Mierzwinski.
Mike, Dewey	Pvt.	Co. A. 128 Inf.	DW	8/30/18	Neillsville, Wis. John Mike (Father).
Mikelajczyk, Joseph	Pvt.	Co. K. 127 Inf.	KIA	8/4/18	834 Burnham Ave., Milwaukee, Wis. Frank Mikelajczyk (Father).
Mikkelson, Johannes S	Pvt.	Co. F. 125 Inf.	KIA	8/2/18	
Miles, Glenn	Pvt.	Co. C. 127 Inf.	KIA	10/4/18	Smithfield, Utah. Gertrude Miles (Wife).
Millar, James	Wag.	Sup. Co. 120 F. A.	DD	....	Lake Geneva, Wis. William Millar.
Miller, David D.	Pvt.	Co. H. 126 Inf.	......	8/30/18	R. F. D. 4, Clare, Mich. Mrs. Mary Miller (Mother).
Miller, Ernest G.	Sgt.	Co. A. 127 Inf.	KIA	10/15/18	East 9th St., Marshfield, Wis. Gustave Fred Miller (Father).
Miller, Francis	Pvt.	Co. F. 126 Inf.	KIA	8/2/18	103 Henrietta St., Jackson, Mich. Frank Miller (Father).
Miller, Frank R.	Pvt.	126 Inf.	DD	9/24/18	R. F. D. 1, Gladstone, Ill. Mrs. Mary Miller (Mother).
Miller, Fred	Pvt.	Mg. Co. 127 Inf.	KIA	9/1/18	Butte, Mont. Samuel Shiner (Friend).
Miller, Hiram	Pvt.	Co. E. 125 Inf.	KIA	10/7/18	Dresden, Ind. William Miller (Father).
Miller, John E.	Corp.	Co. D. 127 Inf.	KIA	8/4/18	1202 S. Spring St., Beaver Dam, Wis. Mrs. Gust. Miller (Mother).
Miller, Leo A.	Pvt. 1cl.	Co. K. 126 Inf.	KIA	8/29/18	Middleville, Mich. Otto B. Miller.
Miller, Leo M.	Corp.	Co. D. 107 Sup. Tr.	DD	6/29/18	
Miller, Oren Grover	Pvt.	Hq. 125 Inf.	KIA	8/6/18	425 Michigan Ave., Detroit, Mich. Mrs. Nellie Miller.
Miller, Pram G.	Pvt.	Hq. 125 Inf.	KIA	8/6/18	425 Michigan Ave., Detroit, Mich. Mrs. Nellie Miller.
Miller, Ray L.	Bug.	Co. L. 127 Inf.	KIA	8/3/18	
Miller, Thomas	Pvt.	Co. B. 125 Inf.	KIA	10/5/18	Viva, Ky. George Miller (Father).
Miller, Ulysses	Pvt.	Co. H. 128 Inf.	KIA	10/20/18	
Miller, Walter B.	Corp.	Co. D. 125 Inf.	DW	8/29/18	417 Sackett Ave., Monroe, Mich. Forest H. Miller.
Miller, Walter R.	Pvt.	Co. C. 126 Inf.	KIA	7/15/18	R. F. D. 21, Plainwell, Mich. Mrs. Cora Miller (Sister).
Miller, William	Corp.	Co. E. 127 Inf.	KIA	7/31/18	613 Division St., Eau Claire, Wis. Fred C. Miller (Father).
Mills, Alfred C.	Pvt. 1cl.	Co. H. 127 Inf.	DW	8/31/18	415 6th Ave., Great Falls, Mont. Robert J. Mills (Brother).
Minehan, Hugh P.	Corp.	Co. M. 127 Inf.	KIA	11/11/18	Garrison, N. Dak. Annie Minehan (Mother).
Minnard, Wibur	Corp.	Co. C. 126 Inf.	KIA	10/5/18	R. F. D. 2, Otsego, Mich. Mrs. Susie M. Minnard.

1. SECOND LIEUTENANT EDWARD A. BURTON, Company D, 128th Infantry. Killed in action August 2nd, 1918, during the Aisne-Marne Offensive.
2. CAPTAIN RALPH H. PERRY, Company B, 128th Infantry. Died November 22, 1918, of wounds received November 10th, 1918, during the Meuse-Argonne Offensive.
3. SECOND LIEUTENANT FRANK C. GODFREY, Company D, 128th Infantry. Killed in action August 30th, 1918, during the Oise-Aisne Offensive.
4. FIRST LIEUTENANT BERNARD L. RICE, Headquarters Company, 128th Infantry. Killed in action August 3rd, 1918, during the Aisne-Marne Offensive.
5. MAJOR HENRY ROOT HILL, Commanding Second Battalion, 128th Infantry. Killed in action October 16th, 1918, while leading his battalion against the enemy position northwest of Romagne, France, during the Meuse-Argonne Offensive.
6. FIRST LIEUTENANT CLARENCE G. NOBLE, Company G, 128th Infantry. Died August 4th, 1918, of wounds received in action during the Aisne-Marne Offensive.
7. SECOND LIEUTENANT SANFORD B. DOLE, Company E, 128th Infantry. Killed in action October 18th, 1918, during the Meuse-Argonne Offensive.
8. SECOND LIEUTENANT CLIFFORD O. HARRIS, Company G, 128th Infantry. Killed in action September 1, 1918, during the Oise-Aisne Offensive.
9. SECOND LIEUTENANT EDWARD H. LOCRE, Company A, 128th Infantry. Killed in action October 18th, 1918, during the Meuse-Argonne Offensive.

265

NAME	RANK	ORGANIZATION	CAUSE	DATE	ADDRESS—NEXT OF KIN
Minus, Alex	Pvt.	Mg. Co. 126 Inf.	KIA	10/5/18	163 Thedore St., Detroit, Mich. Anna Minus.
Mitchell, John A.	Pvt. 1cl.	Co. K. 126 Inf.	DW	8/29/18	Ote, Ky. Mrs. O. F. Watcher.
Mittlestat, Earl C.	Sgt.	Co. C. 120 Mg. Bn.	KIA	8/1/18	New Boston, Mich. Mrs. William Mittlestat.
Mjelde, Olaf	Pvt. 1cl.	Co. K. 127 Inf.	DW	8/31/18	....
Moeller, Edward	Pvt.	Co. E. 125 Inf.	KIA	10/9/18	Bloomfield, Neb. Mrs. Martha Moeller (Mother).
Moenkhouse, Earnest	Pvt. 1cl.	Co. B. 127 Inf.	KIA	10/5/18	R. 1, La Grande. Ore. D. W. Moenkhouse (Father).
Monday, George T.	Pvt.	Co. L. 126 Inf.	KIA	10/6/18	Ivanhoe, Va. Samuel C. Monday (Father).
Monocka, Tony	Corp.	Co. A. 126 Inf.	KIA	10/11/18	R. F. D. 1, Coldwater, Mich. Mrs. Julia Monocka.
Monroe, Elmer	Pvt.	Co. C. 125 Inf.	KIA	10/11/18	Lebanon Junction, Ky. D. E. Monroe.
Monroe, George S.	Pvt. 1cl.	Bty. F. 119 F. A.	KIA	8/22/18	456 Monroe Blvd., So. Haven, Mich. George C. Monroe (Father).
Montgomery, Ira S.	Corp.	Co. G. 126 Inf.	KIA	8/28/18	....
Montley, James E.	Pvt.	Co. B. 126 Inf.	KIA	10/5/18	321 So. Poppleton St., Baltimore, Md. Mrs.Martha M. Montley (Mother).
Mooney, Ralph K.	Pvt.	Co. E. 127 Inf.	DW	8/3/18	R. F. D. 1, Princeton. Ind. Mrs. A. Mooney (Mother).
Moonier, Jesse A.	Pvt. 1cl.	Co. M. 128 Inf.	KIA	8/3/18	Perryville, Mo. Edward Moonier.
Moore, Ampliss M.	Pvt.	Co. E. 125 Inf.	DW	10/8/18	R. F. D. 1, Box 29, Tolee, Ky. Eli Stanton Moore (Father).
Moore, Edwin D.	Pvt. 1cl.	Bat. C. 119 F. A.	KIA	10/21/18	1122 Robin St., New Orleans, La. Mrs. Elsie Ferguson (Mother).
Moore, Francis C.	Pvt. 1cl.	San. Det. 126 Inf.	KIA	10/17/18	1019 E. 75th St., Chicago, Ill. Mrs. C. A. Moore.
Moore, George W.	Pvt.	Co. H. 126 Inf.	KIA	8/2/18	3219 15th St. S., Minneapolis, Minn. Louis Moore (Father).
Moore, James M.	Pvt.	Co. F. 128 Inf.	......	11/10/18	....
More, Jasper M.	Corp.	Co. M. 125 Inf.	KIA	10/9/18	....
Moore, John	Pvt.	Co. E. 127 Inf.	KIA	10/17/18	McMillan, Washington. Merle Greenwood (Cousin).
Moore, Nathan R.	Pvt.	Co. K. 127 Inf.	KIA	10/15/18	R. F. D. 3, Casey, Ark. W. E. Moore (Brother).
Moore, Ralph	Sgt.	San. Det. 102 Mg. Bn.	KIA	10/8/18	Milton, Ind. Jesse Moore (Father).
Moore, Sherman E.	Mech.	Co. K. 126 Inf.	KIA	8/28/18	R. F. D. 3, Ravenna, Mich. Mrs. Anna Crowe (Mother).
Moore, Vinton J.	Corp.	Co. F. 127 Inf.	KIA	7/31/18	Ladysmith, Wis. Vinton Moore (Father).
Moos, Martin A.	Sgt.	Mg. Co. 128 Inf.	KIA	10/6/18	173 Summit Ave., Oconomowoc, Wis. Martin A. Moos.
Moran, Joseph	Corp.	Co. M. 128 Inf.	KIA	8/3 /18	2143 Humbolt Blvd., Chicago, Ill. Mrs. Margaret Moran.
Morgan, Arthur O.	Pvt. 1cl.	Co. I. 128 Inf.	KIA	9/1/18	R. F. D. 1, Topinabee, Mich. Henry Morgan.
Morgan, Ernest P.	Pvt.	Sup. Co. 120 F. A.	DD	....	1927 N. Darien St., Philadelphia, Pa. Mrs. Alice Call.
Morgan, Floyd H.	Pvt.	Co. G. 126 Inf.	DW	....	R. F D. 2, Box 85, New Martinsville. A. E. Morgan. W. Va.
Morgan, Frank	Pvt.	Co. M. 128 Inf.	KIA	10/6/18	126 W. Broad St., Nanticoke, Pa. Mrs. William R. Morgan.
Morris, Budd	Corp.	Co. D. 128 Inf.	DD	10/14/18	Mauston, Wis. Marion Morris.
Morris, John C.	Pvt.	Co. C. 127 Inf.	KIA	9/4/18	Clarkston, Wash. Alec Morris (Father).
Morris, Lyle	Sgt.	Co. C. 128 Inf.	KIA	8/1/18	Berlin, Wis. Mrs. Bert Morris.
Morris, Robert	Pvt.	Co. E. 126 Inf.	DW	10/11/18	Calhoun, Ky. Mrs. Kattie Morris (Wife).
Morrison, George D.	Pvt.	Co. M. 125 Inf.	DW	7/31/18	Germfask, Mich. David F. Morrison.
Morrison, Joseph P.	Corp.	Co. H. 128 Inf.	KIA	10/16/18	R. F. D. 1, Box 101, Ironwood. Mich. Mrs. Julia Morrison.
Moser, Edward L.	Corp.	Co. K. 128 Inf.	KIA	10/16/18	Allens Grove, Wis. Louis Moser.
Mortenson, Sophus	Pvt.	Co. G. 128 Inf.	KIA	10/6/18	2107 Park Ave., New York, N. Y. Marie Mortenson.
Moszcinski, John	Pvt.	Co. I. 127 Inf.	KIA	10/14/18	388 Palmer Ave., Detroit, Mich. Ignac Moszcinski (Father).
Moussa, Walter	Pvt. 1cl.	Co. E. 127 Inf.	KIA	9/2/18	1602 28th St., SW., Superior. Wis. Mrs. K. Thorstenson (Mother).
Moyer, Delbert	Pvt.	Co. M. 125 Inf.	KIA	7/31/18	....
Moyers, Ernie	Pvt.	Bat. B. 324 F. A.	KIA	10/13/18	R. F. D. 1, Cunningham, Ky. Dave Moyers.

Name	Rank	Organization	Cause	Date	Address—Next of Kin
Mrvalevitch, Nickola	Pvt.	Co. I. 125 Inf.	DW	10/9/18	San Diego, Calif. Mrs. Nickola Mrvalevitch.
Mueller, Arthur J.	Corp.	Bat. D. 121 F. A.	DW	10/5/18	1312 25th St., Milwaukee, Wis. Paul Mueller (Father).
Mueller, Herman	Pvt.	Co. C. 127 Inf.	KIA	10/4/18	Box 302, Sheboygan, Wis. August Mueller (Father).
Mulcare, John	Pvt.	Co. D. 128 Inf.	DW	9/2/18	2139 W. 7th St., Cleveland, Ohio. Miss Lilly Mulcare.
Muller, Louis	Corp.	Hq. Co. 128 Inf.	KIA	10/6/18	2149 N. Clark St., Chicago, Ill. Miss Charlotte Muller.
Mulligan, Francis	Pvt.	Co. B. 121 Mg. Bn.	DW	8/8/18	....
Mulligan, Fred	Corp.	Co. M. 128 Inf.	KIA	10/5/18	752 Logan St., Janesville, Wis. Joseph Mulligan.
Munch, Cyril	Corp.	Co. E. 128 Inf.	DW	9/4/18	201 Main St., Toledo, Ohio. Joseph Munch.
Munksgard, Chester H.	Pvt.	Co. A. 125 Inf.	DW	10/13/18	6 Cedar St., Warren, Pa. Mrs. Katie Pederson (Sister).
Murawski, Charles	Pvt. 1cl.	308 Btry. Tr. Arty.	KIA	10/23/18	6920 Rathbun Ave., Cleveland, Ohio. Mrs. Sophie Murawski (Mother).
Muri, Lincoln D.	Corp.	Co. K. 125 Inf.	KIA	8/30/18	Forsythe, Mont. D. J. Muri (Father).
Mureowski, Walter	Pvt.	Co. C. 107 F. S. Bn.	KIA	10/3/18	162 44th St., Pittsburg, Pa. Mrs. Anna Mureowski (Mother).
Murphy, Cornelius	Pvt.	Co. L. 128 Inf.	KIA	11/7/18	274 Avenue B, New York, N. Y. Margaret Patterson (Mother).
Murray, Clayton	Pvt. 1cl.	Co. H. 125 Inf.	KIA	10/7/18	Mackinaw City, Mich. Alonzo Murray.
Murray, Frank	Pvt. 1cl.	Co. D. 126 Inf.	KIA	7/31/18	Kerman, Calif. Mrs. R. DuBois.
Murray, Fred W.	Sgt.	Co. I. 127 Inf.	DW	8/6/18	Menominee, Mich. Miss Josephine Murray (Sister).
Murray, Henry	Pvt.	Co. E. 125 Inf.	KIA	10/18/18	Haworth, Okla. James Albert Murray (Father).
Murray, John E.	Pvt.	Co. B. 125 Inf.	KIA	10/12/18	65 Pine St., Green Island, N. Y. Ames Murray (Brother).
Murray, Mike	Pvt. 1cl.	Co. H. 127 Inf.	DD	9/14/18	Central Junction, Chippewa Falls, Wis. Mrs. M. Murray (Mother).
Murry, Henry W.	Pvt.	Co. E. 125 Inf.	....	10/11/18	Haworth, Okla. James Albert Murry (Father).
Musgerd, Carl N.	Pvt.	Co. G. 128 Inf.	DW	10/8/18	....
Musier, Henry	Pvt.	Co. D. 128 Inf.	KIA	9/1/18	802 Clarence St., Cleveland, Ohio. Mrs. Emma Musier (Mother).
Muth, Karl	Pvt. 1cl.	Co. K. 125 Inf.	KIA	7/31/18	....
Muzzall, Cleater E.	Pvt. 1cl.	Co. B. 125 Inf.	KIA	8/29/18	712 Walnut St., Fulton, Ky. Mr. J. O. Muzzall (Father).
Myers, Carl J.	Pvt.	Bat. D. 120 F. A.	DD	....	....
Myers, George W.	Corp.	Co. K. 125 Inf.	KIA	7/31/18	525 N. Gratiot Ave., Alma, Mich. Charles Myers (Father).
Myers, Howard S.	Pvt.	Co. K. 127 Inf.	KIA	10/15/18	Hendricks, W. Va. Mary C. Myers (Mother).
Nadler, Emil	Corp.	Co. A. 128 Inf.	KIA	....	701 N. Walnut St., Reedsburg, Wis. Fred Nadler (Father).
Nadolski, Walter N.	Corp.	Co. I. 125 Inf.	KIA	7/31/18	1214 S. Monroe St., Bay City, Mich. Julian Nadolski.
Naronjo, Joe R.	Pvt.	Co. B. 127 Inf.	KIA	10/19/18	Espanola, New Mexico. Nanuel Naronjo (Father).
Narbon, Joseph	Pvt.	Co. L. 128 Inf.	KIA	11/7/18	1210 Princeton Ave., Princeton, N. J. Louis Narbon (Father).
Narodzonek, Stanley	Corp.	Co. A. 125 Inf.	KIA	8/5/18	24 Stovel Place, Detroit, Mich. Minnie Narodzonek (Mother).
Nascadi, Angelo	Pvt.	Co. L. 127 Inf.	......	10/18/18	....
Naylor, James R.	Pvt. 1cl.	Co. E. 322 F. A.	KIA	10/10/18	....
Naylor, James R.	Pvt. 1cl.	Co. E. 128 Inf.	KIA	11/10/18	R. F. D. 4, Conway, Ark. Mrs. Lonell T. Naylor (Mother).
Nehrbass, Henry	Pvt.	Co. F. 127 Inf.	KIA	7/31/18	R. F. D. 1, Athens, Wis. John Nehrbass (Father).
Nehring, William G.	Pvt.	Bat. F. 120 F. A.	DD	....	82 4th Ave., Wauwatosa, Wis. E. J. Nehring (Father).
Neilson, Arnold	Pvt. 1cl.	Co. G. 125 Inf.	KIA	10/7/18	Overton, Neb. Alice Neilson (Sister).
Nell, John	Pvt.	Co. B. 125 Inf.	KIA	10/13/18	Edinburg, Ill. George Nell (Father).
Nelson, Albert L.	Pvt. 1cl.	Co. L. 128 Inf.	KIA	8/6/18	Chetek, Wis. Sam Dyrland.
Nelson, Burg	Corp.	Co. E. 128 Inf.	KIA	8/31/18	Sharon, Wis. Art DeGraff.
Nelson, Edward M.	Pvt.	Hq. Co. 128 Inf.	KIA	7/30/18	2010 W. Ohio St., Chicago, Ill. Martha Kregan Nelson (Mother).
Nelson, Fritichof	Pvt.	Co. A. 128 Inf.	KIA	7/1/18	514 Chapin St., Iron Mountain, Mich. August Nelson (Father).

Name	Rank	Organization	Cause	Date	Address—Next of Kin
Nelson, George	Pvt.	Co. C. 128 Inf.	KIA	10/12/18	Angela, Mont. Mrs. Helen Nelson.
Nelson, George	Pvt.	Co. C. 128 Inf.	KIA	10/12/18	Angela, Mont. Mrs. Helen Nelson.
Nelson, Harold C.	Pvt.	Co. A. 121 Mg. Bn.	DW	9/1/18	828 Lake St., Rice Lake, Wis. Mrs. W. O. Nelson.
Nelson, Medes A.	Pvt.	Co. G. 125 Inf.	KIA	10/7/18	Ausable Forks, N. Y. Clara Nelson (Mother).
Nelson, Raymond	Corp.	Co. C. 126 Inf.	KIA	10/5/18	Manton, Mich. Oscar C. Ransom.
Nelson, Walter C.	Pvt.	Co. F. 128 Inf.	KIA	....	Marshall, Minn. William Nelson.
Netcher, William A.	Pvt.	Co. G. 127 Inf.	DW	9/11/18	Trenton, Utah. Mrs. C. S. Netcher (Mother).
Netzel, Edward F.	Pvt.	Co. I. 127 Inf.	KIA	10/4/18	Crivitz, Wis. Alex Netzel (Father).
Newman, Robert E.	Pvt.	Co. A. 125 Inf.	KIA	10/18/18	Valley Station, Ky. Mrs. Emma Newman (Mother).
Nichols, Benjamin	Pvt.	Co. C. 125 Inf.	KIA	10/22/18	Englewood, Tenn. Mary Nichols.
Nichols, Claud A.	Pvt.	Co. L. 125 Inf.	KIA	10/9/18	R. F. D. 1, Tupelo, Miss. Jackson R. Nichols (Father).
Neverdahl, Lawrence W.	Sgt.	Co. H. 128 Inf.	KIA	10/20/18	221 16th Ave., Menomonie, Wis. Tom Neverdahl.
Nichols, Frederic H.	Corp.	Co. C. 107 Sup. Tr.	ACC	2/1/18	221 Congress St., Detroit, Mich. Edward Nichols.
Nichols, Howard	Pvt.	Co. H. 126 Inf.	DW	8/30/18	R. F. D. 1, Weidman, Mich. Allen Nichols (Father).
Nichols, Ramond L.	Pvt. 1cl.	Co. G. 127 Inf.	KIA	8/3/18	1615 Schiller Court, Madison, Wis. Mrs. W. N. Nichols (Mother).
Nicholson, Ray U.	Pvt.	Co. K. 126 Inf.	DD	6/30/18	....
Niskerson, Howard B.	Pvt.	Co. C. 128 Inf.	KIA	10/12/18	Farnam, Neb. Mrs. Cora A. Messersmith.
Niebuhr, George	Pvt.	Co. A. 128 Inf.	KIA	....	Limeridge, Wis. William Niebuhr (Brother).
Niehaus, Fred	Pvt.	Co. E. 126 Inf.	DW	10/5/18	222 Este Ave., Wenton Pl., Cincinnati, Ohio. Adolph Coerling (Brother-in-Law).
Nielson, Niels	Pvt.	Co. B. 125 Inf.	KIA	8/29/18	1822 Duane St., Astoria, Oregon. Jens Nielson (Father).
Ninneman, John	Wag.	Sup. Co. 128 Inf.	KIA	8/29/18	611 Garfield Ave., Wausau, Wis. Herman Ninneman (Father).
Noel, George French Soldier	Pvt.	No. 21, 237 F. A.	DW	9/2/18	....
Norris, Alexander	Pvt.	Co. H. 127 Inf.	KIA	10/13/18	1191 Harrison Ave., Cincinnati, Ohio. Anna Norris (Mother).
Norris, William	Pvt.	Co. F. 125 Inf.	KIA	10/4/18	Shelburn, Ind. Mrs. Anna Norris (Wife).
Notting, Joseph	Pvt.	Co. F. 127 Inf.	KIA	7/31/18	1185 27th St., Milwaukee, Wis. Miss Rose Notting (Sister).
Novek, Frank E.	Pvt.	Co. E. 127 Inf.	KIA	8/1/18	3414 S. Irving Ave., Chicago, Ill. Mrs. Elizabeth Novek (Mother).
Novitske, Walter A.	Pvt. 1cl.	Co. B. 128 Inf.	KIA	....	Ripon, Wis. Mrs. M. Novitske.
Nowack, Fred C.	Pvt.	Co. H. 128 Inf.	KIA	11/10/18	R. F. D. 1, Big Lake, Minn. Ferdinand Nowack (Father).
Nowack, John M.	Sgt.	Co. K. 127 Inf.	KIA	8/4/18	884 Warren Ave., Milwaukee, Wis. Mrs. Rose Nowack (Wife).
Nowatny, John	Pvt. 1cl.	Co. B. 128 Inf.	KIA	7/9/18	R. F. D. 2, Wautoma, Wis. Albert Nowatny (Father).
Nusbaum, Willis	Pvt.	Co. A. 128 Inf.	KIA	11/10/18	R. F. D. 4, Sluffton, Ohio. Daniel Nusbaum (Father).
Nystrom, Caleb	Pvt.	Co. B. 127 Inf.	DW	8/1/18	....
Oakey, Howard G.	Pvt.	Co. G. 127 Inf.	KIA	8/31/18	1214 W. Washington Ave., Madison, Wis. Mrs. C. E. Oakey (Mother).
Oakley, Harley R.	Pvt.	Co. F. 125 Inf.	......	....	R. F. D. 1, Humboldt, Ill. Mrs. Ella Oakley (Mother).
Oakley, George M.	Pvt.	Co. K. 128 Inf.	KIA	11/10/18	Idabel, Okla. B. A. Oakley.
O'Brien, Frank	Pvt.	Co. A. 128 Inf.	KIA	9/1/18	R. F. D. 2, Avora, Wis. Mrs. Mary O'Brien (Mother).
O'Brien, Maurice C. J	Pvt.	Co. F. 127 Inf.	KIA	8/1/18	805 Michigan Av., S. Milwaukee, Wis. Mrs. Patrick J. O'Brien (Mother).
O'Connel, Jeffery A.	Pvt.	107 Eng. Train	DW	8/8/18	....
O'Connell, John V.	Pvt.	Mg. Co. 126 Inf.	KIA	7/31/18	998 2nd Ave., New York, N. Y. Mrs. Margaret O'Connell (Mother).
O'Connor, Eddie	Pvt.	Bat. A. 119 F. A.	KIA	8/10/18	Dunlap, Iowa. Mrs. Mary O'Connor (Mother).
O'Connor, Frank J.	Sgt.	Hq. Co. 125 Inf.	KIA	10/11/18	421 Sheldon Ave., Gd. Rapids, Mich. James O'Connor (Father).
O'Connor, Frank J.	Pvt.	Co. C. 128 Inf.	KIA	8/1/18	Berlin, Wis. John O'Connor.
O'Day, Charles H.	Pvt. 1cl.	Co. B. 127 Inf.	KIA	10/11/18	Adrian, Minn. Mrs. R. M. O'Day (Mother).

Name	Rank	Organization	Cause	Date	Address—Next of Kin
Odee, John	Pvt.	Co. D. 127 Inf.	KIA	7/31/18	1120 8th Ave., Milwaukee, Wis. Rose Odee (Mother).
Odell, Lynn.	Corp.	Co. D. 128 Inf.	DD	3/24/18	....
Odermatt, August	Corp.	Co. H. 127 Inf.	DW	10/13/18	Monroe, Wis. Mrs. Chas. Shutt (Sister).
O'Donnell, Lawrence	Pvt.	Co. E. 126 Inf.	DW	10/9/18	307 Buchman St., Phoenixville, Pa. Mrs. John O'Donnell (Mother).
Oehler, Fred G.	Corp.	Hq. 127 Inf.	KIA	8/30/18	Uhrichsville, Ohio. Paul F. Oehler.
Oertel, Emil L.	Pvt. 1cl.	Co. A. 127 Inf.	KIA	8/4/18	R. F. D. 1, Box 51, Rozellville, Wis. Paul Oertel (Father).
Ogdin, Guy	Sgt.	Co. M. 128 Inf.	KIA	8/30/18	402 2nd St., Edgerton, Wis. Mrs. Geo. L. Ogdin.
Ogletree, Cecil E.	Bug.	Co. C. 120 Mg. Bn.	KIA	8/1/18	458 Distel Ave., Detroit, Mich. Mrs. Dora Merrow.
Oldenburg, Ernest F.	Corp.	Co. M. 125 Inf.	KIA	6/18/18	....
Olin, Charles C.	Pvt.	Co. E. 128 Inf.	KIA	10/14/18	202 George St., Marion, Ohio. Ethel Olin (Wife).
Oliver, Wilson	Pvt. 1cl.	Co. B. 128 Inf.	DW	9/1/18	New France, Mo. J. J. Oliver.
Olk, John E.	Pvt. 1cl.	Amb. Co. 128	KIA	8/29/18	....
Ollnich, Harry	Pvt.	Co. E. 125 Inf.	KIA	7/31/18	....
Olsen, Carl A.	Pvt.	Co. L. 127 Inf.	KIA	10/18/18	34 8th Ave., Spokane, Wash. Cecelia Spurkland.
Olson, Albert	Pvt.	Co. C. 128 Inf.	KIA	10/12/18	Sheyenne, N. D. Andrew Olson.
Olson, Arne B.	Pvt.	Co. L. 127 Inf.	KIA	10/12/18	Castlewood, S. Dak. Mrs. Thorne Olson (Mother).
Olson, Chester W.	Pvt. 1cl.	Co. M. 125 Inf.	KIA	7/31/18	....
Olsson, Herbert T.	Pvt.	Co. K. 125 Inf.	KIA	8/30/18	R.F.D. 2, Bx. 72, Marine-on-St. Croix, Otto Olsson (Father). Minn.
O'Malley, Edward P.	Pvt.	Co. C. 128 Inf.	KIA	10/14/18	....
O'Malley, Martin L.	Sgt.	Co. I. 127 Inf.	DW	9/4/18	....
O'Malley, Thomas	Pvt. 1cl.	Md. 322 F. A.	KIA	10/16/18	....
Opsahl, Colmer T.	Pvt.	Co. D. 127 Inf.	KIA	10/10/18	R. F. D. 2, Spring Grove, Minn. Knut Opsahl (Father).
Orr, John L.	Pvt.	Co. A. 128 Inf.	DW	8/1/18	427 Wrightwood Ave., Chicago, Ill. Mr. James W. Orr (Father).
Orr, Louis D.	Pvt.	Co. I. 125 Inf.	KIA	8/3/18	413 3rd Ave., Great Falls, Mont. Eugene Snider (Friend).
Orr, Russell	Pvt.	Co. G. 126 Inf.	KIA	8/2/18	922 N. Webster St., Saginaw, Mich. Mrs. Catherine Orr (Mother).
Orr, Wifred A.	Pvt. 1cl.	Co. B. 126 Inf.	KIA	8/29/18	515 Pottowattomee St., Tecumseh, Robert Orr. Mich.
Orrick, Jasper	Pvt.	Co. C. 126 Inf.	DW	10/5/18	....
Ortiz, Conception	Pvt. 1cl.	Co. I. 125 Inf.	KIA	10/11/18	Eagle Pass, Texas. Virginia Ortiz.
Orwocke, John	Pvt.	Co. E. 107 Am. Tr.	DR	7/17/18	Empire Block, Platteville, Wis. Wisconsin Zinc Co.
Osborn, Gilbert	Pvt.	Co. A. 125 Inf.	KIA	10/2/18	R. F. D. 6, Robertson, Ill. Samuel Osborn (Father).
Oser, Joseph F.	Pvt.	Co. H. 127 Inf.	KIA	10/7/18	1443 Walnut St., Cincinnati, Ohio. Mrs. Francis Oser (Wife).
Ostrom, Einer	Pvt.	Co. G. 125 Inf.	KIA	10/22/18	22 Sweden Gifle, W. Slottsgatan. Gustav I. Ostron.
Ostrander, Guy W.	Sgt.	Co. D. 126 Inf.	KIA	10/16/18	R. F. D. 1, Brecken Bridge. Albert Ostrander (Father).
Ostrander, Levi	Corp.	Co. E. 125 Inf.	......	8/29/18	90 Will Willett, Attica, Mich. Pearly May Ostrander (Sister).
Osypienski, Wladyslaw	Pvt.	Co. A. 125 Inf.	KIA	8/6/18	98 Nagel St., Hamtramck, Mich. Mrs. Sophia Pytzka (Sister).
Ottinger, Andrew D.	Pvt.	Co. A. 127 Inf.	KIA	7/31/18	Sheridan, Oregon. W. D. Ottinger (Father).
Overholser, Calvin R.	Pvt.	Co. D. 324 F. A.	KIA	10/13/18	....
Owen, Charles	Corp.	Co. H. 128 Inf.	KIA	10/20/18	....
Owens, James	Pvt.	Co. H. 128 Inf.	KIA	11/10/18	Pathfork, Ky. Daniel Owens (Father).
Owens, John H.	Corp.	Co. I. 128 Inf.	KIA	6/13/18	....
Owens, Oliver J.	Pvt. 1cl.	Co. D. 126 Inf.	......	8/29/18	R. F. D. 1, Palestine, W. Va. Joshua Owens (Father).
Ozman, James C.	Pvt.	Co. F. 126 Inf.	KIA	10/9/18	Brookville, Penn. Mr. Joseph Ozman (Father).
Pada, Walter	Corp.	Co. L. 125 Inf.	KIA	7/31/18	Menominee, Mich. Mrs. Mathilda Pada (Mother).

NAME	RANK	ORGANIZATION	CAUSE	DATE	ADDRESS—NEXT OF KIN
Paden, Walter	Pvt.	Co. F. 128 Inf.	KIA	11/10/18	333 E. Warren, Princeton, Ill. John R. Paden (Father).
Padgett, Uriel E.	Pvt.	Co. E. 128 Inf.	KIA	10/5/18	Stithton, Ky. Mrs. Rose Padgett (Stepmother).
Page, Hugh	Pvt. 1cl.	Co. H. 128 Inf.	KIA	8/30/18	765 Ellery St., Detroit, Mich. Mrs. Ida Page (Mother).
Page, H. T.	Pvt.	Co. H. 168 Inf.	DW	10/17/18	....
Pagnani, Nicola	Pvt.	Co. L. 125 Inf.	KIA	7/31/18	Campoli, Sppinno, Casenta, Italy. Mrs. O. Pagnani (Wife).
Pahoon, Herbert A.	Pvt.	Co. M. 125 Inf.	KIA	7/31/18	....
Paine, Burley L.	Corp.	Co. G. 126 Inf.	KIA	8/28/18	52 23rd St., Detroit, Mich. Mrs. Winnie Paine.
Palmer, Harry M.	Sgt.	Co. A. 127 Inf.	KIA	10/6/18	Madison, Neb. Roy Palmer (Father).
Palmer, Jack.	Corp.	Co. B. 127 Inf.	KIA	8/4/18	Townsend, Mont. Mrs. R. McIntyre (Sister).
Palmer, James S.	Pvt. 1cl.	Co. I. 125 Inf.	KIA	8/31/18	200 Edison Ave., Detroit, Mich. Clavin A. Palmer (Father).
Palmer, Leonard	Pvt.	Co. C. 128 Inf.	......	10/20/18	104 Ramsey St., Dawson Springs, Ky. John Palmer.
Palmer, Ralph B.	Pvt.	Co. B. 127 Inf.	KIA	8/2/18	Mistletoe, Mo. Gilbert F. Palmer (Father).
Palmiero, Asparo	Pvt.	Co. G. 127 Inf.	KIA	10/7/18	12 Stanton St., New York, N. Y. Mrs. Garigi Salvatore (Sister).
Pape, Herman	Pvt.	Co. E. 128 Inf.	DD	3/1/18	....
Pardee, Herman O.	Pvt.	Co. E. 125 Inf.	KIA	8/4/18	....
Pargawski, Tony	Pvt. 1cl.	Co. L. 128 Inf.	KIA	8/31/18	821 W. 33rd St., Chicago, Ill. Frank Pargawski.
Parkinson, Homer R.	Corp.	Co. F. 127 Inf.	KIA	10/18/18	Blanchardville, Wis. Dwight E. Baker (Friend).
Parkinson, Leo N.	Corp.	Co. H. 127 Inf.	DW	10/4/18	Blanchardville, Wis. Mrs. Dwight E. Baker (Sister).
Parks, Charley	Pvt.	Co. M. 128 Inf.	DW	9/1/18	Hoyt, Okla. J. H. Parks.
Parks, Clayton A.	Pvt.	Co. H. 128 Inf.	KIA	10/7/18	Route 4, Sauk Center, Minn. Joseph Parks (Father).
Parks, Edward J.	Pvt. 1cl.	Co. A. 127 Inf.	KIA	8/5/18	W. Badersville St., Marshfield, Wis. Stewart Parks (Father).
Parnis, Carlo	Pvt.	Co. B. 125 Inf.	DW	9/1/18	Loggeuno, Per Bosco, Com. Italy. Mrs. Benda Terasa.
Parrish, Henry F.	Pvt.	Co. H. 127 Inf.	DD	2/12/18	Right Angle, Ky. M. B. Parrish (Father).
Parthe, Carl F.	Pvt.	Co. I. 127 Inf.	KIA	10/16/18	Hall Ave., Marinette, Wis. Mr. Carl Parthe, Jr. (Father).
Partridge, Merrett E.	Corp.	Hq. Co. 128 Inf.	KIA	10/17/18	478 Washington St., E. Walpole, Mass. Mrs. Emily Partridge.
Paseka, Andrew J.	Pvt.	Co. C. 128 Inf.	KIA	10/12/18	Wood, So. Dak. Frank Paseka.
Patterson, Arthur C.	1st Sgt.	Co. M. 125 Inf.	KIA	7/31/18	....
Patterson, George	Corp.	Co. D. 125 Inf.	DW	8/30/18	299 Linwood Ave., Detroit, Mich. Mary Kimon (Sister).
Patterson, Oscar M.	Pvt.	Co. M. 128 Inf.	KIA	8/6/18	R. F. D. 6, Mt. Pleasant, Mich. Henry A. Patterson.
Patrick, Clarence A.	Pvt.	Co. L, 125 Inf.	KIA	10/9/18	....
Paulson, Otto A.	Pvt.	Bat. C. 120 F. A.	DW	10/29/18	Malvern, Iowa. C. A. Paulson.
Payne, Everette L.	Pvt.	Co. D. 126 Inf.	KIA	10/10/18	Hand, Ark. Elle Russell.
Payne, Ira	Pvt.	Co. K. 128 Inf.	DW	10/6/18	R. F. D. 6, Richmond, Va. Mrs. Alice Payne.
Payson, Carl F.	Corp.	Co. C. 125 Inf.	KIA	7/31/18	Monroe, Mich. Mrs. Minnie Timbertman.
Pearson, Bernard N.	Pvt.	Co. M. 125 Inf.	KIA	7/31/18	....
Pearson, William B.	Pvt.	125 Inf.	KIA	10/22/18	Gordon, Ala. A. M. Pearson (Brother).
Pentroski, Stanley	Pvt.	Co. E. 126 Inf.	KIA	8/2/18	148 Jacob St., Hamtramck, Mich. Mrs. Helen Tilipiak (Sister).
Paccia, Nicola	Pvt.	Co. G. 127 Inf.	KIA	8/3/18	Cantalupo, Nelsonia, Italy. Mary Domenica Paccia (Wife).
Pederson, Harry J.	Pvt.	Co. C. 128 Inf.	KIA	10/15/18	Skudesnes, Blikshavn, Norway. Peder Pederson.
Pederson, Nels S.	Pvt.	Co. M. 127 Inf.	KIA	8/4/18	Wilmar, Minn. Anna Abrahamson.
Pederson, Oscar	Pvt.	Co. K. 125 Inf.	KIA	7/31/18	Wells, Mich. P. O. Pederson.
Peebles, Charles E.	Pvt.	Co. M. 125 Inf.	KIA	7/31/18	....
Pegues, Nick T.	Pvt.	Co. K. 128 Inf.	KIA	11/10/18	Earle, Ark. Mrs. Maude Pegues.

1. Second Lieutenant Charles Raymond Wilbur, Company B, 126th Infantry. Killed in action October 3rd, 1918, during the Meuse-Argonne Offensive.
2. Second Lieutenant James Vincent Devenny, Company E, 126th Infantry. Killed in action October 9th, 1918, during the Meuse-Argonne Offensive.
3. Second Lieutenant Carl Thompson, 126th Infantry. Killed in action August 31st, 1918, during the Oise-Aisne Offensive.
4. Second Lieutenant John C. Champagne, Company I, 125th Infantry. Killed in action July 31st, 1918, during the Aisne-Marne Offensive.
5. Captain Milburn H. Hawkes, Company D, 125th Infantry. Killed in action September 30th, 1918, during the Meuse-Argonne Offensive.
6. Second Lieutenant Lee N. Wall, Company M, 125th Infantry. Killed in action July 31st, 1918, during the Aisne-Marne Offensive.
7. Second Lieutenant Erk M. Cottrell, Company F, 126th Infantry. Killed in action October 9th, 1918, during the Meuse-Argonne Offensive.
8. Second Lieutenant Otis B. Thomas, Company A, 126th Infantry. Died of wounds August 3rd, 1918, during the Aisne-Marne Offensive.
9. Second Lieutenant Harvey F. Smith, Company K, 125th Infantry. Killed in action October 13th, 1918, during the Meuse-Argonne Offensive.

271

NAME	RANK	ORGANIZATION	CAUSE	DATE	ADDRESS—NEXT OF KIN
Pelagalle, Marco	Pvt.	Co. E. 125 Inf.	KIA	7/31/18	....
Pelissero, Guiseppe	Pvt.	Co. H. 125 Inf.	KIA	7/31/18	354 Middle St., Kenosha, Wis. August Pelissero.
Pelligrino, John	Pvt. 1cl.	Co. G. 125 Inf.	KIA	8/29/18	San Vito La Capo, Italy. Francisco Pelligrino (Father).
Pelowski, Joseph	Pvt. 1cl.	Co. E. 126 Inf.	KIA	....	799 Riopelle St., Detroit, Mich. Miss Pauline Pelowski (Sister).
Pennoyer, H. W.	Pvt.	Co. D. 126 Inf.	KIA	10/5/18	Hamilton, Mont. L. A. Pennoyer (Father).
Perdue, William T.	Pvt.	Co. E. 128 Inf.	KIA	11/10/18	439 Hicks St., Brooklyn, N. Y. Mrs. Mary Riley (Sister).
Perkins, Elmer J.	Pvt. 1cl.	Co. G. 125 Inf.	KIA	7/31/18	....
Perlick, Otto	Sgt.	Co. H. 128 Inf.	KIA	11/11/18	283 Townsend Ave., Detroit, Mich. Mrs. Ida Grill (Sister).
Perou, Charles A.	Pvt.	Co. M. 125 Inf.	KIA	7/31/18	....
Perry, Clarence J.	Pvt.	Co. B. 125 Inf.	KIA	10/13/18	Port Clinton, Ohio. Mrs. Kate Shaefer (Mother).
Perryman, Fred E.	Pvt.	Bat. B. 120 F. A.	DW	10/17/18	431 N. Main St., Tulsa, Okla. Mrs. Laura Perryman.
Pester, Louis	Pvt.	Co. H. 125 Inf.	KIA	10/15/18	2654 E. 67th St., Cleveland, Ohio. Jake Pester.
Peters, Clarence E.	Pvt.	Co. M. 127 Inf.	KIA	8/5/18	925 Spring St., Beaver Dam, Wis. Mrs. Frank Peters (Mother).
Peters, Oliver D.	Pvt.	Co. H. 127 Inf.	KIA	10/7/18	Dewitt, Ark. Mrs. Mary Harrison (Mother).
Peterson, Arnold J.	Sgt.	Co. 127 Inf.	DW	6/30/18	1025 8th St., Beloit, Wis. A. O. Peterson (Father).
Peterson, Arthur	Pvt. 1cl.	Co. H. 127 Inf.	KIA	8/30/18	Nora, Macklaby Oland, Sweden. Per Nelson (Father).
Peterson, Arvie	Pvt.	Co. B. 125 Inf.	DW	8/29/18	Kenesaw, Neb. J. C. Peterson (Father).
Peterson, Charles W.	Pvt.	Co. A. 127 Inf.	KIA	10/12/18	Pine River, Wis. Jens Peterson.
Peterson, Ernest A.	Pvt.	Co. H. 128 Inf.	DW	10/13/18	7243 Greenwood Ave., Chicago, Ill. Gust. Peterson.
Peterson, Matt	Pvt.	Co. L. 125 Inf.	DW	8/1/18	....
Peterson, Viggo	Pvt.	Co. G. 126 Inf.	KIA	10/12/18	Viborg, S. Dak. Mrs. Treona Peterson (Mother).
Petitt, George H.	Pvt.	Co. M. 127 Inf.	KIA	10/15/18	P. O. Box. 205, Ashland, Ill. Charles L. Petitt (Father).
Petri, William S.	Corp.	Co. A. 127 Inf.	KIA	8/5/18	R. F. D. 1, Rozellville, Wis. August Petri (Father).
Petro, Anthony	Pvt.	Co. E. 125 Inf.	KIA	7/31/18	....
Petrowsky, Andrew	Pvt.	Co. G. 126 Inf.	KIA	10/21/18	26 Campbell St., Carnegie, Pa. Welder Petrowsky (Brother).
Petty, John	Pvt.	Co. E. 126 Inf.	DW	10/2/18	Lone Cedar, W. Va. Will Pickering.
Petty, Pat	Pvt.	Co. A. 128 Inf.	KIA	11/10/18	Lonoke, Ark. Thomas F. Petty.
Pfeil, Henry	Corp.	Co. B. 127 Inf.	KIA	10/11/18	29 Madison St., Oshkosh, Wis. J. H. Pfeil (Father).
Pflug, Alfred	Pvt.	Bat. B. 322 F. A.	DD	12/16/18	....
Philbrook, George W.	Pvt. 1cl.	Co. I. 127 Inf.	KIA	8/4/18	South Range, Wis. Mrs. R. P. Philbrook (Mother).
Philbrook, James H.	Sgt.	Co. I. 127 Inf.	KIA	10/17/18	South Range, Wis. Mrs. Mary Philbrook (Mother).
Phillips, Dewey	Pvt. 1cl.	Co. K. 125 Inf.	KIA	8/1/18	427 Hanchett St., Saginaw, Mich. John Phillips (Father).
Phillips, John	Pvt.	Co. D. 127 Inf.	DW	10/5/18	2218 Willis Ave,. Omaha, Neb. James C. Phillips (Father).
Phillip, Vent	Pvt.	Co. L. 126 Inf.	DW	8/7/18	Coopersville, Mich. Fred L. Phillip.
Piaskowski, Frank	Corp.	Co. D. 120 Mg. Bn.	DW	10/6/18	701 Main St., Green Bay, Wis. Joseph Piaskowski (Father).
Pickney, Louis E.	Pvt.	Co. H. 128 Inf.	KIA	10/20/18	Winchester, Tenn. Mr. Louis P. Pickney.
Pierce, Frank	Pvt.	Co. B. 128 Inf.	KIA	10/14/18	R. F. D. 4, Box 80, Pleasanton, Kan.
Pierce, Max O.	Pvt.	125 Amb. Co.	KIA	10/13/18	....
Pierson, Nile	Pvt.	Co. D. 126 Inf.	KIA	8/6/18	Kristjustad, Sweden. Miss Alma Pierson (Sister).
Pietras, Walter	Pvt.	Co. I. 128 Inf.	KIA	9/1/18	5 Duke St., Pontiac, Mich. Joseph Rybach.
Pietrykowski, Louis	Pvt.	Co. D. 125 Inf.	KIA	8/4/18	1780 Tecumseh St., Toledo, Ohio. Grace Gozwiak (Sister).
Piezy, Lawrence	Pvt.	Co. B. 125 Inf.	......	10/4/18	....
Pellington, James	Pvt.	....	......	1/16/18	....

Name	Rank	Organization	Cause	Date	Address—Next of Kin
Pinch, Henry	Corp.	Co. E. 127 Inf.	KIA	10/10/18	Georgetown, Wis. Mary Pinch (Mother).
Pinn, Arthur V.	Pvt.	Co. M. 128 Inf.	KIA	11/8/18	Harwood, Texas. Mrs. Clar Pinn (Mother).
Piper, Elmer L.	Sgt.	Co. K. 125 Inf.	KIA	10/10/18	Goastia, Mich. E. H. Piper (Father).
Pira, Frank	Pvt.	Co. F. 125 Inf.	KIA	10/11/18	Dogliani, Italy. John Pira (Father).
Pittenger, Bearl V.	Sgt.	Hq. 119 F. A.	DW	8/4/18	R. F. D. 4, Muncie, Ind. Jarvis Pittenger (Father).
Pitterle, Frank L.	Corp.	Co. D. 120 Mg. Bu.	KIA	8/30/18	206 3rd St., Watertown, Wis. Mrs. Theresa Pitterle.
Pitts, Albert	Pvt. 1cl.	Co. B. 125 Inf.	KIA	8/29/18	Seligman, Arizona. Harvey B. Pitts (Brother).
Pexley, Loren E.	Pvt.	Med. Det. 125 Inf.	KIA	8/6/18	809 Lawnsdale Ave., Detroit, Mich. Guy L. Pexley (Father).
Pizzini, Louis	Pvt.	Co. K. 126 Inf.	DW	8/29/18	Belt, Montana. John Pizzini (Father).
Plana, Frank	Pvt.	Mg. Co. 125 Inf.	KIA	8/1/18	....
Plassmeyer, Albert J.	Pvt.	Bat E. 322 F. A.	DW	8/1/18	....
Plude, Louis C.	Corp.	Co. E. 128 Inf.	KIA	8/29/18	1412 State St., Milwaukee, Wis. Mrs. Mary Plude.
Plummer, Guy L.	Pvt.	Co. A. 119 Mg. Bn.	KIA	10/15/18	Joliet, Mont. Mrs. N. A. Plummer (Mother).
Poe, Melvin	Pvt.	Co. C. 153 Inf.	DW	10/11/18	Olney, Ky. Bandolo Williams.
Poet, John W.	Corp.	Co. D. 125 Inf.	KIA	8/4/18	75 Chamberlain St., Detroit, Mich. John Poet (Father).
Pohlmann, Francis	Pvt.	Co. E. 126 Inf.	KIA	10/9/18	Brussels, Ill. Barney Pohlmann (Father).
Pohlpeter, Bernard J.	Sgt.	Co. L. 126 Inf.	KIA	10/12/18	1330 6th St., Fort Madison, Iowa. Miss S. Pohlpeter (Sister).
Polak, Max	Pvt. 1cl.	Co. K. 127 Inf.	KIA	10/15/18	1077 12th St., Milwaukee, Wis. Vincent Polak (Father).
Polomis, Peter A.	Pvt.	Co. C. 127 Inf.	KIA	10/14/18	Wausaukee, Wis. Catherine Polomis (Mother).
Polovina, Fred	Pvt. 1cl.	Co. E. 125 Inf.	KIA	7/31/18	....
Polowski, Joseph	Pvt. 1cl.	Co. E. 128 Inf.	DW	....	....
Polubitz, Wyllem	Pvt.	Co. F. 127 Amm. Tr.	DD	6/24/18	....
Ponti, Charles	1st. Sgt.	Co. K. 128 Inf.	KIA	8/3/18	1612 17th St., Superior, Wis. Mrs. Margaret Mary Ponti (Wife).
Pophan, Cecil J.	Pvt.	Co. D. 126 Inf.	KIA	8/1/18	Battletown, Ky. Mrs. Flora B. Padgett.
Porte, Alex	Pvt. 1cl.	Bat. A. 120 F. A.	DW	9/3/18	299 14th St., Milwaukee, Wis. C. E. Porte.
Porter, Horace	Pvt.	Co. K. 128 Inf.	KIA	11/7/18	Bluffton, Yell Co., Ark. Mrs. Anna Porter.
Porter, Ray	Pvt.	Co. E. 128 Inf.	KIA	10/5/18	420 Milton St., Paris, Ill. Mrs. Martha Porter (Mother).
Posharitzky, Stephen	Pvt.	Co. B. 125 Inf.	Suicide	7/16/18	Gordd, Krasnoiarsk, Gubernia, Komit. Pomochia, Ceshenow, Russia. Ivan Posharitzky (Father).
Potter, Harry	Pvt.	Co. F. 125 Inf.	KIA	10/12/18	Brown City, Mich. Mrs. Flora Potter (Mother).
Powell, Joseph	Pvt.	Co. C. 126 Inf.	KIA	10/10/18	R. F. D. 1, Como, Miss. James M. Powell (Father).
Powers, John	Pvt.	Co. F. 126 Inf.	DW	10/4/18	96 Milton Ave., Dorchester, Mass. Miss Sadie Powers (Sister).
Prahl, Louis	Corp.	Co. D. 128 Inf.	KIA	....	R. F. D. 2, Box 71, Berlin, Wis. Edward Prahl (Father).
Prate, Roderick G.	Pvt.	Co. A. 128 Inf.	KIA	8/1/18	Munising, Mich. Joseph Prate (Father).
Pravica, Nickola	Pvt.	Co. B. 125 Inf.	DW	8/29/18	607 Castelar St., Los Angeles, Calif. G. Dabobich.
Preiss, Clarence G.	Pvt.	Co. C. 121 Mg. Bn.	KIA	10/4/18	334 15th St., Milwaukee, Wis. John A. Preiss (Father).
Preissner, Joseph F.	Sgt.	Co. E. 128 Inf.	KIA	8/29/18	1818 State St., Milwaukee, Wis. Theresa Hutl.
Prestegaard, Lars E.	Corp.	Co. M. 127 Inf.	KIA	10/5/18	Voose Vangern, Bergen, Norway. Mrs. Enger Prestegaard (Mother).
Preston, Hobart P.	Pvt.	Co. D. 127 Inf.	DD	10/27/18	....
Price, Dave	Pvt.	Co. H. 128 Inf.	DW	10/6/18	Williamson, W. Va. David W. Price.
Price, Eula	Pvt.	Co. B. 128 Inf.	KIA	11/10/18	Ashland, N. C. Filmore Price.
Price, John	Pvt.	Co. K. 127 Inf.	DW	8/7/18	769 1st Ave., Milwaukee, Wis. Mary Price (Mother).
Price, Thurlow M.	Pvt.	Co. L. 128 Inf.	KIA	11/7/18	P. O. Box 45, Oak Dale, Tenn. Thelma Calyon (Sister).
Preiskorn, Erwin	Corp.	Co. E. 126 Inf.	DW	8/31/18	11 Adams St., Ann Arbor, Mich. Henry Peiskorn (Brother).

Name	Rank	Organization	Cause	Date	Address—Next of Kin
Prime, Dean	Pvt.	Med. Det. 125 Inf.	DW	10/12/18	....
Printz, Frank E.	Mech.	Co. G. 128 Inf.	KIA	8/31/18	423 Normal Ave., Stevens Point, Wis. Mrs. Matt Printz.
Prizzi, Michael	Pvt. 1cl.	Co. G. 126 Inf.	DD	6/23/18	8 Emmett St., Rochester, N. Y. Sam Prizzi (Father).
Procter, Merlin	Pvt.	Co. G. 127 Inf.	DD	4/25/18	....
Prokopowich, John	Pvt.	Co. L. 127 Inf.	KIA	9/2/18	Box 630, Calagorment, Canada. Nick Prokopowich (Brother).
Pruchnofski, Frank	Sgt.	Co. I. 128 Inf.	KIA	9/1/18	632 2nd St., Menasha, Wis. Joe Pruchnofski.
Prybylski, Joseph B.	Sgt.	Co. I. 125 Inf.	KIA	8/28/18	R. F. D. 1, Pinconning, Mich. Michael Prybylski (Father).
Przybylowski, Leonard	Pvt.	Co. F. 127 Inf.	KIA	9/2/18	915 Maple St., Milwaukee, Wis. Victor Przybylowski.
Pukita, Trofin	Pvt.	Co. B. 128 Inf.	DW	10/4/18	23 E. York St., Baltimore, Md. Alexandri Pukita (Brother).
Pullen, James T.	Pvt.	Co. L. 128 Inf.	......	9/23/18	....
Purdy, Williard D.	Sgt.	Co. A. 127 Inf.	ACC	7/4/18	Box 632, Marshfield, Wis. Mrs. Edgar Purdy (Mother).
Purvis, James M.	Pvt.	Co. H. 127 Inf.	KIA	10/10/18	Gunn, Miss. Sam Purvis (Father).
Qualls, James L.	Pvt.	Co. D. 125 Inf.	KIA	10/11/18	Story, Ark. Mrs. Dora Qualls (Mother).
Quereau, Edwin C.	Pvt.	Co. A. 103 Engrs.	DW	8/7/18	....
Quigg, Charles	Stab. Sgt	Bat. C. 120 F. A.	DD	....	824 E. Grand Ave., Eau Claire, Wis. Mrs. J. C. Quigg (Mother).
Raak, Arthur	Corp.	Co. M. 126 Inf.	DW	10/9/18	Herkimer, N. Y. Mrs. Verman Raak (Mother).
Raasch, George	Pvt.	Mg. Co. 128 Inf.	KIA	8/31/18	R. F. D. 1, Oconomowoc, Wis. Dr. N. C. Stuesser (Friend).
Rabenstein, Carl H.	Corp.	Co. A. 128 Inf.	DW	10/10/18	Neillsville, Wis. Carl Rabenstein (Father).
Radcliff, Lilburn	Pvt.	Co. A. 128 Inf.	KIA	11/10/18	Smithfield, Ky. Dack Radcliff (Father).
Radecki, Leon	Pvt.	Co. B. 126 Inf.	KIA	10/5/18	319 Stewart Ave., Gd. Rapids, Mich. Mrs. Klinentyna Gulemlcawski.
Radovich, John	Pvt.	Co. C. 127 Inf.	KIA	10/5/18	2015 Ventura Ave., Fresno, Calif. Mrs. Dora Obradovich (Aunt).
Radovitch, John B.	Sgt.	Co. D. 121 Mg. Bn.	ACC	6/13/18	Fond du Lac, Wis. John Henry (Friend).
Ragan, Arthur E.	Corp.	Co. F. 126 Inf.	DW	10/7/18	....
Raithel, Otto G.	Pvt.	Co. L. 125 Inf.	KIA	10/18/18	Jefferson City, Mo. Julius Raithel (Father).
Ralph, Earl	Pvt.	Co. B. 18 Inf.	DW	9/2/18	Guide Rock, Neb. E. Ralph.
Ramm, Devalois Fred	Pvt.	Co. E. 128 Inf.	KIA	9/1/18	Vigil, Ill. John C. Ramm (Father).
Randall, Carl F.	Pvt. 1cl.	Co. F. 126 Inf.	DW	8/12/18	R. F. D. 5, Ionia, Mich. Soloman J. Randall (Father).
Rankin, Clarence L.	Pvt.	Co. C. 126 Inf.	KIA	8/1/18	R. F. D. 2, Schoolcraft, Mich. Henry Rankin.
Rankin, Raymond	Corp.	Co. L. 126 Inf.	KIA	10/9/18	Coopersville, Mich. John Rankin.
Rannow, Theodore	Pvt.	Co. L. 59 Inf.	DW	8/4/18	....
Rapp, Joseph J.	Pvt.	Co. C. 126 Inf.	KIA	10/10/18	Star Route, Shippensville, Pa. Henry Rapp (Father).
Rasp, Charles J.	Pvt. 1cl.	Co. C. 128 Inf.	KIA	7/2/18	509 McDougall Ave., Detroit, Mich. John Rasp.
Rath, Francis T.	Pvt.	Co. C. 127 Inf.	DW	10/10/18	R. F. D. 2, Defiance, Ohio. W. P. Rath (Father).
Rathburn, Leora A.	Pvt.	Co. M. 125 Inf.	KIA	10/10/18	R. F. D. 1, Box 49, Belle Fourche. James Rathburn (Father). S. D.
Rathbun, William	Corp.	Co. I, 128 Inf.	DW	8/31/18	Sparta, Wis. Jesse Rathbun.
Raustis, John	Pvt.	Co. I. 125 Inf.	KIA	7/31/18	276 Main St., Amsterdam, N. Y. Anna Raustis (Mother).
Rawdon, Lawrence S.	Pvt. 1cl.	Co. M. 127 Inf.	KIA	8/4/18	Malta, Montana. Steve Rawdon (Father).
Raymer, George L.	Pvt.	Co. A. 126 Inf.	......	10/4/18	Gen. Del., Edwards, Mo. Presley Raymer (Father).
Reardon, William S.	Pvt.	Co. M. 128 Inf.	KIA	11/8/18	1969 Chathron Ave., Bronx, N. Y. Julia Reardon.
Rebec, Albert M.	Pvt.	Hq. Co. 125 Inf.	KIA	10/8/18	East Jordan, Mich. Mr. Anthony Rebec (Father).
Rech, Baldwin	Pvt. 1cl.	Co. C. 128 Inf.	KIA	8/1/18	845 14th St., Milwaukee, Wis. Mrs. Catherine Rech.
Redmen, Samuel C.	Pvt.	Co. H. 126 Inf.	KIA	10/5/18	Front Royal, Va. Taylor Redmen.
Reed, Cecil	Corp.	Co. E. 125 Inf.	KIA	8/3/18	406 Lain St., Durand, Mich. Elmira E. Reed (Mother).

Name	Rank	Organization	Cause	Date	Address—Next of Kin
Reed, Seth	Corp.	Co. A. 125 Inf.	DW	9/5/18	R. F. D. 1, Wolverine, Mich. Thomas H. Reed (Father).
Reedy, Austin F.	Pvt.	Co. H. 127 Inf.	KIA	7/31/18	Libby, Montana. Mrs. Joh Reedy (Mother).
Rees, John	Pvt.	Co. B. 125 Inf.	KIA	10/12/18	2028 Peoria Road, Springfield, Ill. Mrs. Rachel Rees (Mother).
Reese, Amose C.	Pvt.	Co. K. 128 Inf.	KIA	....	1739 Sebert St., Philadelphia, Pa. Jesse L. Reese.
Reese, Lester C.	Pvt. 1cl.	Co. B. 125 Inf.	KIA	10/12/18	McMinnville, Ore. Mrs. W. W. Reese (Mother).
Reeser, Harley R.	Sgt.	Co. C. 120 Mg. Bn.	DW	10/4/18	Logansport, Ind. Mrs. Elizabeth Reeser.
Regert, Sam J.	Pvt.	Co. A. 120 Mg. Bn.	KIA	10/4/18	Phillips, Wis. Mrs. Fred Strobel.
Rehling, George C.	Pvt.	Co. F. 127 Inf.	DW	10/5/18	Arlington, Minn. Mrs. Louisia Rehling (Mother).
Reid, Neil W.	Corp.	Co. G. 126 Inf.	KIA	8/2/18	R. F. D. 1, Warren, Mich. J. M. Reid (Father).
Reiff, Myron	Sgt.	Bat. A. 120 F. A.	DW	9/3/18	3406 Walnut St., Milwaukee, Wis. Mrs. P. A. Reiff.
Reiff, Ralph R.	Corp.	Hq. 322 F. A.	KIA	10/30/18	....
Reily, William T.	Pvt.	Co. A. 126 Inf.	KIA	8/1/18	1127 B St. SE., Washington, D. C. Mrs. Ardenia Reily.
Relly, George B., Jr.	Pvt.	Co. B. 126 Inf.	KIA	10/15/18	1236 Cress St., Baltimore, Md. Mary Relly (Mother).
Reinkens, Alfonso	Pvt. 1cl.	Co. G. 126 Inf.	KIA	9/2/18	Montesano, Wash. John J. Reinkens (Father).
Remley, Earl M.	Pvt.	Co. C. 126 Inf.	DW	10/5/18	R. F. D., Russellville, Mo. George em ey (Father).
Rempler, Perry	Pvt.	Co. K. 125 Inf.	DW	10/21/18	R. F. D. 2RFoster, Ohio. Mrs. Ella Rempler (Mother).
Replogla, John	Pvt.	Co. G. 128 Inf.	......	....	....
Reuter, Frederick J.	Pvt.	Co. E. 126 Inf.	KIA	7/29/18	R. F. D. 3, Macton, Maryland. Mrs. Jacob Reuter.
Reynolds, Ralph	Pvt.	Co. C. 127 Inf.	KIA	8/4/18	1209 Dewey Ave., Beloit, Wis. C. A. Reynolds.
Rezak, Martin	Pvt.	Co. L. 128 Inf.	KIA	11/7/18	103 Lincoln St., Butler, Pa. Joseph Rezak (Brother).
Rice, Bertie K.	Corp.	Co. I. 128 Inf.	KIA	11/8/18	Metcalf, Ill. Mrs. Emma Newell (Sister).
Richard, Ramie	Pvt.	Co. G. 125 Inf.	KIA	10/15/18	Creole, La. Mrs. Alice Richard (Wife).
Richards, Samuel	Pvt.	Co. H. 127 Inf.	KIA	10/15/18	Boyero, Colo. Ida Richards (Mother).
Richardson, James M.	Pvt.	Hq. Co. 126 Inf.	KIA	10/20/18	Boone, Iowa. Mrs. Tona Bell Richardson (Mother).
Riches, Albert S.	Sgt.	Co. I. 127 Inf.	KIA	9/1/18	1014 Harrison St., Superior, Wis. S. A. Riches (Father).
Richmond, Benjamin	Corp.	Co. E. 125 Inf.	KIA	8/29/18	Garner Apts., Pontiac, Mich. Robert Garner (Brother-in-Law).
Richmond, Earl G.	Pvt. 1cl.	Co. G. 128 Inf.	KIA	9/1/18	Sturgeon Bay, Wis. Joseph Richmond.
Richmond, Leslie M.	Sgt.	Co. F. 126 Inf.	KIA	8/29/18	Stockbridge, Mich. Mrs. A. L. Richmond (Mother).
Riddle, Henry	Pvt.	Co. D. 125 Inf.	DW	10/19/18	Union Co., Sturgeon, Ky. J. T. Riddle (Father).
Rieck, Victor I.	Pvt.	Mg. Co. 125 Inf.	KIA	10/9/18	P. O. Box 30, Utica, Mich. Herman J. Rieck.
Riemer, Albert W.	Pvt.	Co. M. 127 Inf.	KIA	....	615 Clarke St., Oconto, Wis. Mrs. Fred Riemer (Mother).
Rierson, Ernest H.	Pvt.	Co. E. 128 Inf.	KIA	8/31/18	King, N. Carolina. Mrs. Mary Rierson.
Rietz, Charles	Pvt. 1cl.	Mg. Co. 125 Inf.	KIA	10/18/18	41 Vanderbilt Ave., Detroit, Mich. Mrs. Fred Budnik.
Riffle, Lloyd H.	Pvt. 1cl.	Co. C. 127 Inf.	KIA	7/31/18	2116 Belle Plain Ave., Chicago, Ill. Mrs. R. W. Burdick (Sister).
Riggleman, Charles W	Pvt.	Co. I. 126 Inf.	KIA	10/22/18	Rockingham, Va. Jennie Riggleman.
Rigic, Ferdinand	Mus.	Hq. 322 F. A.	KIA	10/14/18	....
Riggs, Joseph E.	Pvt.	Co. D. 126 Inf.	KIA	8/1/18	Panguitch, Utah. Andre J. Riggs.
Rimstidt, Harry I.	Pvt.	Co. G. 127 Inf.	KIA	8/4/18	642 Pleasant St., Beloit, Wis. Mrs. Lovina Andrews (Mother).
Rinaldi, Scarinei	Pvt.	Mg. Co. 128 Inf.	DW	9/4/18	Peruga, Italy. Agnes Marcluci.
Rineberger, James W.	Pvt.	Co. H. 126 Inf.	KIA	8/28/18	1652 High St., Louisville, Ky. Mrs. Lena Warren (Sister).
Rippberger, Oscar A.	Pvt.	Co. H. 127 Inf.	KIA	7/31/18	25 Whistler St., Freeport, Ill. Mrs. Aloce Rippberger (Wife).
Rising, Joseph	Pvt.	Co. H. 127 Inf.	KIA	10/9/18	1104 2nd Ave., Kalispell, Mont. Mrs. M. Rising (Mother).
Ritzert, Charles T.	Pvt.	Co. G. 125 Inf.	KIA	8/4/18	....

Name	Rank	Organization	Cause	Date	Address—Next of Kin
Roam, Mike	Pvt.	Co. B. 127 Inf.	DW	10/15/18	1269 Water St., Meadville, Pa. Ralph Ditucia (Uncle).
Rease, Camiel	Corp.	Co. D. 125 Inf.	KIA	8/29/18	1072 Bewick Ave., Detroit, Mich. Mrs. R. Rease (Sister-in-Law).
Robb, Vernon M.	Pvt.	Mg. Co. 125 Inf.	DW	8/31/18	Douglas, Neb. Mrs. F. M. Robb (Mother).
Roberts, Bertel	Pvt.	Co. G. 126 Inf.	KIA	10/5/18	Hyden, Leslie Co., Kentucky. Mrs. Lucy Roberts.
Roberts, Earl E.	Corp.	Co. C. 128 Inf.	KIA	11/10/18	46 Pine St., Muskegon, Mich. Mrs. D. L. Roberts.
Roberts, Wyatt	Pvt.	Co. A. 128 Inf.	KIA	10/20/18	Sweetland, W. Va. Mrs. Bara Roberts.
Robertson, Edward A.	Pvt.	Co. A. 128 Inf.	KIA	11/10/18	....
Robinson, Charles	Pvt. 1cl.	Co. F. 127 Inf.	KIA	8/4/18	Gresham, Wis. Ella Quinney (Aunt).
Robinson, John H.	Corp.	Co. L. 125 Inf.	KIA	10/3/18	30 E. Milwaukee St., Detroit, Mich. William Robinson (Father).
Robinson, Trowis W.	Pvt.	Co. C. 125 Inf.	KIA	10/23/18	Harvard, N. Carolina. Charley Robinson.
Roemer, John L.	Pvt.	Co. F. 126 Inf.	......	8/28/18	Raspeburg, Md. John Roemer.
Rogalska, George F.	Pvt. 1cl.	Hq. Co. 128 Inf.	KIA	8/2/18	Apt. 21, 428 Cass St., Milwaukee, Wis. Lydia Lemons Rogalska (Mother).
Rogers, Austin	Pvt.	Co. K. 126 Inf.	KIA	10/16/18	Churchill, Tenn. Harry Rogers.
Rogers, Edward E.	Pvt.	Co. G. 127 Inf.	KIA	10/4/18	Judsonia, Arkansas. Joseph A. Rogers (Father).
Rogers, Samuel	Pvt.	Co. K. 128 Inf.	KIA	11/7/18	Iron River, Wis. Calvin D. Rogers.
Roman, Adam	Pvt.	Co. A. 126 Inf.	KIA	7/31/18	26 Garfield St., Natrona, Pa. Mr. Kostanty Rzewnicki.
Romanzuk, Walter	Pvt.	Co. A. 127 Inf.	KIA	10/15/18	Vilenski, Russia. Pauline Romanzuk.
Romes, Stephens	Pvt.	Co. H. 125 Inf.	KIA	10/15/18	Western Ave., Cheboygan, Mich. Steven Romes, Sr. (Father).
Romely, Earl	Pvt.	Co. C. 126 Inf.	KIA	10/5/18	....
Romotowski, Chester	Pvt.	Co. I. 128 Inf.	KIA	9/1/18	1001 Randolph St., Saginaw, Mich. Zopi Wolkawic.
Roose, Camiel	Corp.	Co. D. 125 Inf.	......	8/28/18	....
Rooney, Thomas	Pvt.	Co. B. 128 Inf.	KIA	10/13/18	1228 La Crosse St., La Crosse, Wis. Thomas Rooney.
Root, George E.	Pvt.	Co. F. 125 Inf.	KIA	8/29/18	110 Edwards St., St. Paul, Minn. Delkia Root (Mother).
Rorabacher, Clare	Corp.	Co. E. 126 Inf.	KIA	10/9/18	Hamburg, Mich. Charles Rorabacher.
Rosati, Antonio	Pvt.	308 Btry. Tr. Arty.	KIA	10/23/18	Union Savings & Trust Co., 1127-1129 Vine St., Cincinnati, Ohio. Vittorio Rosati (Brother).
Rose, Carl	Pvt.	Co. E. 126 Inf.	KIA	10/9/18	Thornwood, W. Va. Mrs. Agnes Rose (Mother).
Rose, Manuel R.	Pvt.	Co. M. 125 Inf.	DW	10/11/18	Milpitas, Calif. Louisa Rose (Mother).
Rose, Orson A.	Pvt. 1cl.	Co. A. 125 Inf.	KIA	10/11/18	R. F. D. 1, Fowlerville, Mich. Eliza Ann Rose (Mother).
Rose, Ralph C.	Corp.	Co. M. 126 Inf.	KIA	10/4/18	140 Main St., Meadville, Mo. Lillian Rose (Wife).
Rosenburger, Leslie	Pvt.	Co. G. 126 Inf.	KIA	10/9/18	Jeffersonton, Va. Mrs. Mary A. Rosenburger (Mother).
Rosenkranz, William J	Sgt.	Co. A. 322 F. A.	DD	12/24/18	....
Rosenzweig, Henry F.	Pvt.	Co. I. 126 Inf.	KIA	....	Morley, Mich. John Rosenzweig (Father).
Rosky, John	Pvt.	Co. H. 125 Inf.	KIA	7/31/18	P. O. Box 38, DeWard, Mich. Thomas McGuire (Friend).
Ross, Edwin	Pvt.	Co. E. 125 Inf.	DW	9/5/18	....
Ross, Lawrence H.	Pvt.	Co. C. 120 Mg. Bn.	KIA	8/1/18	458 Distel Ave., Detroit, Mich. Mrs. Dora Merrow.
Ross, Murdo C.	Corp.	Co. H. 126 Inf.	......	9/2/18	Beauly, Invernesshire, Scotland. Mrs. Mary Ross (Mother).
Ross, William	Pvt.	Co. H. 128 Inf.	DW	10/8/18	Littleton, Ill. Mrs. Maggie Ross.
Rossbach, Fred J.	Sgt.	Co. H. 128 Inf.	DD	3/18/18	....
Rothermel, Richard J.	Corp.	Hq. Co. I. 207 Amm. Tr.	KIA	10/3/18	Plainfield, Wis. Frank A. Rothermel.
Rothfus, Adrian	Sgt.	Mg. Co. 126 Inf.	KIA	7/31/18	1036 Fulton St. SE., Gd. Rapids, Mich. Mrs. Alberta Rothfus (Mother).
Rosseau, Raymond J.	Corp.	Co. L. 127 Inf.	DW	8/31/18	R. F. D. 1, Rhinelander, Wis. Mrs. C. Rousseau (Mother).
Rowe, Jesse	Corp.	Co. M. 125 Inf.	KIA	7/31/18	....
Roy, Charles M.	Corp.	Co. H. 126 Inf.	DD	7/3/18	Jerome, Mich. Calvin, Roy (Father).

1. FIRST LIEUTENANT (FATHER) WILLIAM F. DAVITT, Chaplain 125th Infantry. Killed in action November 11th, 1918, during the Meuse-Argonne Offensive.
2. CAPTAIN MEADE FRIERSON, JR., 125th Infantry. Killed in action August 29th, 1918, while making a reconnaissance before the enemy during the Oise-Aisne Offensive.
3. FIRST LIEUTENANT JOHN HOUSTON STEEN, Medical Department, 125th Infantry. Killed in action August 6th, 1918, during the Aisne-Marne Offensive.
4. CAPTAIN CHARLES A. LEARNED, Company A, 125th Infantry. Killed in action August 5th, 1918, during the Aisne-Marne Offensive.
5. CAPTAIN OSCAR FALK, Company F, 125th Infantry. Died August 1, 1918, of wounds received during the Aisne-Marne Offensive.
6. CAPTAIN MERRITT UDELL LAMB, Regimental Intelligence Officer, 125th Infantry. Killed in action August 29th, 1918, while making a reconnaissance before the enemy during the Oise-Aisne Offensive.
7. SECOND LIEUTENANT JOSEPH M. DUFF, 125th Infantry. Killed in action October 11th, 1918, during the Meuse-Argonne Offensive.
8. CAPTAIN FRANCIS A. BARLOW, Company H, 125th Infantry. Killed in action October 7th, 1918, during the Meuse-Argonne Offensive.
9. FIRST LIEUTENANT CHARLES A. HAMMOND, Company L, 125th Infantry. Killed in action July 31st, 1918, while leading his company against the enemy during the Aisne-Marne Offensive.

277

Name	Rank	Organization	Cause	Date	Address—Next of Kin
Royer, Harry O.	Pvt.	Co. D. 125 Inf.	KIA	10/11/18	R. F. D. 1, Orville, Wayne Co., Ohio. J. F. Royer (Father).
Rozwadewski, Walter	Pvt. 1cl.	Co. D. 125 Inf.	KIA	7/31/18	668 Palmer Ave., Detroit, Mich. Mrs. Mary Rozwadewski.
Rube, Fred K.	Pvt.	Co. I. 127 Inf.	KIA	8/4/18	Kelso, Wash. Mrs. Peter Holleman (Sister).
Ryby, Wilbur M.	Pvt.	Co. C. 127 Inf.	DW	10/8/18	Sellersburg, Ind. Mrs. W. M. Ryby (Wife).
Ruchti, Alfred	Pvt.	Co. H. 127 Inf.	DW	8/2/18	Green County House, Monroe, Mich. Adolph Ruchti (Brother).
Ruedisale, William	Corp.	Co. C. 125 Inf.	DW	8/5/18	900 Van Dyke Ave., Detroit, Mich. W. J. Ruedisale (Father).
Rugg, Harry Geo.	Pvt. 1cl.	Co. E. 125 Inf.	KIA	10/13/18	R. F. D. 1, Remington, Vt. Carrie Thompson (Sister).
Rundquist, Oscar	Sgt.	Co. I. 126 Inf.	KIA	10/9/18	1017 4th Ave., Big Rapids, Mich. Mrs. Olaf Rundquist (Mother).
Runnyon, Joseph W.	Pvt. 1cl.	Co. G. 126 Inf.	KIA	8/5/18	Shelby, N. Carolina. J. C. Runnyon.
Rush, William	Pvt.	Co. G. 128 Inf.	......	11/3/18	
Russell, Charles T.	Pvt.	Bat. E. 76 F. A.	DW	10/5/18	
Russell, Louis A.	Pvt.	Co. M. 126 Inf.	KIA	10/10/18	R. F. D. 3, Cedar Springs, Mich. Byron R. Russell (Father).
Russell, Orrin M.	Pvt.	Co. A. 127 Inf.	KIA	10/12/18	Colfax, Wis. James B. Russell.
Russell, Robert E.	Pvt.	Co. C. 128 Inf.	KIA	10/12/18	Barryville, Va. Mrs. Mary Russell.
Russell, Sim L.	Pvt. 1cl.	Co. H. 126 Inf.	DW	8/28/18	Canmer, Ky. Mrs. A. W. Russell (Mother).
Rust, Daniel T., Jr.	Corp.	Co. M. 125 Inf.	KIA	7/31/18	
Rust, David L.	Pvt. 1cl.	Bat. A. 322 F. A.	DD	12/12/18	
Ruth, William T.	Pvt.	Co. D. 149 Mg. Bn	KIA	....	
Ryan, Arthur	Pvt. 1cl.	Bat. C. 120 F. A.	KIA	8/29/18	516 Euclid Ave., St. Louis, Mo. Patrick Ryan.
Ryan, Bert	Corp.	Co. E. 125 Inf.	KIA	7/31/18	
Sabeen, Merton D.	Corp.	Co. C. 128 Inf.	KIA	8/1/18	New Richmond, Wis. Mrs. A. R. Sabeen.
Sadkowski, Chester	Pvt. 1cl.	Co. C. 125 Inf.	KIA	7/31/18	38 Jackson St., Bridgeport, Conn. Matalyra Zuzuchowski.
Suder, Fred	Pvt.	Co. C. 128 Inf.	DW	10/5/18	
Sage, James E.	Pvt. 1cl.	Co. K. 128 Inf.	KIA	9/1/18	Burke, Idaho. Mrs. Eugene Sage.
Saintom, Nicola	Pvt.	Co. M. 128 Inf.	KIA	10/14/18	
Sakkinen, John P.	Pvt.	Co. G. 125 Inf.	KIA	8/30/18	Box 9, Painesdale, Mich. Peter Sakkinen (Father).
Sakolka, John	Pvt.	Co. A. 126 Inf.	KIA	7/31/18	Wulklanska, Russia. Tuseph Sakolka.
Salazar, Jese C.	Pvt.	Co. A. 128 Inf.	KIA	11/10/18	290 N. Meyer St., Tucson, Ariz. Mrs. Felipa Gonzales.
Sales, Walter H.	Pvt.	Co. H. 127 Inf.	KIA	8/3/18	
Salo, Andrew	Pvt.	Co. G. 128 Inf.	KIA	10/5/18	Van Buskirk, Wis. John Salo.
Salsgiver, Vernet	Pvt.	Co. M. 125 Inf.	KIA	7/31/18	
Saltin, William	Pvt.	Co. L. 126 Inf.	KIA	10/10/18	1214 Langley St., Escanaba, Mich. Mrs. Emma Falt.
Salvator, Benita	Pvt.	Co. K. 30 Inf.	DW	10/4/18	
Salzor, Edward	Pvt. 1cl.	Co. F. 127 Inf.	KIA	8/4/18	Neopit, Wis. Carl Salzor (Father).
Samples, Leonard	Pvt.	Co. B. 128 Inf.	KIA	11/10/18	Route 1, Hatton. Ky. George Samples.
Sandheimier, William	Pvt.	Co. E. 125 Inf.	KIA	7/31/18	
Sanders, Edward L.	Pvt.	Co. A. 125 Inf.	KIA	10/9/18	Brooke, Ky. Berth Sanders (Father).
Sanders, Ralph S.	Pvt.	Co. M. 128 Inf.	KIA	1/8/18	Erlanger, Ky. Mrs. Sanders.
Sanders, Theodore	Pvt.	Co. E. 126 Inf.	KIA	9/1/18	Baltimore. Md. George Sanders (Father).
Sandridge, Marion L.	Pvt.	Co. I. 126 Inf.	KIA	10/5/18	Moormans River, Va. L. L. Sandridge.
Sands, Walter H.	Corp.	Co. L. 128 Inf.	DW	8/16/18	
Sanstrom, Albert	Pvt.	Co. C. 127 Inf.	KIA	9/2/18	1418 6th Ave., Rockford, Ill. Franl Sanstrom (Father).
Sandy, Harry J.	Pvt.	Co. B. 128 Inf.	KIA	11/10/18	Java, S. Dakota. Jim Campbell.

NAME	RANK	ORGANIZATION	CAUSE	DATE	ADDRESS—NEXT OF KIN
Sanson, Joseph	Pvt.	Co. B. 128 Inf.	KIA	11/10/18	Bowling Green, Ky. Joseph J. Sanson.
Santerelli, Angelo	Pvt.	Co. M. 127 Inf.	KIA	8/4/18	Tooele City, Utah. Pasquale Santerelli (Brother).
Sarazen, Aleck	Pvt.	Bat. C. 120 F. A.	DD	....	Bruce, Wis. Mary Sarazen (Mother).
Sather, Ben	Corp.	Co. E. 127 Inf.	KIA	9/2/18	1240 S. Dewey St., Eau Claire, Wis. Mrs. J. Sather (Mother).
Satterlee, Glenn N.	Pvt. 1cl.	Co. C. 128 Inf.	KIA	8/1/18	Hubbardsville, N. Y. C. A. Satterlee.
Satterwhite, Lilbom	Pvt.	Co. F. 128 Inf.	KIA	11/10/18	R. F. D. 1, Hewlett, Va. Frank D. Satterwhite (Father).
Sauvola, Ernest	Pvt.	Co. L. 126 Inf.	KIA	7/31/18	Chassell, Mich. Oscar Sauvola.
Sauvala, Charles	Pvt.	Co. G. 125 Inf.	KIA	7/31/18	....
Savedro, Jose L.	Pvt.	Co. G. 128 Inf.	KIA	10/15/18	....
Sawcheck, Gregory	Pvt.	Co. E. 126 Inf.	DW	8/28/18	Camp St., Lansing, Mich. Jack Moesig (Friend).
Saxe, Chas. E.	Sgt. 1cl.	MD. 107 Engrs.	DD	2/19/18	....
Schener, John	Pvt.	Co. M. 128 Inf.	......	....	701 Louis St., Louisburg, Continton, Ky. Charles Schener.
Saxay, Harry	Corp.	Co. E. 127 Inf.	KIA	9/2/18	Willow Creek, Calif. Kidd Saxay (Father).
Schaedler, August S.	Pvt.	Co. C. 121 Mg. Bn.	KIA	8/31/18	St. Thomas, Mo. Mrs. Sophia Schaedler (Wife).
Schafke, Albert	Pvt.	Co. H. 125 Inf.	DW	10/20/18	Posen, Mich. Mrs. Mary Schafke.
Schanger, Lyman T.	Pvt. 1cl.	Co. E. 125 Inf.	KIA	7/31/18	....
Scheffler, Joseph	Pvt.	Co. M. 127 Inf.	KIA	8/4/18	1048 N. Paulina St., Chicago, Ill. Frank Scheffler (Brother).
Schenck, Oscar K.	Pvt.	Co. H. 128 Inf.	KIA	10/5/18	Cushing, Neb. George H. Schenck (Father).
Scheik, Arthur J.	Pvt.	Co. H. 127 Inf.	KIA	10/7/18	1943 Gravois Ave., St. Louis, Mo. Mrs. Lena Scheik (Mother).
Schielz, Henry	Corp.	Co. A. 127 Inf.	DW	10/8/18	Fenwood, Wis. Mrs. Susan Schielz.
Schireson, Gustav D.	Pvt. 1cl.	Co. A. 128 Inf.	KIA	....	349 N. Main St., Los Angeles, Calif. Jack Schireson (Brother).
Schaikowski, Alois	Corp.	Co. K. 127 Inf.	KIA	8/4/18	496 21st Ave., Milwauke, Wis. John Schaikowski (Father).
Schlosser, Joseph, Jr.	Pvt. 1cl.	Co. F. 127 Inf.	KIA	7/31/18	4008 Lisbon Ave., Milwaukee, Wis. Mrs. J. G. Schlosser (Mother).
Schmees, Leo	Pvt. 1cl.	Co. G. 126 Inf.	KIA	10/14/18	122 Seneca Ave., Detroit, Mich. Mrs. Herman Schmees.
Schmidt, Harry	Pvt.	Co. D. 128 Inf.	KIA	8/30/18	Mildmay, Ontario, Canada. Mrs. Jacob Schmidt.
Schmidt, Hazen	Pvt.	Co. A. 125 Inf.	DW	8/5/18	....
Schmidt, Walter F.	Sgt.	Co. B. 128 Inf.	KIA	8/31/18	212 W. Arndt St., Fond du Lac, Wis. Mrs. Harman Schmidt.
Schmitt, Harry	Pvt.	308 Btry. Tr. Arty.	KIA	10/23/18	4087 E. 56th St., Cleveland, Ohio. Peter Schmitt (Father).
Schmitt, Peter D.	Pvt.	Bat. F. 120 F. A.	ACC	....	1215 Main St., Merrill, Wis. Peter Schmitt (Father).
Schmitt, Thomas	Sgt.	Co. B. 128 Inf.	DW	10/9/18	173 Russell St., Brooklyn, N. Y. Mrs. Anna Finnegan.
Schmitz, Joseph	Pvt.	Co. B. 125 Inf.	DW	10/16/18	2658 Michigan Ave., Detroit, Mich. Mrs. May Schmitz (Mother).
Schmider, John	Pvt.	Co. F. 125 Inf.	......	10/9/18	....
Schnieder, John	Pvt.	Co. F. 125 Inf.	KIA	10/9/18	1908 Montrose St., Cincinnati, Ohio. Mrs. Antoine Schnieder (Mother).
Schniers, Leo	Pvt. 1cl.	Co. G. 126 Inf.	DW	10/14/18	122 Seneca Ave., Detroit, Mich. Mrs. Herman Schniers (Mother).
Schnupp, Carl	Pvt.	Co. B. 127 Inf.	KIA	10/6/18	28 E. Washington Av., Norwalk, O. Richard Schnupp (Father).
Schoenrock, Frank T.	Pvt.	Co. M. 125 Inf.	KIA	7/31/18	....
Schoof, Clark W.	Pvt.	Co. D. 126 Inf.	KIA	8/1/18	R. F. D. A, Washington, Mich. William Schoof (Father).
Schoon, Charles	Corp.	Co. L. 125 Inf.	KIA	7/31/18	739 Wall St., Port Huron, Mich. Mrs. Annie Schoon (Mother).
Schram, Elmore E.	Pvt. 1cl.	Bat. D. 121 Mg. Bn.	DW	8/11/18	127 2nd St., Baraboo, Wis. Mrs. H. Schram.
Schubert, Louis H.	Pvt.	Co. C. 128 Inf.	KIA	10/12/18	Centertown, Missouri. Fred E. Schubert.
Schrech, Andy	Pvt.	Co. E. 125 Inf.	KIA	8/29/18	Tyson, Missouri. Otto Schrech.
Schroeder, August	Corp.	Co. M. 126 Inf.	KIA	10/4/18	Central City, Neb. Miss Salina Matson (Cousin).
Schweikert, Edward L	Pvt.	Co. C. 128 Inf.	KIA	10/15/18	2028 Webster Ave., New York, N. Y. Mrs. Lucy Schweikert.

Name	Rank	Organization	Cause	Date	Address—Next of Kin
Schwenkner, Herman	Corp.	Co. F. 127 Inf.	DW	10/21/18	Shawano, Wis. Fred Schwenkner (Father).
Schukalsky, Anthony	Pvt.	Co. C. 127 Inf.	KIA	7/31/18	R. F. D. 1, Box 65, Beaver, Wis. W. D. Willis (Stepfather).
Schuknecht, Elmer N.	Wag.	Sup. Co. 127 Inf.	ACC	9/22/18	610 Van Buren St., Pt. Washington, William Schuknecht. Wis.
Schulgen, Ernest	Pvt.	Co. A. 128 Inf.	DW	7/1/18	....
Schultz, Carl A.	Pvt.	Co. G. 127 Inf.	KIA	8/3/18	Saco, Montana. Fred Schultz (Father).
Schultz, Charles	Sgt.	Co. K. 125 Inf.	KIA	8/30/18	....
Schultz, Edward	Pvt. 1cl.	Co. A. 127 Inf.	DW	8/5/18	....
Schultz, Herbert J.	Corp.	Co. I. 126 Inf.	DW	10/9/18	1615 W. Mulberry St., Baltimore, Md. Frank Joseph Schultz.
Schultz, John E.	Pvt.	Co. K. 125 Inf.	KIA	7/31/18	926 Hartatt St., Escanaba, Mich. H. A. Schultz.
Schultz, Joseph	Pvt.	Co. B. 128 Inf.	KIA	6/22/18	R. F. D. 1, North Detroit, Mich. Mrs. Mary Schultz.
Schulz, Harry W.	Pvt.	Co. F. 126 Inf.	KIA	10/4/18	633 Adrian Ave., Jackson, Mich. Mrs. A. Schulz (Mother).
Schur, Peter J.	Wag.	Sup. Co. 127 Inf.	DD	10/9/18	1532 Macadam St., Portland, Ore. Peter F. Schur (Father).
Schwartzburg, Gerald W	Corp.	Co. D. 128 Inf.	KIA	8/2/18	North Milwaukee, Wis. W. C. Schwartzburg (Father).
Schyr, Peter J.	Wag.	Sup. Co. 127 Inf.	DD	10/9/18	....
Severson, Harry	Pvt.	Hq. Troop, 32 Div.	DD	2/23/19	....
Schwietzer, Fred	Sgt.	Co. D. 125 Inf.	KIA	10/14/18	13336 Buffalo Ave., Chicago, Ill. John Schwietzer (Father).
Schwindt, Harry	Pvt.	Co. B. 128 Inf.	KIA	10/20/18	Dickerson, N. Dak. Anton Schwindt.
Schwitzenbert, Fred	Pvt. 1cl.	Co. A. 128 Inf.	KIA	8/1/18	Neillsville, Wis. Helen Schwitzenbert (Sister).
Sharpe, James H.	Pvt.	Co. H. 128 Inf.	KIA	10/15/18	R. R. 1, Frankfort, Ky. Mrs. America Spurr Sharpe (Mother).
Scribner, Charles E.	Pvt. 1cl.	Co. B. 128 Inf.	DW	9/1/18	....
Scully, William L.	Corp.	308 Btry. Tr. Arty.	KIA	10/23/18	198 Midland Ave., Columbus, Ohio. Miss Mary Scully (Sister).
Sczepanick, Marion	Pvt. 1cl.	Co. G. 125 Inf.	KIA	8/4/18	....
Seay, Newell P.	Pvt.	Co. L. 128 Inf.	KIA	11/7/18	Route 27, Maysville, Georgia. John A. Seay (Father).
Secrest, Luther Edgar	Pvt.	Co. A. 127 Inf.	KIA	10/15/18	Southmayde, Texas. Mrs. Viola Secrest.
Seeley, Charles A.	Pvt.	Hq. Co. 261 Inf.	DW	10/9/18	....
Sehrt, Allen J.	Pvt.	Med. Det. 127 Inf.	KIA	10/13/18	942 College Ave., Beloit, Wis. Sophia Sehrt.
Seidl, Louis A.	Pvt. 1cl.	Co. A. 127 Inf.	KIA	8/3/18	111 N. Central Ave., Marshfield, Wis. Joseph Seidl (Father).
Seifert, Herbert J.	Pvt.	Co. D. 128 Inf.	KIA	....	Baltimore, Mich. August Seifert.
Seipold, Earl	Pvt. 1cl.	Co. M. 127 Inf.	KIA	9/1/18	613 5th St., Oconto, Wis. Gertrude Seipold (Mother).
Sells, Otto	Corp.	Co. B. 127 Inf.	KIA	8/4/18	1715 Michigan St., Oshkosh, Wis. William Sells (Father).
Selschotter, Julius	Pvt.	Co. 125 Inf.	KIA	8/29/18	601 Clayton St., Flint, Mich. Leone Selschotter (Mother).
Senstad, George K.	Pvt. 1cl.	Co. K. 125 Inf.	KIA	7/31/18	Lakeville, Minnesota. Mrs. C. Senstad (Mother).
Seveille, Walter	Pvt.	Co. M. 126 Inf.	KIA	10/16/18	Mercersburg, Pa. John Seveille.
Shershenuk, Frank	Pvt.	Co. H. 126 Inf.	......	8/28/18	....
Sewell, Whit C.	Pvt.	Co. B. 128 Inf.	KIA	10/14/18	Waldo, Ark. Mrs. Molly Sewell (Mother).
Shaefer, Henry	Corp.	Co. E. 128 Inf.	KIA	8/31/18	1722 Walnut St., Milwaukee, Wis. Mrs. B. Shaefer.
Shanks, Elmer F.	Pvt. 1cl.	Mg. Co. 127 Inf.	KIA	8/1/18	Miami, Florida. Mrs. S. A. Berni (Mother).
Shersheniak, Frank	Pvt.	Co. H. 126 Inf.	KIA	8/28/18	117 Alice St., Hamtramck, Mich. Pete Murzichuk (Friend).
Sharp, Don E.	Pvt. 1cl.	Med. Det. 125 Inf.	KIA	7/31/18	510 Johnson St., Saginaw, Mich. Mrs. S. Sharp (Mother).
Shick, Charles D.	Pvt.	Co. D. 128 Inf.	KIA	10/15/18	Billett, Illinois. Lee Shick.
Sharpley, Sheldon	Pvt.	Co. M. 127 Inf.	DW	8/2/18	McDonald St., Oconto, Wis. Mrs. Alex Sharpley (Mother).
Shaver, Homer T.	Pvt.	Co. I. 128 Inf.	KIA	10/18/18	....
Shaw, Robert C.	Pvt.	Bat. B. 120 F. A.	DD	....	758 Washington St., Portland, Me. Mrs. Fanny Shaw (Mother).

ROLL OF HONOR

Name	Rank	Organization	Cause	Date	Address—Next of Kin
Shea, William	Pvt.	308 Btry Tr. Arty.	KIA	10/23/18	8804 Jeffries Ave., Cleveland, Ohio. Michael Joseph Shea (Father).
Sheehan, John R.	Pvt.	Bat. C. 119 F. A.	KIA	10/23/18	588 Dorchester Ave., S. Boston, Mass. Mrs. Katherine H. Sheehan (Mother).
Shell, Gillis	Pvt.	Co. F. 127 Inf.	......	10/10/18	Woodbine, Ky. Sallie Bailey (Mother).
Sherman, Harry L.	Corp.	Co. A. 126 Inf.	DW	8/1/18	105 W. Chicago St., Quincy, Mich. Mrs. Lillia Sherman.
Sherman, William H.	Sgt.	Co. G. 126 Inf.	......	8/27/18	Bad Axe, Mich. Nelson Sherman (Father).
Sievers, Edwin	Pvt.	Co. D. 125 Inf.	......	10/18/18	....
Sinnatt, Ray	Sgt.	Bat. A. 121 F. A.	DW	10/1/18	866 Astor St., Milwaukee, Wis. Thomas Sinnatt (Father).
Shinkle, Leonard	Pvt.	Co. K. 128 Inf.	KIA	10/10/18	....
Shinn, Harley F.	Pvt.	Co. D. 125 Inf.	KIA	10/10/18	....
Shirey, Meria	Pvt.	Co. M. 128 Inf.	DW	10/15/18	Guin, Alabama. J. F. Shirey.
Shirley, Arthur L.	Corp.	Co. A. 128 Inf.	KIA	11/10/18	Lawrence, Neb. W. B. Shirley (Father).
Shovan, Earl J.	Pvt.	Co. G. 125 Inf.	KIA	10/7/18	Skanee, Mich. Mrs. J. Shovan (Mother).
Shrigley, Lloyd	Corp.	Co. M. 125 Inf.	KIA	7/31/18	....
Shubert, William A.	Pvt.	Hq. Co. 127 Inf.	KIA	10/16/18	R. F. D. 3, Box 84, Elgin, Ill. Albert Shubert (Father).
Shull, Charles R.	Pvt. 1cl.	Co. K. 126 Inf.	KIA	....	Cascade, Montana. Mrs. D. D. Jamison (Mother).
Shuttlesworth, James H	Pvt.	Co. B. 128 Inf.	KIA	11/10/18	Worthington, W. Va. Mrs. Hattie Shuttlesworth.
Sierplenski, Felix	Pvt.	Co. D. 128 Inf.	KIA	9/2/18	55 Holborn St., Detroit, Mich. Walter Sierplenski.
Sigorski, Julius	Pvt. 1cl.	Co. F. 125 Inf.	KIA	7/31/18	....
Sikors, Frank	Pvt.	Co. K. 127 Inf.	KIA	10/14/18	751 5th Ave., Milwaukee, Wis. John Sikors (Brother).
Sijka, Paul	Pvt.	Co. L. 128 Inf.	KIA	11/7/18	458 Martin St., Detroit, Mich. John Sijka (Brother).
Siberberg, Joseph	Pvt. 1cl.	Co. H. 128 Inf.	KIA	8/31/18	457 Mitchell St., Milwaukee, Wis. Benjamin Rosenberg.
Simons, Ritchie	Pvt.	Co. C. 125 Inf.	DW	10/1/18	R. F. D. 1, Berea, Ritchie Co., W. Va. Mrs. Victoria Simons (Mother).
Simonsen, Adolph	Pvt.	Co. A. 128 Inf.	KIA	11/10/18	369 E. Main St., Cory, Pa. Elsie Anderson (Aunt).
Simonson, Gaylor T.	Pvt.	Co. C. 126 Inf.	KIA	9/1/18	Agee, Neb. Lawrence Simonson.
Simonson, Richard L.	Sgt.	Co. C. 128 Inf.	KIA	8/1/18	Hudson, Wis. Andrew Simonson.
Sims, Wilbur	Pvt.	Co. I. 126 Inf.	DW	10/10/18	R. F. D. 1, Branch, Mich. James Sims.
Sinaveski, Kazimer	Pvt.	Co. A. 126 Inf.	KIA	7/31/18	941 Russell St., Detroit, Mich. Louis Sinaveski.
Sinclair, Harold	Pvt.	Co. I. 127 Inf.	KIA	10/12/18	Baker, Montana. Dean Sinclair (Father).
Sines, Benton	Corp.	Co. M. 126 Inf.	KIA	10/10/18	Johnston, Ohio. Mrs. Ben Sines.
Sinniger, George C.	Pvt. 1cl.	Hdqs. 128 Inf.	DW	11/10/18	18th & Bennett Sts., La Crosse, Wis. Anton Sinniger.
Siuba, Benny	Pvt.	Co. D. 128 Inf.	KIA	8/1/18	155 36th St., North Milwaukee, Wis. Lloyd W. Place (Father).
Sizemore, Noah	Pvt.	Co. F. 127 Inf.	KIA	10/7/18	Roark, Ky. Bud Sizemore (Brother).
Sizer, Walter	Pvt.	Co. G. 127 Inf.	KIA	8/3/18	King, Montana. Mary Seuser.
Skaggs, Emery	Pvt.	Co. C. 126 Inf.	KIA	10/25/18	Barnrock, Johnson Co., Kentucky. John C. Skaggs (Father).
Skaggs, Otto R.	Pvt.	Co. K. 126 Inf.	KIA	10/16/18	Litchfield, Ky. Rebecca Well.
Skaleski, Charles J.	Corp.	Co. F. 127 Inf.	KIA	8/1/18	R. F. D. 1, Oneida, Wis. Mrs. Ed. Sijich (Sister).
Skibski, Frank A.	Pvt.	Co. L. 127 Inf.	KIA	10/19/18	3217 Warsaw St., Toledo, Ohio. John Skibski (Father).
Skinner, Harold C.	Pvt.	Co. A. 127 Inf.	KIA	7/3/18	McMinnville, Ore. C. J. Skinner (Father).
Sky, John A.	Corp.	Mg. Co. 127 Inf.	KIA	8/1/18	....
Slaney, Maurice	Pvt. 1cl.	Batt. A. 120 F. A.	DW	8/6/18	179 Belair Place, Milwaukee, Wis. Mrs. W. J. Holleran.
Slattery, John J.	Sgt.	308 Bt. T. M.	KIA	10/23/18	833 W. Broad St., Columbus, Ohio. Mrs. Anna Slattery (Mother).
Slining, Ole	Pvt. 1cl.	Co. E. 127 Inf.	KIA	7/19/18	....
Slonina, Andrew	Corp.	Co. K. 127 Inf.	KIA	9/1/18	....

NAME	RANK	ORGANIZATION	CAUSE	DATE	ADDRESS—NEXT OF KIN
Smalor, Paul W.	Pvt. 1cl.	Co. M. 125 Inf.	KIA	8/30/18	....
Smith, Albert	Pvt.	Co. C. 128 Inf.	DW	8/30/18	....
Smith, Albert H.	Pvt.	Co. K. 128 Inf.	KIA	10/16/18	Edgehill, Mo. Eyhel Shy.
Smith, Benjamin F.	Pvt.	Co. L. 125 Inf.	KIA	10/9/18	....
Smith, Charles E.	Pvt.	Co. F. 127 Inf.	KIA	10/29/18	706 6th St., Milwaukee, Wis. Herman Smith (Father).
Smith, Clyde R.	Pvt.	Co. A. 125 Inf.	KIA	8/29/18	R. F. D. 3, Winfield, Ala. J. N. Smith (Father).
Smith, Clyde	Pvt.	Co. K. 128 Inf.	KIA	10/16/18	....
Smith, David, R.	Pvt.	Co. D. 128 Inf.	KIA	10/13/18	Tullahoma, Tenn. James A. Smith.
Smith, Eldridge D.	Pvt.	Co. B. 125 Inf.	KIA	10/11/18	Wytheville, Pa. William D. Smith (Father).
Smith, Emery N.	Pvt.	Co. A. 120 Mg. Bn.	DW	10/11/18	44 North St., Nazareth, Pa. Gideon Smith (Father).
Smith, Everett	Pvt. 1cl.	Co. D. 125 Inf.	KIA	8/4/18	La Grange, Ky. Miss Eva Smith (Sister).
Smith, Finck	Pvt.	Co. D. 125 Inf.	KIA	10/21/18	....
Smith, Garret	Sgt.	Co. K. 126 Inf.	KIA	8/2/18	420 Fremont Ave., Gd. Rapids, Mich. Mrs. J. Siden (Sister).
Smith, George A.	Corp.	Co. G. 125 Inf.	KIA	8/29/18	Ontonagon, Mich. Andrew Smith (Father).
Smith, Gilbert W.	Pvt.	Co. B. 125 Inf.	KIA	10/4/18	R. F. D. 3, Niota, Tenn. Mrs. Lucy Smith (Wife).
Smith, Harrison B.	Pvt.	Co. M. 125 Inf.	KIA	10/8/18	707 Fisher St., Peoria, Ill. Louise Smith (Sister).
Smith, Harold	Pvt.	Co. D. 121 Mg. Bn	KIA	10/17/18	2004 Vintin St., Omaha, Neb. S. H. Smith (Father).
Smith, Howard	Pvt.	Mg. Co. 125 Inf.	KIA	8/29/18	R. F. D. 4, Milford, Mich. George W. Ormsbee (Grandfather).
Smith, Ira H.	Pvt.	Co. C. 127 Inf.	KIA	10/19/18	1359 Lewis St., Santa Clara, Calif. Mrs. Ida Smith (Mother).
Smith, John K.	Pvt.	Co. B. 125 Inf.	KIA	10/9/18	Bierne, Ark. Mrs. A. J. Smith (Mother).
Smith, John S.	Pvt.	Supp. Co. 125 Inf.	DD	5/24/18	....
Smith, Leo J.	Pvt. 1cl.	Co. B. 107 Eng.	DD	1/26/18	....
Smith, Lester J.	Pvt.	Co. F. 126 Inf.	KIA	10/9/18	R. F. D. 1, Covington, Va. John Osborne Smith (Father).
Smith, Millard	Pvt.	Co. K. 128 Inf.	KIA	9/1/18	511 Va St., Farmville, Va. L. A. Smith.
Smith, Phillip C.	Pvt. 1cl.	Co. B. 128 Inf.	DD	3/25/18	....
Smith, Richards E.	Corp.	Co. I. 126 Inf.	KIA	10/9/18	Otia, Mich. Albert Butter.
Smith, Robert K.	Bug.	Co. H. 126 Inf.	KIA	8/4/18	414 Pingree Ave., Detroit, Mich. Mrs. Thomas Smith (Mother).
Smith, Robert	Pvt. 1cl.	Bat. F. 120 F. A.	DD	....	J. J. Mitchell Est., Lake Geneva. Arthur Smith (Father). Wis.
Smith, Russel J.	Pvt.	Bat. E. 32 F. A.	KIA	10/23/18	....
Smith, Tink	Pvt.	Co. D. 125 Inf.	KIA	10/14/18	R. F. D. 1, Dallas, Ga. Jim S. Smith (Brother).
Smith, Wilson J.	Pvt.	Co. H. 127 Inf.	KIA	10/7/18	....
Smith, William	Pvt.	Co. E. 128 Inf.	KIA	11/10/18	Barbourville, Ky. James Smith (Father).
Smith, William P.	Pvt. 1cl.	Co. D. 126 Inf.	KIA	7/3/18	Winton, Iowa. Mrs. J. P. Campbell (Friend).
Smotzer, Andrew	Pvt.	Co. D. 126 Inf.	KIA	10/4/18	Philipsburg, Pa. Mrs. Julia Smotzer (Mother).
Sneed, John A.	Pvt.	Co. M. 128 Inf.	KIA	11/8/18	Eagle Springs, N. C. Mrs. F. S. Sneed (Mother).
Snell, Harry E.	Pvt.	Co. I. 125 Inf.	KIA	10/20/18	Harrisburg, N. C. C. A. Snell (Father).
Snyder, Charles E.	Corp.	Co. F. 126 Inf.	KIA	8/25/18	1709 S. 10th St., Waco, Texas. Miss Margaret Kissler (Friend).
Snyder, George F.	....	Bat. D. 323 F. A.	......	9/18	628 Center Ave., Butler, Pa. Mrs. Geo. F. Snyder (Wife).
Snyder, John Mathias	Pvt.	Co. E. 128 Inf.	KIA	10/6/18	....
Sole, Arthur A.	Pvt.	Co. F. 128 Inf.	KIA	9/1/18	1125 Johnston St., Saginaw, Mich. Mrs. Anna Kasehoot (Mother).
Soles, Walter H.	Pvt. 1cl.	Co. A. 127 Inf.	KIA	7/31/18	Richfield Road, Marshfield, Wis. William H. Soles.
Solomon, Max	Pvt.	Co. D. 125 Inf.	KIA	8/28/18	413 Hastings St., Detroit, Mich. Mrs. Joseph (Cousin).
Soltis, Michael A.	Pvt.	Co. D. 125 Inf.	KIA	10/10/18	29 N. 6th St., W. Terre Haute, Ind. Mr. Louis Soltis (Father).

1. First Lieutenant John A. Chapman, Company C, 120th Machine Gun Battalion. Died September 12th, 1918, of wounds received in action August 29th, while directing the disposition of his guns against the enemy during the Oise-Aisne Offensive.

2. First Lieutenant Harry M. Keiser, 125th Infantry. Killed in action July 31st, 1918, during the Aisne-Marne Offensive.

3. First Lieutenant Lisle P. Amberland, Medical Department, 125th Infantry. Killed in action August 6th, 1918, during the Aisne-Marne Offensive.

4. Second Lieutenant Everett S. Fick, Company K, 125th Infantry. Killed in action August 1st, 1918, during the Aisne-Marne Offensive.

5. Major Ira D. MacLachlan, 2nd Battalion, 125th Infantry. Died of wounds October 31st, 1918, during the Meuse-Argonne Offensive.

6. First Lieutenant William H. Rust, Company K, 125th Infantry. Killed in action October 10th, 1918, during the Meuse-Argonne Offensive.

7. Second Lieutenant Herbert J. Sheldon, Headquarters 125th Infantry. Killed in action October 10th, 1918, during the Meuse-Argonne Offensive.

8. Second Lieutenant Albert S. Ross, Company K, 125th Infantry. Killed in action October 9th, during Meuse-Argonne Operations.

9. Second Lieutenant Phillip M. Shelly, Company F, 125th Infantry. Killed in action October 10th, 1918, during the Meuse-Argonne Offensive.

NAME	RANK	ORGANIZATION	CAUSE	DATE	ADDRESS—NEXT OF KIN
Sonn, Edward H.	Corp.	Co. B. 128 Inf.	KIA	8/31/18	Oakfield, Wis. Mrs. Henrietta Sonn.
Sorenson, John	Pvt.	Co. F. 128 Inf.	KIA	10/10/18	....
Sortum, Andrew	Pvt.	Co. B. 128 Inf.	KIA	8/4/18	Albee, S. Dakota. Esten A. Sortum (Father).
Soulis, Angeles J.	Pvt.	Co. E. 125 Inf.	KIA	7/31/18	....
Sours, Emry	Pvt.	Co. I. 126 Inf.	KIA	10/9/18	Axin, Mich. Levi D. Sours.
Sowards, Arthur	Corp.	Co. E. 127 Inf.	KIA	9/2/18	1015 Grand Ave., E. Eau Claire, Wis. Mrs. Arthur Sowards (Wife).
Spargimino, Meze	Pvt.	Co. M. 127 Inf.	KIA	10/20/18	149 West St., Salt Lake City, Utah. Joe Spargimino (Brother).
Sparks, Reese D.	Pvt. 1cl.	107 T. M. Batt.	KIA	6/30/18	Gimlet, Ky. George Sparks.
Spencer, Frank	Pvt.	Co. L. 125 Inf.	KIA	7/31/18	1419 Willow St., Pt. Huron, Mich. William G. Spencer (Father).
Spencer, Robert	Corp.	Co. G. 127 Inf.	KIA	8/3/18	....
Sperle, Michael	Pvt.	Co. A. 128 Inf.	KIA	11/10/18	Napoleon, N. Dak. Michael Sperle (Father).
Spicknell, Walter	Pvt.	Co. F. 126 Inf.	KIA	8/30/18	Roseland, Neb. Mrs. Lillie Spicknell (Mother).
Sprightly, Richard L.	Pvt.	Co. L. 127 Inf.	KIA	9/2/18	Beloit, Wis. R. J. Sprightly (Father).
Sproul, Harold J.	Pvt.	Bat. B. 120 F. A.	DD	....	Windsorville, Me. James W. Sproul (Father).
St. Anthony, Frank	Pvt.	Co. F. 125 Inf.	KIA	8/30/18	Faribault, Minn. Mrs. Katie Ives (Friend).
St. Peter, Fred	Mech.	Co. L. 125 Inf.	KIA	7/31/18	633 Almyra St., Menominee, Mich. Mrs. Mary St. Peter (Mother).
Stack, Fred	Corp.	Co. C. 126 Inf.	KIA	8/1/18	23 W. 43rd St., Chicago, Ill. Mrs. R. Holker.
Staff, Bibe	Pvt.	Co. H. 126 Inf.	KIA	8/30/18	Gulnare, Ky. John B. Staff (Father).
Stafford, Edward A.	Corp.	Co. L. 126 Inf.	KIA	8/2/18	325 S. Terrace St., Muskegon, Mich. Mrs. Marguret D. S'afford.
Stamitz, Herman E.	Pvt. 1cl.	Co. F. 125 Inf.	KIA	7/31/18	....
Stamp, Clifford	Pvt.	Co. E. 125 Inf.	DW	10/9/18	Rankin, Ill. Ira Stamp (Father).
Stanton, Guy M.	Pvt.	Co. B. 128 Inf.	KIA	7/9/18	....
Stapski, Stanislaw	Pvt.	Co. F. 107 Am. Tr.	KIA	10/6/18	811 1st Ave., Milwaukee, Wis. Frank Stapski (Brother).
Starbuck, Harry	Pvt. 1cl.	Co. A. 127 Inf.	KIA	8/5/18	Gowen, Mich. Harry Starbuck (Father).
Stauber, John	Pvt.	Co. L. 125 Inf.	KIA	7/31/18	Menominee, Mich. Michael Stauber (Father).
Stauppacher, LeRay	Corp.	Co. F. 128 Inf.	DW	10/15/18	Blanchardville, Wis. Mrs. Marion Stauppacher (Mother).
Stearns, Ford	Pvt. 1cl.	Hdq. Co. 126 Inf.	KIA	10/9/18	410 La Grave Ave., Gd. Rapids, Mich. Mrs. Nettie Stearns.
Stearns, Walter	Pvt. 1cl.	Hdq. Co. 128 Inf.	DW	10/10/18	1641 E. Stark St., Portland, Ore. J. O. Stearns (Father).
Stedwell, Roland	Pvt.	Mg. Co. 125 Inf.	DW	10/12/18	Carbon Hill, Ohio. Mrs. Elizabeth Stedwell.
Steeves, Raymond	Corp.	Co. B. 128 Inf.	KIA	10/20/18	143 Mary Ave., Fond du Lac, Wis. Mr. J. D. Steeves.
Steffe, Paul E.	Corp.	Co. F. 126 Inf.	KIA	8/31/18	Newaygo, Mich. J. W. Steffe.
Stegal, Jessie D.	Pvt.	Co. C. 126 Inf.	KIA	7/15/18	Seneca, Wis. M. W. Stegal (Father).
Steinberg, Henry F.	Corp.	Co. D. 125 Inf.	KIA	10/14/18	422 Cooper Ave., Detroit, Mich. Mrs. T. Steinberg (Mother).
Steinborn, Emil W.	Sgt.	Co. D. 127 Inf.	KIA	10/10/18	1418 22nd St., Milwaukee, Wis. Lucie Steinborn (Mother).
Stekelberg, William C.	Corp.	Co. G. 127 Inf.	KIA	7/31/18	407 Washburn Place, Madison, Wis. Mrs. Anna Rowley (Sister).
Stenseth, Jalmer L.	Pvt.	Co. C. 127 Inf.	DR	5/21/18	....
Stepke, Eugene J.	Pvt.	Co. A. 126 Inf.	DW	10/7/18	6th St. Indiana Ave., Glassport, Pa. Anna Stepke (Mother).
Sterling, Robert L.	Pvt.	Co. D. 127 Inf.	KIA	10/12/18	R. F. D. 7, Marysville, Tenn. Samuel A. Sterling (Father).
Stettler, Floyd L.	Pvt.	Co. K. 128 Inf.	KIA	11/7/18	DuPont, Ohio. Mrs. Ruth Stettler.
Stevans, Raymond R.	Pvt.	Co. A. 126 Inf.	KIA	8/1/18	Churubusco, N. Y. James B. Stevens (Father).
Stever, Helmet	Pvt.	Co. D. 121 F. A.	KIA	8/5/18	Milan, Wis. Herman Stever.
Steves, Raymond E.	Pvt.	Co. B. 128 Inf.	KIA	10/20/18	....
Steward, Russell H.	Pvt.	Mg. Co. 125 Inf.	KIA	9/30/18	R. F. D. 4, Nelsonville, Ohio. Norman Steward.

Name	Rank	Organization	Cause	Date	Address—Next of Kin
Stewart, Iver V.	Pvt. 1cl.	Co. A. 128 Inf.	KIA	9/1/18	R. F. D. 1, Gothenburg, Neb. A. F. Stewart (Father).
Stewart, Irving J.	Pvt. 1cl.	Co. I. 128 Inf.	DD	2/6/18	....
Stewert, William H.	Pvt.	Co. B. 127 Inf.	KIA	10/7/18	R. F. D. 3, Greenville, Pa. Clara A. Stewert (Mother).
Stimay, Matt	Corp.	Co. G. 125 Inf.	KIA	8/29/18	Box 636, Painesdale, Mich. Mat Stimay (Father).
Stinson, Ernest B.	Pvt.	Co. H. 126 Inf.	KIA	8/4/18	Monroe, Ky. Sam T. Stinson.
Stipsky, Vincent M.	Pvt.	Co. G. 126 Inf.	KIA	10/1/18	Stuttgart, Ark. Julias Stipsky (Father).
Stoewer, Charles	Corp.	Co. E. 126 Inf.	KIA	10/9/18	3419 O'Donnel St., Canton, Md. Mrs. Augusta Stoewer (Mother).
Stokes, Arthur T.	Corp.	Co. G. 126 Inf.	KIA	8/30/18	10 Marine Tr., Co. Dublin, Kingston. Mrs. H. Stokes (Mother).
Stolling, William C.	Pvt.	Co. E. 126 Inf.	KIA	7/31/18	....
Stomner, Martin A.	Corp.	Co. I. 128 Inf.	KIA	8/31/18	506 59th St., Seattle, Wash. Andrew Stomner.
Stone, Ed.	Pvt.	Co. E. 127 Inf.	KIA	10/17/18	....
Stone, Fred	Pvt.	Hdq. Co. 314 Inf.	DD	10/3/18	....
Stone, Verne E.	Pvt. 1cl.	Co. B. 128 Inf.	KIA	8/31/18	R. F. D. 7, Memphis Me. E. W. Stone (Father).
Stone, Walter	Corp.	Co. B. 128 Inf.	KIA	9/2/18	Bay View, Wash. H. E. Stone.
Stonecipher, Norman	Pvt.	Co. M. 125 Inf.	KIA	10/11/18	715 E. Chester St., Jeffersonville, Ind. Mary E. Stonecipher (Mother).
Storey, Elmer	Pvt.	Co. L. 125 Inf.	KIA	10/9/18	....
Storey, William C.	Pvt.	Co. K. 128 Inf.	KIA	11/10/18	2112 S. 11th St., Springfield, Ill. Mrs. Mary Storey.
Stover, Roy H.	Pvt.	Co. A. 126 Inf.	KIA	8/4/18	R. F. D. 1, Luray, Pa. William Stover (Father).
Stovall, Shelby	Pvt.	Co. L. 127 Inf.	KIA	10/15/18	Graham, Ky. Oda Stovall.
Stowasser, Harold	Sgt.	Co. B. 121 Mg. Bn.	KIA	8/4/18	Necedah, Wis. J. S. Stowasser (Father).
Straightwell, Wesley G.	Pvt.	Co. A. 126 Inf.	KIA	8/4/18	R. F. D. 61, Brookville, Pa. George Straightwell (Father).
Strand, Cornel B.	Sgt.	Co. A. 107 F. S. Bn	DW	10/12/18	430 16th St., Milwaukee, Wis. B. Strand.
Stover, Mack D.	Pvt.	Co. A. 128 Inf.	KIA	11/10/18	Grimms, W. Va. Alfred Stover (Father).
Strand, Otis W.	Corp.	Co. M. 128 Inf.	DW	8/30/18	....
Stratham, James A.	Corp.	Bat. D. 322 F. A.	DD	12/7/18	....
Stratton, Arthur E.	Pvt.	Mg. Co. 125 Inf.	KIA	8/3/18	301 Forth St., Nelsonville, Ohio. Ephraim Stratton.
Stratton, Walter R.	Pvt.	Co. M. 125 Inf.	KIA	10/11/18	Grand View, Mont. Lucus Stratton (Brother).
Struber, Herman	Pvt.	Co. D. 128 Inf.	KIA	9/1/18	Romeo, Mich. Charles Struber (Father).
Strong, Judson	Pvt. 1cl.	Co. C. 120 Mg. Bn	KIA	10/1/18	Francis Hospital, Waterloo, Iowa. Thomas Strong.
Stronghoener, William H.	Pvt.	Co. F. 127 Inf.	KIA	10/5/18	Gerald, Mo. Theodore Stronghoener (Brother).
Stracham, James G.	Corp.	Bat. D. 322 F. A.	DD	12/7/18	....
Strunk, Freeman	Pvt.	Co. F. 128 Inf.	KIA	10/7/18	Parkers Lake, Ky. Mrs. Freeman Strunk (Wife).
Stuart, Arthur J.	Corp.	Co. M. 125 Inf.	KIA	7/31/18	....
Sturla, Pietro	Pvt.	Unknown	KIA	8/4/18	....
Sucicie, Herbert C.	Pvt.	Co. G. 127 Inf.	KIA	9/2/18	318 Wayhoset St., Providence, R. I Mrs. Gray (Friend).
Sukut, August	Pvt.	Co. A. 127 Inf.	KIA	11/10/18	R. 1, Box 27, Lhr. N. Dak. August Sukut (Father).
Sullivan, Charles	Sgt.	Co. I. 128 Inf.	DW	7/20/18	....
Sullivan, Daniel	Pvt.	Co. M. 125 Inf.	DW	7/31/18	....
Summers, William	Pvt.	Co. G. 127 Inf.	KIA	10/7/18	Star Route, Mt. Sterling, Ky. James Summers (Father).
Sund, Bernt H.	Pvt.	Co. B. 128 Inf.	DW	10/9/18	....
Sutfin, David L.	Pvt.	San. Det. 126 Inf.	KIA	10/10/18	316 E. South St., Kalamazoo, Mich.
Sutherland, Fred	Pvt.	Co. B. 128 Inf.	KIA	10/17/18	Box 117, Keansburg, N. J. Jacob Fries.
Sutter, Ernest	Bug.	Co. D. 127 Inf.	DW	6/15/18	....

—·—

NAME	RANK	ORGANIZATION	CAUSE	DATE	ADDRESS—NEXT OF KIN
Svetlik, Henry P.	Corp.	Co. C. 128 Inf.	KIA	8/1/18	Cadott, Wis. W. B. Svetlik.
Sweet, Harold	Pvt.	Hdq. Co. 125 Inf.	KIA	10/17/18	East Jordan, Mich. Mrs. Nellie Sweet (Mother).
Swiedarke, Wilbur A.	Pvt.	Co. H. 128 Inf.	DW	8/1/18	....
Swierczynaski, John	Pvt.	Co. B. 126 Inf.	KIA	10/11/18	1367 Duboise St. Joseph Swierczynaski.
Swift, Claude	Corp.	Co. F. 128 Inf.	DW	12/6/18	....
Swift, Lloyd N.	Pvt.	Co. E. 125 Inf.	KIA	10/9/18	R. F. D. 2, Hardin, Ky. W. D. Swift (Father).
Swift, Lonnie	Pvt.	Co. B. 128 Inf.	KIA	10/14/18	Tilford, Ky. M. M. Swift (Father).
Swiney, Nath	Pvt.	Co. G. 125 Inf.	KIA	10/14/18	Livingston, Ky. Mrs. Eva Swiney (Mother).
Swischer, Basil	Pvt.	Bat. A. 147 F. A.	DD	7/23/18	....
Szczepanski, Leo	Pvt.	Co. M. 125 Inf.	KIA	7/31/18	....
Tackowiak, Joseph	Pvt.	Co. K. 127 Inf.	KIA	8/30/18	....
Tahlier, Joseph	Pvt.	Co. I. 127 Inf.	KIA	10/16/18	Wausaukee, Wis. Emile Tahlier (Father).
Talbert, Harry H.	Pvt.	Co. B. 128 Inf.	KIA	10/14/18	Revillo, S. Dak. Albert Krause, Jr.
Talbot, Guy	Pvt.	Bat. A. 322 F. A.	DD	12/19/18	....
Tallroth, Leo	Pvt. 1cl.	Bat. B. 120 F. A.	KIA	8/7/18	539 Clement Ave., Milwaukee, Wis. Helmer Tallroth.
Tande, Ludvig	Pvt.	Co. G. 127 Inf.	KIA	8/3/18	Tande, Mont. Ole Tande (Father).
Tanner, Harold E.	Pvt. 1cl.	Bat. A. 120 F. A.	KIA	8/6/18	6702 Greenfield Ave., West Allis, Wis. Albert F. Tanner.
Tanson, Edwin A.	Pvt.	Co. E. 127 Inf.	KIA	7/30/18	Silverton, Oregon. Mrs. A. Tanson (Mother).
Tasson, Nick	Pvt.	Co. L. 125 Inf.	KIA	7/31/18	787 S. Pine St., Ishpeming, Mich. Mrs. Nazarino Mose (Sister).
Tate, Isaac	Pvt.	Co. F. 362 Inf.	DW	10/10/18	....
Taylor, Edward A.	Pvt.	Co. F. 127 Inf.	KIA	9/3/18	Minburn, Iowa. Mrs. Armanda Taylor (Mother).
Taylor, Harry M.	Pvt.	Co. C. 126 Inf.	DW	10/12/18	Kidds Fork, Va. Frank L. Taylor (Father).
Taylor, Ralph C.	Corp.	Bat. A. 119 F. A.	ACC	7/4/18	R. F. D. 3, Mt. Pleasant, Mich. J. C. Taylor (Father).
Taylor, Walter I.	Pvt. 1cl.	Co. E. 125 Inf.	KIA	7/21/18	....
Teichler, John	Sgt.	Co. L. 125 Inf.	KIA	7/31/18	Menominee, Mich. Edward Teichler (Brother).
Terry John P.	Pvt.	Co. G. 125 Inf.	KIA	8/29/18	Aquilla, Texas. Mrs. Lee Gregory (Mother).
Teunis, John W.	Sgt.	Bat. C. 119 F. A.	KIA	10/11/18	Spring Lake, Mich. Mrs. Herman Teunis (Mother).
Therkildsen, Niels	Pvt.	Mg. Co. 361 Inf.	DW	10/10/18	....
Thomas, Clarence E.	Pvt.	Co. K. 128 Inf.	KIA	11/10/18	R. F. D. 4, London, Ohio. Isabell J. Thomas.
Thomas, David F.	Pvt. 1cl.	Co. I. 125 Inf.	KIA	10/10/18	Box 42, Rowley, Iowa. David F. Thomas.
Thomas, Emil	Pvt.	Co. C. 125 Inf.	KIA	8/27/18	770 24th St., Detroit, Mich. Mrs. Minnie Thomas (Mother).
Thomas, Harold L.	Pvt. 1cl.	Co. B. 128 Inf.	DW	8/31/18	....
Thomas, John T.	Pvt. 1cl.	Co. A. 125 Inf.	DW	10/11/18	Goliad, Texas. John Thomas (Father).
Thomas, Walter E.	Pvt. 1cl.	Co. K. 128 Inf.	KIA	11/10/18	Palmyra. Wis. Will Thomas.
Thomas, Walter E.	Pvt. 1cl.	Co. L. 128 Inf.	KIA	8/4/18	314 S. Euclid Ave., Oak Park, Ill. Stedman Thomas (Father).
Thompson, Alfred M.	Pvt.	Co. A. 128 Inf.	KIA	11/10/18	....
Thompson, George	Pvt. 1cl.	Co. C. 128 Inf.	KIA	8/1/18	Dalton, Wis. John Thompson.
Thompson, Henry B.	Pvt.	Co. L. 125 Inf.	KIA	7/31/18	3510 Canal St., Milwaukee, Wis. John Thompson (Father).
Thompson, Perie	Sgt.	Co. C. 126 Inf.	DW	10/20/18	1020 Reed St., Kalamazoo, Mich. Mrs. Eliza Thompson.
Thorne, Charles E.	Pvt. 1cl.	Bat. C. 147 F. A.	KIA	9/29/18	Pierre, So. Dak. Al. Thorne.
Thanton, Ernest M.	Pvt.	Co. B. 128 Inf.	DW	10/12/18	Thornton, Idaho. Mrs. Minnie Thanton.
Thurlow, Gordon G.	Corp.	Mg. Co. 127 Inf.	DW	8/4/18	10 Fountain Pl., New Rochelle, N. Y. Mrs. H. M. Thurlow (Mother).

1. First Lieutenant Elmer S. Terhune, Battery B, 121st Field Artillery. Killed in action October 8th, 1918, during the Meuse-Argonne Offensive.
2. Second Lieutenant William D. Morgan, Company E, 128th Infantry. Killed in action November 9th, 1918, during the Meuse-Argonne Offensive.
3. First Lieutenant Harold J. King, 128th Infantry. Killed in action October 10th, 1918, during the Meuse-Argonne Offensive.
4. Second Lieutenant Andrew S. Dineen, 128th Infantry. Died of wounds received November 10th, 1918, during the Meuse-Argonne Offensive.
5. Major John A. Street, Commanding First Battalion, 128th Infantry. Killed in action October 18th, 1918, during the Meuse-Argonne Offensive.
6. Second Lieutenant Ray E. Bostick, Company C, 126th Infantry, Killed in action August 1st, 1918, during the Aisne-Marne Offensive.
7. Second Lieutenant Carl A. Johnson, Company M, 126th Infantry. Killed while repulsing an enemy raid in the trenches in Alsace June 23rd, 1918.
8. Captain Orville L. Anderson, Company E, 128th Infantry. Killed in action August 1st, 1918, while leading his company against Hill 230 during the Aisne-Marne Offensive.
9. Second Lieutenant Arthur I. Keller, Company I, 126th Infantry. Killed in action August 1st, 1918, during the Marne Offensive.

NAME	RANK	ORGANIZATION	CAUSE	DATE	ADDRESS—NEXT OF KIN
Tice, Clarence J.	Pvt.	Hq. Co. 127 Inf.	DW	10/8/18	2320 Cherry St., Milwaukee, Wis. Maggie Lovejoy (Aunt).
Tidball, Jack T.	Pvt.	Co. I. 126 Inf.	KIA	10/16/18	Fayerre, Ark. Mrs. Charles Tidball.
Tiegs, Emil	Pvt.	Co. F. 127 Inf.	KIA	7/30/18	Shawano, Wis. Miss Anna Tiegs (Sister).
Tieman, William O.	Pvt.	Co. E. 128 Inf.	DD	12/14/18	....
Tieman, Raymond	Pvt. 1cl.	Co. C. 126 Inf.	KIA	8/1/18	640 Forrest Ave., Hamilton, Ohio. Phillip Tieman, Sr. (Father).
Timm, Adolph	Pvt.	Co. G. 127 Inf.	KIA	8/3/18	Ontario, Wis. Mrs. J. O. Timm (Mother).
Tira, Fiorengo	Pvt.	Co. B. 125 Inf.	KIA	7/31/18	Bx. 1292, Renton, Wash., or Domenica Tira, S. Giorgis, Canavise, Italy. Louis Delaurenti.
Titus, Lloyd	Pvt. 1cl.	Co. F. 128 Inf.	KIA	10/2/18	Munith, Mich. Mrs. Bertha Titus (Mother).
Tobin, Wilson H.	Pvt.	Co. B. 127 Inf.	KIA	10/11/18	Washington, Va. Kemnel G. Tobin (Father).
Toby, Williard	Pvt.	Co. L. 125 Inf.	KIA	7/31/18	Taylorville, Calif. Mrs. Jennie Toby (Mother).
Tollefson, Leland A.	Corp.	107 Tr. Motor Bty.	DW	8/17/18	624 Badger Ave., Antigo, Wis. Mrs. Marh Tollefson (Mother).
Toloknianik, Iowan	Pvt.	Co. E. 126 Inf.	KIA	7/29/18	Russia. Mrs. Anna Toloknianik.
Tolsma, Jacob	Sgt.	Co. G. 128 Inf.	KIA	8/3/18	....
Tomanski, Barney	Sgt.	Co. K. 127 Inf.	KIA	9/1/18	814 10th Ave., Milwaukee, Wis. Andrew Tomanski (Father).
Tomczak, Chester	Pvt.	Co. A. 127 Inf.	DW	8/6/18	764 Becher St., Milwaukee, Wis. Ben Tomczak (Father).
Tomilson, Fred M.	Pvt.	Co. C. 127 Inf.	KIA	8/4/18	10 E. 6th St., Portland, Oregon. Mrs. Mary Tomilson (Mother).
Toskan, Gus S.	Pvt.	Co. E. 127 Inf.	KIA	10/5/18	116 E. Main St., Medford, Oregon. Peter Toskan (Brother).
Town, Eskay D.	Pvt.	Co. M. 126 Inf.	KIA	8/2/18	R. F. D. 1, Casnovia, Mich. Mrs. Minnie Town (Mother).
Tracey, Louis B.	Pvt. 1cl.	Hq. Co. 125 Inf.	KIA	8/4/18	Sand Lake, Mich. Mrs. Louis Salsgiver.
Trautmann, Otto	Pvt.	Co. M. 125 Inf.	KIA	10/29/18	117 70th St. N., St. Paul, Minn. Mrs. Sophia Trautmann (Mother).
Traylor, Andrew J.	Pvt.	Co. K. 126 Inf.	KIA	8/28/18	Stepstone, Ky. Sam Traylor.
Trepozynski, Frank A.	Pvt.	Co. M. 125 Inf.	KIA	7/31/18	1320 Junction Ave., Owasso, Mich. Minnie Trepozynski (Mother).
Trierweiler, Nick	Pvt. 1cl.	Co. A. 127 Inf.	KIA	8/5/18	312 W. 4th St., Marshfield, Wis. August Trierweiler (Father).
Trites, Edmund S.	Corp.	Co. C. 120 Mg. Bn.	KIA	8/29/18	306 McKinster, Detroit, Mich. J. S. Trites.
Troester, Carl F.	Pvt.	Co. C. 125 Inf.	KIA	10/9/18	Sidney, Ohio. Mrs. Louis Troester (Mother).
Trombley, Jerome	Pvt.	Co. E. 125 Inf.	ACC	7/18/18	....
Trout, Homer B.	Pvt. 1cl.	Co. E. 125 Inf.	KIA	10/9/18	Shawmut, Ark. Viola Trout (Wife).
Trowbridge, William K	Sgt.	Co. D. 125 Inf.	KIA	10/16/18	4 E. 1st St., Monroe, Mich. Clement Trowbridge (Brother).
Truckey, Antoine J.	Pvt.	Co. M. 125 Inf.	KIA	7/31/18	....
Tucker, Arthur J.	Corp.	Co. D. 125 Inf.	DD	10/12/18	506 Cherry St., Anaconda, Mont. C. Tucker (Father).
Tucker, Edward C.	Pvt.	Co. B. 127 Inf.	KIA	10/9/18	R. F. D. 2, Lynchburg, Tenn. William C. Tucker (Father).
Tunis, Guy A.	Pvt.	Co. D. 127 Inf.	KIA	10/19/18	Route 1, Winamac, Indiana. Elmus Tunis (Father).
Turley, Clarence L.	Corp.	Co. I. 128 Inf.	DW	8/31/18	....
Turley, Joe R.	Pvt.	Co. B. 128 Inf.	KIA	10/14/18	....
Turner, George	Corp.	Co. H. 126 Inf.	DW	9/1/18	1389 Hastings St., Detroit, Mich. Miss Hazel Turner (Sister).
Tweedale, Elmer J.	Pvt.	Co. A. 121 Mg. Bn.	KIA	8/4/18	Sturgeon Bay, Wis. Samuel Tweedale.
Tweite, Alfred L.	Pvt.	Co. E. 127 Inf.	KIA	10/5/18	R. F. D. 2, Barron, Minn. Martha Tweite (Mother).
Twomey, Michael P.	Corp.	Co. C. 126 Inf.	KIA	8/1/18	711 3rd St., Kalamazoo, Mich. Mrs. A. Twomey.
Tyler, Albert H.	Pvt.	Co. B. 121 Mg. Bn.	KIA	8/2/18	Prairie du Chien, Wis. Seroy L. Tyler (Brother).
Tyler, Alvin	Pvt.	Co. C. 127 Inf.	DW	10/6/18 about	Pocahontas, Ark. William Tyler (Father).
Udych, John	Pvt.	Co. A. 128 Inf.	KIA	9/1/18	677 McKinstry St., Detroit, Mich. Rosa Maach (Half-Sister).
Udell, Michael J.	Corp.	Co. M. 125 Inf.	KIA	7/31/18	....
Ulrich, Dan F.	Pvt. 1cl.	Co. C. 128 Inf.	KIA	8/1/18	312 Brown St., Ionia, Mich. Mrs. Cora Harner.

Name	Rank	Organization	Cause	Date	Address—Next of Kin
Underwood, David H	Pvt. 1cl.	Co. B. 126 Inf.	KIA	8/31/18	Tecumseh, Mich. Cyrus J. Underwood (Father).
Underwood, Walter A.	Pvt.	Co. F. 126 Inf.	KIA	8/3/18 about	R. F. D. 1, Grass Lake, Mich. Mrs. Hattie Underwood.
Upton, Grover C.	Pvt.	Co. C. 127 Inf.	KIA	10/20/18	R. F. D. 1, Prairie Point, Miss. Tom Upton (Father).
Upton, Philley H.	Corp.	Co. I. 126 Inf.	KIA	10/9/18	R. F. D. 1, Bradley, S. Dak. Homer Upton.
Urbaniak, Steve	Pvt.	Co. I. 127 Inf.	DW	8/11/18	....
Urbanschack, Richard	Pvt.	Co. B. 119 Mg. Bn	DW	10/5/18	....
Vance, Nurl S.	Pvt.	Mg. Co. 126 Inf.	KIA	10/16/18	Hurricane, W. Va. Mrs. Mahulda Burton (Mother).
Vandegarde, Joseph H	Corp.	Co. M. 128 Inf.	KIA	8/30/18	6043 S. Honore, Chicago, Ill. Mrs. Eva Vandegarde.
Vandegezelle, Isaac	Bug.	Co. C. 126 Inf.	KIA	10/15/18	Hokzaroost Burg, Zeeland, Netherlands. Mrs. Susana Vandegezelle.
Vonder Heide, Cornelius	Pvt. 1cl.	Hq. Co. 126 Inf.	KIA	10/9/18	152 Page St., Gd. Rapids, Mich. P. S. Vonder Heide (Father).
VanDeHoming, Leonard	Pvt. 1cl.	Co. M. 128 Inf.	DW	9/30/18	R. F. D. 1, Alma, Mich. Mrs. Val Cryder.
Vanderhoof, Harvey W.	Pvt.	Co. G. 127 Inf.	DW	8/4/18	Enid, Mont. Allie Vanderhoff (Brother).
Van Dyke, Wynard	Pvt.	Co. K. 126 Inf.	KIA	8/29/18	1531 Roosevelt Av., Gd. Rapids, Mich. Melvin Van Dyke (Father).
Van Eimeren, Everhart	Pvt. 1cl.	Bat. C. 120 F. A.	KIA	8/29/18	640 Hawthorne Ave., S. Milwaukee, Wis. Martin Van Eimeren.
Van Ells, Ándrew V.	Wag.	Sup. Co. 127 Inf.	DW	8/10/18	514 Main St., Pt. Washington, Wis. Andrew Van Ells (Father).
Van Handel, Rudolph	Pvt. 1cl.	Co. C. 127 Inf.	KIA	10/19/18	734 N. 3rd St., Sheboygan, Wis. Mrs. Peter Van Handel (Mother).
Van Horsen, William	Sgt.	Co. L. 126 Inf.	DW	Unknown about	430 Slayton St., Gd. Haven, Mich. William Van Horsen.
Van Huizen, Albert	Bug.	Co. A. 128 Inf.	KIA	9/1/18	Owen, Wis. Jerry VanHuizen (Father).
Van Voorhees, Simon	Pvt.	Co. K. 125 Inf.	DW	8/31/18	....
Van Wert, Peter	Pvt.	Co. I. 125 Inf.	KIA	7/31/18	2501 Center Ave., Bay City, Mich. Mrs. Margaret Luxton.
Varga, Paul	Pvt. 1cl.	Co. H. 126 Inf.	KIA	8/4/18	23 Thaldens St., Detroit, Mich. Rev. Andrew Daniel.
Vermecky, John F.	Pvt.	Co. C. 128 Inf.	KIA	8/1/18	297 Harold Ave., Johnstown, Pa. George Vermecky.
Varno, Antonio	Pvt.	Co. A. 126 Inf.	DD	9/18/18	2148 2nd Ave., New York, N. Y. Mrs. Libarto Varno (Mother).
Vath, Raymond	Pvt.	Co. M. 128 Inf.	KIA	10/20/18	514 Wilker Court, New York, N. Y. Miss Veromea Vath.
Vegnapoulos, Constantine	Pvt.	Co. E. 127 Inf.	KIA	10/17/18	264 Main St., Springfield, Mass. Nicholas Vegnapoulos (Brother).
Velliquette, Cosmas C	Corp.	Co. F. 127 Inf.	DW	10/11/18	Limestone, Ohio. Mrs. Caroline Velliquette (Mother).
Verner, James	Pvt.	Co. L. 125 Inf.	KIA	10/21/18	....
Vetraino, John	Pvt. 1cl.	Co. F. 125 Inf.	KIA	10/18/19	85 Haley St., Detroit, Mich. Dominico Vetraino (Brother).
Vibbert, Edward T.	Pvt. 1cl.	Co. M. 125 Inf.	KIA	7/31/18	....
Villalevos, Chris.	Pvt.	Co. E. 125 Inf.	KIA	7/31/18	....
Villeneauve, Alexander	Pvt.	Co. A. 121 Mg. Bn	KIA	8/6/18	2709 Pardridge Ave., Marinette, Wis. —, Villeneauve (Father).
Vingere, Roy	Sgt.	Co. B. 128 Inf.	KIA	8/5/18	Sparta, Wis. Thomas C. Rice.
Voss, Arthur F.	Pvt.	Co. D. 127 Inf.	KIA	6/17/18	....
Voss, John B.	Pvt.	Co. G. 128 Inf.	DW	10/7/18	Albany, Minn. Mrs. Anna Voss.
Vurn, Joseph	Saddler	Bat. F. 147 F. A.	KIA	8/31/18 about	Parker, S. Dak. Frank Vurn (Father).
Wache, August C.	Pvt.	Co. E. 128 Inf.	KIA	10/16/18 about	820 Malone St., West Hoboken, N. J. Mrs. Charles Wache.
Wade, Percy C.	Pvt.	Co. C. 128 Inf.	KIA	10/16/18	Elliston, Mo. William E. Wade.
Wade, William C.	Pvt. 1cl.	Co. L. 125 Inf.	KIA	7/31/18	1203 Lincoln Ave., Pt. Huron, Mich. Louis G. Blunt (Friend).
Wagner, Frank	Pvt. 1cl.	Bat. B. 322 F. A.	DD	12/24/18	R. F. D. 2, Lewisburg, Ohio. John Wagner (Father).
Wagner, Lester W.	Corp.	Co. F. 127 Inf.	KIA	9/1/18	Markesan, Wis. William Wagner (Father).
Wagoner, Westley C.	Pvt.	Co. I. 128 Inf.	ACC	5/4/18	....
Waite, Francis	Pvt.	Co. G. 128 Inf.	KIA	9/1/18	Owatonna, Minn. Ben Chladek.
Waitekunas, John	Pvt.	Co. D. 125 Inf.	DW	8/30/18	127 Cardoni Ave., Detroit, Mich. Mrs. Sylvia Bizanskas.

NAME	RANK	ORGANIZATION	CAUSE	DATE	ADDRESS—NEXT OF KIN
Wakeman, Albert	Corp.	Co. C. 107 F. S. Bn.	KIA	8/31/18	Big Rapids, Mich. Mrs. C. E. Wakeman (Mother).
Walker, Charles L.	Pvt. 1cl.	Co. B. 127 Inf.	KIA	10/18/18	R. F. D. 2, Hillsboro, Ore. Mrs. A. W. Walker (Mother).
Walker, John	Pvt.	Hq. Co. 125 Inf.	DW	10/11/18	R. F. D. 2, Applegate, Mich. John Walker (Father).
Walker, John Thomas	Pvt.	Co. I. 125 Inf.	KIA	7/31/18	28 Franklin Crt., Battle Creek, Mich. Mrs. Helen G. Walker (Wife).
Walker, Lemual A.	Pvt.	Mg. Co. 125 Inf.	KIA	10/11/18	R. F. D. 2, Northville, Mich. Mrs. Bettie Walker.
Wallace, William B.	Pvt.	Co. E. 127 Inf.	KIA	10/9/18	R. F. D. 7, Frankford, Ind. Hugh A. Wallace (Father).
Wallen, John	Pvt.	Co. C. 127 Inf.	KIA	9/2/18	Abo, Finland. Erika Wallen (Father).
Wallis, Henry D.	Pvt. 1cl.	Co. A. 127 Inf.	KIA	8/5/18	Greenwood, Wis. Leroy Wallis (Brother).
Walling, Carl W.	Corp.	Hq. Co. 147 Inf.	DW	8/30/18	235 Halsey St., Portland, Oregon. Mrs. Carl W. Walling (Wife).
Walsh, Edward	Pvt.	Co. M. 125 Inf.	KIA	10/11/18	609 Alder St., Anaconda, Mont. Patrick Walsh (Brother).
Walters, George J.	Pvt.	Co. M. 126 Inf.	KIA	10/4/18	2372 Rohs St., Clifton Heights, Cincinnati, Ohio. Miss Lillian Walters.
Walton, William B.	Pvt.	Co. F. 126 Inf.	DW	10/15/18	Stevensville, Va. Mrs. Mary A. Walton.
Wangen, Carl	Sgt.	Co. E. 127 Inf.	KIA	9/1/18	1215 State St., Eau Claire, Wis. Iver Wangen (Father).
Ward, Benjamin C.	Pvt.	Co. D. 126 Inf.	KIA	10/11/18	Vanalstyne, Texas. M. C. Hunnicutt.
Ward, Clarence V.	Corp.	Co. D. 126 Inf.	KIA	7/31/18	Portland, Mich. Mrs. R. J. Ward.
Warner, Charles A.	Pvt.	Co. L. 126 Inf.	Suicide	4/27/18	....
Warner, John E.	Pvt.	Co. B. 119 Mg. Bn.	KIA	8/29/18	R. F. D. 1, Olympia, Wash. John A. Warner (Father).
Warren, Millard F.	Pvt.	Co. G. 128 Inf.	KIA	8/4/18	Trade, Tenn. William Warren (Father).
Washburn, Charles	Pvt.	Co. E. 126 Inf.	KIA	9/2/18	304 Byron Road, Howell, Mich. George Washburn.
Washburn, Earl	Pvt.	Co. C. 126 Inf.	DW	10/5/18 about	Whittemore, Mich. Enoch Washburn (Uncle).
Wasserberger, Charles	Corp.	Co. A. 128 Inf.	KIA	9/1/18	Neillsville, Wis. Charles Wasserberger, Sr. (Father).
Watkins, Harry T.	Corp.	Co. A. 126 Inf.	KIA	8/4/18	Allen, Mich. William Watkins.
Watkins, Leonard L.	Pvt.	Co. K. 127 Inf.	KIA	10/20/18	R. 1, Fulton, Ark. Lee Watkins (Father).
Watson, Elmer T.	Pvt.	Co. M. 125 Inf.	KIA	10/11/18	....
Watson, Henry	Pvt.	Co. D. 126 Inf.	KIA	8/30/18	R. F. D. 2, Sherwood, Mich. Mrs. Elemine Watson (Mother).
Watson, Leonard	Sgt.	Co. M. 125 Inf.	KIA	10/15/18	....
Watson, Robert	Pvt.	Co. E. 128 Inf.	KIA	11/10/18	74 Main St., Inkerman, Luzerne C, Pa Mrs. Margaret Watson.
Way, Travis S.	Pvt.	Co. L. 128 Inf.	KIA	9/1/18	Hunting Park, Calif. George Way.
Waybrant, Albert	Corp.	Co. M. 125 Inf.	KIA	7/31/18	....
Weaver, Carl O.	Corp.	Co. G. 126 Inf.	KIA	10/5/18	713 Grove Ave., Petoskey, Mich. Mrs. George A. Weaver (Mother).
Weaver, Charles S.	Pvt.	Mg. Co. 125 Inf.	DW	10/12/18	1129 New Hampshire Ave. W., Washington, D. C. Mrs. N. N. Neck (Mother).
Webb, Roy Adair	Pvt.	Co. L. 128 Inf.	KIA	11/7/18	Box 341, Shamrock, Oklahoma. Mrs. Della Shouse (Mother).
Weber, Herman F.	Corp.	Co. L. 128 Inf.	KIA	11/7/18	Mykawa, Tex. Mrs. Mary Weber (Mother).
Weeks, George T.	Pvt.	Co. G. 128 Inf.	KIA	9/1/18	Womble, Ark. John William Weeks (Father).
Wertman, George	Pvt.	Co. L. 126 Inf.	KIA	10/1/18	921 Canefield Av. S. W., Gd. Rapids, Mich. Mrs. Delia Wertman (Mother).
Weese, Wilbur W.	Pvt.	Co. G. 125 Inf.	KIA	10/6/18	Beverly, W. Va. Park Weese (Father).
Weide, Christigen	Pvt.	Co. F. 128 Inf.	DW	10/14/18	Remus, Mich. Louis Weide.
Weigell, Carl	Sgt.	Bat. A. 120 F. A.	KIA	10/15/18	138 18th St., Milwaukee, Wis. August Weigell.
Weigel, Moritz	Pvt.	Co. F. 127 Inf.	KIA	8/1/18	Shawano, Wis. Gustave Weigel (Father).
Weisgerber, Clifton G	Sgt.	Co. C. 126 Inf.	KIA	8/30/18	716 Wealthy Ave., Gd. Rapids, Mich. Mrs. Maymire L. Barton.
Weiss, Adolph C.	Pvt.	Med. Det. 125 Inf.	KIA	8/6/18	518 Hermansau St., Saginaw, Mich. J. A. Weiss (Father).
Weiss, William	Pvt.	Bat. F. 121 F. A.	DW	8/21/18	2109 Clarence Ave., Racine, Wis. Fred Weiss.

1. Second Lieutenant Paul T. Settle, Company A, 120th Machine Gun Battalion. Died November 14th, 1918, of wounds received October 8th during the Meuse-Argonne Offensive.
2. First Lieutenant Harry W. Fenelon, Company L, 127th Infantry. Died August 18th, 1918, of wounds received in action during the Aisne-Marne Offensive.
3. Second Lieutenant Harry B. Mauger, Company A, 127th Infantry. Killed in action October 18th, during Meuse-Argonne Operations.
4. First Lieutenant Tolman D. Wheeler, Company G, 127th Infantry. Died of wounds September 6th, 1918, during the Oise-Aisne Offensive.
5. Captain James Cook, 120th Machine Gun Battalion. Killed in action July 30th, 1918, while making a reconnaissance before the enemy during the Aisne-Marne Offensive.
6. First Lieutenant David Stubbs, Company A, 127th Infantry. Killed in action August 6th, 1918, during the Aisne-Marne Offensive.
7. Second Lieutenant Lloyd O. Beaton, Headquarters Company, 119th Field Artillery, Killed in action August 30th, 1918, during the Oise-Aisne Offensive.
8. Second Lieutenant William S. Feustel, Battery B, 147th Field Artillery. Died August 7th, 1918, of wounds received during the Aisne-Marne Offensive.
9. Second Lieutenant Stacy L. Harding, Battery B, 120th Field Artillery. Killed in action October 11th, 1918, during the Meuse-Argonne Offensive.

291

Name	Rank	Organization	Cause	Date	Address—Next of Kin
Welmerink, William E	Pvt. 1cl.	Co. M. 126 Inf.	KIA	8/2/18	856 Watson St. S. W., Gd. Rapids, John Welmerink (Father). Mich.
Wellner, Louis	Pvt. 1cl.	Co. A. 127 Inf.	KIA	10/4/18	Marshfield, Wis. Mr. George Wellner (Father).
Wells, Benjamin E.	Pvt.	Co. C. 125 Inf.	KIA	10/22/18	732 Malivax, Petersburg, W. Va. Mrs. E. W. Wells.
Welsh, Frederick	Pvt.	Co. I. 126 Inf.	KIA	10/9/18	Homing Falls, W. Va. Oscar L. Welsh.
Welsh, James	Pvt. 1cl.	Co. H. 128 Inf.	KIA	11/10/18	16th & Williams St., Omaha, Neb. Miss Hazel Welsh.
Welsh, Lorein A.	Pvt.	Co. G. 127 Inf.	KIA	7/31/18	Breckenridge, Mo. Bessie Welsh (Sister).
Welton, Gale	Pvt.	Co. C. 121 Mg. Bn.	KIA	8/31/18	Sextonville, Wis. Mrs. Carrie Welton (Mother).
Wenzel, Byron W.	Pvt.	Co. A. 126 Inf.	KIA	8/27/18	104 S. Grave St., Sturgis, Mich. Mrs. Ida Wenzel.
Werner, Edward	Pvt.	Co. M. 125 Inf.	KIA	7/31/18	....
Wescott, Ira L.	Sgt.	Co. M. 126 Inf.	KIA	10/9/18	Grandville, Mich. L. D. Wescott (Father).
West, Ernest S.	Pvt.	Co. I. 125 Inf.	KIA	10/21/18	142 E. Thornton St., Akron, Ohio. Charles West.
West, Lynn M.	Pvt.	Co. L. 127 Inf.	KIA	8/4/18	Walworth, Wis. Mrs. Edna F. West (Mother).
Wezesenski, Edward	Corp.	Co. D. 127 Inf.	KIA	8/31/18	R. F. D. 2, Randolph, Wis. Mrs. Joseph Wezesenski (Mother).
Whalen, Loy	Pvt.	Co. F. 125 Inf.	KIA	10/2/18	719 S. Main St., Mattoon, Ill. Mrs. Sarah Whalen (Mother).
Wharren, Williamson G	Pvt.	Co. D. 126 Inf.	KIA	8/30/18	Highwood, Mont. Tom Wharren (Brother).
Wheaton, Benjamin P	Pvt.	Co. D. 120 Mg. Bn.	KIA	10/9/18	38 Malbone Ave., Newport, R. I. Mrs. E. Wheaton.
Wheeler, George H.	Pvt.	Co. H. 125 Inf.	KIA	10/13/18	Camden, W. Va. Mrs. Elizabeth B. Wheeler.
Wheeler, Thomas M.	Pvt. 1cl.	Co. A. 127 Inf.	KIA	10/15/18	Hollis, Long Island, N. Y. Mrs. Joe B. Wheeler.
Whichser, Emil	Corp.	Co. H. 127 Inf.	DW	Unknown	....
Whipple, David O.	Pvt.	Co. H. 128 Inf.	KIA	11/10/18	R. D. 4, Portland, Ind. Mrs. Susie Whipple (Mother).
Whisler, Homer	Pvt.	Co. I. 126 Inf.	KIA	10/9/18	R. F. D. 11, Ottaway, Ohio. Mrs. Mary Whisler.
White, Leonard J.	Pvt.	Co. G. 126 Inf.	KIA	10/1/18	Debush, Va. W. A. White (Father).
Whitehurst, Walter	Pvt.	Co. G. 125 Inf.	DW	10/11/18	Butler, Ind. Mary M. Whitehurst (Mother).
Witemore, Wilbur	Pvt.	Med. Det. 125 Inf.	KIA	8/6/18	R. F. D. 3, Bangor, Mich. Fred C. Witemore (Father).
Wicklund, John	Corp.	Co. E. 127 Inf.	KIA	7/31/18	127 Water St., Eau Claire, Wis. Charles Wicklund (Father).
Widdifield, Clarence P	Corp.	Co. K. 125 Inf.	KIA	7/31/18	607 Church St., Lynchburg, Va. De Alphonso Widdifield (Father).
Widener, William G.	Corp.	Co. F. 1st Am. Tr.	DW	10/6/18	....
Wiebusch, William	Pvt.	Co. E. 125 Inf.	DW	10/10/18	Somerville, Texas. J. F. Wiebusch (Father).
Wietem, Derk J.	Pvt.	Co. F. 126 Inf.	KIA	10/9/18	Node, Wyo. Mrs. Carrie Wietem (Wife).
Wilcox, Allen C.	Pvt.	Co. E. 127 Inf.	KIA	8/3/18	918 12th St., Arcata, Calif. H. C. Wilcox (Father).
Wilczynski, Adam Albert	Pvt.	Co. I. 125 Inf.	KIA	7/31/18	76 Adison Ave., Detroit, Mich. Jo ephine Mary Wilczynski (Wife).
Wilke, Arthur	Sgt.	Co. D. 120 Mg. Bn.	KIA	10/9/18	530 Greenfield Ave., Milwaukee, Wis. Mrs. P. Wilke.
Wilker, Albert A.	Corp.	Co. B. 125 Inf.	KIA	8/29/18	R. F. D. 2, Box 40, c/o Mrs. Frank Shibley, Elyria, Ohio. Freda Wilker (Sister).
Wilkerson, Valmer	Pvt.	Co. A. 125 Inf.	DW	9/1/18	R. F. D. 6, Lafayette, Ala. William Wilkerson (Father).
Wilkins, George A.	Pvt. 1cl.	Med. Dept. 120 F. A.	DD	....	....
Wilkinson, Harry D.	Corp	Co. L. 125 Inf.	KIA	7/31/18	Rockford, Mich. Mrs. Hattie Wilkinson (Mother).
Wilks, Clyde L.	Pvt.	Co. I. 125 Inf.	DW	6/6/18	....
Willar, Clarence	Pvt.	Co. G. 127 Inf.	DW	8/31/18	....
Williams, Daniel C.	Pvt.	Co. G. 127 Inf.	DW	8/30/18	305 E. 85th St., New York, N. Y. Nellie Rally Williams (Wife).
Williams, Ernest	Pvt.	Co. C. 126 Inf.	KIA	7/15/18	R. F. D. 2, Canton, Pa. Burnett Williams (Brother).
Williams, Franklin C.	Sgt.	Bat. C. 120 F. A.	DD	4/3/18	376 Kane PL, Milwaukee, Wis. Frank J. Williams (Father).
Williams, Harry	Corp.	Co. B. 127 Inf.	KIA	9/3/18	Bisher, Mont. J. S. Williams (Father).
Williams, Hugh R.	Pvt.	Hq. Co. 127 Inf.	KIA	10/12/18	R. F. D. 1, Rochester, Wash. Mrs. Elizabeth Williams (Mother).

Name	Rank	Organization	Cause	Date	Address—Next of Kin
Williams, Julius	Pvt.	Co. M. 125 Inf.	KIA	7/31/18	....
Williams, Robert Wells	Pvt.	Hq. 64 Inf. Brig.	DD	3/11/18	Camp Douglas, Wis. Lt. Col. Chas. R. Williams (Father).
Willis, Frank	Pvt.	Co. C. 125 Inf.	KIA	8/29/18	508 Main St., St. Joseph, Mich. Louis Willie (Brother).
Wilson, Fay M.	Corp .	Co. C. 107 F. S. Bn	KIA	10/14/18	Waupaca, Wis. W. L. Wilson (Father).
Wilson, Fred C.	Ptv. 1cl.	Hosp. 126- 107 San. Tr.	KIA	10/31/18	110 34th St., Milwaukee, Wis. Mrs. Charles C. Wilson.
Wilson, Harry V.	Pvt.	Co. C. 126 Inf.	KIA	8/1/18	505 3rd St., N. W., Washington, D. C. Charles B. Wilson (Father).
Wilson, John	Pvt.	Co. M. 127 Inf.	KIA	10/20/18	Crab Orchard, Ky. James Wilson.
Wilson, Lewis	Corp.	Co. D. 128 Inf.	KIA	8/2/18	Mauston, Wis. Mrs. Gene Lulu Señogles (Mother).
Wilson, William L.	Pvt.	Co. L. 128 Inf.	KIA	11/10/18	Route 5, Coshocton, Ohio. Jesse Wilson (Father).
Winch, Ray	Corp.	Co. A. 127 Inf.	KIA	8/5/18	901 East 9th St., Marshfield, Wis. Carlton Winch (Father).
Windl, Lawrence	Pvt. 1cl.	Co. D. 127 Inf.	KIA	9/1/18	608 B. St., Jefferson, Wis. Joe Windl (Father).
Winkler, Arthur E.	Pvt.	Co. G. 128 Inf.	KIA	8/3/18	....
Winner, Charles A.	Pvt.	Co. L. 126 Inf.	SIW	3/27/18	....
Winslow, John M.	Pvt.	Co. D. 125 Inf.	DW	10/13/18	1435 1st St. N. W., War Trade Road, Washington, D. C. Miss Ethel Clara Winslow.
Winsper, Carl V.	Pvt.	Co. B. 128 Inf.	KIA	10/14/18	....
Winger, Courtlin	Pvt.	Hq. Co. 125 Inf.	KIA	10/13/18	McNeil, Ark. Mrs. Fannie Winger (Wife).
Wireman, Lindsey	Pvt.	Co. I. 127 Inf.	KIA	10/21/18	Oil Springs, Ky. Mr. Abe Wireman (Father).
Wirketis, Peter	Pvt.	Co. D. 126 Inf.	KIA	8/2/18	2130 W. 22nd St., Chicago, Ill. Zappa Gentilaite (Friend).
Witte, William	Pvt.	Co. B. 125 Inf.	DW	10/10/18	504 L St., Louisville, Ky. Mrs. Catherine Witte (Mother).
Wludarski, Sladyslaw	Pvt.	Co. H. 126 Inf.	KIA	8/30/18	943 Milwaukee Ave., Detroit, Mich. Mrs. Stanley Gorecki (Cousin).
Woleford, Frank	....	Co. M. 126 Inf.	DD	Unknown	....
Wojciechowski, Alex Aloyz	Sgt.	Co. I. 125 Inf.	KIA	7/31/18	1523 S. Monroe St., Bay City, Mich. Mrs. Stelle Wojciechowski (Mother).
Wolfe, Lawrence	Corp.	Co. A. 125 Inf.	DW	10/5/18	42 Norvall St., Detroit, Mich. Rose Wolfe (Mother).
Wolfe, Edward J.	Pvt. 1cl.	Co. B. 127 Inf.	KIA	8/5/18	1020 Bellevue, Seattle, Wash. Mrs. E. J. Wolff (Mother).
Wolff, Verne O.	Pvt.	Co. D. 125 Inf.	DW	8/30/18	....
Wolinski, Sol.	Pvt.	Co. M. 126 Inf.	DD	9/20/18	185 Ave. C, New York City, N. Y. Mrs. Bessie Goldberg.
Wolman, Ben	Pvt.	Co. D. 121 Mg. Bn.	KIA	8/31/18	Wautoma, Wis. Louis Wolman.
Womac, Claude	Pvt.	Co. C. 125 Inf.	KIA	10/23/18	Athens, Tenn. M. Womac.
Wood, Archie B.	Pvt.	Co. L. 128 Inf.	KIA	11/7/18	536 Main St., Clarksville, Tenn. David B. Wood (Father).
Wood, Clark	Sgt.	Co. A. 126 Inf.	KIA	10/9/18	321 W. Cushman, Three Rivers, Mich. John W. Wood.
Wood, Fred E.	Pvt.	MD. 322 F. A.	KIA	10/16/18	....
Wood, James A.	Pvt. 1cl.	Co. M. 125 Inf.	KIA	7/31/18	Reed St., Warren, Mass. James Wood (Father).
Woods, Leo V.	Corp.	Co. C. 127 Inf.	DW	8/6/18	....
Woolford, Charles E.	Pvt.	Co. E. 125 Inf.	KIA	7/31/18	....
Woodville, Henry H.	Pvt.	Co. G. 126 Inf.	KIA	10/1/18 about	Indiantown, Orange Co., Va. Mrs. Julia A. Woodville (Mother).
Woodworth, Earl F.	Pvt. 1cl.	Co. E. 128 Inf.	KIA	10/15/18	526 E. Main St., Owosso, Mich. Mrs. Cora Woodworth (Mother).
Woolridge, William	Pvt.	Co. M. 125 Inf.	KIA	8/4/18	....
Worcester, Thomas F.	Pvt.	Co. H. 128 Inf.	KIA	10/15/18	....
Wortz, Peter P.	Corp.	Co. G. 126 Inf.	KIA	8/27/18	704 Theodore Ave., Detroit, Mich. Mrs. Anna Wortz (Mother).
Wozenski, Julius	Pvt.	Co. A. 128 Inf.	KIA	8/1/18	296 Evline St., Hamtramck, Mich. Frank Wozenski (Father).
Wrasse, Earl G.	Corp.	Co. E. 127 Inf.	KIA	7/31/18	306 14th St., Milwaukee, Wis. Mrs. Frank W. Wrasse (Mother).
Wray, Willie A.	Pvt.	Co. G. 126 Inf.	KIA	10/21/18	Wirtz, Franklin Co., Va. Mr. David Wray (Father).
Wright, Charles H.	Pvt.	Co. C. 125 Inf.	KIA	6/30/18	1224 Dorr St., Toledo, Ohio. Lina Ida Baley (Sister).

Name	Rank	Organization	Cause	Date	Address—Next of Kin
Wright, Elmer F.	Corp.	Co. K. 128 Inf.	KIA	10/6/18	Whitewater, Wis. Mr. Frank Wright.
Wright, George W.	Pvt.	Co. D. 125 Inf.	KIA	10/11/18	R. F. D. 1, Ferrum, Va. John W. Wright (Father).
Wright, Preston M.	Pvt. 1cl.	Co. E. 127 Inf.	KIA	9/2/18	Hostess, House, Vancouver, Wash. Mrs. Robert K. Wright (Mother).
Wright, Roy S.	Pvt.	Co. C. 128 Inf.	KIA	8/4/18	....
Wright, Walker	Pvt.	Bat. C. 120 F. A.	DD	9/12/18	Ripley, W. Va. Jessie M. Wright (Sister).
Wynt, Max	Pvt.	Co. D. 128 Inf.	KIA	8/3/18	....
Yaney, Phillip R.	Mech.	Co. L. 126 Inf.	KIA	10/5/18	368 Pine St., S. Muskegon, Mich. Phillip Yaney.
Yarno, James A.	Pvt.	Co. M. 127 Inf.	DW	8/3/18	....
Young, Bain E.	Pvt.	Co. I. 125 Inf.	KIA	8/1/18	....
Young, Edward J.	Pvt.	Co. M. 125 Inf.	KIA	7/31/18	....
Zackow, Harold M.	Pvt. 1cl.	M. D. 127 Inf.	KIA	9/1/18	....
Zahn, Alfred	Pvt. 1cl.	Co. F. 128 Inf.	KIA	8/3/18	....
Zajicek, Robert O.	Pvt.	Co. L. 128 Inf.	KIA	9/1/18	....
Zaleski, John	Pvt.	Co. A. 126 Inf.	KIA	7/31/18	....
Zane, Ralph L.	Pvt.	Co. F. 126 Inf.	DW	9/1/18	....
Zaneni, John	Pvt.	Mg. Co. 361 Inf.	DW	10/9/18	....
Zenewich, John	Pvt.	Co. C. 125 Inf.	KIA	8/29/18	408 Perry St., Bowery PL, Phil., Pa. Nikols Zenewich (Brother).
Zenus, Anthony	Pvt.	Co. F. 126 Inf.	DW	7/29/18	16 10th St., Dayton, Ohio. Joseph Smith (Friend).
Zeuske, Emil C.	Pvt.	Co. F. 127 Inf.	DW	9/15/18	Shawano, Wis. Mrs. Amilia Merkes (Sister).
Zilmar, Glen	Sgt.	Co. H. 127 Inf.	DW	8/1/18	....
Zimmerlie, George W.	Pvt.	Co. E. 127 Inf.	KIA	7/19/18	....
Zimmerman, Henry	Sgt.	Co. M. 127 Inf.	KIA	8/4/18	....
Zimmerman, Victor	Pvt.	Co. H. 127 Inf.	KIA	7/31/18	....
Zitterman, John J.	Pvt.	Co. H. 126 Inf.	DW	9/20/18	....
Zive, Samuel	Pvt. 1cl.	Co. K. 126 Inf.	KIA	8/29/18	....
Zubin, Julius	Pvt.	Co. D. 128 Inf.	KIA	8/31/18	....
Zuckowski, Antoine	Pvt.	Co. K. 125 Inf.	KIA	8/1/18	....
Zullo, Antonio	Pvt.	Co. B. 128 Inf.	KIA	8/31/18	....

1. Major William F. Mehl, 127th Infantry, died at Waco Texas, October 22, 1917.
2. Captain Alfred E. Gaartz, Co. D, 120th Machine Gun Battalion, killed in action August 29, 1918, during the Oise-Aisne Offensive.
3. First Lieutenant Herbert Jones Taylor, Co. M, 125th Infantry, died of wounds September 2, 1918, during the Oise-Aisne Offensive.
4. First Lieutenant Alexander E. Shiells, Co. E, 107th Engineers, died of disease, February 17, 1919.
5. Second Lieutenant George E. Harris, 120th Field Artillery, died of wounds, October 13, 1918.
6. Second Lieutenant Paul K. LeBaron, Supply Co. 120th Field Artillery, died October 14, 1918.

Consolidated Casualty Report

	Killed in Action and Died of Wounds.		Wounded—All Degrees.		Missing.		Non-Battle Casualties.	
	OFFICERS	MEN	OFFICERS	MEN	OFFICERS	MEN	OFFICERS	MEN
ALSACE	2	54	19	238	....	2	....	....
AISNE-MARNE .	66	715	161	3,184	....	12	....	....
OISE-AISNE	15	470	132	1,855	....	14	(NOTE—Includes Died of Disease, Prisoners of War, Accidentally Injured, Drowned, etc.).	
MEUSE-ARGONNE..	37	1,141	132	4,525	....	82		
EAST OF THE MEUSE..	7	153	17	505	....	24	....	....
	127	2,533	461	10,352	....	134	12	317

GRAND TOTAL—13,936

DISTINGUISHED SERVICE CROSS.

125TH INFANTRY.

Lt. Col. Guy M. Wilson, D. S. C.
Capt. Geo. S. Crabbe, D. S. C.
Capt. C. M. Williams, D. S. C.
Chaplain Thos. E. Swan, D. S. C.
Capt. Chas. Follis, D. S. C.
Capt. Meade Frierson, D. S. C.
1st Lt. Harry S. Wheat, D. S. C.
1st Lt. Herman Moyse, D. S. C.
1st Lt. Chas. A. Hammond, D. S. C.
1st Lt. Harry M. Keiser, D. S. C.
1st Lt. Merritt Wilson, D. S. C.
1st Lt. Herman Crites, D. S. C.
1st Lt. Robert E. Motley, D. S. C.
1st Lt. Francis A. Barlow, D. S. C.
1st Lt. Levi Stevens, D. S. C.
2nd Lt. William S. Brittain, D. S. C.
2nd Lt. Samuel Snowden, D. S. C.
2nd Lt. Edgar A. Jennings, D. S. C.
1st Sgt. Russell V. Somes, D. S. C.
Sgt. Ivan Smith, D. S. C.
Sgt. Carl F. Payson, D. S. C.
Sgt. John Teichler, D. S. C.
Sgt. Paul H. Rediker, D. S. C.
Corp. Arthur G. Stuart, D. S. C.
Corp. Robt. E. Craidge, D. S. C.
Corp. Theodore T. Cariery, D. S. C.
Corp. Gustave Micalka, D. S. C.
Corp. Alden Bush, D. S. C.
Corp. Matt Stevens, D. S. C.
Corp. Clarence Smith, D. S. C.
Pvt. 1cl. Everett C. Dressell, D. S. C.
Pvt. 1cl. Wilfred V. Seeler, D. S. C.
Pvt. 1cl. Arthur Heritier D. S. C.
Sgt. Joseph A. Madden, D. S. C.
Pvt. Jacob Masson, D. S. C.
Pvt. Marcus Armijo, D. S. C.
Pvt. Pontiac Williams, D. S. C.
Pvt. Fred Connette, D. S. C.
Pvt. Andy Skrypeck, D. S. C.
Pvt. Harold J. Devereaux, D. S. C.
Pvt. Bernard Schultheis, D. S. C.
Pvt. Nelson Burleigh, D. S. C.
Pvt. Joseph Isaacs, D. S. C.
Pvt. Harry Roley, D. S. C.
Pvt. George McFarling, D. S. C.
Pvt. Harry Ollrich, D. S. C.

Pvt. Edward T. Wibbert, D. S. C.
Pvt. Franciszak, D. S. C.
Corp. Elmer W. Brennan, D. S. C.
1st Sgt. Michael Castura, D. S. C.
Corp. Raymond Henry, D. S. C.
Corp. Geo. H. Pohl, D. S. C.
Pvt. Roy C. Mark, D. S. C.
Pvt. John Mecom, D. S. C.
Pvt. Wm. Holzgiebe, D. S. C.
Mechanic Eino I. Jarvi, D. S. C.
Pvt. Lionel Goodman, D. S. C.
Pvt. Victor Andryowski, D. S. C.
Pvt. Chas. T. Ritzert, D. S. C.
Pvt. John Heikkinen, D. S. C.
Pvt. Michael F. Connelly, D. S. C.
Corp. Fred C. Stein, D. S. C.
Pvt. Harry Thrall, D. S. C.
Pvt. 1cl. William Reese, D. S. C.
Pvt. Hazen Wilson, D. S. C.
Pvt. 1cl. Mike Kaminski, D. S. C.
Pvt. 1cl. Dewey Phillips, D. S. C.
Corp. Thos. M. Purdon, D. S. C.
Pvt. Walter B. Brown, D. S. C.
Pvt. Frank B. Holmes, D. S. C.
Corp. Fred Clay, D. S. C.
Sgt. Wm. A. Monroe, D. S. C.
Pvt. 1cl. Leonard St. James, D. S. C.
1st Sgt. James McDonald, D. S. C.
Corp. Harlow B. Emerson, D. S. C.
Sgt. Earl Adelspberger, D. S. C.
Pvt. 1cl. Frank Lewis, D. S. C.
Pvt. Conception Ortiz, D. S. C.
Bugler Olius Berkompas, D. S. C.
Pvt. Geo. Bullian, D. S. C.
Corp. Wm. B. Bell, D. S. C.
Corp. Wm. A. Belongea, D. S. C.
Pvt. Richard C. Anderson, D. S. C.
Corp. Isaac Chandler, D. S. C.
Bugler Geo. Deeaire, D. S. C.
Sgt. Walter L. Chellis, D. S. C.
Pvt. David H. Underwood, D. S. C.
Pvt. Franciszak Dudzinski, D. S. C.
Sgt. Emery Hawks, D. S. C.
1st Sgt. A. H. Griswold, D. S. C.
Pvt. Lyman N. Morrison, D. S. C.

126TH INFANTRY.

Colonel Joseph B. Westnedge, D. S. C.
Lt. Col. James O. Cathcart, D. S. C.
1st Lt. Leo. J. Crum, D. S. C.
1st Lt. Philip Tindall, D. S. C.
1st Lt. Harold J. King, D. S. C.
1st Lt. Chas. E. H. Bates, D. S. C.
1st Lt. Edgar L. Burton, D. S. C.
2nd Lt. James M. Wilson, D. S. C.
Sgt. Rancy R. Kain, D. S. C.
Sgt. Orrie Thompson, D. S. C.
Sgt. Dougald Ferguson, D. S. C.
Sgt. Wm. Lizinski, D. S. C.
Pvt. 1cl. John G. Zeldam, D. S. C.
Pvt. Steven V. Chipman, D. S. C.
Sgt. Robert J. Kline, D. S. C.
Sgt. Alexander Salik, D. S. C.
Sgt. Carl Banks, D. S. C.
Corp. Frank R. Raymond, D. S. C.
Pvt. Albert R. Neitzel, D. S. C.
Pvt. Albert S. Krzywa, D. S. C.
Pvt. Chas. L. Beck, D. S. C.
Pvt. Wm. A. Edsall, D. S. C.
Pvt. Frederick W. McClemmens, D. S. C.
Sgt. John G. Fowle, D. S. C.
Corp. Ernest A. Sheer, D. S. C.
Sgt. Maxwell E. Smith, D. S. C.
Sgt. Arthur Aamot, D. S. C.
Corp. Henry F. Dye, D. S. C.
Pvt. Wm. E. Hurst, D. S. C.
Sgt. Geo. A. Hopkins, D. S. C.
Pvt. Lonso L. Fuller, D. S. C.
Sgt. Wm. Liniger, D. S. C.
Sgt. Oscar A. Rundquist, D. S. C.
Pvt. 1cl. Howard A. Waite, D. S. C.
Sgt. Harold A. Dawson, D. S. C.
Corp. Laurel Shore, D. S. C.
Pvt. Harry Swift, D. S. C.
Sgt. Ira L. Westcott, D. S. C.

127TH INFANTRY.

Col. Russell C. Langdon, D. S. C.
Major Wm. G. Watkins, D. S. C.
Capt. John D. Spencer, D. S. C.
1st Lt. Herman W. Steinkraus, D. S. C.
1st Lt. Ray C. Dickop, D. S. C.
1st Lt. Henry S. Blomberg, D. S. C.
Pvt. Olaf Olsen, D. S. C.
Sgt. Frank Glomski, D. S. C.
Pvt. 1cl. Jos. A. Chayie, D. S. C.
Pvt. 1cl. Wilfred Lloyd, D. S. C.
Sgt. Ray Rolain, D. S. C.
Corp. Jesse Marlin, D. S. C.
Pvt. Helmuth Dewitz, D. S. C.
Pvt. Chas. Holmes, D. S. C.
Corp. Clarence Lake, D. S. C.
Pvt. Jos. Mueller, D. S. C.
Sgt. Walter Siebert, D. S. C.
Pvt. Emil Buckendahl, D. S. C.
Pvt. Mike Curti, D. S. C.
Pvt. Arthur L. Stuckrad, D. S. C.
Sgt. Max P. Thalke, D. S. C.
Sgt. James McSorley, D. S. C.
Sgt. Louis Witte, D. S. C.
Pvt. Henry W. Wetzel, D. S. C.
Sgt. Willard D. Purdy, D. S. C.
Pvt. Edwin Austin, D. S. C.
Pvt. James C. Hix, D. S. C.

128TH INFANTRY.

Major Frank L. Gottschalk, D. S. C.
Major Daniel J. Martin, D. S. C.
Major Henry R. Hill, D. S. C.
Capt. Clifford E. Bischoff, D. S. C.
1st Lt. Clarence G. Noble, D. S. C.
1st Lt. Walter O. L. Peterson, D. S. C.
1st Lt. Alexander L. Nicol, D. S. C.
2nd Lt. Richard W. Austerman, D. S. C.
2nd Lt. Oscar T. Slagsvol, D. S. C.
Sgt. Arthur Schultz, D. S. C.
Sgt. Max P. Thalke, D. S. C.
Corp. Clarence L. Turley, D. S. C.
Pvt. Clem Anthony, D. S. C.
Pvt. Lonso L. Fuller, D. S. C.
Pvt. Geo. W. Langham, D. S. C.
Pvt. Samuel Shaskan, D. S. C.
Major Chas. L. Sheridan, D. S. C.
Corp. Claude R. Roberts D. S. C.
Pvt. 1cl. Herman Plauman, D. S. C.
Pvt. Raymond Genicke, D. S. C.
Corp. Earl M. Curnow, D. S. C.
Pvt. Maurice L. Mathey, D. S. C.
Pvt. Lynn Blossom, D. S. C.
Pvt. Wm. A. Jacobson, D. S. C.
Pvt. Clarence J. McNulty, D. S. C.
Pvt. Alabel Blumenthal, D. S. C.
Pvt. Mack Dudley, D. S. C.
2nd Lt. John M. Regan, D. S. C.
Sgt. Elmer Evenson, D. S. C.
Corp. Chester C. Kromer, D. S. C.

121ST MACHINE GUN BATTALION.

1st Sgt. Paul J. Gaston, D. S. C.
Sgt. Herman Korth, D. S. C.

The Division Commander and Staff at the Presentation of Distinguished Service Crosses, Dierdorf, Germany.

107TH *ENGINEERS.*

2nd Lt. Geo. Winfield Kuhlman, D. S. C.   2nd Lt. James Stanley Solton, D. S. C.

107TH F. S. BATTALION.

Sgt. John Lamb, D. S. C.
Sgt. 1cl. Geo. Burr, D. S. C.

Corp. Donald D. Palmer, D. S. C.
Pvt. Edw. Pelkey, D. S. C.

120TH *FIELD ARTILLERY REGIMENT.*

2nd Lieut. Stacey L. Harding, D. S. C.
Sgt. Frank M. Holt, D. S. C.
Wagoner Nick Adler, D. S. C.
Corp. Frank I. Fox, D. S. C.
Corp. Floyd Prescott, D. S. C.

Pvt. 1cl. Joseph Biwan, D. S. C.
Pvt. 1cl. Harold J. Drotning, D. S. C.
Pvt. Lee O. Prescott, D. S. C.
Pvt. Stephen H. Faatz, D. S. C.

121ST *FIELD ARTILLERY REGIMENT.*

Sgt. Albert B. Brown, D. S. C.

147TH *FIELD ARTILLERY REGIMENT.*

Sgt. Hobart M. Bird, D. S. C.
Corp. Albert J. Reed, D. S. C.

Pvt. 1cl. Chas. E. Thorne, D. S. C.

107TH AMMUNITION TRAIN.

Wagoner James A. Norton, D. S. C.
Pvt. 1cl. Walter J. Raleigh, D. S. C.

Pvt. 1cl. John F. Shedlewski, D. S. C.

158TH *FIELD ARTILLERY BRIGADE.*

2nd Lt. John Morrison, D. S. C.
Corp. John M. Crocker, D. S. C.

Corp. Elvin L. Pierson, D. S. C.
Pvt. Urban V. Craft, D. S. C.

"The Division Commander and Staff and Decoratees Reviewing the Division."
(DIERDORF, Germany.)

301

322ND, 323RD FIELD ARTILLERY REGIMENT.

Pvt. 1cl. Joe J. Donahue, D. S. C.
Sgt. John M. Crocker, D. S. C., Hq. Co.

Corp. Elvin L. Pierson, D.S.C., Battery "A."
Pvt. Urban V. Craft, D. S. C., Hq. Co.

308TH TRENCH MOTOR BATTERY.

Capt. Don. R. McCil, D. S. C.
2nd Lt. Roy B. Foreman, D. S. C.
2nd Lt. Harold Burns, D. S. C.
Sgt. Chas. S. Hoover, D. S. C.

Sgt. Horace L. Holloway, D. S. C.
Sgt. Elver J. Dowles, D. S. C.
Corp. Carl F. Turkopp, D. S. C.

UNATTACHED.

1st Lt. Maurice J. V. Ritt, D. S. C.
2nd Lt. Verne E. Rogers, D. S. C.

Corp. Jean Babtiste Carrere, D. S. C.

DISTINGUISHED SERVICE MEDAL.

Major General W. M. Haan, Div. Hq., D. S. M.
Major General Wm. Lassiter, Div. Hq., D. S. M.
Brigadier General Edwin B. Winans, 64th Inf., D. S. M.
Brigadier General G. LeRoy Irwin, 57th F. A. Brig., D. S. M.
Colonel Robt. McC. Beck, Jr., Div. Hq., D. S. M.
Colonel Russell C. Langdon, 127th Inf., D. S. M.
Colonel Robt. B. McCoy, 128th Inf., D. S. M.
Colonel G. E. Seaman, Div. Surgeon, D. S. M.
Colonel Joseph B. Westnedge, 126th Inf., D. S. M.
Lt. Col. Philip Zink, 127th Inf., D. S. M.

MEDAILLE MILITAIRE.
125TH INFANTRY.
1st Sgt. Wm. B. Scheffler.

LEGION OF HONOR—FRANCE.

Major General William G. Haan............................Division Commander.
Major General William Lassiter............................Division Commander.
Major General J. A. Le Jeune................................64th Infantry Brigade.
Major General Robert Alexander ....63rd Infantry Brigade.
Brigadier General William D. Connor........................63rd Infantry Brigade.
Brigadier Adrian S. Fleming ....158th Field Artillery.
Brigadier General G. LeRoy Irwin...........................57th Field Artillery.
Brigadier General Frank R. McCoy..........................63rd Infantry Brigade.
Brigadier General Edwin B. Winans.........................64th Infantry Brigade.
Colonel Robert McC. Beck, Jr...............................Chief of Staff.
Colonel Harold C. Fiske....................................107th Engineers.
Colonel Russell C. Langdon.................................127th Infantry.
Colonel William M. Morrow..................................125th Infantry.
Colonel Jerome G. Pillow...................................Ass't Chief of Staff, G-3.
Colonel George M. Russell..................................Acting Chief of Staff.
Colonel Gilbert E. Seaman..................................Division Surgeon.
Lt. Col. Paul B. Clemens ....Ass't Chief of Staff, G-2.
Lt. Col. John H. Howard....................................Ass't Chief of Staff, G-1.
Lt. Col. John Scott..Division Signal Officer.
Lt. Col. Guy M. Wilson.....................................125th Infantry.
Lt. Col. Allen L. Briggs...................................Ass't Chief of Staff, G-3.
Captain Clifford E. Bischoff...............................128th Infantry.
Captain James Wilson ....125th Infantry.

CROIX DE GUERRE.

DIVISION HEADQUARTERS, HEADQUARTERS TROOP, AND DETACHMENT.

Major General W. M. Haan, C. G.
Major General Wm. Lassiter, C. G.
Colonel Robt. McC. Beck, Jr., C. G.
Colonel H. B. Fisk, C. G.
Colonel Jerome G. Pillow, C. G.
Lt. Col. John H. Howard, C. G.
Lt. Col. John Scott, C. G.
Colonel G. E. Seaman, C. G.
Lt. Col. G. W. Garlock, C. G.
Lt. Col. Paul B. Clemens, C. G.
Lt. Col. Chas. R. Williams, C. G.
Lt. Col. James Scott, C. G.
Major Fred C. Best, C. G.
Major Wm. H. Holmes, C. G.
Major Chas. S. Harrison, C. G.
Major Patrick Dunigan, C. G.
Major Robt. Connor, C. G.
Major Edgar H. Campbell, C. G.

Capt. Frank Ward, C. G.
Capt. Wm. J. Niederpruem, C. G.
Capt. John C. Crandall, C. G.
Capt. Herbert Shonk, C. G.
Capt. LeRoy Pearson, C. G.
Chaplain Wm. P. O'Connor, C. G.
Capt. Daniel L. Thompson, C. G.
Capt. Chas. F. Bowen, C. G.
Lt. Ernest H. Barrow, C. G.
Lt. Camille Morvant, C. G.
Lt. Harold J. Lance, C. G.
Lt. F. F. Malloy, C. G.
Sgt. J. Irl Croshaw, C. G.
Sgt. William L. Barrard, Jr., C. G.
Sgt. Fred R. Starr, C. G.
Corp. Perry R. Shisler, C. G.
Pvt. 1cl. Frank Stafford, C. G.
Pvt. Vernon L. Downer, C. G.

63RD INFANTRY BRIGADE, HEADQUARTERS.

Lt. John P. Gregg, C. G.

Lt. Col. John J. Burley, C. G.

125TH INFANTRY.

Lt. Col. Guy M. Wilson, C. G.
Major Milton L. Hinkley, C. G.
Major Alfred E. Lemon, C. G.
Capt. C. M. Williams, C. G.
Capt. Joseph M. Donneley, C. G.
Capt. Oscar Falk, C. G.
Capt. C. M. Williams, C. G.
Chaplain Wm. F. Davitt, C. G.
1st Lt. Levi Stevens, C. G.
1st Lt. Harry S. Wheat, C. G.
1st Lt. Herman Moyse, C. G.
1st Lt. Chas. A. Hammond, C. G.
1st Lt. Harry M. Keiser, C. G.
Lt. Chas. A. Keskey, C. G.
Lt. Joseph Jenkinson, C. G.
1st Lt. Francis A. Barlow, C. G.
1st Lt. Ray C. Dickop, C. G.
1st Lt. Wm. F. Weine, C. G.
Lt. John L. Hynan, C. G.
Lt. Wm. Ward, C. G.
2nd Lt. William S. Brittain, C. G.
2nd Lt. John J. Bruenn, C. G.
Corp. Marion Ross, C. G.
Sgt. William Quilliam, C. G.
Sgt. Clyde O. Helgeson, C. G.
Sgt. Alfred N. Platt, C. G.
Sgt. Darwin D. Martin, C. G.
Sgt. Anthony Kwiathkowski, C. G.
Sgt. Harry Beuker, C. G.
Corp. Everett C. Dressell, C. G.
Corp. Herman Yokie, C. G.
Pvt. 1cl. Arthur Allen, C. G.

Sgt. Harold Burley, C. G.
Pvt. James A. Burlingame, C. G.
Pvt. Fred A. Lepire, C. G.
Pvt. Clarence Hunter, C. G.
Pvt. Paul A. Moore, C. G.
Pvt. Wm. Phillips, C. G.
Pvt. Emile Jensen, C. G.
Pvt. Harry Hill, C. G.
Pvt. John Canavan, C. G.
Pvt. Antone Markiando, C. G.
Pvt. Wm. E. Ferris, C. G.
Pvt. Etinne Badeaux, C. G.
Pvt. 1cl. Henry M. Bradow, C. G.
Cook Daniel Pratt, C. G.
Mechanic Ivan Wardell, C. G.
Pvt. Burton G. McSivean, C. G.
Pvt. 1cl. Fred Rosencrance, C. G.
Bugler Lester C. Reese, C. G.
Pvt. George Pearson, C. G.
Sgt. Jos. A. Lefebre, C. G.
Sgt. Manuel Vicau, C. G.
Sgt. Chas. B. Orr, C. G.
Corp. Alphonse Bergen, C. G.
Corp. Virgil V. Sabourin, C. G.
Corp. Arthur Adams, C. G.
Corp. Albert Neault, C. G.
Pvt. 1cl. Wm. E. Hurst, C. G.
Pvt. 1cl. Joseph Hilbig, C. G.
Pvt. Benhard A. Schultheis, C. G.
Sgt. Harold Springer, C. G.
Sgt. Russel Fisk, C. G.
Sgt. Carl F. Payson, C. G.

125TH INFANTRY—Continued.

Sgt. Ivan Smith, C. G.
Corp. Isaac Chaudler, C. G.
Pvt. 1cl. Arthur Heritier, C. G.
Pvt. Fred Connette, C. G.
Pvt. Geo. Decaire, C. G.
Pvt. Carl O'Neil, C. G.
Pvt. Edw. T. Vibbert, C. G.
Corp. Elmer W. Brennan, C. G.
Corp. Alden Bush, C. G.
Corp. Paul H. Rediker, C. G.
Corp. Clarence Smith, C. G.
Pvt. Nelson Burleigh, C. G.
Pvt. Devereaux, C. G.
Pvt. Harry Foley, C. G.
Pvt. Wilfred Seeler, C. G.
Pvt. Pontiac Williams, C. G.
Sgt. Walter L. Chellis, C. G.
Sgt. Edgar H. Jennings, C. G.

Corp. Morris D. Mist, C. G.
Corp. Matt Stevens, C. G.
Pvt. Joseph Madden, C. G.
Pvt. Harry Thrall, C. G.
Sgt. Horace H. Sole, C. G.
Sgt. Fowler, C. G.
Sgt. Edw. J. MacHugh, C. G.
Sgt. Samuel Snowden, C. G.
Sgt. Orville Weir, C. G.
Corp. Harlow B. Emerson, C. G.
Corp. T. Cariepy, C. G.
Pvt. Richard C. Anderson, C. G.
Pvt. Harry W. Dennison, C. G.
Pvt. Joseph Isaacs, C. G.
Pvt. Stuart P. Tice, C. G.
Corp. Barnel C. Carr, C. G.
Mechanic Philip R. Janey, C. G.
Corp. Clyde O. Martinson, C. G.

126TH INFANTRY.

Colonel Joseph B. Westuedge, C. G.
Major Wm. Rankin, C. G.
Major Wm. Henry Burke, C. G.
Lt. Leland E. Wheeler, C. G.
Lt. Walter L. Shirley, C. G.
Lt. Jacob Cohen, C. G.
2nd Lt. James Blaney, C. G.
2nd Lt. Donald Perry, C. G.
Corp. Clarence L. Hinkle, C. G.
Sgt. Wm. E. Hamilton, C. G.
Pvt. 1cl. Okey Price, C. G.
Pvt. John C. Casey, C. G.
Pvt. Albert L. Luce, C. G.
Sgt. Richard Lauder, C. G.
Corp. Henry G. Griffin, C. G.
Corp. Glenn Graves, C. G.
Pvt. 1cl. James Taylor, C. G.
Pvt. 1cl. Wendell Wilson, C. G.
Pvt. 1cl. Chas. F. Comska, C. G.
Pvt. Frank W. Fresse, C. G.
Sgt. Mathew Post, C. G.
Sgt. James D. Babcock, C. G.
Sgt. Arthur B. Pehrson, C. G.

Sgt. Ben F. Fogelsong, C. G.
Sgt. Alexander Salik, C. G.
Corp. Geo. Pohl, C. G.
Corp. Gustave Michalka, C. G.
Sgt. Dougald Ferguson, C. G.
Sgt. Arthur E. Hawks, C. G.
Sgt. Raney R. Kain, C. G.
Sgt. Wm. Luzinski, C. G.
Sgt. Orrie Thomson, C. G.
Sgt. Roy Webster, C. G.
Pvt. Geo. S. Downing, C. G.
Pvt. ——— Shipman, C. G.
Sgt. Vonk, C. G.
Corp. Jerrold B. Thompson, C. G.
Pvt. Isidore Vissilo, C. G.
Pvt. John J. Zeldam, C. G.
Sgt. Bugler Theo. Kutchinski, C. G.
Sgt. Lyman T. Covell, C. G.
Sgt. Geo. Rinaldi, C. G.
Corp. Lewis Hudson, C. G.
Mechanic Guthfort Cournmer, C. G.
Sgt. Wallace J. Waltman, C. G.
Sgt. William R. Smith, C. G.

120TH MACHINE GUN BATTALION.

2nd Lt. Louis H. Carlson, C. G.
Pvt. Logan A. Sond, C. G.

Pvt. Nick Lucero, C. G.

127TH INFANTRY.

Colonel Russell C. Langdon, C. G.
Lt. Col. P. J. Zink, C. G.
Major John F. Stevens, C. G.
Capt. Wilbur K. Black, C. G.
Capt. Martin Ackerson, C. G.
Capt. Arnold A. Gritzmacker, C. G.
Capt. Guy V. Anderson, C. G.
Capt. Stephen Boon, Jr., C. G.

Lt. Garlon E. Harrington, C. G.
Lt. Frank Krukar, C. G.
Lt. Harmon Chas. Padon, C. G.
Lt. Rogers T. Cooksey, C. G.
Lt. Willfred Page, C. G.
Lt. James W. Stiggleman, C. G.
1st Lt. Stanley A. Jewasinski, C. G.
1st Lt. Wm. F. Weine, C. G.

127TH INFANTRY—Continued.

2nd Lt. J. Kenneth Rutherford, C. G.
2nd Lt. Moriss Togstad, C. G.
2nd Lt. Roy W. Kelley, C. G.
2nd Lt. Laverne E. Deal, C. G.
Sergt. Olaf Olsen, C. G.
Pvt. Paul Florine, C. G.
Corp. Frank Plain, C. G.
Sgt. Peter La Fromway, C. G.
Sgt. Wm. K. Larson, C. G.
Corp. August C. Meyer, C. G.
Corp. Ralph Rand, C. G.
Sgt. Frank Glomski, C. G.
Pvt. Richard E. Charles, C. G.
Pvt. Wm. J. Kirkpatrick, C. G.
Pvt. Oliver O. Grant, C. G.
Pvt. 1cl. Jos. A. Chayie, C. G.
Corp. Carl Rasmessen.
Sgt. Floyd Hughes, C. G.
Sgt. Isadore Rheuaume, C. G.
Sgt. Wm. N. Waugh, C. G.
Sgt. Floyd F. Brown, C. G.
Cook Erwin Kunath, C. G.
Cook Leo Kick, C. G.
Pvt. Wm. H. Price, C. G.
Sgt. Wm. J. Huempfner, C. G.
Sgt. Bernard Allen, C. G.
Sgt. Frank Bufka, C. G.
Sgt. Chas. R. Schmidt, C. G.
Sgt. Lawrence Gauthier, C. G.
Sgt. Rudolph Kallies, C. G.
Pvt. 1cl. Arthur Wolfe, C. G.
Pvt. 1cl. James Faulds, C. G.
Pvt. 1cl. Alfred Swens, C. G.
Pvt. Chas. Huling, C. G.
Pvt. Guy Whitman, C. G.
Pvt. Bert Harper, C. G.
Pvt. Donald K. Brown, C. G.
Pvt. Venanzio Guilio, C. G.
Pvt. John F. Hart, C. G.
Pvt. John Anderson, C. G.
Pvt. Lester Rondeau, C. G.
Corp. Arthur Deel, C. G.

Corp. Bert Williston, C. G.
Corp. Wm. Taylor, C. G.
Corp. Eitel Meyer, C. G.
Corp. Geo. H. Rowe, C. G.
Pvt. 1cl. Louis Lafave, C. G.
Pvt. 1cl. Joseph Adamski, C. G.
Pvt. 1cl. Melvin Mercord, C. G.
Pvt. 1cl. Hjalmer Hanson, C. G.
Mechanic Carl A. Larsen, C. G.
Pvt. Edw. J. Riley, C. G.
Cook Robert H. Morris, C. G. .
Corp. Alvin Bocher, C. G.
Pvt. 1cl. Wm. Tolkren, C. G.
Sgt. Vincent P. Kielpinski, C. G.
Sgt. Paul G. Bonack, C. G.
Sgt. Joseph Witeck, C. G.
Sgt. Tom Xygogasrepolos, C. G.
Sgt. William Watt, C. G.
Sgt. Jacob Borski, C. G.
Sgt. Stanley Tarzuyski, C. G.
Corp. Marshall Rumary, C. G.
Pvt. 1cl. Joseph Milicki, C. G.
Corp. Thos. Stafford, C. G.
Corp. Alexander Legault, C. G.
Pvt. 1cl. Wm. J. Ashmun, C. G.
Pvt. 1cl. Louis Schlegel, C. G.
Sgt. Wm. H. Bruce, C. G.
Sgt. Benjamin G. Bilter, C. G.
1st Sgt. Richard Arndt, C. G.
Sgt. Ellsworth Hay, C. G.
Sgt. Howard C. Coates, C. G.
Sgt. Alfred Erhardt, C. G.
Sgt. George Abell, C. G.
Sgt. Marek, C. G.
Pvt. 1cl. Wilfred Lloyd, C. G.
1st Lt. John D. Spencer, C. G.
Sgt. Rolain, C. G.
Pvt. Alexander J. Lurye, C. G.
Corp. Alfred J. Weyandt, C. G.
Pvt. 1cl. Wm. Schneider, C. G.
Pvt. 1cl. Cyrus McKenzie, C. G.
Corp. John Tremain, C. G.

128TH INFANTRY.

Colonel Henry A. Meyer, C. G.
Major Lewis A. Moore, C. G.
Major Orra L. Norris, C. G.
Major Emil G. Prellivitz, C. G.
Major Frank L. Gottschalk, C. G.
Capt. Carl Hanton, C. G.
Capt. John D. Ewing, C. G.
Capt. John M. Scantleton, C. G.
Capt. Leo. Schwanekamp, C. G.
Capt. Rantz F. Snoberger, C. G.
Capt. Clifford E. Bischoff, C. G.
Capt. Wm. R. Doctor, C. G.
Capt. Earl L. Hemenway, C. G.
Lt. Frank E. Machus, C. G.
Lt. Archibald A. Walker, C. G.
1st Lt. John R. Devall, C. G.
Lt. Francis L. Gullickson, C. G.
2nd Lt. Oscar T. Slagsvol, C. G.

Sgt. Arthur Schultz, C. G.
Sgt. Max P. Thalke, C. G.
Corp. Clarence L. Turley, C. G.
Pvt. Clem Anthony, C. G.
Sgt. Walter Peterson, C. G.
Corp. Claude R. Roberts, C. G.
Pvt. 1cl. Herman Plauman, C. G.
Sgt. Raymond H. Kraft, C. G.
Sgt. Jess Ford, C. G.
Corp. Mike Rouchena, C. G.
Sgt. Wm. G. Hunter, C. G.
Corp. Floyd C. Hanson, C. G.
Sgt. Severin Setter, C. G.
Sgt. Ralph W. Bock, C. G.
Sgt. Forest Touton, C. G.
Pvt. 1cl. Phil Case, C. G.
Pvt. 1cl. John Anton Staudinger, C. G.
Pvt. 1cl. John Bonneville, C. G.

128TH INFANTRY—Continued.

Pvt. lcl. Hilton E. Dressel, C. G.
Corp. Mack Dudley, C. G.
Corp. Joseph Poland, C. G.
Corp. Grover Jones, C. G.
Corp. Martin L. Kuklinski, C. G.
Pvt. Joseph Mattrass, C. G.
Sgt. John Peters, C. G.
Sgt. Frank Murphy, C. G.
Sgt. Geo. P. Banann, C. G.
Sgt. Ernest P. Coleman, C. G.
Sgt. Roy Meadows, C. G.
Sgt. James K. Briggs, C. G.
Sgt. Max A. Draheim, C. G.
Pvt. Michael Kempinski, C. G.
Pvt. Thos. L. Lawton, C. G.
Corp. Carl Koutnik, C. G.
Corp. John Nelson, C. G.
Cook Benjamin J. Bradshaw, C. G.
Pvt. Joseph W. Powell, C. G.
Pvt. Wm. J. Hilt, C. G.
Pvt. Frank J. Bell, C. G.
Pvt. Paul Piehler, C. G.
Pvt. Chas. E. Coulin, C. G.
Bandmaster Webster G. Needles, C. G.
Pvt. Arnold E. Erling, Jr., C. G.
Pvt. Albert Peralta, C. G.
Pvt. Roy Marley, C. G.
Pvt. Floyd W. Sieber, C. G.
Pvt. Raymond Genicke, C. G.
Sgt. Rollin B. Curtiss, C. G.
Sgt. Robert S. Finkle, C. G.
Sgt. Arthur R. Klein, C. G.
Sgt. Louis E. Wilpolt, C. G.
Sgt. Arthur Streich, C. G.
Sgt. Christ Christianson, C. G.
Corp. John Maciejwski, C. G.
Corp. Chester Kromer, C. G.
Corp. Russell Smith, C. G.

Corp. Walter Thomds, C. G.
Corp. Frank A. Southworth, C. G.
Corp. Harvey C. Bohli, C. G.
Corp. John Horvath, C. G.
Corp. Erwin A. Olson, C. G.
Corp. John Junk, C. G.
Corp. Alphonsus Cavanaugh, C. G.
Corp. Cecil L. Lolmaugh, C. G.
Corp. Lloyd Mosler, C. G.
Corp. Mike Jankowski, C. G.
Corp. Edwin A. Cable, C. G.
Corp. Myrl O. Platt, C. G.
Pvt. lcl. Archie Black, C. G.
Pvt. lcl. Mike Gentino, C. G.
Pvt. lcl. Dominick Geomo, C. G.
Pvt. Lynn Blossom, C. G.
Sgt. Edward Becker, C. G.
Sgt. Geo. B. Schultz, C. G.
Sgt. Elmer Evenson, C. G.
Sgt. Harry Peterson, C. G.
Sgt. Harris A. Hallenbeck, C. G.
Sgt. Earl A. Goldsmith, C. G.
Sgt. Clarke A. Trimble, C. G.
Sgt. Chas. Gislason, C. G.
Sgt. Clyde B. McAuley, C. G.
Sgt. Emil F. Kabat, C. G.
Sgt. Irving Roberts, C. G.
Sgt. Adolph Knutson, C. G.
Corp. Carl L. Curnow, C. G.
Pvt. Clarence G. Ston, C. G.
Pvt. Geo. W. Langhan, C. G.
Pvt. lcl. Geo. L. Croce, C. G.
Pvt. Pete Anderson, C. G.
Corp. Peter L. Dimouich, C. G.
Pvt. Clyde E. Howell, C. G.
Pvt. lcl. Wm. O. Morgan, C. G.
Pvt. lcl. Donald Swartout, C. G.
Corp. James P. Ewing, C. G.

121ST MACHINE GUN BATTALION.

Lt. Col. Dan. L. Remington, C. G.
Capt. John C. Graham, C. G.
Capt. John G. Brunkhorst, C. G.
Capt. John McCullum, Jr., C. G.
Lt. Austin A. Peterson, C. G.
Lt. Daniel M. Erickson, C. G.
Lt. Allen S. Harrison, C. G.
1st Sgt. Paul J. Gaston, C. G.
Sgt. Herman Korth, C. G.
Sgt. Jos. D. Phelan, C. G.

Sgt. Elmer C. Aune, C. G.
Sgt. Jos. Halter, C. G.
Corp. Wm. A. Stone, C. G.
Corp. Nathan Wilson, C. G.
Pvt. lcl. Jacob Tautges, C. G.
Pvt. lcl. Albin C. Ness, C. G.
Pvt. Richard Blumke, C. G.
Pvt. Francis J. Dunn, C. G.
Pvt. Sillas F. Wallen, C. G.
Pvt. Donald C. Hume, C. G.

119TH MACHINE GUN BATTALION.

Major Wm. A. McCulock, C. G.
Capt. Edw. S. Reynolds, C. G.

Bugler Orville Scheffner, C. G.
Pvt. Robert J. Coey, C. G.

DISTINGUISHED SERVICE DECORATIONS

32ND MILITARY POLICE COMPANY.

2nd Lt. Fred J. Mattingly, C. G.
Sgt. Chas. E. Walker, C. G.
Mess Sgt. Norman Sever, C. G.
Pvt. Edw. Freidel, C. G.

Pvt. Paul M. Wedvick, C. G.
Pvt. Harry R. Rayburn, C. G.
Pvt. Ray D. May, C. G.
Pvt. Harry M. Bently, C. G.

107TH ENGINEERS.

Name.
Colonel L. H. Callan, C. G.
Lt. Col. C. S. Smith, C. G.
Major Edgar C. Barnes, C. G.
Major R. A. Loveland, C. G.
Major James W. Shaw, C. G.
Capt. Sinclair H. Lorain, C. G.
Capt. Arthur Knowles, C. G.
Capt. Harold B. Schmidt, C. G.
Capt. C. U. Smith, C. G.
Capt. T. Dodson Stamps, C. G.
Lt. Henry H. Hart, C. G.
Lt. Andrew T. Sweet, C. G.
Lt. Robert H. Sauds, C. G.
2nd Lt. Chas. Hemberger, C. G.
2nd Lt. James Stanley Cotton, C. G.
2nd Lt. Wm. N. Pearce, C. G.
Master Engr. Chas. F. Akin, C. G.
Master Engr. A. Bartlett King, C. G.
Sgt. Wm. A. Hartman, C. G.

Name.
Sgt. Frederick C. Brown, C. G.
Sgt. LeRoy S. Barber, C. G.
Sgt. Lester H. Edwards, C. G.
Sgt. Roland B. Hackin, C. G.
Sgt. Robert M. Hoagg, C. G.
Sgt. Cliff Hendrickson, C. G.
Sgt. Albert J. Jackson, C. G.
Sgt. Howard R. Winterbottom C. G.
Sgt. Jean A. Thibeau, C. G.
Sgt. Lawrence W. Evins, C. G.
Sgt. Elmer J. Jestila, C. G.
Sgt. Harold S. Brown, C. G.
Corp. Raymond W. Hackett, C. G.
Corp. Wm. A. Ward, C. G.
Corp. Wm. J. La Plante, C. G.
Corp. Wallace L. Anderson, C. G.
Pvt. 1cl. Jerry L. Allen, C. G.
Pvt. 1cl. Wm. P. Murphy, C. G.
Pvt. 1cl. Hans P. Christensen, C. G.

107TH FIELD SIGNAL BATTALION.

Lt. Col. Wm. Mitchell Lewis, C. G.
Lt. Elmer G. Meyer, C. G.
Sgt. John Lamb, C. G.
Sgt. John W. Dollar, C. G.
Sgt. Warham A. Kuehlthau, C. G.
Sgt. 1cl. Ivan L. Allen, C. G.
Sgt. Louis G. Komarek, C. G.

Sgt. Frank A. Mateja, C. G.
Corp. Wafford Dry, C. G.
Pvt. 1cl. Harry D. Hunter, C. G.
Pvt. 1cl. Frank E. Root, C. G.
Pvt. 1cl. Ernest E. Ross, C. G.
Pvt. Peter J. Proten, C. G.
Pvt. Elmer G. Weller, C. G.

147TH FIELD ARTILLERY REGIMENT.
(41st U. S. Div.)
Attached to 32nd Division, American Expeditionary Force.

Colonel Boyd Wales, C. G.
Capt. Richard A. Dorer, C. G.
Capt. Thos. W. Watson, C. G.
Capt. Geo. F. Weber, C. G.
1st. Lt. Arthur Bergstrom, C. G.
1st Lt. Wallace Burton, C. G.
1st Lt. James Gay, C. G.
1st Lt. Alvin M. Knutson, C. G.
2nd Lt. Lawrence I. Champe, C. G.
Sgt. Solomon Hoy, C. G.
Sgt. Earl C. Kieselhorst, C. G.
Sgt. Ayres H. Larrabee, C. G.
Sgt. David Levy, C. G.
Sgt. Warren L. Cooper, C. G.
Sgt. Leo L. Denbo, C. G.
Sgt. Edward Hardy, C. G.
Sgt. James H. Heffron, C. G.
Sgt. Thos. F. Pitts, C. G.

Sgt. Francis W. Rollins, C. G.
Sgt. Floyd R. Young, C. G.
Musician Carl W. Bahr, C. G.
Musician Wilbur B. Koplitz, C. G.
Corp. Wm. MacMahon, C. G.
Corp. Clifford E. Pole, C. G.
Corp. Frank B. Ritchey, C. G.
Corp. Arthur J. Anderson, C. G.
Corp. Arlo W. Bredberg, C. G.
Corp. Frederick G. Bunch, C. G.
Corp. Chas. M. Dalby, C. G.
Corp. Roy E. Dunn, C. G.
Corp. Nelles K. Egner, C. G.
Corp. Earl Henderson, C. G.
Corp. Philip T. Lee, C. G.
Corp. Ernest C. Lord, C. G.
Corp. Geo. Meats, C.G.
Corp. Edgar C. Morford, C. G.

147TH FIELD ARTILLERY REGIMENT—Continued.

Corp. Frank C. MacClaffin, C. G.
Corp. Lars Sand, C. G.
Corp. Roy C. Stone, C. G.
Corp. Oscar Voyen, C. G.
Pvt. 1cl. Arthur Anderson, C. G.
Pvt. 1cl. Harley Gamber, C. G.
Pvt. 1cl. Homer Heath, C. G.
Pvt. 1cl. Walter W. Jennerjahn, C. G.
Pvt. 1cl. Harry A. Millener, C. G.

Pvt. 1cl. Walter MacCrum, C. G.
Pvt. 1cl. Humert C. MacGee, C. G.
Pvt. 1cl. Carl L. Pitts, C. G.
Pvt. 1cl. Ernest L. Reck, C. G.
Pvt. 1cl. Chas. E. Stoddard, C. G.
Pvt. 1cl. Donald A. Young, C. G.
Pvt. Geo. Kongle, C. G.
Pvt. Carlyle Ogders, C. G.
Pvt. Ernest A. Stauffacher, C. G.

107TH AMMUNITION TRAIN.

Driver James A. Norton, C. G.
Pvt. 1cl. Walter J. Raleigh, C. G.

Pvt. 1cl. John F. Shedlewski, C. G.

57TH FIELD ARTILLERY BRIGADE.

Major James Gilson, C. G.

322ND FIELD ARTILLERY REGIMENT.

Pvt. Urban V. Craft, Hq. Co., C. G.

120TH FIELD ARTILLERY REGIMENT.

Capt. Miles D. Cottingham, C. G.
1st Lieut. Thomas J. Uhl, C. G.

Priv. Theodore Jaussen, C. G.

107TH SANITARY TRAIN.

Capt. Geo. B. Beach, C. G.
Sgt. Carl H. Smith, C. G.
Pvt. 1cl. Wm. Cline, C. G.
Pvt. 1cl. Dick Hamstra, C. G.

Pvt. 1cl. Wm. M. Koehler, C. G.
Pvt. 1cl. Kazimier Marcinkowski, C. G.
Pvt. 1cl. John Hall, C. G.

BELGIAN DECORATIONS.

2nd Lt. Edgar A. Jennings, Co. M, 125th Inf. Belgian War Cross.
Sgt. Horace H. Cole, Co. B, 125th Inf. Chevalier of the Order of Leopold II.
Bugler Geo. Decaire, Co. G. Belgian Military Dec.
Corp. Morris D. Mist, Co. A, 125th Inf. Belgian Military Dec.
Corp. Wm. B. Bell, Co. I, 125th Inf. Belgian War Cross.
Capt. James MacNickam Wilson, 126th Inf. Decoration of Chevalier of the National Order.
Sgt. Geo. Rinaldi, Co. G, 126th Inf. Chevalier of the Order of Leopold II.
Sgt. Lyman T. Covell, Co. L, 126th Inf. Chevalier of the Order of Leopold II.

DIVISION CITATIONS.

HEADQUARTERS, 32ND DIVISION.

Sgt. William A. Jank.
Sgt. Emerson B. Wood.
Pvt. 1cl. Fred Ten Hoore.
Bat. Sgt. Major Francis E. Prokop.
Pvt. 1cl, Dave N. Pierson.
Army Field Clerk Frank Milani.
Army Field Clerk Robert L. Jacobson.
Pvt. John Abraham Blomster.
Corp. Fred A. Yeager.
Bat. Sgt. Major John J. Chisholm.
Bat. Sgt. Major Peter P. Walsh.
Pvt. Dewit Bonebrake.
Pvt. John E. Collins.
Pvt. Niels C. Anderson.
Pvt. 1cl. Class Edwin P. Gibson.
Reg. Sgt. Major Peter Johnson.
Pvt. 1cl. Stuart A. Wendell.
Reg. Sgt. Major Joseph M. Noll.
Pvt. 1cl. John P. Mallow.
Bat. Sgt. Major Joseph H. Haebig.
Bat. Sgt. Major Irl F. Bratten.
Army Field Clerk George W. Carncy.
1st Lt. E. K. Barr.
Bat. Sgt. Major Barnard T. Campbell.
Sgt. Hy Mullaney.
Sgt. Martin Hendricks.
Sgt. Joseph Dirmeier.
Pvt. 1cl. John N. Schaack.
Pvt. 1cl. Henry W. Thompson.
Sgt. Hilding Olson.
Sgt. Julian Ramsey.
Pvt. 1cl. James Harland Hyde.
Wag. Wm. K. McLaggan.
Pvt. 1cl. Clyde W. Albright.
Pvt. Ole Matson.
Horseshoer Roy J. Fuller.
Corp. Joseph G. Rogers.
Pvt. 1cl. Elmer J. Nygaard.
Pvt. Fay A. Raefsnyder.
Pvt. Melville Rhodes.
Wag. Gordon I. Gce.
Wag. Anders Kolberg.
Wag. Maynard B. Reed.
Wag. Harry T. Gnat.
Wag. James H. Ellis.

Wag. Nisholas Keup.
Wag. Robert I. Knutson.
Wag. Fred D. Miles.
Wag. Ora Sands,
Wag. Charles B. Hill.
Pvt. 1cl. Lewis D. Adams.
Pvt. Stanley Zukowski.
Pvt. Martin T. Thoreson.
Pvt. 1cl James D. Blythin.
Pvt. William C. Northamer.
Sgt. Warren B. Niles.
Lt. Colonel Frank H. Fowler.
Capt. LeRoy Pearson.
Capt. Daniel D. Thompson.
1st Lt. Frederick F. Malloy.
Colonel Harold C. Fisk.
Colonel Jerome G. Pillow.
Lt. Col. John H. Howard.
Lt. Colonel Paul B. Clemens.
Major Fred C. Best.
Capt. Carl Hanton.
Capt. Charles F. Bowen.
Lt. Col. Charles R. Williams.
Lt. Col. James R. Scott.
Lt. Col. John Scott.
Lt. Col. Wm. Mitchell Lewis.
Lt. Col. James A. Howell.
Major Joseph E. Barzyinski.
Major Robert Connor.
Major William Woodlief.
Major Thomas E. Blood.
Major Charles R. Harrison.
Major Luther G. Beckwith.
Major Lewis A. Moore.
Major Amos H. Ashley.
Major Alexander W. Fluegel.
Major Edward D. Arnold.
Capt. Walter M. Gaudynski.
Capt. John A. Crandall.
Capt. Fred B. Rhyner.
Capt. William J. Niederpruem.
Capt. William J. Brennan.
Capt. Harvey F. Wiles.
1st. Lt. Harold J. Lance.
Capt. Robert L. Wiley.

107TH ENGINEERS.

Regimental Sergeant Major Walter Belau.
Master Engineer, Sr. Grade, Samuel E. Johnson.
Master Engineer, Sr. Grade, Roy O. Papenthien.

Bat. Sgt. Major Norman L. Johnson.
1st Sgt. Arthur F. Miller.
Sgt. 1cl. Melvin W. Dock.
Sgt. Michael P. Marino.
Colonel Luke H. Callan.

107TH SANITARY TRAIN.

Major William Johnston.
Capt. Luther N. Schuetz.
Capt. Harry W. Sargeant.
Capt. William J. Hanley.
Wagoner Frank F. Howe.
Major John A. Sullivan.
Capt. Raymond L. Kenney.
Capt. William J. Ryncarson.

Corp. Carl C. Glave.
Corp. Thomas McAneny.
Wag. Earle W. McGovern.
Pvt. 1cl. Erwin E. Carl.
Pvt. 1cl. Earle A. W. Frank.
Pvt. Benjamin B. Cieslinski.
Pvt. John Drury.
Pvt. Lloyd Geesey.

119TH MACHINE GUN BATTALION.

Sgt. Evald N. Nelson.
Pvt. 1cl. Harry A. Newbury.
Pvt. 1cl. William Jouett.
Pvt. 1cl. William E. Menard.
Mech. George H. Streeter.

Pvt. 1cl. Harry Wald.
Pvt. 1cl. Isreal Socular.
Pvt. John Borysiewicz.
Corp. Vernis K. Shuttelworth.

VETERINARY MOBILE SECTION.

Pvt. 1cl. Alvin Madison.

Pvt. Frank C. Bassett.

128TH INFANTRY.

Capt. Lewis J. Donovan.
1st Lt. Edmund T. Szaskos.
1st Lt. Lee A. Brown.
1st Lt. Talma A. Scott.
1st Lt. James T. Harris.
Mess Sgt. Severin Setter.
Sgt. John L. Harris.

Sgt. Sigwald Steen.
Sgt. Fred Galoff.
Sgt. Herbert L. Hadden.
Sgt. Albert Siebers.
Sgt. Otto Olsen.
Sgt. Clyde O. Helgeson.
Corp. Joseph Bruce.

127TH INFANTRY.

Colonel Russel C. Langdon.
Capt. Stephen Boon.
1st. Lt. Stanley A. Jowasinski.
1st Lt. Tolman D. Wheeler.
2nd Lt. Roy M. Kelley.
2nd Lt. R. E. Barclay.
Sgt. Williard D. Purdy.

Corp. Ruben J. Cain.
1st Lt. John G. Purtillo.
Sgt. Edward Krawczyk.
Pvt. Albert R. Guernsey.
Corp. Carl Tullberg.
Pvt. Guy Whiteman.
Pvt. Albert R. Guernsey.

HEADQUARTERS 63RD INFANTRY BRIGADE.

1st Lt. R. G. Carter.
1st Lt. A. C. Baltzer.
Wag. Perce J. Cox.
Pvt. 1cl. Leon Scheurelberg.

Pvt. 1cl. Cressie N. Johnson.
Regt. Sgt. Major Rodney D. Schopps.
Wag. Charles M. Wolfe.

DISTINGUISHED SERVICE DECORATIONS

120TH MACHINE GUN BATTALION.

Capt. Claude C. Manly.
1st Lt. Wm. O. Chamberlain.
1st Lt. Fred A. Dietz.
1st Lt. Odin T. Rovelstad.
1st Lt. Walter H. Sheup.
1st Sgt. Loren Coon.
Sgt. Samuel Kontas.
Sgt. Harry H. Peck.
Sgt. Harold R. Schindrick.

Sgt. Ernest C. Lyle.
Sgt. Patrick J. Kelly.
Sgt. Peter J. Drazage.
Corp. Mark O. Lover.
Corp. James C. Monroe.
Corp. Oscar Lambert.
Corp. Forest D. Sherman.
Wag. Earle T. Wood.
Pvt. 1cl. John Pontoskl.

126TH INFANTRY.

Colonel Joseph B. Westnedge.
Major James T. Potter.
Capt. Charles R. Myers.
Capt. Otto K. Budder.
Capt. Fred W. Jamoska.
Capt. Roscoe L. Graves.
Capt. William Haze.
Capt. Joseph A. McDonald.
Capt. Burton P. Harrison.
1st Lt. C. H. Modie.
1st Lt. John R. DeVall.
1st. Lt. George H. Bunnell.
1st Lt. Patrick Sweeney.
2nd Lt. Donald E. Perry.
Regt. Sgt. Major Milton K. Abell.
Bn. Sgt. Major John M. Lofstrom.
1st Sgt. David Carpe.
1st Sgt. Wm. Owen.
2nd Lt. Joseph A. Sobie.
Sgt. 1cl. Benjamin S. Beck.
Supply Sgt. Arthur E. Hawks.
Mess Sgt. Herman P. Cuser.
Sgt. John G. Fowle.
Sgt. George Rinaldi.

Sgt. Cornelius J. Vonk.
Sgt. Frank M. Townsend.
Sgt. Lyman T. Covell.
Sgt. Roy Webster.
Sgt. Theodore Kutschinski.
Sgt. Russell A. Fuller.
Sgt. Part A. Dove.
Sgt. Paul E. Slauthter.
Sgt. Heral Gardiner.
Sgt. Harry A. Smith.
Sgt. Ransome Garter.
Sgt. John DeBoer.
Corp. Banrell C. Carr.
Corp. Lewis Hudson.
Corp. Jerrold B. Thomson.
Mech. Cuthbert Couryner.
Mech. Phillip R. Vaney.
Mech. Erik Vettergren.
Pvt. Wilson M. Stirdivant.
Pvt. George S. Downing.
Pvt. Isidoro Vissillo.
Pvt. Charles A. Carlon.
Pvt. Walter Rhenow.

125TH INFANTRY.

Colonel Edward G. Heckel.
Major Augustus H. Gansser.
Capt. Charles A. Learned.
1st Lt. Charles Giles.
1st Lt. Dudley P. Ranney.
1st Lt. Wm. H. Rust.
2nd Lt. William Ward.
Bn. Sgt. Major Lyle C. Pratt.
1st Sgt. Wm. B. Scheffler.
Sgt. Emery Hawks.
Sgt. Guy L. Young.
Sgt. Herbert B. Collins.
Sgt. William Wines.
Sgt. Aaron L. Gensiver.
Sgt. Napoleon J. Beaune.
Sgt. Darwin D. Martin.
Sgt. Lawrence LaPorte.
Corp. Morris D. Mist.
Corp. Ernest O'Brien.
Corp. Michael Coyne.
Corp. Wm. H. Emmick.
Corp. Leonard A. Unson.
Corp. Archie J. Finley.

Corp. Clyde C. Martinson.
Corp. Joseph Frommert.
Mech. Christian A. Stillmeyer.
Pvt. 1cl. James A. Brennan.
Pvt. 1cl. Chester Smith.
Pvt. 1cl. Robert J. Ahearn.
Pvt. 1cl. Fred W. Kalkbrenner.
Pvt. 1cl. Anton Marchiando.
Pvt. 1cl. James S. Palmer.
Pvt. Angus Teeple.
Pvt. Alfred B. Anderson.
Pvt. Charles Reifschneider.
Pvt. John Redmond.
Pvt. Hugh Laughlin.
Pvt. Donald A. Smith.
Pvt. Walter Bastedo.
Pvt. Marcus Armijo.
Pvt. Samuel Williams.
Pvt. Elmer A. Brashaw.
Pvt. Alva Cook.
Pvt. John Adams.
Pvt. Wm. Fleming.

107TH SUPPLY TRAIN.

Corp. Lynn S. Savage.
Corp. Henry M. Rider.
Sgt. Vernon Kelly.
Corp. Simon P. Hilebrandt.
Sgt. Hilton A. Doege.
Sgt. Thomas Weir.
Pvt. Joseph Bizunowicz.
Sgt. Dayton C. Baldwin.
Corp. Guy Wiseman.
Corp. David M. Rickerd.
Corp. Harry P. Vanderburg.
Corp. Sigmund Kudlicki.
Pvt. 1cl. Dale D. V. Whitney.

Corp. Simon P. Hillebrandt.
Corp. Joseph Gilders.
Pvt. John Baniszewski.
Corp. Edward F. Paul.
Pvt. Walter E. Taylor.
Corp. Frank Polomares.
Corp. Richard Thornton.
Corp. Albert J. Krause.
Pvt. Merle G. Vantassel.
Corp. Roy E. Pottle.
Pvt. Herman H. Seeley.
Sgt. Galen D. Moyer.
Sgt. George A. Borgenhelmer.

119TH FIELD ARTILLERY.

1st Lt. Milton Shaw, M. C., San. Det. 119th F. A.
1st Lt. William E. Wilson, M. C., San. Det. 119th F. A.
2nd Lt. Lloyd C. Beaton, 119th F. A. (Dec'd).
Sgt. Glenn J. Brook, 297352, Batt. C, 119th F. A.
Sgt. Jesse A. Lamson, 296930, Hq. Co., 119th F. A.
Sgt. Bearl V. Pittinger, 297481, Hq. Co., 119th F. A.
Sgt. Lee H. Crippen, 297350, Batt. C, 119th F. A.
Sgt. Harold D. Graham, 197199, Batt. F, 119th F. A.
Sgt. Archie C. Norris, 296927, Hq. Co., 119th F. A.
Sgt. Robert Elliott, 297494, Batt. D, 119th F. A.
Sgt. Benjamin E. Hartsig, 297475, Batt. D, 119th F. A.
Corp. Raymond H. Moore, 297706, Batt. E, 119th F. A.
Corp. Paro M. Thomas, 296956, Hq. Co., 119th F. A.
Corp. Joseph M. Lambert, 297401, Batt. C, 119th F. A.
Cook Carl M. Marietta, 297452, Batt. C, 119th F. A.
Cook Claude V. Jack, 297445, Batt. C, 119th F. A.
Pvt. Thomas R. McBride, 297566, Batt. D, 119th F. A.
Pvt. 1cl. Charles Sieger, 297657, Batt. E, 119th F. A.
Pvt. Walter W. Holt, 1634070, Batt. D, 119th F. A.
Pvt. Jesse Sawyer, 297580, Batt. D, 119th F. A.
Pvt. 1cl. William J. Christie, 4631, San. Det., 119th F. A.
Pvt. Guy S. Gongwer, 4117, San. Det., 119th F. A.
Pvt. James R. Jollie, 626532, Batt. D, 119th F. A.
Pvt. Robert D. Chisholm, 828050, Batt. C, 119th F. A.
Pvt. Wilbur E. Schaefer, 1434933, Batt. C, 119th F. A.
Pvt. John E. Feighner, 4118, San. Det., 119th F. A.
Pvt. 1cl. George R. Koopman, 297784, Hq. Co., 119th F. A.
Mech. Orville J. Collins, 1435704, Batt. D, 119th F. A.

ABBREVIATIONS AND MILITARY TERMS.

A. E. F.................American Expeditionary Forces.

Axis of Liaison...........The line on which telephone, telegraph lines or other means of communication are to be extended.

A. C. I. ....Advance Center of Information. A point in advance of a Post of Command, designated in orders, where messages and information may be sent.

Barrage ....A wall or curtain of fire, fired by artillery or machine guns.

Brig. ....Brigade.

Bn. ....Battalion.

Bound ....A word used in French Orders—"to advance by bounds" meaning advancing in regulated distances according to a schedule.

Btry. ....Battery. An artillery unit corresponding to a company of infantry.

Bridge Head ....The holding of a sufficient amount of territory on the enemy side of a river to enable friendly troops to construct bridges and cross, or cross troops on bridges already built.

Bus Move ....A move of troops by motor. A Bus is a covered motor truck with seats along each side and accommodating from 18 to 30 men each. The French call a truck a "camion." The British call it a "lorry."

"Bucks" ....Private soldiers.

Bois ....The French word for Wood or Woods.

Casualty ....A man or animal, killed, wounded or missing in action.

Co. ....Company.

C. O. ....Commanding Officer.

Col. ....Colonel.

C. G. ....Commanding General.

Cote ....The French word for Hill.

C. of S. ....Chief of Staff.

D-Day ....The day an attack or movement is to take place. Generally mentioned in secret orders which can be prepared long in advance of the day of an action. When the proper time for the attack arrives, notice is sent out that D-Day for the attack prescribed in such and such an order will be 4 July 1918—for example. (The same definition for H-Hour- except that the hour is named instead of the Day). For example, H-Hour and D-Day will be 5:30 A. M. 4 July 1918.

Dump ....A designated place for the storage or assembling of rations, forage, ammunition or other supplies.

Div. ....Division.

Dug In or Dig In........The construction of individual shelters—"fox" or "funk" holes.

D. S. ....Detached Service.

Evacuate ....To send back. Evacuating the wounded means sending them to hospitals or dressing stations in rear of the firing line. Sick men are counted as "evacuations" but not as "casualties."

Eng. ....Engineer.

Field Tn. ....Field Train.

F. A. ....Field Artillery.

F. O. ....Field Order—Orders issued in the Field.

Fox Hole ....An individual shelter, generally a hole in the ground in the side of a hill, ditch or embankment away from the enemy.

Funk Hole ....Same as a fox hole.

Ferme ....The French word for Farm.

G. S. ....General Staff.

313

G-1 ....The first section of the General Staff; the section having the administration, supply and co-ordination of all the services of an organization.

G-2 ....The second section of the General Staff; the section which collects all information of the enemy, and produces and distributes maps.

G-3 ....The third section of the General Staff; the section responsible for the training of an organization and of its operation during combat.

G. H. Q. ....The General Headquarters of the American Expeditionary Forces.

"Hommes 40 Chevaux 8"..On nearly all French box cars, this phrase is painted. It means that the capacity of the car is 40 men or 8 horses.

H-Hour ....See definition to D-Day.

15 Hours ....The system of designating time in the French Army and adopted by us. By its use, it is unnecessary to state A. M. or P. M. thereby eliminating possible mistakes;—15 hours may be easily understood as 3 P. M. or 23:30 Hours as 11:30 P. M.

Hq. ....Headquarters.

H Plus 3 hours...........Three hours after an attack commences.

Inf. ....Infantry.

Infirmary ....Where medical treatment is rendered to minor cases of illness or injury. A First Aid station, etc.

I. D. ....French designation for the Infantry troops of a division. An Infantry division is abbreviated D. I. Thus the 32nd D. I. U. S. is the Thirty-Second American Infantry Division.

Jump Off Line...........A line from which the Infantry launches an attack.

J. A. ....Judge Advocate. The Staff Officer having charge of legal matters.

"Kriembilde Stellung" ...The name of a strong German position; the main line of resistance corresponding to the Hindenburg Line. By "position" is meant a line of prepared trenches, in front of which were masses of strong Wire entanglements to obstruct the advance of our troops.

Kamerad ....The German term for "I surrender."

Km. ....Kilometer. In France and Germany distances are measured by kilometers instead of miles. A kilometer is five-eighths of a mile.

Liaison ....Communication. "Liaison was good" means the transmission of messages and information was rapid and satisfactory. "Getting in liaison with the Division on our right" means that the Division Commander or his agent had visited the Division on our right and that the plans of both organizations had been discussed—or in other words, each was made familiar with the plans of the other.

Lieut-Col. ....Lieutenant Colonel.

Machine Gun Nest........Several machine guns in different locations but in close proximity to each other.

MM. ....Millimeter (.039 of an inch). The term used in describing the caliber of artillery pieces.—French 75s, German 77s, French 155s, etc.

M. S. T. U. ....Motor Supply Truck Unit. A truck repair shop.

M. O. R. S. ....Mobile Ordnance Repair Shop. A repair shop for repairing artillery, small arms and other ordnance.

M. P. ....Military Police.

M. C. ....Medical Corps.

M. D. ....Medical Department.

M. G. ....Machine Gun.

M. T. O. ....Motor Transportation Officer.

"Minnie" ....The nickname for the German minnenwerfer—a trench mortar.

N. G. ....National Guard.

N. A. ....National Army.

RD -7.6

ABBREVIATIONS AND MILITARY TERMS

Non-Coms. . . . . Non-Commissioned Officers.

N. C. O. . . . . Non-Commissioned Officer.

No Man's Land. . . . . The land between the trenches of opposing forces.

O. P. . . . . Observation Post. A post from which the movements or actions of the enemy are observed.

Objective . . . . Successive lines which troops are to take or advance to according to schedule.

"Over the Top". . . . . The phrase used by troops in describing their start to an attack. (Over the top of the trench.)

O. D. . . . . Olive Drab.

O. O. . . . . Operation Officer. Ordnance officer.

P. C. . . . . Post of Command. Sometimes the same place as the Headquarters of an organization. Generally in combat the headquarters, the supply and administrative branch, is left behind in some convenient place where it can function without annoyance from the enemy, while the Commanding Officer, with part of his staff, go forward to be nearer the front line that he may better direct the operations. This forward location or Headquarters is called the Post of Command, or P. C.

Poilu . . . . A private in the French Army; the French doughboy.

Panels . . . . A piece of white cloth, or paper, used to signal from the ground to an airplane. Carried by the infantry. When a friendly airplane flies over and calls for the signal, the panels are shown. The observer in the plane marks their location on his map, flies back and drops the map at headquarters, thus locating the front line.

P. W. E. . . . . Prisoner of War Enclosure.

Q. M. C. . . . . Quartermaster Corps.

Runner . . . . A messenger.

R. H. . . . . Railhead. A railway station where the replacements and supplies of a camp or Division are received from warehouses in the rear.

Replacements . . . . Men, animals or material sent forward to replace those killed, wounded, or broken and worn out.

Ration . . . . The food for one man or one animal for one day. For example, 1000 rations means food for 1000 men for one day.

R. T. O. . . . . Railway Transportation Officer.

R. L. O. . . . . Regimental Liaison Officer.

S. O. S. . . . . Service of Supply, formerly known as the Line of Communications. The service responsible for the supply of all troops of an army.

Sanitary Train . . . . The Medical Organization of a Division, Corps or Army. It consists, in a Division, principally of four Ambulance Companies and four field hospitals.

Sector . . . . A section or area alloted to and occupied by an Army, Army Corps, Division, Brigade, Regiment or other organization.

"In Square so-and-so." . . . A kilometer square referred to on a map. French maps are generally laid off in kilometer squares to facilitate the reading of co-ordinate. In sending messages, it was sometimes easier to refer to some woods or a cross road "in Square 64" than to name the co-ordinates.

S. C. . . . . Signal Corps.

Triage . . . . The French term for a casualty Clearing Station, where the casualties were classified as "transportable," "non-transportable," and "slightly wounded, not to be evacuated."

Take off line. . . . . A line or position from which an attack is to be launched.

Tn. . . . . Train.

T. S. F. . . . . Radio or wireless telegraphy.

T. P. S. . . . . Earth telegraphy.

CPSIA information can be obtained
at www.ICGtesting.com
Printed in the USA
BVOW11s1117270717
490292BV00019B/328/P